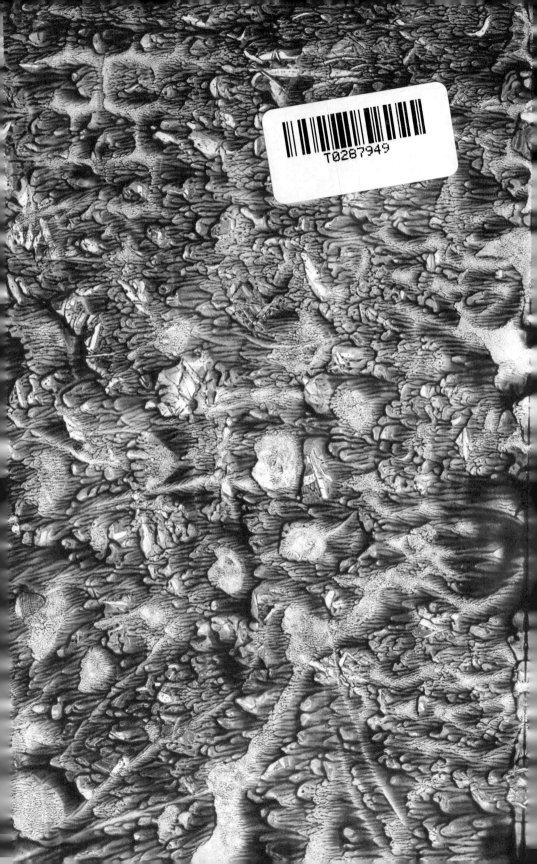

Naked Lunch @ 50

Naked Lunch @ 50
anniversary essays

edited by
oliver HARRIS and
ian MACFADYEN

Southern Illinois University Press
Carbondale

Copyright © 2009 by the Board of Trustees,
Southern Illinois University
Printed in the United States of America

12 11 10 09   4 3 2 1

The endpapers were created by Philip Taaffe.
The interior geometric motifs were created by Keith Albarn.
Cover illustrations: Photograph of William Burroughs by Allen Ginsberg, 1957, reproduced from *With William Burroughs: A Report from the Bunker* (New York: Seaver, 1981) by Victor Bockris, with permission of the Allen Ginsberg Trust and the Wylie Agency, Inc.; photograph of Tangier, by Oliver Harris; Burroughs at his typewriter, photographs by Allen Ginsberg, 1953, Allen Ginsberg Papers, Stanford University, with permission of the Allen Ginsberg Trust and the Wylie Agency, Inc.; photograph of Burroughs by Anthony Balch, 1960–61, with permission of the William Burroughs Estate and the Wylie Agency, Inc.

Library of Congress Cataloging-in-Publication Data
Naked lunch at 50 : anniversary essays / edited by Oliver Harris and Ian MacFadyen.
    p. cm.
  Includes bibliographical references and index.
  ISBN-13: 978-0-8093-2915-1 (cloth : alk. paper)
  ISBN-10: 0-8093-2915-8 (cloth : alk. paper)
  ISBN-13: 978-0-8093-2916-8 (pbk. : alk. paper)
  ISBN-10: 0-8093-2916-6 (pbk. : alk. paper)
  1. Burroughs, William S., 1914–1997. Naked lunch. 2. Burroughs, William S., 1914–1997—
Anniversaries, etc. I. Harris, Oliver (Oliver C. G.) II. MacFadyen, Ian, 1952–
  PS3552.U75N336 2009
  813'.54—dc22   2008039686

The paper used in this publication meets the minimum requirements of American National Standard for Information Sciences—Permanence of Paper for Printed Library Materials, ANSI Z39.48-1992. ♾

We dedicate this book to:

alan ANSEN
sinclair BEILES
wallace BERMAN
paul CARROLL
gregory CORSO
robert CREELEY
john yerbury DENT
allen GINSBERG
maurice GIRODIAS
brion GYSIN
michael HOROVITZ
leroi JONES
jack KEROUAC
madame RACHOU
irving ROSENTHAL
barney ROSSET
richard SEAVER

And all those who otherwise
aided and abetted the creation and
dissemination of *Naked Lunch* . . .

contents

 **preface**

t is a book unlike any other. Famous, infamous, derided, and banned but also recognized as a work of genius. For fifty years, it has tantalized, shocked, baffled, and inspired. It simultaneously holds a significant place in postmodern literature while retaining its iconic, underground allure, resisting diverse critical attempts to define and explain it. It is an aberrant concoction, stylistically brilliant and structurally disorienting, obscene and blasphemous and yet satirically cathartic and redemptive. A drug book—*the drug book*—which also happens to be morally admonishing. A systematic program of speaking the unspeakable. The exorcism of a violent death and years of addiction. A lacerating satire on conformity and authoritarianism and a grotesque indulgence in derangement and possession. The Leviathan of the Nuclear Age and a fairground chamber of horrors. A book of ideas, a book about language, viruses, and control. A *queer* book and a work of reportage—as straight as it comes. It is the Caliban of the Canon and the Prospero of the Avant-garde.

Fifty years after its original publication and in a new heated-up millennium, it still has the power to shock and delight but remains as mysterious and illusive as ever. Ungraspable and delirious, it challenges the critical orthodoxies and politically correct sensibilities of our time. In the twenty-first century, its stature, paradoxically, is as assured and yet as debatable as ever, as if its place in the world is fated to be stellar but unstable, controversial, and finally unassimilable. A dark star, indeed. In certain respects, it is increasingly problematic and challenging, its sexual proclivities and apparent colonialist callousness guaranteed to dismay our cultural and moral arbiters. Which is as it should be: the desire to shock, to rub one's face in human ordure, is the book's strategic, perpetual motor. At the same time, its pre–cut-up montage assemblage, its viral obsessions and sexual hard-core, its concern with dehumanized control apparatuses (medical, political, technological, criminal, as well as those deeply implanted in the psyche) make it a prophetic post-postmodern blueprint for our chaotic digital age, our ravaged, murderous planet, and our terrifying yet unimaginable future. Unforgettable and unwished-for, uncanny and utterly unbridled, Gentle Reader, Ladies and Gentlemen of the Jury—marks, agents, collaborators, Paregoric Babies of the World: welcome to *Naked Lunch*. A book—*the book*—like no other.

William S. Burroughs was, of course, more than a one-book writer, and the experiments in creativity that followed publication of *Naked Lunch* in 1959 exceeded and challenged both the conventions of authorship and the literary career. And yet the one book that—inevitably, rightly—stands for the strange power of Burroughs' oeuvre has itself received surprisingly little direct, detailed attention. Paradoxically, *Naked Lunch* has deterred head-on critical engagement at the same time as it has been *taken as read*. The present book of essays therefore not only marks an important commemorative occasion, the last in a series of three Beat milestones, following the fiftieth anniversaries of "Howl" and *On the Road*, but directly addresses a serious critical omission. Our aim was not to be exhaustive—an impossibility given the sheer complexity of the origins, history, and text of *Naked Lunch* and the extreme responses it has engendered—but to ask a diversity of readers for their own specialized, critical takes. We may have thought at the beginning of the project that we knew what we wanted—to create through a number of historical, professional, and subjective perspectives a multiplicity of differing interpretations and analyses—but we also knew that we could not anticipate how the contributors would respond, individually and collectively, to the invitation and to the challenges involved.

We hoped to discover the different ways in which the book is read right now, at this moment in time, fifty years down the line from its first publication, and to reflect changes in the way the book is understood, remembered, and appreciated. We asked a number of artists and writers and musicians with a special interest in Burroughs and *Naked Lunch* to contribute alongside known Burroughs scholars and leading academics, drawing upon their own areas of expertise and their very different cultural backgrounds and generational experiences. The international lineup not only pays homage to Burroughs' own travels between continents but also tracks the worldwide influence of his book.

It was this promising if risky mix, deliberately juxtaposing writers from very different milieus, which was our starting point. We believed that the pejoratively branded academic writer and the often unfairly excluded artist could in the collective context of the book reveal not only their shared interests but the overlapping and interconnection of their approaches—the scholar as artist, the artist as critic.

We have tried to make possible a shared space for the grain of each voice to come through and have preserved disagreement and disparity as the very lifeblood of that original democratic ethic now so evidently debased and abused all around us. Inevitably, the essays connect and intersect, often echo and sometimes contradict one another—"back and forth in and out fore and aft"—rather than keeping their places under neatly contrived categories and headings. The guiding principles fit loosely, flexibly, giving the individual essays space to breathe, not an agenda to follow. The various scholarly, critical, and personal approaches here use the vantage of fifty years to reengage with the text in all its wild hybridity and heterogeneity and to remap the long and curious histories of both its making and reception. Preceding the essays and grounding the retrospective vantage points of their investigation, Jonas Mekas's diary extract from 1958 provides a primary document of singular historical value: written as an impassioned response to early published sections of *Naked Lunch*, his piece gives a viscerally potent and quite literal starting point for all that follows. In between the spaces opened up by the essays run the Dossiers, offering drifting points of entry, oblique snapshots, fragmentary and provisional sketches suggestive of the work that remains unsaid and undone, the territories left unexplored—"Well, as you can plainly see, the possibilities are endless like meandering paths in a great big beautiful garden. I was just scratching that lovely surface when I am purged by Party Poops . . . Well, '*son cosas de la vida*'" (25).[1]

Note

1. For convenience, except where indicated, all references to the text are to the most readily available edition, *Naked Lunch: The Restored Text,* edited by James Grauerholz and Barry Miles (New York: Grove, 2003).

 **acknowledgments**

We would like to thank the following for their important contributions, which we very much appreciate: Keith Seward, for envisioning the book's cover design and for his creativity and technical expertise; Keith Albarn, for his perfect, permutated motifs; Philip Taaffe, for his brilliant endpapers, and Raymond Foye, for all his help in making them a part of the book; Benn Northover, for his vital assistance and creative liaison; Jeremy Reed, for his revealing poem-portrait of Burroughs which concludes the book; Lou Reed, for his words and for his support of Burroughs' work over many years; Terry Wilson, for his special knowledge and unrivalled understanding and for the generous loan of rare archival material.

We would also like to thank Karl Kageff, Barb Martin, Kathy Kageff, and everyone at Southern Illinois University Press for helping us to realize our vision of a book worthy of the occasion. Thanks to Andrew Hussey and Isabelle Schmitt at the University of London Institute in Paris for all their help with the 2009 Burroughs homage in Paris.

We want to acknowledge the generous permissions to reproduce images granted by James Grauerholz of the William Burroughs Estate and Peter Hale of the Allen Ginsberg Trust. We would also like to thank Jeff Posternak of the Andrew Wylie Agency, J. P. Donleavy, Shay Howell, Brigitte Murphy, John de St. Jorre, Patrick Kearney, Rick Gekoski, Virginia McGillycuddy, and Neil Pearson for helping to secure permission to reproduce the letter from Maurice Girodias. And, our thanks to Isaac Gewirtz and his staff at the Henry W. and Albert A. Berg Collection of English and American Literature, New York Public Library, to Polly Armstrong and all the staff of the Special Collections Department at Green Library, Stanford University, and to Karen Cook at the Kenneth Spencer Library, University of Kansas, for expediting the reproduction of images for this book. And for financially supporting this research, we also gratefully acknowledge the David Bruce Centre for American Studies and the Research Institute for Humanities at Keele University.

Very special thanks to all those who have helped in so many ways: Inge Bakkenes, Philippe Baumont, Philippe Boulet, Jamie Fettis, José Féréz Kuri, Jean Fischer, Louise Landes Levi, Simon Lilly, Richard Livermore, Robert and Morna McFadyen, Malcolm McNeill, Andrew Morley, Michael Hrebeniak, Simon Prager, Nick Rogers, Carol Rothman, John Tytell, Simon Vinkenoog and Edith Vinkenoog, Regina Weinreich, Andrew Whittingham, and Eddie Woods. To Kathelin, Chili, Tango, John, Elisabeth, Ros, and everyone at the Institute of Ecotechnics and the October Gallery, London. And to Ira Cohen who told us, "I remember reading *Naked Lunch* for the first time. I had never read anything like it. And I feel the same way today."

To our contributors who made the journey with us—*Salud*.

To Alison—"J'ai trouvé le secret de t'aimer, toujours pour la première fois."—Ian

To Jenny, Ella, Mia, and Nina—with love, Oliver

Naked Lunch @ 50

In Defense of Perversity: Diary Entry, 1958

jonas MEKAS

In a bastard standardized conformist sick society, perversity becomes a force of liberation. Horror and degradation for the professors, guardians of Morality, it is a drop of Holy Spirit, a ray of salvation.

One has to hit on the very head. The time has come when the action of the silent wisdom, when the truth takes a form of anarchy, and exaggeration, and negation. This subconscious, in its organic protest against the dehumanizing tendencies, sprouts and bursts and spits out its venom.

Young Angry Men are necessary not because they are bringing a new philosophy. No—others will bring it in right time. Their function is to destroy. They came against their own will, to begin to clean the rotten swelling of their age. They are the subconscious of their (our) own age.

Beat and Angry generation is a protest. Not everybody in this generation is angry and beat. Generations get their markings from a few who express their generation clearest. They are being forced by the total subconscious of their generation to utter, to shout, to cry, to beat out their truths, suspicions, hopes, loneliness, warnings, prophesies. They are the true voices of their generation. Those are sensitive voices. They are pervert—they are not normal. Normality is conformist, money-minded, dead, Eisenhowered, and Mamieed, and Futurized, Harperized, deodorized. To be beat today is to be abnormal, to go against the normality, conformity, to be immoral, to be perverse.

Even the sexual pervert today is an innocent and helpless protest against the bourgeois morality and unsensitivity. Better a pervert than a businessman. A pervert is an innocent, beating, crying himself, not the others.

When the society is unlivable, the brave will die. The innocent will jump out the window, cut their innocent veins, suck in their innocent blood, or dream themselves out in the leaves of marijuana. The unsensitive ones will survive and become Mamies, salesmen, atomic pirates, Dulleses, professors, Wouks.

Listen to the songs, on radio, jukeboxes, cheap songs, true songs. Popular American song is the saddest thing in America, or maybe in the world. Listen to their sacred sadness. There was never such sadness in the songs of a large, strong nation: they always came from the trampled small nations, poor, beaten on the paths of war, famine. Now it is in America. An anguished sadness, a suicide sadness, a loveless sadness. Or listen to the jazz. It is a kind of silent, hidden, sad crying out, for oneself, somewhere very deep. Or look at the paintings of de Kooning. There is the same suicide sadness, and cry: he paints his heart out, the heart of his generation. The businessmen do not realize that these songs, and jazz, and de Koonings are also pervert: they demask their dead happy Peale's *Reader's Digest* smiles. The popular art and the modern art sing the truth, as all perversity today does.

Isn't it then that the Mamies, the Eisenhowers, the salesmen, and the atomists, and the Wouks and professors are the real perverts? Aren't they who go against the truth of life, love, and death? Aren't they who smear their Old Age in Mademoiselle's fashions and wilt without tasting it, in anguish? Aren't they who made love into dating and partnership? Life into business? The true perversity of our age? Aren't we the holy ones?

Isn't Elvis Presley a half-saint, who showed the absurdity of his parents' generation by exaggerating their ideals, by buying two three four cars? All ideals and truths of our fathers become fake and lie when lit up: rotten, evil, yellow puke.

So let us be beat and angry, and pervert: if that helps to dethrone the falsity and rottenness of morality and puked way of living. It is more honest today to be confused than to be sure (when the time is for dethroning). It is more honest to destroy than to build (there is not yet a clean place for building). It is more honest to be delinquent (and juvenile) than to learn and accept the ways of living in lies and pukes and garbage.

Holy are the delinquent thoughts and deeds and insubordination, disrespect, and hate for their ways of living, for their philosophies, for all work (for the perpetuation of the dump); holy is beat and zen and angriness and perversity.

This perversity doesn't deny the need of moral values. It only shows the corruption of the existing moral values. It is the first anxiety in which the new moral values will be born, in suffering and in angriness.

Let us, then, deny and destroy, so that, perhaps, some of us will find again and keep, until it will be needed again, the truth of life, the spontaneity, the joy, the freedom, exultation, soul, heaven and hell. Let us free ourselves for perversity, become James Deans, and Presleys, and Parkers, and Osbornes, de Koonings, Kerouacs, Bernard Shaws, and Millers, Genets, Villons, Rimbauds—to learn the dynamics of the holy perversity, not to be bound into the dump of the XX-century normality.

Thus I spit into the generation that has produced me, and this is the holiest spit of my generation.

This piece was my diary entry after reading the first chapters of *Naked Lunch* in *Big Table* magazine. I remember very vividly the occasion. It was electrical. I ran to Louis Brigante and Storm DeHirsch, editors of a literary monthly, *Intro Bulletin,* and we read it again together, and then we got drunk. To us, it seemed like a new beginning in American literature. We thought it was an event of monumental proportions. We could not sleep that night.

dossier ONE
ian MACFADYEN

Files Comprising: Deposition, Thomas And Charlie, High, Skip Tracer, Shamanic, Journey Of A Lost Soul, Amsterdam And A New York State Of Mind, City, White Masks, Smiling Damned, The Boulevard Of Crime, Paris Au Fils Du Temps, Paris Please Stay The Same, The Naked City, Lupita/Coatlicue, Death Candy, The Mexico Gimmick, The Final Shrug, Mexican Time, A Spectral Dimension.

Deposition

We're in Paris, rue Git-le-Coeur, on the trail of *Naked Lunch*—looking for clues, checking out the key sites half a century down the line. Oliver frames another shot, attempting to homage a fifty-year-old photograph—but the figure in that picture, William Burroughs, has definitively quit the scene, walking away like his hero John Dillinger in *Naked Lunch*—"Don't ever look back, kid . . ." (190). Still, that's what we're driven to do, though the London, Paris, and Tangier scenes are gone forever. The old Beat Hotel is now a smart hotel with a bidet in every suite, the Turkish toilets ripped out along with the artworks and the poems on the walls. What are we looking for, and what is left to find? It appears a hopeless quest, but we have no choice, we're hooked, and that book will never be done with us, as we will never be done with it. Check out the sources, pay calls on those few left who still remember, follow up all possible angles, then return once again to that text which is a Tantalus, seemingly forever beyond our reach. So, let the pieces fall where they may, these hunches and hints and guesses, snapshots and notes collected here in Dossiers which others may consult as they set off on their own readings, their own investigations, their spirited attempts to travel through time. This is a trail of some sort . . . and from it radiate the traces of an endless fascination.

Thomas And Charlie

"'Thomas and Charlie,' I said. / 'What?' / 'That's the name of this town. Sea level . . . '" (14). This mysterious, oblique exchange refers to the town Tamazunchale, 220 miles north of Mexico City, pronounced "Thomas 'n' Charlie." But what is the significance of this name? Both "Thomas" and "Charlie" are slang expressions related to narcotics. Thomas comes from Tom Mix (signifying a fix), Tom becoming "Thomas" just as Charlie, a euphemism for cocaine ("C" for Cocaine) became "Charles" in Britain. The two words also have sexual connotations, Charlie meaning cunt, derived from Cockney rhyming slang (Charlie Hunt is "a right cunt") while "Tom" means a prostitute, and the term was taken up by homosexuals to signify available trade through its reference to the penis (John Thomas=cock). The interlocutory "'What?'" is a double take, pointing to the hidden significance of these two words, their multiple coded meanings encapsulating in an extraordinary way the operations of slang in narcotics parlance and sexual euphemism.

High

The writer Terry Wilson has made the connection between the Thomas and Charlie section of *Naked Lunch* and a passage in Alain Gheerbrant's 1953 book *The Impossible Adventure*: "We pressed on for several hours and Pierre and I kept our eyes on the mountain ahead which grew larger and larger. 'Cierro Mono,' said Catire" (185). *Naked Lunch* is an aberrant take on travel writing and the tale of adventure, and Burroughs' geographical references contain secret, hip connotations. The reference to "Sea level" in the Thomas and Charlie episode designates physiological response to altitude, and immediately after providing this information, Lee takes a fix, making a correspondence—and also a demarcation—between barometer and syringe, between the equilibrium outside and inside the body, between current pressure and how "high" one is, or needs to be. Tamazunchale is high in the mountains, a place of rivers and lakes and forest, and it was an important stop for tourists driving from the U.S. border to Mexico City on the old Pan American Highway (MEX-85). Because of the hard driving on the winding, two-lane road and the morning mists, drivers would often stop there, sixty-six miles from the border, before heading south to Mexico City. Lee and his partner have driven all night, and this is their stop-off point to swap driving duties and take a fix—getting high on the Highway. Burroughs takes us there—we *feel* that clammy mist, *hear* those dawn dogs, and a river runs through it, water trickling, pouring, cascading, filling the atmosphere with liquid sound . . .

Skip Tracer

Lee attempts to shed his own skin, taking flight in old Packards and Fords, escaping the "rancid magic" of slot machines and the ceremonial sites and inhuman rites of the prehistoric Americas—both are dead zones, stripped of eros, the life spirit of youth snuffed out, and the mound-building peoples will continue to bury themselves alive forever. It is the ultimate stasis of the "earthbound ghost" (11). Lee is literally driven *out of the past*, with echoes of Jacques Tourneur's 1947 *noir* masterpiece. This is a bravura performance by Burroughs and is crucially important in the book—the America that resurfaces as memories and flashbacks throughout the rest of the text is that old evil land, that dirty U.S. drag seeping back through blood-soaked cottons and withdrawal delirium, and this section is its true source, the terrible, broken origin. Wherever Lee goes, that abstract paranoid American Evil pursues him like a ghostly skip tracer, never to be shaken off, and we feel Burroughs' repulsion for this shadowy, creeping repossessor. This is what defines Lee as a profoundly *noir* creation—for him, there can be no escape from the unnameable horror, he is desperately, inextricably bound to a hateful time and place, even though he is burning up the road map. Indeed, Lee's account of the drive is a compulsive return to the curse of the past, and *Naked Lunch* is itself a doomed attempt to escape the "ghosts" of haunted memory and the resident "evil" (11) of possession. It is Lee, resurrected from the grave, who appears as the demonic Skip Tracer at the end of *Queer*—and in *Naked Lunch*, he is literally pursuing himself, chasing himself *out of the picture*, leaving that old Packard burned-out and terminally *off the road*.

Shamanic

Psychic delirium flips into slapstick, the trance journeys of *yagé* and the dreams of *kif* splinter into vaudeville routines, physical degradation and anguish transform into ecstatic trips out-of-the-body, out of the self. Burroughs is like those shamans whose recapitulations take off into inspired tale-telling, the rites of exorcism switching to pantomimic mockery, terrifying transports and trickster mischief inextricably entwined in the process of being *carried away*. Everything is sacred. Nothing is sacred. And the shaman *laughs*.

Journey Of A Lost Soul

The traumatized amnesiac, the junkie on the lam, the criminal hero, the adventurer as remittance man, the Private Dick who files his report but never intervenes—Lee is characterized by his moral absence and shadow existence, the quality of both being there and not there. He is the ghosting in the machine, as well as the ghostwriter's revenant double, he flickers in and out of vision like a disturbance of the light, a break in the scanning pattern, a flaw in transmission. He has a hole inside him, where his soul should be. But "soul-loss" and the "soul-journey" are anthropologically equivalent, and it is this very absence which defines the nature of his quest. As Paul Zweig notes, "Someone who is 'absent' has become unstuck from his body" (86), and this may be the result of some traumatic act or part of a spiritual initiation. The "holes" created by "illness, hysterical seizures, sudden changes of fortune, fainting, dreams, even death" are "intrusions from or into the spirit world" (87). In this sense, Lee is on a spiritual quest and needs to heal a hidden wound, to reconstitute his human form and feeling. He is ostensibly working for Islam Inc., but his investigations and peregrinations tell a different story—he is looking for something ineffable, unnameable, and he is quite unaware of the intention of this journey which will in any case end in failure and abandonment. His fate is to be cast back into the past, back into damage and despair, through a hole in space-time.

Amsterdam And A New York State Of Mind

We meet Eddie Woods at Café Berne and visit Simon and Edith Vinkenoog in their Amsterdam apartment. Eddie and Simon both knew Burroughs and speak of his work with admiration, and it's clear that *Naked Lunch* had a 1960s European countercultural influence quite distinct from its reception and history in America. Burroughs believed that artists are "the most powerful members of society because their dreams will come to life in a thousand ways in a thousand places" (S. Wilson, 12), and he spoke of the "conduits and connections" through which the dreams pass, the *lieux de mémoire* which they create throughout the world. Leslie Dick acknowledges the key role which

Burroughs' work played in the New York art scene of the late 1970s and early 1980s and notes the simultaneous reemergence and reappropriation of Situationist *détournement*—"what used to be known as 'cultural terrorism' is central to the period I remember" (112). Burroughs' return to New York from London was propitious—his influence was feted, and *Naked Lunch* took on a new lease of life, a New York incarnation which would eventually lead to the recontextualization of the book in cyber culture, connecting it with digital sampling and the post-punk aesthetic. As a result, *Naked Lunch* would be seen as a "cut-up" book—and what matters is not that this is historically and technically incorrect but that this understanding changed the ways in which the book was understood and read.

City

Burroughs' description of The Composite City is immediately followed by "*Notes from* yagé *state,*" Burroughs adding, "The City and the Meet Café written in state of *yagé* intoxication . . . " (91). Here the city's diseased, polyglot fecundity, the "blood and substance of many races" (92), flows in waves, through epidemics, everything merging, condensing, and then expanding in an organic melée. This is the Interzone of interpenetration and interconnectivity, the city as human mass and mess, the endless permutations of the human image flickering and writhing with hybridized life as they appear and disappear in time, the Great Wheel of Being transformed into a Coney Island Ferris Wheel flying off into space. Readers and critics continue to call this Interzone "Tangier," but it very definitely is not—it is the visionary city of all life, the drift and detritus of continents over and through millennia, the ineluctable, perilous human pilgrimage which Burroughs would call "The Biological Film."

White Masks

Naked Lunch leaves us in no doubt about the author's poisonous antipathy—this is a text of cultural derogation, as if Burroughs took upon himself the role of racist, capitalist oppressor, the white foreigner who would play the part which he believed had been allotted to him by the "native" inhabitants. This intensification of difference, literally at the expense of the *other*, is only too clearly exposed in *Naked Lunch*'s scenarios of inferiority and subordination, where the market place facilitates the trade in cut flesh, the literally colonized human body. Burroughs' rebarbative stance is cynical and shameless—but is it a role played out as a strategy in the fiction, to let us see just how ugly the Ugly American can be? Well, his letters suggest otherwise, though he may well indeed have been playing devil's advocate there. It may be that the desire for drugs and sex stigmatized the foreign Tangerine, isolating and deculturing him, while fueling racism in a kind of reflexive displacement of undesirability—he adopts the white mask of the colonialist and *authorized* exploiter as a form of self-protection and as a refutation of innocence, his own and that of others, in order to become both inviolate and the excoriated *other*.

Smiling Damned

Burroughs is knowingly contradictory and complicit, like his friend in Tangier, the criminal Paul Lund, of whom his biographer Rupert Croft-Cooke wrote, "It would not be far from the truth to say that he has been a criminal for fun" (7). Baudelaire's *Au Lecteur* pays homage to another who would "turn the earth to scraps and swill, / swallow it whole in one great, gaping yawn" while "smoking his hookah"—"Hypocrite lecteur, mon semblable, mon frère!" (qtd. in Lyu, 84). Burroughs celebrates man's sheer perversity, and he knows that in extreme adversity man is capable of absolutely anything. As Defoe wrote, "You will not only rob your Neighbour, but if in distress, you will EAT your neighbour, ay, and say Grace to your Meat too . . . " (qtd. in Zweig, 104-5).

The Boulevard Of Crime

Burroughs knew Carné and Prévert's 1945 film *Les Enfants du Paradis*, their great homage to the Funambules of the Boulevard du Temple, and his novel, too, is a homage to popular, unruly, "underground" entertainment, with its own rioting *gamins* and the mockery of the "Jocrisse" or dupe waiting to be rubed, and its own "bespattered, beggarly, filthy and drunken" audience of willing vaudeville participants (Jones, 39), characters derived from popular trickster figures and buffoons, scenarios mixing high and low, the scatological and vital, the unbridled and poetic. *Naked Lunch* resounds to the infernal satanic laughter of the carnival's performing devil and is in the subversive tradition of maniacal desecration which Baudelaire praised as surpassing satire because it will "cast off all its hatred in an explosion of gaiety" (Jones, 23), laughter rising up to the joy of sheer excess.

Paris Au Fils Du Temps

In 1959, four hundred thousand people in Paris lived in unheated furnished rooms and derelict dwellings. Five hundred thousand buildings had no water, one and a half million had no private toilet, and half of the waste was emptied untreated into the Seine while garbage piled up, and infestation was rife. Burroughs inhabited milieus virtually unchanged since the days of Hemingway and Miller, though he could turn a corner and there was the future, heralded by a poster for an Yves Klein exhibition at the Galerie Iris Clert—blue transcendence, a leap into the void, the technological recreation of Eden. Paris was both a City of Ghosts, acted out by Kenneth Anger in the cemetery of Père Lachaise, and the consolatory promise of a new prosperity on the American model, a consumerist spectacle to distract from the dismantling of the French colonial empire. Godard would employ the new steel-and-glass modernist buildings of Paris as the interplanetary sets for the pop-culture future in his film *Alphaville* (1965), and the Lee of *Naked Lunch* is the ironic, iconic prototype of Godard's version of Lemmy Caution—traveling through galaxies in a Ford Galaxy, a refugee from a *noir* world already being turned into a nostalgic cult art form but out of place and out of time in the fabulous Fifth Republic. For both guys, every Metropolis is a Necropolis.

Paris Please Stay The Same

Walking the streets of late 1950s Paris, Burroughs can only have experienced the same abrupt and irreconcilable urban transitions which the Situationists lamented, every *dérive* a detour into a shrinking, vanishing no man's land. The Future was a work-in-progress, a Spectacle to be excoriated, while the Past was mourned as it was eradicated or turned into chic street museums. Many years later, Burroughs would croon Maurice Chevalier's "Paris, Stay The Same" as a hopeless elegy to the city he had known. In *Naked Lunch*, the city is both medieval and ultramodern, primitively osmotic and technologically streamlined, continually remaking itself or being torn apart. "'They are rebuilding the City.' / Lee nodded absently . . . 'Yes . . . Always . . .'" (196).

The Naked City

Like following the detectives in Jules Dassin's 1948 film *The Naked City*, we track Lee's footsteps as he drifts through the criminal city, piecing together its morphology out of the rotten body parts. It is a nightmare trawl through the urban mess and sprawl, a mapping of cancerous bureaucracies, malignant narcotics departments, atrophied suburbs, backwater courthouses, immigrant ghettoes, electronic psychiatric institutes, docksides stacked with counterfeit garbage, wasteland motels and splattered hospital wards . . . The Situationists' homage to Dassin's film took the form of a map, also called *Naked City*, its nineteen sections skewing the city through an act of *détournement*, the sections linked by red arrows known as *plaques tournantes*, which topographically reroute the orientation, traversal, and experience of different milieus. But in *Naked Lunch*, there is no such liberation of the subject through psychogeographic disorientation. Lee appears and disappears by happenstance, with no *plaques tournantes* to deploy him—the turntable he's on is a great whirligig which spins him around and around with increasing velocity through the city's vortex of maleficent zones. Although the *dérive* is essentially directionless, Lee is blown off the Situationist map—he is entirely displaced, lost in space, with no direction home.

Lupita/Coatlicue

Burroughs describes Lupita the pusher as "an Aztec Earth Goddess" (14). The reference is to Coatlicue, the all-devouring, monstrous fertility spirit with gravedigging claws, a necklace of hearts and skulls, and a skirt of serpents. Burroughs' junk goddess is a street Death Deity—"Lupita" is the alias he provides for drug dealer Lola La Chata—with the power to dole out "her little papers of lousy shit" (14). But Burroughs' invocation of the archetypal is telling—the flashcuts of Mexico which appear throughout *Naked Lunch* draw upon a baroque iconography of the monstrous and delirious, a homage which nevertheless testifies to an unbridgeable cultural gulf.

Death Candy

The sugar skull becomes a crystal skull, the carnivalesque mockery of mortality is transformed into the primal spectacle of death, *Fiesta* reveals the Aztec sacrificial rite as the victim is spread upon a limestone altar and "ejaculates in a rainbow against the rising sun" (68). Mexico is portrayed in *Naked Lunch* through casual street shootings and random sex murders, but the mythic, too, is invoked: "'Death was their Culture Hero,' said my Old Lady looking up from the Mayan codices [. . . .] The Ouab Days are upon us" (194), this ethnological reference taking its place in the "Atrophied Preface's" homage to the mythopoetics of Eliot's *The Wasteland*.

The Mexico Gimmick

Lee's hipster armoring provides no protection beneath the unsheltering sky. He has only his cover stories—the stories of *Naked Lunch* itself, in effect—to provide him with the requisite "identity." As Benway explains to him, this identity "gimmick"—a counterpart to the "Mexico

[...] gimmick" (17) of scoring under cover of another party's government *script*—erases "real" identity and merges the vacant subject with the appropriately *scripted* cover story. Lee is the junky whose life is necessarily one of estrangement and deception, a ghost at the feast, participant as actor, spectator as revenant, the agent floating through the sets and stages of hostile and indifferent cultures—*Visto por ojos extranjeros*. And it is in Mexico that his fate, the contractual living death of outsider-hood, is sealed.

The Final Shrug

Like the expression "Mektoub," which Burroughs discovered in Paul Bowles' work, "*Son cosas de la vida*" (25) mixes fatalistic resignation and sublime indifference, a supreme detachment which runs throughout *Naked Lunch* to hilarious and horrible effect, from Andrew Keif sitting by the roadside stirring blood with a stick, to the judge's adage, "Be just and if you can't be just, be arbitrary" (5). This pragmatism is both funny and deadly, and it is one of the most important rhetorical devices in the book, employed repeatedly to devastating effect. All moral and ethical judgment is terminally deferred *with a shrug*— blithe opportunism, heartless insouciance, and a complete disregard of scruple are axiomatic. Conscience is an alien concept in *Naked Lunch*, and its absence is at odds with the polemical critique and moralizing tone of the introduction. Urged on by Burroughs' self-justificatory prolegomena, readers have only too knowingly yet helplessly applied the critique of the "Deposition" to a text which definitively refuses all ethical condemnation or moral justification.

Mexican Time

"Entering Mexico, a northerner arrives in another time zone, a passage that requires much more than the resetting of a watch. Mexican time, densely textured, encompassing myriad rhythms, ancient and contemporary, melding much more fluidly between life and death, easily allows the assumption that all time zones, actual and imagined, must exist somewhere within it" (Ritchin, 271).

A Spectral Dimension

In a conference paper addressing the history of Burroughs' manuscripts prior to *Naked Lunch*, Oliver Harris observes, "Burroughs planned to make a composite text out of material that overlapped the end of *Junky*, all of *Queer* and all of 'In Search of Yage.' The result would have been a narrative based on events lasting two-and-a-half years, from April 1951 to August 1953, taking in both of Burroughs' journeys through Latin America and, most significant of all, emphatically bounded by Mexico City as a place of not just one but *two* departures and *two* returns. That's to say, Mexico City would have been at the beginning, the middle, and the end. In this composite of 'Junk,' 'Queer,' and 'Yage'—a trilogy that might be said to exist in a kind of spectral, parallel dimension of unrealized potentiality—the Mexican connection could hardly have had greater prominence." In *Naked Lunch*, Mexico is all but lost in the shuffle and cut, but the spectral dimension and the composite of manuscripts are taken up and applied to a point of radical, dizzying extremity.

The Beginnings of *"Naked Lunch,* an Endless Novel"

oliver **HARRIS**

Caveat Lector

The mythology began to circulate and to seduce even before the book itself, starting with Allen Ginsberg's famous dedication to *Howl and Other Poems* in October 1956. From this point on, an image of *Naked Lunch* would always precede the real thing and, for the image-hungry, replace it altogether. Simultaneously, this is an appalling irony and part and parcel of Burroughs' great work, which is both the genuine article—a one-off, not-to-be-missed revelation of such toxic brilliance and convulsive beauty that it stains the mind and stirs up the soul—*and* a mockery, a scam that mercilessly exposes our insatiable desire for the tricks and treats of the image. Make no mistake, the mythology is more than a trashy accessory to the *rara avis* of *Naked Lunch*; it is its natural accomplice, its viral double, there from the very beginning, bait for rubes and cognoscenti alike.

While most punters take the mythology rather than open the book—if it's really so mad, bad, and dangerous to read, why go to all the trouble?—the unspoken truth for the rest of us is that we need the myths to make sense of the text, to redact this unmanageable contrariety, to save us from this traumatic *Thing*. Above all, the mythology synthesizes the bewildering bricolage of the book, magically transforming multiple pieces that cannot be mastered into Burroughs' singular "masterpiece," explaining *Naked Lunch* entirely in terms of its extra-textual origins. But do not be deceived: while these apocrypha make how we read the text depend upon false assumptions about how Burroughs wrote it, the precise genesis of his writing is what we really need to discover and understand. For fifty years, the genetic fables at the heart of *Naked Lunch*'s mythology have led us around in circles, mystifying the very basis to interpretation by turning fact and fiction, life and legend into a fast revolving door. From this trap, there can be no final exit. But if Burroughs scholarship is to make a *beginning*, is to reach through the myths to grasp the true material origins of *Naked Lunch* as title, manuscript, text, and publication—then Ginsberg's dedication is itself the place to begin.

"William Seward Burroughs, author of NAKED LUNCH, an endless novel which will drive everybody mad" (Ginsberg, *Collected Poems*, 802). Despite being so familiar, or maybe because of it, nobody has taken seriously the precise wording of Ginsberg's dedication or the significance and particular circumstances of its writing. For here were three important beginnings in one: this was the first appearance in print of Burroughs' own name as an author (preceding by three months his "Letter from a Master Addict" in the *British Journal of Addiction*, later appended to *Naked Lunch*), the first appearance in print of the title *Naked Lunch* (preceding by twelve months "From *Naked Lunch*, Book III: In Search of Yage" in *Black Mountain Review*), and the first appearance of both name and title together (preceding by eighteen months the "Excerpt" published in *Chicago Review*). All of these significant debuts were staged by Ginsberg's one-line dedication. Equally, bear in mind that before writing "Howl," Ginsberg had been working at Towne-Oller in San Francisco, the latest position in a five-year career in market research. Ginsberg's dedication was not just mythmaking but an agent's act of marketing—and one as successful as any other during a decade of his tirelessly promoting Burroughs' work, from *Junky* (first published as *Junkie*) in 1953 to *The Yage Letters* in 1963 via *Naked Lunch* in 1959.

In effect, Ginsberg's dedication launched a teaser campaign, and it's a safe bet that Gary Lee-Nova was not alone among readers at that time in experiencing, "due to the dedication in 'Howl,' a buzz—accompanied by a sense of frustration" generated by the advance promotion of an unavailable product (28). While Ginsberg's training in sales campaigns gave him an eye for the power of adverts to tantalize and stimulate new desires, his uniquely intimate knowledge of Burroughs and his writing enabled him to draft the perfect—that is to say, utterly *perverse*—advertisement, as only a sucker would believe in, let alone desire, a novel that never ended except by driving you insane. . . . Ginsberg's dedication is therefore *hype* in not only its modern public relations sense, as blatantly exaggerated sales promotion but also in the hipster or criminal sense of a con man's routine—as in *Naked*

Lunch, which talks the talk of both the underworld and the ad man's world and glosses "The Hype" as a variety of the "short-change con" (166). In sum, Ginsberg promoted *Naked Lunch* in exactly the same, openly double-dealing terms as Burroughs' own *routines* and specifically anticipated the very beginning of his narrative. Here *caveat emptor* becomes *caveat lector* as the aggressive equation of telling tall stories with selling fake products (catnip passed off as marijuana) acts as a warning to the reader who witnesses Lee's hustling performance—a performance aimed at the perfect mark for The Hype: "an advertising exec type fruit" (3).

The publicity generated by its censorship trial made *Howl* an unforeseen bestseller and ensured that by the time the trial ended, in October 1957, thousands of readers first knew Burroughs not only from his profoundly enigmatic portrait in Kerouac's *On the Road*—published a month earlier—but also through Ginsberg's equally enigmatic dedication, which tied the mysterious allure of the man to the mystery of his writing. Ginsberg's phrasing was of a piece with Kerouac's representation of Burroughs as a figure of ambivalent fascination but went one better in actually defining the term in relation to his work: for what could be more fascinating than the impossible paradox of an "endless novel which will drive everybody mad"? In just eight words, Ginsberg seems to have captured the reading experience of *Naked Lunch* as an utterly compelling yet maddeningly elusive text, one you can never pin down and that won't let you go.

Ginsberg's dedication drew on his unique knowledge of Burroughs' then-unpublished—indeed, then *unpublishable*—writing, but his trope of madness already had a history, going back to his earlier poem "On Burroughs' Work": "A naked lunch is natural to us [. . . .] Don't hide the madness" (*Collected Poems*, 114). Like his dedication, Ginsberg's poem has sometimes been taken to "describe" *Naked Lunch;* but the poem dates from November 1954 and so begs even more visibly the question of the text's material history. In other words, in late 1954 or in spring 1956—when he drafted the dedication—what existed of the book published in summer 1959? The answer depends on a precise chronology of the text's composition, a material history that, fifty years on, scholars have only just begun to work out. Certainly, in the case of "On Burroughs' Work," the answer is simple: almost nothing. And even by 1956, all that Ginsberg could have seen added up to a small fraction of the book we know (the short "Interzone" section, most of "Hospital" and "Hauser and O'Brien," parts of "Islam," and a number of important routines, including "The Talking Asshole").

However disturbing, this is actually an answer to the wrong question. Far more disturbing is the answer to the real question: to what in 1956 did the title *Naked Lunch* refer? For Ginsberg—like Burroughs and Kerouac—did not mean the book we know at all. On the contrary, at this stage, the title *Naked Lunch* still referred to a three-volume manuscript made up of "Junk" (i.e., *Junky*), "Queer," and "Yage" (hence "From *Naked Lunch*, Book III: In Search of Yage"), that Burroughs and Ginsberg assembled in New York in fall 1953 (fulfilling Burroughs' plan for a composite text sketched in Mexico that August). Ironically, the logical critique of Ginsberg's dedication—that it misleadingly describes the unfinished *Naked Lunch* as if it already existed—does not apply, because what it actually described did indeed exist.

All of a sudden, Ginsberg's influential and apparently astute descriptions of *Naked Lunch* appear in another light, as unintended mystifications that only an accurate historical knowledge can identify and dispel. Here, however, we encounter the paradox in his definition of *Naked Lunch* as a maddeningly elusive and endless object of fascination. The year before, French philosopher Maurice Blanchot had theorized fascination in *L'Espace littéraire* (1955), observing that the hypnotically indecisive enigma "ruins in me the power of knowing, the right to grasp" (31). Blanchot's point is that fascination has nothing to do with a simple split between fact and fantasy, reality and illusion but to do with the limits of knowledge itself. As the story of the origins of *Naked Lunch*'s title will demonstrate, such limits are especially meaningful when seeking the true scene behind the genetic myths that Burroughs himself promoted.

There Emerged Instead . . . *Naked Lunch*

The received version of *Naked Lunch*'s origins is so well known because it appears in the most prominent place in the book: its very first paragraph. Through the "Deposition"—typically referred to as "the introduction"—*Naked Lunch* begins, therefore, in a dry, factual manner, by drawing attention to its own beginnings: "I have no precise memory of writing the notes which have now been published under the title *Naked Lunch*. The title was suggested by Jack Kerouac" (199). However, not one of these beginnings—of book, text, and title—are what they appear to be.

Fifty years on, the first of these genetic claims is still almost universally believed, even though Burroughs scholarship has long since shown that the grain of truth in it—he did write "notes on sickness and delirium" and may well have had no "precise" memory of *all* he wrote (199)—only makes the story more a falsification than an outright fiction. The same goes for Burroughs' other claim about the title—that it was suggested by Kerouac—which at first sight appears too minor and vague to matter but that actually serves a double symbolic function. First, it confirms Burroughs' denial of conscious responsibility for his book. Second, it insists that the truth of the title—"NAKED Lunch—a frozen moment when everyone sees what is on the end of every fork"—is a kind of accidental collaboration of intentions and interpretations, revealed through an absolutely literal reading of the result: "The title means exactly what the words say" (199). Whatever Burroughs reveals here with one hand he hides with the other, although to grasp his game we need to consider the true history of the title's origins in relation to the two mythic versions in which it exists.

Burroughs tells one version most succinctly in his essay "Remembering Jack Kerouac." Here, he recalls first meeting Kerouac in New York during the mid-1940s and says he was the one "who kept telling me I should write and call the book I wrote *Naked Lunch*" (*Adding Machine*, 178). The second version, familiar enough to be cited in many Burroughs obituaries, describes an entirely different scenario, although the details vary so much that it's effectively several scenarios in one. The most common account is best summed up under the subhead "Scrawl of 'Naked Lust' Becomes 'Naked Lunch'" that appeared in the *New York Times* obituary of 3 August 1997: the title that Kerouac suggested came "from Ginsberg's misreading a bit of manuscript in Mr. Burroughs' scrawl, which actually referred to 'naked lust.'" In one variant, the manuscript that contained "Bill's hurried handwriting" is identified as *And the Hippos Were Boiled in Their Tanks,* the novel cowritten in New York by Burroughs and Kerouac in 1945 (Amburn, 94). In the most popular variant, what's misread is the very title of the manuscript later published as *Naked Lunch*. Neither of these accounts stands up under questioning. Even if Burroughs wrote "naked lust" in *Hippos* in 1945—and the manuscript evidence strongly suggests he didn't—then how to explain the gap of almost a decade before the first reference to "Naked Lunch" in any of the voluminous correspondence between Kerouac, Ginsberg, and Burroughs? Even more obviously, the idea that Ginsberg misread the manuscript's *title* falls apart not just because it was never referred to as "Naked Lust" but because this could only have taken place in spring 1957, when he and Kerouac visited Burroughs in Tangier—some three years after the title was already in use. No: the title emerged precisely in time to name his three-volume "Junk," "Queer," and "Yage" manuscript in fall 1953.

This recycled tale makes the naming of *Naked Lunch* a minor curiosity of unlikely errors, and that is why it's so important to correct it. For the slapdash origins of its title implies a reading of Burroughs' whole book in the same terms, as simply thrown together by chance and error—a crudely reductive reading that has nonetheless stuck. That the story is in any case "possibly apocryphal"—as the *LA Times* obituary noted (3 August 1997)—disguises the true symbolic significance of the question of the title's origins; which is to say how remarkably little is known about *Naked Lunch*'s provenance in general and how much of what we think we know turns out to be wrong. Which brings us to the real scene of the title's creation. Fadeout to 206 East Seventh Street, number 16, third-floor rear apartment, early September 1953 . . .

It was very likely about a month before Ginsberg took a rightly famous series of photographs of Burroughs and Kerouac posing on the couch, at the kitchen table, by the window, and on the rooftop of his Lower East Side apartment. With a nice historical irony, Olympia Press later used one portrait of Burroughs, posed behind a row of books by the fire-escape window, on the inside flap of the first edition, so materially connecting the published text of *Naked Lunch* back to the origins of its title that fall of 1953. But there was probably no posturing or horseplay for Ginsberg's Kodak Retina this day. Instead, they were reading through the manuscripts of "Queer" and "Yage" that Burroughs had written over the past eighteen months, having just returned to the city for the first time in six years. Kerouac possibly spotted the mistake Ginsberg made because in fact Kerouac already knew the manuscript. Indeed, he had been staying with him in Mexico City during early May 1952 when Burroughs was typing it up from longhand notes. The relevant lines appear dead center on page twenty-six of Burroughs' sixty-two-page first draft, very rough manuscript of "Queer": "As Lee stood aside to bow in his dignified old world greeting, there emerged instead a leer of nakedlust wrenched in the pain and hate of his deprived body" (cf. *Queer*, 18).[1] The origins of the title are still to do with Ginsberg's misreading and then Kerouac suggesting it, but the specific material context changes everything.

To begin with, Ginsberg's mistake does not come from any "difficulty deciphering" Burroughs' supposed scrawl (Amburn, 94). The typescript makes it clear that Ginsberg's mistake arises because of its precise conjuncture with Burroughs' own mistake in typing, that ran together "naked" and "lust," and the coincidence that the very next word was "wrenched," to produce the misreading "naked lunch." In other words, the title is a collaboratively authored, composite text, the simultaneously inspired and mechanical product of chance circumstance and slips in conscious intention, clinched by Kerouac's suggestion they take it literally. Burroughs' version of events in the "Deposition" is misleadingly incomplete but not entirely inaccurate. The double accident of Burroughs' typing and Ginsberg's reading has a further symbolic significance that becomes apparent when we take into account both the larger context of this particular page within *Queer* and the moment in fall 1953 that gave rise to the creation of "naked lunch."

The scene takes place in the Ship Ahoy, based on the real-life Bounty Bar in Mexico City, where William Lee's "leer of naked lust" is directed towards Allerton, based on Burroughs' reluctant young lover Lewis Marker. The biographical background confirms the drama and psychological point of this scene, which is clearly condensed in the full phrase, "there emerged instead a leer of naked lust." That is to say, Burroughs was recording how the truth reveals itself apparently despite or against conscious intentions: the very effort to channel and contain his feelings forces Lee "instead" to let slip his naked desire. In this sense, the scene precisely anticipates the novel's increasingly manic routines, which themselves dramatize the comic-horror return of the repressed in Lee's seduction of Allerton. The leer of lust is therefore a mistake full of meaning. In Freudian terms, Ginsberg's metamorphosis of *lust* into *lunch* is not an innocent or meaningless mistake either but is another instance of *parapraxis,* an accident that reveals the unwelcome truth. And this is because, by the time Ginsberg read the words out loud in his apartment, the desire that Burroughs felt for Marker had suddenly shifted onto Ginsberg, so that Ginsberg effectively found himself cast in the position of Allerton in *Queer.* Burroughs' desperation had forced Ginsberg into accepting what he described that September as a "great psychic marriage" (*As Ever,* 154), but the pressure was too great for it to last. Ginsberg's misreading is therefore highly *motivated* and in an obvious way disavows the undesired lust—the drive to *schlup* Ginsberg—that Burroughs now felt for him; but it also inescapably reaffirms it, because what Burroughs termed *schlupping*—which features first in *Queer* and then *Naked Lunch*—was a fantasy of devouring the body of his elusive object of desire and so very much a matter of making lust into lunch. Quite literally, *that's* what's on the end of the fork.

In retrospect, it's no coincidence that it was while researching the genetic history of *Junky,* in 2001, that I discovered "naked lunch" in the manuscript of "Queer" and knew I had found the Secret in material and symbolic form. After all, until the belated publication of *Queer* in 1985, readers of *Naked Lunch* could only look back to *Junky* as its point of origin. But the passage from *Junky* to *Naked Lunch* is simply inexplicable without *Queer,* which provides the missing link in Burroughs' extraordinary transformation as a writer. This is because of the emergence of the comic-horror routine in *Queer* as Burroughs' special form. And, as I have shown elsewhere,[2] the routines that Lee delivers to Allerton with the aim of seducing him had their hidden origins in Burroughs' desperate, desire-driven epistolary courtship of Lewis Marker in spring and summer 1952. The letter routine is the secret history that locates the beginnings of *Naked Lunch* within the writing of *Queer.*

Having read the manuscript of "Queer" and been Burroughs' only emotional support throughout the crisis of his relationship with Marker, in fall 1953 Ginsberg knew all about what he had called the "black magic" of Burroughs' letter routines (*Letters,* 128). In fact, as soon as Burroughs arrived in New York, Ginsberg reported that he was creating these "literary symbolic psychic fantasies daily" (*As Ever*, 154). The difference was that now they were aimed directly at Ginsberg himself. And so the events of September 1953, which ended with Burroughs' departure for Europe and North Africa, predicted the dark creativity of his letter writing to Ginsberg from Tangier between 1954 and 1956. During these three years, *Naked Lunch* developed out of an intense, fertile, and finally unresolved conflict between multiple forms of writing, as Burroughs tried and failed to impose coherence on material that was unstable, hazardous, and perplexing even to himself; so the letter cannot explain the genesis of the text as a whole. But it was the main engine of textual production during those first three years, and a key to determining the book's textual politics—that is, its relationship to and effect on the reader. And "the reader" was, almost exclusively, Allen Ginsberg.

When he claimed in 1956 that *Naked Lunch* would "drive everybody mad," Ginsberg was therefore generalizing from his own long experience of Burroughs' epistolary habit: as he had told Kerouac in November 1954, he was being "driven to distraction" by Burroughs and "got so mad" because of "the letter spectre zipping around" him, "sometimes 3 a.m."[3] Just days later, Ginsberg wrote "On Burroughs' Work," a context that casts the poem and its conclusion—"Don't hide the madness"—in an entirely different light. And if behind the dedication from 1956 there lies "On Burroughs' Work" from 1954, then behind the poem there lies the epistolary madness of Burroughs' original black-magic routines from 1952. For Burroughs had haunted Marker with the same "letter spectre," prompting Ginsberg in late May to warn Burroughs that his manuscript of "Queer" was writing "from the inside of the madman,"[4] adding in his journal next day the telling conclusion: "Don't bother to cover up madness" (*Book of Martyrdom*, 382). In short, Ginsberg's dedication to "Howl" described Burroughs' new work-in-progress by returning to the desire-driven, epistolary-powered queer center to his original three-volume *Naked Lunch*.

The End

Reconstructing the real scene of *Naked Lunch*'s origins brings us back to the account given by Burroughs in the "Deposition." In its legal sense, this tells no lies but is nevertheless wholly misleading, literally leading us in one genetic direction—towards Kerouac, notes, and junk addiction—all the better to avoid a far more revealing one—away from Ginsberg, the epistolary, and sexual desire. Paradoxically, this misdirection of the reader points to the truth of Burroughs' strategy here and throughout *Naked Lunch*. For in giving with one hand what he takes back with the other, Burroughs *shows his hand*. The "Deposition" itself is divided into two halves to insist on the inevitable falsifications of narrative, to make plain both its epistemological limits and its self-interested motivations. The second half—subtitled, with a surreptitious wink at the epistolary form, "Post Script" (207)—brazenly comes on to the reader with carny delight—*"Bill's Naked Lunch Room. . . . Step right up"* (208)—so as to undermine the trust we have invested in Burroughs' apparently straight narration of facts in the first. From tempting credulity to inviting skepticism, the "Deposition" warns the reader to steer between the false choices and equal seductions of Scylla and Charybdis (209), between the hard rock of authoritative, objective knowledge and the whirlpool of total subjectivity and relativism. Offering a "word to the wise guy" (210), the "Deposition" ends by insisting that we do not know what we think we know.

Bearing in mind the warning he gave Conrad Knickerbocker in 1965, that "there is no accurate description of the creation of a book, or an event" (Lotringer, 71), scholarship has to grasp the caveat built into Burroughs' own genetic accounts. In "Remembering Jack Kerouac," the point is that he immediately follows his claim for the title's origins by calling it into question: "Trying to remember *just where and when* this was said is like trying to remember a jumble of old films [. . .] I see a bar on 116th Street [. . .] Or was it in New Orleans [. . .] or was it later in Mexico by the lake in Chapultepec Park . . ." (*Adding Machine*, 178; my emphasis). Parodying the entire genre of the genetic anecdote, Burroughs dismisses the definitive account as a myth like any other—in which case my own reconstruction of the real scene must be taken as not objective and authoritative but motivated and inconclusive. "And speaking *Personally*," as Burroughs insists we must in the second half of his "Deposition" (207), after twenty-five years of scholarship and obsession, I wouldn't have it any other way. For the other side to arguing that all interpretation is based on material assumptions is to admit that even the most material research remains interpretive. And so, because *Naked Lunch* will never be explained *away* by its history, the task for scholarship is to do on a larger scale for Burroughs what Barry Miles, in his variorum facsimile edition of "Howl," did over twenty years ago for Ginsberg. This is less about securing the canonical status of Burroughs' masterpiece—an ambivalent tribute at best—than about establishing the basic knowledge required to understand the text in light of its complex manuscript and textual histories.

Take the "Deposition": it not only begins with a falsified account of *Naked Lunch*'s beginnings, it is itself a false beginning to Burroughs' book. This is because it was never intended as an introduction, was written and published separately after the first Olympia edition, was then included for the Grove edition only at the suggestion of its editors, and because Burroughs himself accepted it on condition it appear in an appendix, that is, *after* the end of his text. One of the most important corrections in the restored edition of 2003 was to at last relocate the "Deposition" to its proper position and to give supporting documentary evidence (see 249). The publication of any book is shaped to some extent by collaborations and contingencies, but *Naked Lunch* is determined by them from start to finish. Most obviously, the precise editorial roles played by Ginsberg, Kerouac, and Alan Ansen in Tangier during 1957, by Ginsberg, Brion Gysin, and Sinclair Beiles in Paris during 1958 and 1959, or by *Chicago Review* and *Big Table* editor Irving Rosenthal have yet to be documented or analyzed in regard to their decisive impact on Burroughs' book. And what makes these factors so important is how they relate to the long and tortuous history of its writing. In both form and theme, the effects of Burroughs' unresolved conflict between exercising control and embracing spontaneity can be seen and felt on every page of *Naked Lunch*. And just as contingencies were decisive in the origins of the title, so are they central to the story of how the book achieved its final form—courtesy of the supposedly arbitrary sequence in which the French printers returned to Burroughs sections of the galley proofs in July 1959.

"By some magic," Burroughs recalled, "the chapters had fallen into place, and the only change was to shift the 'Hauser and O'Brien' section from the beginning to the end" (qtd. in *Naked Lunch*, 240). Significantly, the first half of this anecdote is often recycled without the qualifying second half. Leaving out the detail falsifies the entire anecdote, however, making Burroughs seem a blind believer in chance, when his point is precisely that he embraced contingency while exercising choice. But the mythic version of *Naked Lunch* prefers to keep it vivid and simple. If this is how "magic" becomes mystification, what about Burroughs' inverting of his text's "beginning" and "end"? When he first drafted it in February 1955, Burroughs had seen "Hauser and O'Brien" as "one beginning" to his novel (*Letters*, 267). Between 1957 and 1959, it was located—suspended like a junkie's fantasy between two "Habit Notes"—in the "Hospital" section, which always appeared towards the end of his manuscript, never the beginning, even when the running order changed. At some point, he cut the second half (published separately as "The Conspiracy" in 1960) and wrote a new, two-page conclusion. His decision in July 1959 to move "Hauser and O'Brien" to the end gave *Naked Lunch* a coherent, first-person, narrative frame, because the last lines—"The Heat was off me from here on out"—now seemed to return to the very first line—"I can feel the heat closing in" (181, 3). At the last minute, Burroughs had created a perfect symmetry and apparent teleology, giving support to claims for the deliberate architectural design of *Naked Lunch* as a whole—but only by concealing the multiple and contradictory genetic histories of his manuscript.

"When they walked in on me that morning at 8 o'clock" might have been the first line of *Naked Lunch*—but so might "The only native in Interzone who is neither queer nor available is Andrew Keif's chauffeur," "The Word is divided into units," or "Stay away from Queens Plaza, son," because, at one time, all headed manuscripts destined to become *Naked Lunch*. The many *Naked Lunch*es that might have been are matched by the multiple, different, versions that do exist. Take just the first section, "And Start West." With numerous small differences, it appeared in three magazines (*Chicago Review*, *Big Table*, and *Jabberwock*) before the Olympia edition, while the Grove, Calder, and restored editions of *Naked Lunch* also show numerous small differences. A basic comparative analysis of just this one section in magazine and book form has, therefore, twenty-one textual permutations. And while the differences are mostly small—punctuation, layout, spelling, typos—small is not necessarily minor or insignificant, especially given the sheer number of them. There are, for example, over *two hundred* differences between "And Start West" as published in *Chicago Review* and *Jabberwock*—evidence that the obscure Edinburgh magazine had in fact used a completely different manuscript.[5]

The full history of "And Start West" is particularly important, because it reveals how *Naked Lunch* came to begin with that resonant first line and stunning opening caveat lector. Was this really determined arbitrarily by the Olympia Press printers in July 1959? Certainly, *Naked Lunch*'s entire history dictated that its published form would only be decided by some contingent circumstance, and had Maurice Girodias been slower or quicker to act, another, quite different *Naked Lunch* would have appeared. The constant changes across future editions are a material extension of that original instability and a true measure of the unbound, perverse, and inexhaustible vitality of Burroughs' creation. "This novel *is happening*," he wrote in October 1957 (*Letters*, 375)—and it *still is*. And so it's ironic to note that the first and last words of the Paris Olympia edition falsified the "endless" history predicted by Ginsberg, mysteriously adding a definite article to Burroughs' title—*The Naked Lunch*—and, on the final page, bringing it to a false closure with "THE END" (226).

Notes

1. "Queer" Ms., Box 1, Folder 13, William S. Burroughs Archive, the Henry W. and Albert A. Berg Collection of English and American Literature, New York Public Library, Astor, Lenox, and Tilden Foundations.

2. See *William Burroughs and the Secret of Fascination* (Carbondale: Southern Illinois UP, 2003).

3. Allen Ginsberg to Jack Kerouac, 9 November 1954, Allen Ginsberg Collection, Harry Ransom Humanities Research Center, University of Texas, Austin.

4. Ginsberg, journal entry for 30 May 1952, series 2, notebooks and journals, box 4, folder 1, Allen Ginsberg Papers, Stanford University.

5. Thanks to Lizzie MacGregor of the Scottish Poetry Library for obtaining a copy of *Jabberwock* (1959). The title "And Start West" appeared in *Jabberwock* but was not used in *Naked Lunch* until the restored edition, edited by Grauerholz and Miles.

Works Cited

Amburn, Ellis. *Subterranean Kerouac: the Hidden Life of Jack Kerouac*. New York: St. Martin's, 1998.

Blanchot, Maurice. *The Space of Literature*. Translated by Ann Smock. 1955. Lincoln: U of Nebraska P, 1982.

Burroughs, William S. *The Adding Machine*. London: Calder, 1985.

———. "Excerpt: *Naked Lunch*." *Chicago Review* 12.1 (Spring 1958): 25–30.

———. "From *Naked Lunch*, Book III: In Search of Yage." *Black Mountain Review* 7 (Autumn 1957; issued Spring 1958): 144–48.

———. "Letter from a Master Addict to Dangerous Drugs." *British Journal of Addiction* 53, no. 2 (January 1957): 119–31.

———. *The Letters of William S. Burroughs, 1945–1959*. Edited by Oliver Harris. New York: Viking, 1993.

———. *The Naked Lunch*. Paris: Olympia Press, 1959.

———. *Queer*. New York: Viking, 1985.

Ginsberg, Allen. *Collected Poems, 1947–1980*. New York: Viking, 1985.

———. *The Book of Martyrdom and Artifice: First Journals and Poems, 1937–1952*. Edited by Juanita Liebermann-Plimpton and Bill Morgan. New York: De Capo, 2006.

Ginsberg, Allen, and Neal Cassady. *As Ever: The Collected Correspondence of Allen Ginsberg and Neal Cassady*. Edited by Barry Gifford. Berkeley, CA: Creative Arts, 1977.

Lee-Nova, Gary. "Reading Burroughs since the Beginning." *Beat Scene* 53 (summer 2007): 28–38.

Lotringer, Sylvère, ed. *Burroughs Live: The Collected Interviews of William S. Burroughs 1960–1997*. Los Angeles: Semiotext(e), 2001.

"Room for One More": The Invitation to *Naked Lunch*

robert **HOLTON**

(T)he present stress of our most gifted talents on private studies of pathology is also symptomatic of the larger, the national disease.
—Maxwell Geismar, 1958

Control, bureaucracy, regimentation, these are merely symptoms of a deeper sickness that no political or economic program can touch. What is the sickness itself?
—William Burroughs, 1955

Some lunches are "by invitation only." Although William Burroughs' *Naked Lunch* is not so formal or exclusive, an invitation is nonetheless provided in the form of the introductory essay: "Deposition: Testimony Concerning a Sickness." Of course, as Burroughs himself observes, readers "can cut into *Naked Lunch* at any intersection point" (187), and while the cutting metaphor is appropriate to the culinary title, attendance generally begins with the "Deposition." This introduction has been part of the text since the 1962 Grove Press edition, and, although it may have been added primarily to mollify American censors, it has come to function as an invitation to the lunch itself. Invitations and introductions possess an ambiguous status, because both are part of the larger process of the meal or text and yet remain quite separate. As Oliver Harris notes, this one may belong in the genre of "false prefaces" (187), designed to draw readers in rather than to give a genuine account of the text's origins. Like all good invitations though, the "Deposition" is both attention-catching and memorable: Carol Loranger observes that it was a focus of discussion during the obscenity trial that greeted its initial American publication, that it continues to provide a number of the most frequently cited passages, and that it tends to stay in the minds of casual readers. And, as any good invitation should, it attempts to make its recipient, the reader, feel included and to elicit a sense of anticipatory desire.

It is an understatement, perhaps, to point out that *Naked Lunch* is hardly to everyone's taste. Burroughs warns that the details to follow are "brutal, obscene and disgusting" as well as "repulsive" (205), and its fantastic scenes of graphic violence and transgressive sexuality exceeded anything that had been published at that point. Whatever individual pathologies might have led Burroughs himself to this, it is worth considering the motives that led so many postwar readers to take up an invitation to consume such strange and disturbing fare. While it may have been the most extreme, *Naked Lunch* was not the only postwar text to explore this zone. Nelson Algren's gritty novel of addiction and despair, *The Man with the Golden Arm* (1949), won the first National Book Award, and many subsequent American writers surveyed a terrain of decadence, substance abuse, violence, criminality, and sexual "deviance" that stands in marked contrast to the relative affluence and security of postwar life. Burroughs' invitation is explicit: "Room for One More Inside, Sir," he declares in his carnival barker voice, "Step right up" (208). But it is not immediately clear why so many would venture into a space offering immersion in waste and filth, the deviant and the abject.

The central figure in the "Deposition" is a version of Burroughs himself, of course, and his confessional narrative, whatever its fidelity to truth, traces his movement from abjection to knowledge. The nadir in this trajectory, "the end of the junk line," occurs in a room "in the Native Quarter of Tangier" (202). This is presented as the culmination of junkie existence, the moment of truth, and, in a sense, it is this abject moment that grounds Burroughs' authorial position, that generates the inverse social capital on which his authority is based. The term *junk* itself appropriately enough refers both to heroin and waste, and the junkie is a figure of wasted humanity, social refuse. Burroughs specifies that the room was in the Native Quarter, a detail carrying racialized connotations of an existence far removed from productive, middle-American culture. Burroughs had, in fact, closely studied *The Decline of the West*, in which Spengler described those who associate with the native "fellahin" as "wasteproducts" (185). Filthy and surrounded by rising heaps of garbage, without basic amenities such as light and water, his body turned "fibrous grey," the junkie is the epitome of uselessness and nonproductivity: "I did absolutely nothing. I could look at the end of my shoe for eight hours" (202–3). Human relations are reduced to fantasies of checking the pockets of dead friends for money as, helpless in the face of addiction and its ineluctable physiological and economic rhythms, he has hit bottom. "Wouldn't you?" he asks repeatedly, by way of invitation. "Yes," he affirms, "you would" (201).

Postwar America, with its unprecedented emphasis on adjustment and productivity, was the subject of David Riesman's influential 1950 study *The Lonely Crowd*. In it, he argued that a new form of subjectivity had emerged, an unprecedented form of conformist adjustment. Fueled by the work of writers Erich Fromm, C. Wright Mills, William Whyte, and others, debates on these topics raged throughout the 1950s and 1960s as Americans came to terms with Cold War limits on dissent, a newly affluent economy, the proliferation of suburbs and malls and consumer goods, the rapidly expanding influence of mass media, and a myriad of other phenomena whose overall effect appeared to be an increasing cultural homogeneity. As Fredric Jameson has remarked in a sweeping but useful generalization: "What then dawns is the realization that no society has ever been as standardized as this one" (17). Riesman argued that the new conformists, more or less adjusted to these conditions, were becoming the defining force in American culture. Dissent, which in the 1930s had been organized along political lines, shifted instead to more broadly cultural forms in response not only to McCarthyism but also to a general postwar loss of faith in political solutions. As a result, many who resisted the tide of conformist adjustment instead sought out what Jameson refers to as vantage points or fantasy subject positions (17) from which the mainstream could be considered. For Burroughs (and his readers) the figure of the junkie, both inside and outside the social system and replete with signifiers of waste as well as of truth, provided an inviting and enabling perspective.

In defining adjustment, Riesman uses the counterexample of the maladjusted, whom he refers to as the "anomics," a group including the misfits, the eccentrics, those who cannot fit in, and those who will not fit in, that assortment of individuals existing beyond—or perhaps beneath—the reach of adjusted conformity: drug addicts, sexual "deviants," criminals, the mentally ill, and so on. Collectively, estimates Riesman, "the anomics—ranging from overt outlaws to 'catatonic' types who lack even the spark for living, let alone rebellion—constitute a sizable number in America" (290). Curiously, Burroughs' junkie bridges these opposites in his recourse to criminal behavior on one hand and his heroin-induced immobility on the other. One quality shared by anomic outlaws and catatonics both, despite manifest differences, is nonproductivity; indeed, the idea that such people represent a form of social waste recurs with some frequency. Riesman notes that in Marxist discourse, anomics are generally referred to as the *lumpenproletariat*, a group Marx disparages as "scum, offal, refuse" (149). In *Multitude*, for example, Michael Hardt and Antonio Negri observe that lumpens are often characterized as "unproductive social parasites—thieves, prostitutes, drug addicts, and the like" (190).

The "Deposition" presents Burroughs as an exemplary anomic, and while this can hardly be considered adjusted, neither is it a position of resistance in any straightforward manner. Rejected as useless by capitalism, anomics contribute no revolutionary potential to socialism. Despite its sordid nature, anomia both appealed to the voyeuristic instinct and, more important perhaps, pointed to the emerging postwar desire for a space outside the conformist network of productive socioeconomic relations that was establishing an unprecedented homogeneity at the level of culture and at the level of individual subjectivity. Herbert Marcuse, often critical of apolitical alienation, allowed that lumpen refuse nevertheless "exist[s] outside" the centripetal center and "violates the rules," adding almost grudgingly that their "opposition is revolutionary even if their consciousness is not" (256). Revolutionary or not, the unproductive lumpens became the subject of much interest in the 1950s and 1960s as heterogeneous spaces seemed to be vanishing. In these circumstances, the spaces of lumpen anomia in all their bizarre manifestations appeared increasingly worthy of investigation. "To be unique or grotesque," Jameson observes, "a cartoon figure, an obsessive, is [. . .] not to be usable in efficient or instrumental ways" (101).

A similar argument was made in the 1960s by Susan Sontag, who recognized that revolutionary politics were bound to fail because of the government's superior force. Instead, in true 1960s style, she recommended sex, drugs, and anything else that would make people less suitable as functionaries in the "bureaucratic machine," anything that "unfits, maladapts, a person for the American way of life" (186). This interest in anomic positions, ranging from horrified fascination to outright advocacy, was a prominent feature of postwar cultural life because it offered the possibility of pushing against the encroachments of modern adjustment, of escaping from what Burroughs describes as the "lifeproof houses" of the "vast subdivision," where the "antennae of television [reach up] to the meaningless sky" (11). A number of postwar writers, from Nelson Algren to Ken Kesey, and particularly the Beat writers, represented lumpens and anomics as inhabitants of a zone of reaction and potential refuge, if not actual resistance. Georges Bataille directly connects "the *heterogeneous* world" with "unproductive expenditure": "This consists of everything rejected by *homogeneous* society as waste [. . .] the waste products of the human body and certain analogous matter [. . .] the numerous elements or social forms that homogeneous society is powerless to assimilate [. . .] those who refuse the rule" (142). Unassimilability is crucial here: in remaining outside the normative structures of social ontology, the lumpens constitute a space in which, according to Jeffrey Mehlman, "heterogeneity, in its unassimilability to every dialectical totalization, is affirmed." Even in Marx himself, the explicit condemnation of the lumpens is, Mehlman argues, belied by the linguistic exuberance of his prose, which, as he describes the lumpens in *The Eighteenth Brumaire*, registers an "exhilaration," an "almost Rabelaisian verve," and a "proliferating energy" (13).[1]

As this indicates, there can arise in such discussions a temptation to overlay a peculiar and desperate form of hope on the figure of the lumpen. Jameson puts it this way: to accept being unusable and maladjusted may open the door to "a Utopia of misfits and oddballs in which the constraints for uniformization and conformity have been removed and human beings grow wild like plants in a state of nature" (99). Opening this door to the garden of anomia, then, provides a space for those "who, no longer fettered by the constraints of a now oppressive sociality, blossom into the neurotics, compulsives, obsessives, paranoids, schizophrenics, whom our society considers sick but who, in a world of true freedom, may make up the flora and fauna of 'human nature' itself" (99). While maintaining the heuristic value of the lumpen position, Burroughs could hardly be accused of an excess of utopian optimism, and the notion that a space of "true freedom," anomic or otherwise, might be located in the world of *Naked Lunch* seems bitterly out of place. The fact that their opposition is neither utopian nor revolutionary is made abundantly clear in Burroughs' insistent representation of addicts as exemplary and helpless figures in the "pyramid of junk" (200), as miserable pawns in a structure homologous with modernity's widespread systems of oppressive and manipulative power. Participating in neither the processes of production nor the politics of resistance, the abject figure of the wasted junkie becomes instead a figure of truth in an introduction saturated with complex, and sometimes contradictory, discourses of truth.

The title itself, attributed to Kerouac, refers to a meal where "everyone sees what is on the end of every fork" (199), the abattoir that resides unacknowledged, as it were, in the shadow of many graceful meals. The implication is that this meal's "frozen moment" will be a moment of truth, that readers who take up this peculiar invitation will find the lunch revelatory. The naked truth is to be encountered, with neither distractions to diffuse it nor euphemisms to render it palatable. This extends the truth claim more broadly: not only is the author's wasted anomia to be frankly revealed but this exposé also will extend outward to reveal the truth of everyone's condition, fork-holders and lunch-eaters everywhere. This was confirmed by Allen Ginsberg in his censorship-trial testimony: the term *naked*, he explained, "relates to nakedness of seeing, to be able to see clearly without any confusing disguises, to see through the disguise." If this presents truth and nothing but the truth, as required by the legal swearing-in ritual, the title's second word connects it to the whole truth: the "'Lunch,'" Ginsberg continued, "would be a complete banquet of all this naked awareness" ("Boston Trial"). The nakedness Burroughs insists on ("The title means exactly what the words say: NAKED Lunch" [199]) is far removed from the innocent state of prelapsarian unconcealment this can connote and instead involves the kinds of awful truth some might prefer not to face except from the safe distance of a literary account.

The text of *Naked Lunch* itself purportedly results from the "detailed notes" (199) Burroughs took while undergoing the delirium, a kind of fieldwork of which he has subsequently retained no memory. This disavowal, which he later called into question (211), has the effect of increasing the truth claim because it suggests that the notes collected here constitute an account of the experience that is unmediated, uncensored, and undistorted by retrospective considerations. While it is clear that sickness and delirium were negative conditions, these can nonetheless make possible the opening of a door to truth. The link between the image of the anomic lumpen as a form of human waste and the idea of truth was a strong one in the postwar period because it allowed the assertion of a zone whose immediacy remained uninsulated by middle-class protections, whose reality could not be shielded by bourgeois euphemisms and hypocrisy—unlike the compromised content provided by "that long newspaper spoon" (205). The appetite for such forms of truth was shaped by the cultural dynamics of postwar America, a period defined at one level by its shiny hygienic surfaces, its relentless and shallow optimism, and its tendency to narrowed and homogenized discursive possibilities. At another level, though, the period was defined by the reaction against all this, as debates about conformism and alienation emerged as significant cultural spaces in which the meaning of modernity itself was dissected.

From J. D. Salinger's Holden Caulfield to John Updike's Rabbit Angstrom and beyond, literature presented characters fleeing from the compromising homogeneity of the center in search of some more-authentic centrifugal experience. If the pressures of conformity are to be understood truthfully, Algren wrote, readers and writers will have to look unflinchingly at "the enormous reservoir of sick, vindictive life that moves like an underground river beneath all our boulevards" (35). Or as Adrienne Rich puts it in "Open Air Museum" (1964), waste constitutes a "sacred field" and a "Cry of truth among so many lies" as we come "Face to face with the flag of our true country" (63–64). Burroughs' invitation promises this and more, because the specific details of lumpen anomia are, he promises, related to much larger truths: "there are many junk pyramids feeding on peoples of the world," he asserts, and this "is the mold of monopoly and possession" (200). The claim, then, is that heroin addiction exists in a homological or even allegorical relation to the human condition and thus, by seeking the truth of the former, we will find crucial truths of the latter.

"There has to be something somewhere that does not deceive," Michel de Certeau has argued, and the "positioning of the subject under the sign of *refuse* is the point where 'true' discourse is imprinted" (39–40). This sense of truth is cultivated in the first section of *Naked Lunch* through vocabularies conventionally associated with facticity and objectivity: the legal, the mathematical, and the scientific. A *deposition* is a legal term alluding to testimony given under oath and thus sworn to be true, for example, and much of what follows draws on the clinical vocabulary of medical research. Heroin is "quantifiable and accurately measurable" (200), he argues, and his next book will consist of a "mathematical extension" of this to encompass the wider range of applications because "they all obey basic laws" (205). Throughout, Burroughs' references to algebra, to formulae, to the economics of consumerism, and so on suggest rigor and precision. Furthermore, the opening lines reference an awakening, a familiar metaphor drawing on a transition from a state of unknowing to a condition of true knowledge, from unconsciousness to conscious awareness. Moreover, the transition is described as one from sickness to health, a "recovery." The awakened and now-healthy Burroughs claims to be "calm and sane" following an ordeal including "delirium" and refers to himself as a survivor (199). If the center of the "Deposition" may be said to be the abject junkie in Tangier whose "field of vision" has become "a grey screen always blanker and fainter" (203), the first part of the "Deposition" concludes with a hope for the transparency of truth: "If man can *see*" (205).

Although the introduction initially situates the text in terms of a desire to ameliorate a public-health issue, there is, of course, a different impulse also at work and, in the second section, a less-distanced and more-directed rhetoric brings the reader closer to experiential reality. His claim is more personal, is grounded in having been a junkie, having lived through experiences only barely imaginable for most readers, and returned, like Melville's Ishmael, to tell his tale of obsession—albeit one of white powder rather than a white whale. The opening initiates a set of oppositions that reinforces the overall sense of truth: legal/illegal, science/irrationality, sanity/delirium. Although one side of these oppositions carries a comforting legitimacy, and

Burroughs initially pitches it as though this were really the main point, it is centrifugal force that draws readers in and constitutes the core of the book's appeal. This is a very different category of truth, one that whets the readerly appetite for the confessional, the sordid, the delirious, and the trangressive, for a truth unavailable inside conformity's secure zones. If truth is a major stake in this account, it lies finally not with those who stand outside and exercise reason but with the recovering addict, the one who exists quite literally "post script": "A condition of total exposure is precipitated when the Kicking Addict cannot choose but see smell and listen" (207). Truth as reason makes its appearance but is displaced by the awful truth. One side frames the discussion in the rhetoric of math and economics as though it were containable within the realms of the quantifiable and the predictable; the other side moves toward the uncontainable categories of the sublime and the grotesque.

Julia Kristeva observes that abjection is a border condition of proximity to that which must be rejected in order that life is sustained, yet the sublime and grotesque tend to erode those very borders (3). At one level, the general direction of the first section of the "Deposition" is straightforward in its rejection of junk, lumpen anomia, and refuse. The cautionary tone and public-spirited injunction to rid the world of this sickness seem clear, but as a new voice takes over, the tone of the "Post Script" section becomes more insidious, closer to an invitation than to a rejection, and shifts from the measured and distanced articulation of the objective observer to the baiting and cynical attitude of a con-man/carnie huckster. Hints of this are present in the earlier section, particularly when he breaks into the second person to describe the dissolution of basic boundaries defining the body and personal identity: he notes, for example, "Whether you sniff it smoke it eat it or shove it up your ass the result is the same" (200), and later he declares, "You would lie, cheat, inform on your friends, steal, do *anything* to satisfy total need" (201). In both cases, the *you* implicates the reader and, in the "Post Script," when Burroughs drops the tone of distanced objectivity and slips into character, repeatedly addressing "you," this is even more pronounced and compromising.

The second-person rhetoric is repeated seven times over nine pages, once as a subtitle, and it has the effect not only of inviting the reader into Burroughs' world but also of insinuating the reader's complicity, an attraction to the brutal, the obscene, the disgusting, and the repulsive. In the end, Burroughs uses these techniques to invite readers into a literary experience, not necessarily to become human refuse. The textual immersion in the abject is thus a second-order abjection in which readers confront that truth without actually enduring it. As Kristeva puts it, this is "an impure process that protects from the abject only by dint of being immersed in it" (29) through a complex process of attraction/repulsion. A similar idea of protection/immersion comes up in another of the invitations contained in the "Post Script"—albeit with heavy Burroughsian irony: "Only way to protect yourself against this horrid peril is come over HERE and shack up with Charybdis. . . . Treat you right kid" (209). Charybdis, of course, is anything but protective, and there is always the danger that immersion in abjection's "horrid peril" will prove irreversible.

The danger is an integral part of the appeal, of course, and the "Deposition's" invitation combines the cautionary and the seductive in a rhetorical tension that continues to attract (and repel) readers decades after the initial postwar circumstances in which it was written. Fifty years after the publication of *Naked Lunch*, our social preoccupation with drug use (a preoccupation shared by users and opponents alike) has continued unabated, and Burroughs' text has maintained its cultural currency. There is always "Room for One More," Burroughs reminds us as he beckons us in.

Note

1. In a remarkable passage, Marx provides a list of representative lumpens:

> Alongside decayed roués with dubious means of subsistence and of dubious origin, alongside ruined and adventurous offshoots of the bourgeoisie, were vagabonds, discharged soldiers, discharged jailbirds, escaped galley slaves, swindlers, mountebanks, lazzaroni, pickpockets, tricksters, gamblers, maquereaux [pimps], brothel keepers, porters, literati, organ grinders, ragpickers, knife grinders, tinkers, beggars—in short, the whole indefinite, disintegrated mass, thrown hither and thither, which the French call la bohème. (149)

Works Cited

Algren, Nelson. *Nonconformism: Writing on Writing*. New York: Seven Stories, 1996.

Bataille, Georges. *Visions of Excess: Selected Writings 1927–1939*. Translated and edited by Allan Stoekl. Minneapolis: U of Minnesota P, 1985.

"The Boston Trial of *Naked Lunch*." Realitystudio.org, http://realitystudio.org/texts/naked-lunch/trial/ (accessed August 2007).

de Certeau, Michel. *Heterologies: Discourse on the Other*. Minneapolis: U of Minnesota P, 1986.

Hardt, Michael, and Antonio Negri. *Multitude: War and Democracy in the Age of Empire*. New York: Penguin, 2004.

Harris, Oliver. *William Burroughs and the Secret of Fascination*. Carbondale: Southern Illinois UP, 2003.

Jameson, Fredric. *The Seeds of Time*. New York: Columbia UP, 1994.

Kristeva, Julia. *Powers of Horror: An Essay on Abjection*. New York: Columbia UP, 1982.

Loranger, Carol. "'This Book Spill Off the Page in All Directions': What Is the Text of *Naked Lunch*?" *Postmodern Culture* 10, no. 1 (September 1999). http://www3.iath.virginia.edu/pmc/text-only/issue.999/10.1loranger.txt (accessed August 2007).

Marcuse, Herbert. *One-Dimensional Man: Studies in the Ideology of Advanced Industrial Society.* Boston: Beacon, 1991.

Marx, Karl. *The Eighteenth Brumaire of Louis Bonaparte.* New York: International, 1963.

Mehlman, Jeffrey. *Revolution and Repetition: Marx/Hugo/Balzac.* Berkeley: U of California P, 1977.

Rich, Adrienne. *The Fact of a Doorframe: Poems Selected and New 1950–1984.* New York: Norton, 1994.

Riesman, David. *The Lonely Crowd.* New Haven: Yale UP, 1950.

Sontag, Susan. "Some Thoughts on the Right Way (for Us) to Love the Cuban Revolution." *The Uptight Society: A Book of Readings,* edited by Howard Gadlin and Bertram E. Garskof, 186–94. Belmont, CA: Brooks/Cole, 1970.

Spengler, Oswald. *The Decline of the West.* 2 vols. Translated by Charles Francis Atkinson. New York: Knopf, 1926.

dossier TWO
ian MACFADYEN

Files Comprising: Portrait Of The Author As An Invisible Man, Trauma, A Strong Black Medicine, Tourette's, Absent From The Scene, Vineland, *Yagé* And The Oblivion Sign, Delirious Transcription, Frozen Moments, The Blue Movie, Flowers, Chinoise, The Shooting Of Joan, Joan, Checkpoint, In Memory Of Identity, Private Dick.

Portrait Of The Author As An Invisible Man

H. G. Wells' malevolent, havoc-wreaking creation becomes that feared and fascinating monstrosity which leaks phantasmatically through the media. James Hillman: "The invisible becomes 'alien' [. . .] Our modern passages are so narrow and with such low ceilings, the invisibles must twist themselves into freakish shapes in order to come through" (109).

Trauma

There was a traumatic incident in Burroughs' childhood which he was never able to clearly recall or reconstruct. Burroughs' repeated declaration that he will "unlock [his] word hoard" (192) mimics "the talking cure" of psychoanalysis, inviting the return of the repressed, the uncovering of a buried truth, while parodying the process of regression which is itself infantilized by Doctor Benway: "'Take baby walkabout Switchboard'" (24). When Burroughs expresses his desire to be a recording instrument, adding, "I do not presume to impose 'story' 'plot' 'continuity'" (184), it is because a traumatic event may have been "recorded," but it is not accessible through cause-and-effect narrative and cannot therefore be decoded: it is a *record* without a history. The ticker-tape splicing and disruption of the "Atrophied Preface" is a radical method of free-association seeking some kind of hidden truth, though Burroughs' professed confessional is undercut by his revival of the fake carny God routine, the Radio Cairo Prophet's declamatory sales pitch drowning out revelation with a tide of pseudotestimonial babble and entropic feedback. It is a deranged séance, the voices of the dead and Burroughs' own past words filling Dead Air Time—ciphered, screened, cut off, lost in the cacophony.

A Strong Black Medicine

Naked Lunch was not the abolition of the demonic but its ultimate creation, not a spiritual exit visa but an impasse of the truly monstrous.

Tourette's

Compulsively, convulsively speaking the unspeakable, Burroughs' narrative voices create a Tourette's text, both strategically and helplessly breaking linguistic taboos. Don't eat your own words—spill them, disgorge them, it's the visceral, uncontrollable urge to rupture and shock, not a "discourse" but an uncensored eruption of the nervous system, an apoplexy of pure, impure, liberating filth. Don't say it! But I *must*. ... We submit to the overthrow of all taste and decorum in Burroughs' text, we are readers transformed into galvanized performers of a great echolalia, gleefully parroting linguistic pandemonium. "'Possession' they call it . . . " (184). This is what it feels like to be possessed by the unspeakable which speaks through you, in your very own name, to be a vessel merely for the transmission of hateful logomania.

Absent From The Scene

Because his work was confessional, De Quincey knew that the public would seek an image of the author of *Confessions of an English Opium Eater*. He appears to oblige in the text, providing a portrait for every reader—it's a stormy winter night, a room piled with five thousand books, a fire is burning in the hearth, its flames reflected in the glass decanter of ruby-colored laudanum . . . but the author "himself" is entirely absent from the scene, a central invisibility. Alina Clej writes that the "Opium-Eater appears to be a fictional construct, a potential or hypothetical self—an empty sign, the locus of all imaginary inscriptions" (110). In *Naked Lunch*, this absence is abject—empty ampule boxes, the toe of the author's shoe, "a grey screen always blanker and fainter" (203). *N'existe pas:* something other than the existential junkie's *cris de coeur,* it is the absence which guarantees nothing less than absolute literary authenticity, the validation of an *immaculate* conception.

Vineland

In *Suspiria de Profundis* (1845), De Quincey writes of "those parasitical thoughts, feelings, digressions, which climb up with bells and blossoms round about the arid stock" (qtd. in Clej, 109), and Burroughs' own vine blooms with brilliant flowers of evil in orchidaceous splendor and concealing entanglement. In both cases, the confession of guilt and error, blindness and mourning is overrun, overwhelmed by an excess of rampant foliage. In *Naked Lunch*, the vine is *Bannisteriopsis,* climbing until its flesh-pink flowers reach the sun, greedily smothering all in its climb and spread. The *yagé*-inspired sections of the text take the form of labyrinthine dream detours and explosions of phantasmagoria, feeding off the poisonous roots of confession.

Yagé And The Oblivion Sign

It may be that this "heroin book" is really a *yagé* book, Burroughs, sloughing off his junkie skin, changed utterly. His old version of himself, Lee, is a ghost who doesn't even realize that he is truly a revenant—Burroughs has made him so and then takes leave of that character. In this sense, Lee is not Burroughs' "alter ego" as so often presumed—he is the repudiated one, the abandoned lost soul, an oblivion sign. If Lee is the old ghost self, then Burroughs the writer of *Naked Lunch* is now someone quite other—he sees the truth of his junk past, he writes and replays this past as fiction, as the telling of stories, and he unravels and fragments and erases it, he is not just the Master Addict but a master of space and time, free to travel, to enter and go out, he has a privileged, panoramic view of space and time and the mutations and metamorphoses of life—beautiful, hideous, terrifying, and blissful. He has become writer as *seer.*

Delirious Transcription

The history of the book's creation is thrown into question by the writer's claim in the 1960 introduction, "Deposition: Testimony Concerning a Sickness," that he has "no precise memory of writing these notes" (199). The use of the term *notes* is significant, suggesting words scribbled in sickness and delirium on a bedside table, while the word *precise* here is strategically *imprecise*. This disavowal of intentionality, which even Burroughs would later admit was an exaggeration, preferences a hemorrhage of the imagination and the *unconscious transcription* of delirium over intentionality. It is paradoxically both a disclaimer and a deposition guaranteeing the pure authenticity of the self-begotten text, a work beyond literary caesarian, moral control, and aesthetic intervention. The introduction and the appendix are retroactive mission statements and constitute post-"recovery," post facto explanations and justifications of a book whose production circumvents memory, created through a time which is lost, ideally beyond recall—as if *written before remembering*.

Frozen Moments

The pre–cut-up fragmentation in *Naked Lunch* reveals an attraction to the part-object, the isolated phrase evidently removed from its context and reconfigured—a process of continual fetishistic detachment/reattachment, the referent made anew, only to testify to an ultimate loss. It is a fetishistic operation to which, significantly, Burroughs would become addicted, an obsessive replaying of severance and reconstitution, without cease, without limit. *I do not remember / I must always forget.*

The Blue Movie

Sylvère Lotringer describes the orgy as a permanent spectacle of habitual perversity fed by "the obsessive fear of all those who monstrously consume themselves, out of sheer self-exhaustion, in order to better disappear" (19). Strangulation procures simultaneous orgasm and death, speeding up the porn production and distribution line—sex as sacrifice, libido and death instinct inextricably intertwined. The detritus is reingested, the abject endlessly recycled, as in de Sade. There can be no final money shot, just as there will never, ever be a truly definitive blue-movie *wrap.*

Flowers

The first, 1949 English translation of *Our Lady of the Flowers* was passed from Annette Michelson to Alan Ansen and then on to Burroughs and the Beats. The book's poetic artifice and erotic arabesques run through the fabric of *Naked Lunch*, but above all Burroughs, like Genet, desires to seduce the reader while seeking moral condemnation—the lover must become an adversary, fascination lead to excoriation. Parodying the Book of Job, Genet sought "the delicious enemy quite disarmed" (qtd. in T. Wilson, 167), and Lee and Sailor's lubricious *coming on* to the perfect mark, rube, or john, is a wising-up process for the sheer loathing to come. Genet philosophized an erotics of treachery, and in *Naked Lunch*, "all Agents defect and all Resisters sell out" (172), and desire is inseparable from ravishment. You're so beautiful—I'm going to rip you to shreds.

Chinoise

Chinese in *Naked Lunch* personifies the inhuman, racial other, and its mimicry is the author's final, parting shot in the book—"No glot . . . C'lom Fliday" (196). The Chinese cannot be blindsided, according to this conceit, the old *Chinoise* has no opium today, he has shut his little shop—and so it is over, the con stops here, no more junk, no more illusion, seen through. But the junkie will wait forever, even when tapering off on the Chinese cure—hop and Wimpole's tonic—and the racist image of the inscrutable Oriental remains, part of the old drug mythos, straight out of Sax Rohmer's 1919 *Dope,* a sensationalist novel which Burroughs professed to despise.

The Shooting Of Joan

"The shooting of Joan" is a phrase used by journalists, critics, and fans which may even predate Burroughs' own phrasing in the introduction to *Queer.* But those commentators didn't know "Joan," and besides, in a world of commonplace shootings, we need to reinstate the shattering impact of that single bullet. Derek Marlowe: "There was a noise of little importance as if someone had clicked their tongue . . . and then it was no longer a kiss but a penetration, a penetration into the flesh and into the skull as the .38 bullet pierced the bone and exploded behind the forehead, pushing and pushing through cells and tissue and blood and brain, tunnelling a course from left to right, eliminating dreams and hopes and things to do, cancelling memories, loves, silly mistakes, scratching out fears, ecstasies, caresses, swivelling and spinning, boring ceaselessly onwards, eliminating, eliminating past, eliminating present, future, nullifying, purging, bringing to a halt a lifetime in a split-second irrevocably and absurdly, before the missile, no larger than a jelly bean one bought as a toddler, reappeared through the left eye sucking out a cargo of liquid and mucus and blood, emerging neatly between long eyelashes to continue its trajectory into the warm summer air. It left nothing. A nothingness. It simply killed and as it killed, its victim was aware, surprisingly, of the smell, the delicate fragrance of honeysuckle" (229).

Joan

baby what is happening will you pass the glass
pour me something special something that will last . . .
take all your ideals and throw them in the flood
all your knives and needles were no substitute for love
when it's goin' going gone
                                        —Eric Andersen, "Goin' Gone"

A very particular death has been seen to haunt the text—the death of Joan Burroughs. She is a ghost we try to glimpse in this supernatural horror story, like Ginsberg's poignant dream account of Joan's ghostly visitation. There is that still but fractured space at the heart of *Naked Lunch*'s whirling mosaic of evil, destruction, and chaos—the life unmentioned, the death unspoken which occurs *offstage,* in another country, another time . . . *La mujer invisible* . . . But the crime scene remains in the Dossiers. . . . See those ashtrays on the floor, the four empty bottles of Oso Negro gin. . . . The stale, sweet smell of booze and a bullet. . . . The clickety-clack of the record stuck in its groove . . . Mexicano or Lester Young . . . The dust in the folds of the blind . . . Dirty glasses . . . And the Star .380 automatic, abandoned where it was last placed *in time* . . . Too late, too late, too late . . . *Naked Lunch* is not a "How-To" book (187)—it is a How-NOT-To book. It is not a *permisso* note, it is an injunction—*You do not know yourself, know yourself you must.* This is a book in which *everything is permitted*—and yet it is an urgent warning against the risks of losing conscious awareness, of realizing the lethal potential of subconscious urges. Burroughs polemically and satirically admonishes and then runs riot, goes on a killing spree, and it is the profound tension between the cautionary reprimand and the unleashing of instinct which makes the book so ambiguous, contradictory, disorienting, and disturbing, the junkie's interminable inner dialogue played out as the oppositional essence of all psychic life—Don't do it! / But I *must.*

Checkpoint

Cronenberg inserts the shooting of Joan not once but twice, the second take at a frontier checkpoint—and this shooting becomes the transition from one existence to another. It's an appalling idea—it guarantees that the traveler's passport is in order. He is now free to go, because he has already, definitively, crossed the line.

In Memory Of Identity

Lee didn't have a deprived childhood, he had no childhood at all—he arrived preternaturally old on the page, in a wrinkled raincoat, lighting a Methuselah with his Lucifer, tired of all this already, just passing through, born under a bad sign.

Private Dick

Lee is a private dick hired by Burroughs to investigate The Burroughs Case, he's a downbeat shamus from whom the truth will be systematically screened and withheld. Well, that was why he was hired in the first place. His collection of notes, reports, *Dossiers,* entitled *Naked Lunch*, will be taken over, "completed" and signed-off by Burroughs himself: "Now I, William Seward, will unlock my word hoard . . . " (192). Another smokescreen, naturally. From the very beginning the case was an elaborate hoax, a bizarre cover story, a series of quite unbelievable, Chandleresque alibis, the creation of a book—both strategic and chaotic, written in blood and yet written *as if by another*—into which the client hoped to disappear forever, true confession as terminal vanishing act, that old routine. But it didn't quite work out that way.

William S. Burroughs as "Good Ol' Boy": *Naked Lunch* in East Texas

rob **JOHNSON**

'm on the *Naked Lunch* inter-American highway, just outside of Houston, Texas, driving North on I-45 towards the New Waverly exit, the same exit Billy Burroughs would take to his "ranch" in Pine Valley, ten miles from Coldspring, Texas, the seat of San Jacinto County and home of *Naked Lunch*'s "County Clerk." This is just one stop on the *Naked Lunch* highway, which begins in Mexico City, crosses Texas into Louisiana, and terminates in New Orleans. Burroughs describes the entire trip in a spectacular three-page passage in *Naked Lunch* (abbreviated below):

> And the junk was running low. So there we are in this no-horse town strictly from cough syrup. And vomited up the syrup and drove on and on, cold spring wind whistling through that old heap around our shivering, sick sweating bodies [...] On through the peeled landscape, dead armadillos in the road and vultures over the swamp and cypress stumps. Motels with beaverboard walls, gas heater, thin pink blankets. Itinerant short con and carny hype men have burned down the croakers of Texas. [...] Came at last to Houston where I know a druggist. I haven't been there in five years but he looks up and makes me with one quick look and just nods [...] "A quart of PG and a hundred nembies."
> [...] Shooting PG is a terrible hassle [...] So we pour it in a Pernod bottle and start for New Orleans past iridescent lakes and orange gas

flares, and swamps and garbage heaps, alligators crawling around in broken bottles and tin cans, neon arabesques of motels, marooned pimps scream obscenities at passing cars from islands of rubbish . . . New Orleans is a dead museum. [. . .] We stock up on H and backtrack for Mexico. Back through Lake Charles and the dead slot-machine country, south end of Texas, nigger-killing sheriffs look us over and check the car papers. Something falls off you when you cross the border into Mexico, and suddenly the landscape hits you straight with nothing between you and it, desert and mountains and vultures [. . .] Drove all night, came at dawn to a warm misty place, barking dogs and the sound of running water. "Thomas and Charlie," I said. "What?" "That's the name of this town. Sea level. We climb straight up from here ten thousand feet." [. . .] Mexico City where Lupita sits like an Aztec Earth Goddess doling out her little papers of lousy shit. (12–14)

Burroughs was making this drive in the mid- to late 1940s, long before the completion of the interstate-highway system. En route to his east Texas "ranch" from his farmland in Pharr, located in deep south Texas near the Mexican border, Burroughs drove (using the old highway numbers) Highway 281 North to Alice, Texas, then took Highway 59 North over to Beeville (where he was arrested in 1948 by the notoriously racist south Texas Sheriff Robert "Vail" Ennis) and on up through Victoria, Texas, into Houston. There, he headed his Jeep north on Highway 75 (now Interstate 45) and just past Conroe exited onto a county road connecting New Waverly and Coldspring (now Highway 150). If he was bound for New Orleans, he drove Highway 90 east through Beaumont and Vidor (where, as recently as 1993, the Ku Klux Klan marched against the integration of public housing), crossing the Sabine River on a swing bridge at Orange, Texas, and entering Louisiana on a two-lane road lined with nightclubs, casinos, and whorehouses ("marooned pimps scream obscenities at passing cars"). Past Lake Charles ("dead slot-machine country"), he drove at sea level through the swamps south of Grand Lake via Highway 90, which took him by a southerly route into New Orleans. Returning to Mexico City, back through Houston, Burroughs headed the Jeep south on Highway 59 to Laredo, described by Jack Kerouac in *On the Road* as "the bottom and dregs of America" (249). South of the border, from Nuevo Laredo to Mexico City, he toured the recently completed (in 1937) 770-mile leg of the Pan American Highway. The last major stop on the old highway before Mexico City was Tamazunchale ("'Thomas and Charlie,' he said"), site of an old Aztec town.

Driving the far-northern outskirts of Houston's famously unzoned sprawl (where churches sit next to topless bars), I already feel my junk antenna picking up signs of Burroughs amidst the shopping centers and pine trees—a car dealership run by a "No Bull" Bill (who is probably less honestly named than Kerouac's "Old Bull Lee"), a highway sign indicating it's another twenty-three miles to Conroe, Texas (where Billy Burroughs Jr. was born in 1947), and a billboard sponsored by the Huntsville, Texas, Chamber of Commerce urging tourists to stop at the "Ol' Sparky" museum, "Ol' Sparky" being Texas's original electric chair ("Senators leap up and bray for the Death Penalty with inflexible authority of virus yen," says Lee in *Naked Lunch* (186).

Exiting I-45 and turning off onto Highway 150, approximately fifty miles north of Houston, you are on the country road Herbert Huncke described driving in 1947—"a black macadam road which began twisting and turning [. . .] through countryside sparsely dotted with small farms and occasional houses along the road" (156). The description holds true, even today. It's still isolated country, beyond the reach of cell-phone towers as you near Coldspring, and it's still country populated by Hoots, Ellisors, and Gilleys, families whose names appear in Burroughs' works and who were his closest neighbors (although they lived over a mile away) on Winters Bayou. Living in a falling-down cabin on ninety-nine acres bordering this swampy bayou, Burroughs planned to take advantage of the thick underbrush and privacy of his land to cultivate a domestic crop of opium poppies (Huncke, 148). It was one of many get-rich-quick schemes he plotted in the 1940s. However, it turned out to be better country for making moonshine, as his neighbors the Ellisors did, than it was for growing poppies.

Back then, in the late 1940s, driving east towards Coldspring and just before crossing Winters Bayou, you passed a small general store run by Andrew Ellisor, the nephew of one of Burroughs' neighbors, Arch Ellisor. Burroughs evidently spent a good bit of time at this store listening to Andrew, Arch, and other east Texans spin yarns. Did you ever hear about old Ma Lottie from back in the swamps, who kept her dead daughter's body in her house for ten years before it was discovered? Or about the cattle rustler who was killed by a falling tree when he passed out drunk and his campfire burned through the tree he was under? Welcome to *Naked Lunch* country. As Burroughs himself says, the world of *Naked Lunch* is "a kind of midwestern, small-town, cracker-barrel, pratfall type of folklore, very much part of my own background" (Lotringer, 71). At Andrew's store near Pine Valley, Burroughs might literally have been sitting around a cracker barrel hearing Ma Lottie stories. In *Naked Lunch*, students in an English Lit class scream for more "Ma Lottie," interrupting the professor's dull lecture on Coleridge's *The Rime of the Ancient Mariner* (72–73).

In respect to how such odd biographical and geographical details find their way into *Naked Lunch*, Ted Morgan makes a simple but profound judgment of the novel: "What gives the book credibility is that Burroughs is writing out of his own experience. He's been there. The situation of the society is his situation. Every page is strewn with autobiographical clues, which the uninformed reader would not recognize" (352). When I wrote my own microbiography of Burroughs, *The Lost Years of William S. Burroughs: Beats in South Texas*, I found Morgan's comments to be true: "Billy" was all over the South Texas Valley, but only someone very familiar with the place would be able to decipher that aspect of his work. I assumed the same was true of east Texas, where he lived for over a year and which appears as a setting (if you know what to look for) throughout his works.

Burroughs himself is upfront about how east Texas inspired one of the great scenes in his works: "The County Clerk sequence in *Naked Lunch* derived from contact with the County Clerk in Cold Spring, Texas. It was in fact an elaboration of his monologue, which seemed merely boring at the time, since I didn't know yet that I was a writer" (*Adding Machine*, 19).

Burroughs met the county clerk of San Jacinto County, James D. Browder, in November of 1946, when he filed General Warranty Deed #741 for the purchase of ninety-nine acres along Winters Bayou known as the "old Brooks place." The following scene from *Naked Lunch*'s "County Clerk" reflects the actual language and facts of the warranty deed, but the monologue is also clearly (as Burroughs says) an "elaboration":

> "Well, Chester Hoot tore that nigger shack down and rebuilt it just back of his house up in Blood Valley. [. . .] Well it was just where the nigger shack used to be, right across from the old Brooks place floods out every spring, only it wasn't the Brooks place then . . . belonged to a feller name of Scranton. Now that piece of land was surveyed back in 1919 . . . I reckon you know the man did the job too . . . Feller name of Hump Clarence used to witch out wells on the side . . . Good ol' boy too, not a finer man in this Zone than Hump Clarence." (147)

I've visited the old courthouse in Coldspring where something like this monologue was originally delivered in front of Burroughs, and I can imagine Burroughs, an obvious "city feller," sitting down with this member of an "old blood" east Texas family and going through the process of buying land in the area. It would have been an initiation and a kind of interrogation, with the clerk droning on and on about the history of the property all the way back to Adam or at least back to the Hoots, Brookses, and Ellisors, all of whom are named as former owners of Burroughs' property in the general warranty deed.

Today, the land is (ironically) owned by one of County Clerk Jim D. Browder's nephews. He knows Burroughs was a miscreant and that he grew marijuana on the land. "Maybe that's why your cattle are acting so weird," the current owner's daughter has joked to her father. It's no joke, however, that they don't want people interested in Burroughs poking around their land. And why would they. While today Jim Browder is remembered as having been a "nice old man," and the family, whose descendants are everywhere in San Jacinto County, is a "fine" one, Burroughs portrays the county clerk as an anti-Semitic, un-Reconstructed racist who is nonetheless "getting that coon pone" steady from a "yaller girl" (146). It is in fact (as Allen Ginsberg points out) one of the most scathing—and uncensored—portraits of a racist penned up to that point in American literature.

The clerk's most offensive (and funniest) story in this respect is about a couple visiting Coldspring from Texarkana:

> They burned that ol' nigger over in Cunt Lick. Nigger had the aftosa and it left him stone blind . . . So this white girl down from Texarkana screeches out:
>
> "Roy, that ol' nigger is looking at me so nasty. Land's sake I feel just dirty all over."
>
> "Now, Sweet Thing, don't you fret yourself. Me an' the boys will burn him."
>
> "Do it slow, Honey Face. Do it slow. He's give me a sick headache."
>
> So they burned the nigger and that ol' boy took his wife and went back up to Texarkana without paying for the gasoline and Old Whispering Lou runs the service station couldn't talk about nothing else all fall: "These city fellers come down here and burn a nigger and don't even settle up for the gasoline." (147)

This scene is not one often pulled out for analysis, although in the *Naked Lunch* trial Allen Ginsberg specifically cites it by way of arguing that the book is a "moral" one, an argument that just confuses the judge: "Don't you realize he is making a parody of the monstrous speech and thought processes of a red-necked Southern, hate-filled type, who hates everybody, Jews, Negroes, Northerners. Burroughs is taking a very moral position, like defending the good here, I think" (*Naked*, 1987, xxx).

Among contemporary reviewers of the novel, Mary McCarthy is the most sensitive to such racially charged material in the book and makes the insightful comment that racism is portrayed in the book as yet another addiction: "The South is addicted to lynching and nigger-hating, and the Southern folk-custom of burning a Negro recurs throughout the book as a sort of Fourth-of-July carnival with fireworks" (359). Lynchings and burnings are, in fact, repeatedly depicted in the book in a variety of creative ways. For example, when the "Complete All American Deanxietized Man" (a horrible—not by accident—*black* centipede) is brought into a medical conference, a "fat, frog-faced Southern doctor" orders: "Fetch gasoline! [. . .] We gotta burn the son of a bitch like an uppity Nigra!" (88). Other examples specifically compare participation in such violent rituals to an addictive behavior. In "Ordinary Men and Women," "Red Necks in black Stetsons and faded Levis tie a Nigra boy to an old iron lamppost and cover him with burning gasoline . . . The junkies rush over and draw the flesh smoke deep into their aching lungs . . . They really got relief" (106). Many of these images are overtly sexual, such as the "pornographic" hangings and human pyrotechnics in "A. J.'s Annual Party." Even these "pornographic" scenes, though, are connected to the book's depictions of lynching and human immolation in the South by the inclusion of parallel details, such as gasoline dowsing and a bayou setting: "Masturbating end-over-end, three thousand feet down, his sperm floating beside him, he screams all the way against the shattering blue of sky, the rising sun burning over his body like gasoline, down past great oaks and persimmons, swamp cypress and mahogany, to shatter in liquid relief in a ruined square paved with limestone" (83).

Images of lynching and human immolation in the novel recur almost as regularly as images of needles and drug addiction. There are several well-known explanations for this, and I'd like to add one that is perhaps not self-evident: Burroughs was a Southerner. More precisely, in St. Louis, he says he was raised on the "borderline between North and the South" (Lotringer, 514). He calls his mother a "Southern Belle" (which, as a type, he despised), and his maternal grandfather is described by Ted Morgan as a "Bible-thumping, fire-and-brimstone Southern clergyman" (19–20). However, among Burroughs' critics, Barry Miles is the only one I am aware of who connects Burroughs' obsession with lynchings and burnings in *Naked Lunch* with his Southern upbringing. As Miles points out, Burroughs "grew up with media stories of hangings in Missouri" (*El Hombre Invisible*, 104).

Indeed, such Southern-style *Grand Guignol* would have been a part of the St. Louis culture in which he was raised. In the winter of 1931, when Burroughs was completing his senior year at a private academy in St. Louis, the *St. Louis Post Dispatch* ran front-page stories about the lynching of Raymond Gunn in Maryville, Missouri. Gunn was accused of murdering a local schoolteacher, and a mob tied him to the roof of the schoolhouse and burned him alive ("Negro Slayer of Teacher"). It was the sixth lynching of its type in the last ten years in Missouri, according to the *Post Dispatch* ("Maryville Lynching Sixth"). Even as late as 1942, an accused rapist named Cleo Wright was seized by a mob in Sikestown, Missouri, and dragged behind a car to his hometown community, where his body was burned "beyond recognition" to the approval of hundreds of white onlookers, including children (Capeci, 863).

Such horrible scenes from the Jim Crow–era South clearly (as Miles points out) make their way into the world of *Naked Lunch*. Most readers and critics, however, do not focus on the more distinctly Southern scenes of lynching; rather, they focus on the highly sexualized gallows artistry in "A. J.'s Annual Party." As is well known, Burroughs was compelled to defend the literary value of the latter's "pornographic" scenes, which repeatedly depict hanged men spontaneously ejaculating: "These sections are intended to reveal capital punishment as the obscene, barbaric and disgusting anachronism that it is. As always the lunch is naked. If civilized countries want to return to Druid Hanging Rites in the Sacred Grove or to drink blood with the Aztecs and feed their Gods with blood of human sacrifice, let them see what they actually eat and drink" (205). Perhaps Burroughs really is making a statement against capital punishment here, but the necessity of defending the "pornographic" execution scenes in the book had the unfortunate effect of taking the focus off the far more "obscene, barbaric and disgusting" (and topical) scenes of Southern, mob-style justice—the real lunch that needed to be eaten nakedly in the 1940s and 1950s.

The novel serves up just such a naked lunch, quite literally. In the "outtakes" to the appropriately titled "Black Meat" section (added for the restored edition of the novel in 2003), there is an implied connection between the Meat Eaters (eating, after all, a black carcass) and a Southern sheriff who takes pride in slow-cooking (barbecuing) his victims: "Nothing like a good *slow* Nigga Burnin' to quiet a town down for a piece. . . . And folks go around all dreamy and peaceful looking and sorta sleepy like they just ate something real good and plenty of it" (268). Historian Trudier Harris quotes a participant in the real-life burning of a man named "Shine" Wilson in the 1940s: "Funniest thing I ever smelled was him a burnin', and the way his flesh cooked it sizzled same as if we was a cookin' a pig or a cow" (10). These scenes of cannibalism are described in many contemporary newspaper accounts of Negroes being lynched and burned; in one, a young woman who has just watched a mob complete the burning of a black man in Mississippi says, "I'm hungry. . . . Let's get something to eat" (Patterson, 127).

Now this voice of the Southern Sheriff ("Nothing like a good *slow* Nigga Burnin'") in *Naked Lunch* was, evidently, more than just a routine: it was a submerged part of Burroughs' personality. Beginning in 1945, Burroughs had undergone hypnoanalysis and narcoanalysis with Dr. Lewis David Wolberg, who uncovered multiple personas in Burroughs' psyche. There was a St. Louis aristocrat, a lesbian governess, an inscrutable Chinaman, and "Old Luke"—a tobacco farmer whom Allen Ginsberg said had the personality of a "psychotic Southern sheriff." Old Luke liked to sit on his porch and watch the catfish come down the river, occasionally bothering himself to catch one, then lustily killing and cleaning it: *"Ever gut a catfish?"* (Miles, *Ginsberg,* 71). Fishing for catfish on the banks of Winters Bayou, Burroughs was, eerily, the very image of Old Luke.

With Old Luke just below the surface, east Texas must have appealed strongly to Burroughs' inner redneck, which—and I speak from experience—is very close beneath the skin of any white man raised in or around the South. It is easy to fall into this persona, and it's sometimes necessary for communication and even survival. In *Naked Lunch*, for example, Lee channels this inner redneck and makes an anti-Semitic comment to the county clerk in order to seal the deal for his property: "Well [. . .] you know yourself all a Jew wants to do is doodle a Christian girl. . . . One of these days we'll cut the rest of it off." The clerk, humored, says he "talk[s] right sensible for a city feller" and instructs one of his six assistants to "take care of him. . . . He's a good ol' boy" (148).

Neal Cassady, visiting the "ranch" in the summer of 1947, didn't quite know how to take Burroughs' Southern, racist, good-ol'-boy routine. In the famous taped sessions that are transcribed in *Visions of Cody*, Cassady tells Jack Kerouac the following east Texas story. There wasn't really a lot to do on the "ranch," and so Burroughs and his visitors spent the mornings listening to music and reading: "he'd be reading and I'd be reading [. . .] and so then he said, 'What do you think of that *Really the Blues?*' 'Oh, it's alright I guess.' [. . .] 'The guy's just nowhere,' you know what he's saying, 'this Mezzrow character' [Mezz Mezzrow, author of *Really the Blues*]—Oh no! then he said: 'Sure a nigger lover ain't he?' You know, he he he, just like that" (120). By way of explaining these racist statements to Jack Kerouac, who had never been to Burroughs' east Texas ranch, Cassady says Burroughs was merely imitating a man identified in *Visions of Cody* as "Jimmy Low," the owner of a general store down the road (probably the country store owned by Andrew Ellisor). When he was younger, though, Cassady says such racist talk from Burroughs "amazed" him: "I used to look at him as though to *take* him seriously, you're not supposed to take him seriously, you don't know what he's saying about—and he'll say these horrible things" (Kerouac, *Visions of Cody*, 120).

While researching his life in south Texas, I'd been puzzled myself by this persona of Billy Burroughs—the racist, the colonialist. Like the judge in the *Naked Lunch* trial—and Neal Cassady and Allen Ginsberg, who believed Burroughs' anti-Communist rants in his south Texas letters were "just a W. C. Fields act" (*Letters*, 57n32)—early critics couldn't see how a man could create characters like the county clerk and not be that kind of person. John Willett wrote in his famously wrong-headed 1963 review entitled "Ugh," "[S]uch things are too uncritically presented, and because the author gives no flicker of disapproval the reader easily takes the 'moral message' the other way" (43).

This was an important aspect of the early criticism of *Naked Lunch*: Was it a moral book (as satire or parody or "pamphlets" as Burroughs called it), merely a disgusting book or art for art's sake? Robin Lydenberg argues *Naked Lunch* is a book beyond "good and evil," taking Burroughs at his word that he was neither a "political" nor "moral" writer (3–8). Burroughs did, in fact, have a low opinion of "morality" and was, like the heroes of *Naked Lunch*, an apolitical "factualist." Still, it's obvious to anyone reading the "County Clerk" routine that while Burroughs appears to be having a bit too much fun telling these racist and anti-Semitic jokes, he is hardly condoning such opinions.

What, though, were Burroughs' moral views (if any) on the race question of the mid- to late 1950s? To be fair, you need to consider what Burroughs or any other writer said about the issue *at the time*, not even a few years later, when the Civil Rights movement was in full swing. Certainly, no Beat writer during this time period wrote anything remotely political about the South and the race issue. Although Allen Ginsberg refers to the case of the Scottsboro Boys in "America," he does not list Southern racism and segregation as one of the evils besetting America in his first overtly political essay, 1959's "Poetry, Violence, and the Trembling Lambs" (he does, however, compare the poor oppressed junkies of the world to Jews in Nazi Germany). Even black writers, in the mid- to late 1950s, were hardly writing what would come to be seen as Black Power literature (as A. Robert Lee argues [307]). Black Power didn't exist in the 1950s. "Remember," Burroughs told an interviewer in the late 1980s, "40 years ago [. . .] no one questioned the right of a cop to beat up a nigger. All that is gone in the last 40 years" (Lotringer, 548).

One of the few statements on race (outside his fiction) made by Burroughs at the time of *Naked Lunch*'s publication is found in a 1961 interview with Gregory Corso. Corso pushed Burroughs to discuss the issue of white "supremacy," but you can see in Burroughs' reply how he sidesteps the topicality of the question and includes white supremacy as an example of a larger debate (a typical rhetorical move by Burroughs, by the way, but also a typical white/Southern strategy of avoiding the topical issue of race in favor of debating "essential" questions related to race): "The essence of White Supremacy is this: they are people who want to keep things as they are. That their children's children's children might be a different color is something very alarming to them—in short, they are committed to the maintenance of the static image. The attempt to maintain a static image, even if it's a good image, just won't work" (Lotringer, 46). *Naked Lunch* had made a similar point, a couple of years earlier, in its attack on cancerous bureaucracies: "Bureaucracy is wrong as a cancer, a turning away from the human evolutionary direction of infinite potentials and differentiation and independent spontaneous action to the complete parasitism of a virus" (112). Similarly, in "Islam Incorporated and the Parties of Interzone," Burroughs accuses the Liquefactionists, who are racists like the county clerk, of forcing us to "deny our protoplasmic core," a core that allows us "to maintain a maximum of flexibility without falling into the morass of liquefaction" (140). From the point of view of the Factualist, the "moral" outrage one feels about Southern racists burning and torturing "Nigras" is a response to a larger threat—the threat of how racism stifles change, evolution, progress, differentiation, and randomness.

It is not too far off base to suggest, though, that just as Kerouac projected his own liberation fantasies onto Negroes and was rightly accused by Norman Podhoretz and others of "romanticizing" them, so, too, did Burroughs see in blacks his own factualist way of viewing the world. The first factualist in his oeuvre may well be the man he calls Clutch in *Junky* and in "Davy Jones" (in *Exterminator!*): "He was known as Clutch because of a deformed hand. He was skeleton thin composed cool and aloof with the other prisoners. And insolent to the narcs. 'Old Monkey climbing up on your back boy?' said a narc clapping him jovially on the back. 'I don't know what you're talking about now,' said Clutch coldly. The narc dropped his hand and turned away coughing." Burroughs describes a similarly insolent black man in what appears to be an autobiographical incident from his childhood, when "Audrey" would spend his Saturdays hanging out at the courthouse. A fifteen-year-old black boy is accused of armed robbery but tells the judge, "saucily," "I'm not guilty." When the judge asks if the boy has any relatives in the courtroom, the black man in front of Audrey, Davy Jones, says, "I'm the boy's father. He's not the type to do that." The judge stammers back that he is the type, but the black man repeats, "He's not the type." No one tells him to address the judge as your honor or stand when he addresses the judge, and Audrey realizes this is because they "were afraid of him. Davy Jones father and son and Clutch destroy the whole white world" (*Exterminator!* 17–19).

Clutch's voice is the voice of *Junky*—direct, unemotional, and factual. *Naked Lunch* is (largely) not written in that voice, although its philosophical point of view (factualism) is pure Clutch. Its voice is instead that of the good ol' boy, whose solution to all problems is gasoline and a match: "So I shoot that old nigger and he flop on his side one leg up in the air just a-kicking." "Yeah, but you ever burn a nigger?" (Clem and Jody in *Naked Lunch*, 133).

In spite of the Clems and Jodys of the world, there is justice in the universe of William S. Burroughs. The Southern "Negro" finally exacts his revenge against all of the "nigger-killing sheriffs" in a scene found in

"Twilight's Last Gleamings" (in *Exterminator!*). In the story, a motley crew of "conspirators" is set on "turn[ing] the clock back to 1899 when a silver dollar bought a good meal or a good piece of ass" (86). The conspirators stop to gas up their car in a Southern town, and when no one comes to service the car, Jones ("a Negro castrated in the cradle") gets out to fill the tank:

> At this moment the owner of the filling station, a Nigger-killing lawman with six notches in his gun, comes out a side door.
> LAWMAN: "Get away from that pump, boy."
> JONES: "Yahsuh boss." (He drenches the lawman with gasoline and sets him on fire.) (89)

Pure fantasy, of course. Even today, fifty years after the publication of *Naked Lunch*, the east Texas where Burroughs lived in the 1940s is still Klan country. Just two years ago (at the writing of this essay), the White Camelia Knights of the Ku Klux Klan marched through downtown Tomball, Texas (about twenty miles from Coldspring), and held an "informational" meeting in the town's Community Center. The Tomball police force protected the Klan's right to assemble at the center, even though the meeting was designated a "Whites Only" event ("Galveston County Residents").

Coldspring, Texas, Postcard: Half a mile off the town square, just north of the San Jacinto County Courthouse, is the old Coldspring Jail. It's a turn-of-the-century, two-story, brick jailhouse, well preserved and looking like a movie set. What really catches my eye, though, is a huge oak tree down the hill from the courthouse, one of the biggest oak trees I have ever seen in Texas. Its hundreds of limbs wind sinuously from the massive, main trunk, gradually attenuating and bending down to the ground like bony fingers trailing the dirt. It's a frightening tree. A sign in front of it reads: "Hanging Tree: Once Used to Dispense Justice." I see dozens of "strange fruit," swaying from any of a hundred limbs that could be used for that purpose.

There's no one working the jail, although the sign says it's open. After about ten minutes, a man appears. "You want to see the jail?" He's about my age (forties) and is wearing a heavy-metal T-shirt. He looks a little like the hitchhiker in the original *Texas Chainsaw Massacre*. I get the private tour of the cell house, empty and echoing our lone presence. Upstairs, he directs me into one of the actual cells and then suddenly pulls a heavy lever that momentarily locks me inside. "You been in prison?" he asks me. I shake my head no. "I was in a spell," he says. "You never forget that sound of the bars shuttin' on you."

Before I leave, I ask my guide about the "Hanging Tree." "When was the last time anyone was hanged from that tree?" "Well," he strokes his chin, "must a been 'bout the time they fired up Ol' Sparky in Huntsville." We both laugh. On a chance, I then ask, "You don't have any pictures of anyone hanging from that tree, do you?" He gets my meaning. I've told him I grew up in Pasadena, Texas. He grew up in Cleveland, Texas. Our high-school football teams had met in regionals one year, in the Astrodome. "Any pictures?" he asks. "Well, if we did," he says, almost winking, "they wouldn't be for public consumption, now would they?" No, I say, I guess not. We share a chuckle as I leave.

Because after all, it turns out, me, I'm a good ol' boy, too.

Works Cited

Burroughs, William S. *The Adding Machine*. New York: Arcade, 1986.

———. *Exterminator!* New York: Viking, 1973.

———. *Last Words: The Final Journals of William S. Burroughs*. Edited by James Grauerholz. New York: Grove, 2000.

———. *The Letters of William S. Burroughs, 1945–1959*. Edited by Oliver Harris. New York: Viking, 1993.

———. *Naked Lunch*. New York: Grove, 1987.

Capeci, Dominic J., Jr. "The Lynching of Cleo Wright: Federal Protection of Constitutional Rights during World War II." *Journal of American History* 72, no. 4 (March 1986): 859–87.

Charters, Ann, ed. *Beat Down to Your Soul*. New York: Penguin, 2002.

"Galveston County Residents Accuse Tomball of Racism at Klan Event." *Tomball Magnolia Tribune*, online edition, tribunenews.com/index_20050816.aspx (accessed September 2007).

General Warranty Deed #741. Office of the County Clerk, San Jacinto County Courthouse, Coldspring, Texas.

Ginsberg, Allen. "Poetry, Violence, and the Trembling Lambs." *Deliberate Prose: Selected Essays 1952–1995*, edited by Bill Morgan, 3–5. New York: HarperCollins, 2000.

Harris, Trudier. *Exorcising Blackness: Historical and Literary Lynching and Burning Rituals*. Bloomington: Indiana UP, 1984.

Huncke, Herbert. *Herbert Huncke Reader*. Edited by Benjamin Shafer. New York: Quill, 1998.

Johnson, Rob. *The Lost Years of William S. Burroughs: Beats in South Texas*. College Station, TX: Texas A&M UP, 2006.

Kerouac, Jack. *On the Road*. New York: Penguin, 2000.

———. *Visions of Cody*. New York: Penguin, 1993.

Lee, A. Robert. "Black Beats: The Signifying Poetry of LeRoi Jones/Imamu Baraka, Ted Joans, and Bob Kaufman." In Charters, *Beat Down to Your Soul*, 303–28.

Lotringer, Sylvère, ed. *Burroughs Live: The Collected Interviews of William S. Burroughs, 1960–1997*. Los Angeles: Semiotext(e), 2001.

Lydenberg, Robin. *Word Cultures: Radical Theory and Practice in William S. Burroughs' Fiction*. Urbana: U of Illinois P, 1987.

"Maryville Lynching Sixth in Missouri in Last Ten Years." *St. Louis Post Dispatch*, 12 January 1931, 2A.

McCarthy, Mary. "Burroughs' *Naked Lunch*." In Charters, *Beat Down to Your Soul*, 356–64.

Miles, Barry. *El Hombre Invisible*. London: Virgin, 2002.

———. *Ginsberg: A Biography*. New York: Simon and Schuster, 1989.

Morgan, Ted. *Literary Outlaw: The Life and Times of William S. Burroughs*. New York: Holt, 1988.

"Negro Slayer of Teacher Lynched at Maryville, Missouri, Burned With Schoolhouse." *St. Louis Post Dispatch*, 12 January 1931, 1–2A.

Patterson, Orlando. "Rituals of Blood: Sacrificial Murders in the Postbellum South." *Journal of Blacks in Higher Education* 23 (Spring 1999): 123–27.

Podhoretz, Norman. "The Know-Nothing Bohemians." In Charters, *Beat Down to Your Soul*, 481–93.

Willett, John. "Ugh." In *William S. Burroughs at the Front: Critical Reception, 1959–1989*, edited by Jennie Skerl and Robin Lydenberg, 41–44. Carbondale: Southern Illinois UP, 1991.

Tangier and the
Making of *Naked Lunch*

allen **HIBBARD**

Burroughs is in Tangiers I don't think he'll come back it's sinister.
—Allen Ginsberg, "America"

There would be no *Naked Lunch,* at least not in the form we know it, without Burroughs' sojourn in Tangier from 1954 to 1958. The historical/geographical context of the novel's making has itself been a key, but often problematic, aspect of the text's creation and its reception. This juncture, half a century after the novel's original publication, offers a new horizon from which we might profitably take a fresh look at the critical connection between Tangier and *Naked Lunch.* What I suggest at the outset is that the very nature of changing conditions in Tangier as it moved from international-zone status toward integration within a newly independent Morocco, is registered in both the novel's making and its final form. Moreover, just as this time was a critical turning point in Moroccan history, it was also a pivotal turning point in Burroughs' own work, an important transitional phase between the early, linear narrative style of *Junky, Queer,* and *The Yage Letters* and the subsequent disjunctive, nonlinear, antirepresentational style of the cut-up phase (*The Soft Machine, The Ticket That Exploded*, and *Nova Express*) influenced by Brion Gysin, whom he first met in Tangier.

Various stories and accounts of the time Burroughs spent in Tangier while he was composing and assembling *Naked Lunch* have circulated widely in biographies, collections of letters, and books devoted to expatriate life in the city. Indeed, strands of the story have been woven together to create a durable and familiar pattern with legendary, even mythic, qualities. Burroughs left Latin America in August of 1953, disinclined to settle in the United States. His decision to make Tangier his destination may in part at least be attributed to his acquaintance with Paul Bowles' novels *The Sheltering Sky* and *Let It Come Down* as well as the kind of carefree expatriate lifestyle associated with Tangier at the time. During his first year in Tangier, however, Bowles seemed aloof. Lonely, depressed, and heavily addicted, Burroughs speculated that the well-established, genteel writer might not have wanted anything to do with him because of his associations with unsavory characters and contraband substances. Bowles was also gone off and on during the mid-1950s, traveling by ship to Ceylon (Sri Lanka) and other places. Still, the city on the northwest tip of Africa had enough to hold Burroughs. After all, he had a habit to feed, and drugs were readily available. So, too, were boys.

Burroughs' letters from the period, especially those to Allen Ginsberg, contain evidence of these fluctuations of mood, descriptions of interactions with local characters (including his Spanish-speaking lover Kiki), and shifting responses to the city, along with accounts of the novel's development and early versions of routines that wound their way into the novel. As early as 1955, Burroughs had begun coaxing Ginsberg to visit him in Tangier, often extending the promise of boys and including in his letters chunks of the manuscript he then referred to as "Interzone." By late 1956 and early 1957, Burroughs stepped up his campaign. Besides his keen interest in seeing Ginsberg, he needed help compiling the novel.

The visit of Ginsberg, Jack Kerouac, Peter Orlovsky, and Alan Ansen to Tangier in 1957 is a key aspect of the legend. Ted Morgan, describing the scene of Burroughs and his friends working on the novel there in Tangier as a "writer's equivalent of a quilting bee," notes, "Over a period of two months working steadily, they integrated and edited and typed the material which was an incredible mosaic of Bill's fantasies over the past three years, until they had about 200 pages of finished manuscript typed in duplicate" (265). Burroughs continued to generate material for the novel after his friends left and handed over the job of peddling the novel to Ginsberg. By the time he left Tangier in January 1958 to join Ginsberg, Orlovsky, and Gregory Corso in Paris at 9 Rue Git-le-Coeur (famously known as the Beat Hotel), the city had left its indelible mark on the writer and the novel he wrote there.

Although it is a critical commonplace to acknowledge the connection between Tangier and *Naked Lunch*, the specific ways the city influenced Burroughs' vision have only recently begun to be examined. "[C]ritics have in one way or another avoided a serious inquiry into the relationship between Burroughs' major text and his response to Tangier," Brian T. Edwards writes in *Morocco Bound*, a study that explores the Moroccan context of the novel more thoroughly than any to date (159). For instance, Barry Miles makes virtually no mention of the Moroccan political scene during the time Burroughs was in Tangier. Ted Morgan mentions riots in the International Zone prior to independence (255) and an anxious state of "independence jitters" but stops short of noting how these events might have affected Burroughs (261). Burroughs' expatriation has most often been situated vis-à-vis the cultural landscape in the United States during the late forties and early fifties, marked by the onset of the Cold War, containment policies, the McCarthy hearings, increasing consumerism, growth of suburbs, and social conservatism.

This, although important to bear in mind, is only part of the story. A more comprehensive account of the part Tangier plays in the novel must begin with an examination of the unfolding political drama in Morocco at the time Burroughs was in the city and move toward a consideration of how this scene influenced Burroughs' vision. Burroughs found himself in Morocco at one of the most pivotal moments in modern Moroccan history—when the country, after a long period of struggle, finally threw off colonial rule and established its independence in the form of a modern monarchy. During and after World War II, the French protectorate, established in 1912, was already showing signs of fragility and weakness, challenged by the rise of the Moroccan independence movement, supported to a large extent by Sultan Mohammad. The deposition in 1953 of the sultan, who was exiled to Madagascar, "only hastened the end of French rule" (Pennell, *Morocco: From Empire*, 160). Nationalists (Istiqlal and other groups) kept up pressure with assassination attempts, attacks on Europeans, and bombings (such as a major one in Casablanca), precipitating French relinquishment of control. In November of 1955, arrangements were made for the sultan to return to Morocco. Morocco officially became an independent state, under the leadership of King Mohammed V, on 2 March 1956. In April, Spain acceded most of its territories, and in July, the international zone in Tangier was annexed by the new Moroccan state. By 1961, all vestiges of the international zone had been dismantled.

Burroughs' ambivalent attitude toward political changes transpiring during his stay in Morocco is displayed in letters and the novel. On the one hand, in contrast to some of his fellow expatriates who seemed to lament the loss of the colonial period, Burroughs remained open to possibilities for change; on the other, he registers a degree of skepticism toward the nationalists' motives. "I have no nostalgia for the old days in Morocco, which I never saw," he writes to Ginsberg on 29 October 1956. "Right now is for me" (*Letters*, 337). In the same letter, he included a playful piece titled "Jihad Jitters" that dramatized local resistance to the French. Several months later, as he tried to persuade Ginsberg and Kerouac to visit him in Tangier, Burroughs seeks to allay fears (apparently mainly on Kerouac's part) no doubt generated by press accounts of political instability in the country prior to independence. On 28 January 1957, he writes to Ginsberg: "Tell Jack that Paul Bowles, who is very much afraid of violence, live [*sic*] twenty years in Morocco and wouldn't live anywhere else, is afraid of Mexico—where he spent a year" (*Letters*, 351). These remarks are made on either side of Sidi Mohammed's first *Fête du Trône* speech given in an independent Morocco, on 18 November 1956.

Readers of *Naked Lunch* will no doubt recall episodes that respond to events going on around Burroughs in Tangier. The section entitled "Ordinary Men and Women" opens with a scene depicting "Luncheon of Nationalist Party on balcony overlooking the Market" (101). A character simply identified as "Party Leader" (supposedly associated with the nationalist movement and seeking support for the cause) surveys the market and remarks to his interlocutor, referred to simply as Lieutenant: "*Ordinary* men and women going about their ordinary everyday tasks. Leading their ordinary lives. That's what we need . . . " (102). The description of the party leader—who creates the impression of a "successful gangster in drag," dressed in a *djellaba*, hairy legs showing, wearing Western-style shoes, smoking a cigar, and drinking whisky—is satirical. That the character is given no proper name suggests that he is simply playing a prescribed role. "What do you think about the French?" the P.L. asks a hustler who shows himself more concerned with his own business than political issues. Likewise, the leader seems more concerned about gaining recruits for the nationalist cause (for the enhancement of his own position) than the real needs of so-called ordinary men and women.

The skeptical view of political actors and their motives revealed here and elsewhere in the text is consistent with Burroughs' libertarian views and his distaste for bureaucracy and organized, dogmatic political movements. Pointing to riot scenes and other comments, Edwards aptly notes, "What is inspiring to Burroughs about the ensuing chaos is not violence per se but the possibility for disrupting the established order that rioting and chaos present. He sees revolution as opportunity, not as the replacement of one control mechanism with another" (171). Like Frantz Fanon, who was witnessing the effects of French colonization and resistance to it in Algeria in the 1950s, Burroughs seemed aware that colonial mentalities and practices would not so easily be dislodged.

Given the significance of Tangier in the making of *Naked Lunch*, it is surprising that the place does not figure more prominently and recognizably than it does in the novel. Indeed, we might recall that the opening scene features the narrator vaulting a turnstile at Washington Square Station in New York trying to shirk a narc. While the setting of *Naked Lunch*—rather like that in the film *Blade Runner*—is a surreal phantasmagoria, a cornucopia of cultures, still the presence of Tangier in that mix is evident, with a proliferation of signifiers pointing to the Arab city. The first time we get a glimpse of a setting vaguely resembling Tangier is in "The Black Meat." The opening of the scene features a meeting between the junky Sailor and the shoeshine hustler. No specific place is indicated at first, though we slide into a cafe "built into one side of a stone ramp at the bottom of a high white canyon of masonry" (44). The Sailor leaves and "drifted down into the Plaza": "All streets of the City slope down between deepening canyons to a vast, kidney-shaped plaza full of darkness. Walls of street and plaza are perforated by dwelling cubicles and cafés, some a few feet deep, others extending out of sight in a network of rooms and corridors" (45). Something of the landscape of Tangier, with streets running down to the Grand Socco or the public space overlooking the Straits on the Boulevard Pasteur, can be felt here. The scene, however, quickly becomes surreal and multilayered, vertical, with a "criss-cross of bridges, catwalks, cable cars" where traffickers in the black meat—centipedes—ply their trade, almost invisibly (45).

Hassan's Hospital "adjoining cemetery" in the following section ("Hospital") clearly is a rendition of the Jewish-run Benchimol Hospital, in Tangier (near the Marshan), which Burroughs checked into to help cure his junk sickness. In a "withdrawal nightmare," the narrator, "seized by a convulsion of urgency," throws a "pitcher of boiling acid" into the face of "a slight, short Arab dressed in a brown djellaba with grey beard and grey face" (47). The notorious "Hassan's Rumpus Room" and "Islam Incorporated" (if only by their names) also suggest connections to Arab history and culture, even if they do not specifically refer to Tangier.

The novel moves in postmodern fashion, never really resting in one particular geographical place, never settling, shifting kaleidoscopically with brief fragmentary glimpses of Venice, New York, Chicago, Houston, New Orleans, Mexico, Scandinavia, Paris. What results, then, is a kind of Foucauldian "heterotopia," or—to use Burroughs' own terms—a "composite city," a notion he actually hatched during his 1953 travels in Peru, in relation to his experimentation with *yagé*:

The blood and substance of many races, Negro, Polynesian, Mountain Mongol, Desert Nomad. Polyglot Near East, Indian, and new races as yet unconceived and unborn, combinations not yet realized, passes through your body. You make migrations, incredible journeys through jungles and deserts and mountains [. . .] across the Pacific in an outrigger canoe to Easter Island. The Composite City, Near Eastern, Mongol, South Pacific, South American where all Human Potentials are spread out in a vast silent Market. (*Letters*, 182–83)

Although Burroughs may have had a notion of the "composite city" before he landed in Tangier, the dream-like quality of the North African city provided an ideal place for the vision to blossom. He describes the synergy between the city and his vision for the novel in a letter to Kerouac and Ginsberg in 1955.

In Interzone it might or might not be a dream, and which way it falls might be in the balance while I watch this tea glass in the sun . . . The meaning of Interzone, its space-time location is at a point where three-dimensional fact merges into dream, and dreams erupt into the real world . . . The very exaggeration of routines is intended to create this feeling. In Interzone dreams can kill—Like Bangutot—and solid objects and persons can be unreal as dreams . . . (*Letters*, 300)

Tangier has left its imprint on *Naked Lunch* in significant ways beyond being the site of composition/assemblage and containing textual references to the city. The city's character, particularly at this moment in its history, can be felt in the novel's innovative aesthetic and style, its dream-like quality, its syncopated rhythms, its fractured structure. Again, Burroughs describes his purposes in a letter to Ginsberg: "The fragmentary quality of my work is *inherent* in the method and will resolve itself so far as necessary. Tanger novel will be Lee's impressions of Tanger, discarding novelistic pretext of dealing directly with his characters and situations" (*Letters*, 251). Oliver Harris' characterization of the connection between the novel's aesthetic and Tangier is spot on:

He was interested in a form that reproduced his experiences both of Tangier and of his work's composition: his drug-induced sensitivity to the place's strange collage of histories and cultures resulted in sudden, heightened intersections of dream and reality; and this corresponded to the fusions and reversals of past and future, fact and fantasy, that came about from transcribing, cutting, and selecting from a mass of fragmentary material drawn from his letters. (introduction, Burroughs, *Letters*, xxxiv–xxxv)

Clearly, the novel does not attempt to represent the city realistically as in Paul Bowles' novel *Let It Come Down* (1952), where the landscape of the novel is neatly and recognizably aligned with the physical geography of the place. Burroughs' fragmented, surreal vision of the city in some more oblique yet central way captures its intrinsic qualities and responds to its rhythms and feelings rather like Alfred Chester's novel *The Exquisite Corpse*, also written in Tangier, in the early sixties. While Bowles, in the tradition of nineteenth-century realists, constructed a linear, orderly progression of events, neatly and rationally plotted, Burroughs by his own confession was unable to write a conventional novel—"It's hopeless, Jack," he wrote to Kerouac on 7 December 1954. "I can't write in a popular vein" (*Letters*, 242). The difference between Bowles' Tangier novel and Burroughs' no doubt stems from differences in the two men's literary and aesthetic sensibilities. The differences might also be accounted for by the changes occurring in the city during the 1950s. *Let It Come Down* depicts a Tangier operating according to practices related to its status as an international city, before the riots of 1952 and the subsequent rise of nationalist fervor, before the gradual dissolution of American citizens' extraterritorial rights in the city. *Naked Lunch*, by contrast, embodies the character of a city in flux.

Sensitized as we now are to notions of how Orientalist discourse is produced and circulated, and informed as we are by postcolonial theory, we might certainly scrutinize Burroughs' representations of Tangier and portrayals of Moroccan characters in the novel. It is difficult, in the end, however, to come up with a clear and unequivocal assessment of Burroughs' attitudes toward Tangier, for his attitudes are anything but clear and unequivocal. Indeed, any sustained acquaintance with Burroughs and his work yields an appreciation of its complexity, its ambivalence. Edwards suggests that despite Burroughs' "Orientalist framework," he nonetheless "may from this position imagine a contestatory position that undoes the more particular U.S. political position in Tangier and within cold war domestic culture" (174). Moreover, I would suggest the very form of the novel—the way it defies traditional, realistic means of representation—can be thought of as a means of insisting on a complexity that refuses to participate in easy binary distinctions, by continually resisting the urge to assign stable, fixed identities. Burroughs is, above all, a satirist par excellence, a critic of sham, a creative talent seeking new ways to represent experiences with the Other, taking things to the extreme, challenging the very premises of representation itself.

For the past fifty years, the image of Tangier as a seedy, sordid, decadent city has stubbornly persisted, often in association with *Naked Lunch*, a novel prone perhaps to reinforce the image. On the first pages of *Tangier:*

City of the Dream, Iain Finlayson notes that "a lurid history of Tangier vice, crime and scandal, most of it inflated far beyond the petty, banal reality, continue to colour the popular imagination" (3). A sentence later we read: "Seedy, salacious, decadent, degenerate—Tangier is inevitably identified with 'Interzone,' William Burroughs' fevered, fictional, drug-inspired evocation of the boomtown years of Sodom-on-Sea" (4). Michelle Green's gossipy *The Dream at the End of the World: Paul Bowles and the Literary Renegades in Tangier*, published just a couple of years before the Finlayson book, portrays a glamorous, libertine expatriate world given to excess against an exotic background. It is only recently, as we have moved into the twenty-first century, particularly with Brian Edwards' fine study, that we have begun to look beyond or behind sensationalized or glamorized portrayals of the city to consider more closely the connections between historical realities and literary form.

As Tangier changes, so, too, will our views of *Naked Lunch*. At the time Burroughs resided in the city, its population was between 160,000 and 180,000. Today, Tangier is a congested city of nearly a million people, by some estimates. The nature of the expatriate community has vastly changed in a city now fully integrated into the political, social, and economic fabric of Morocco. The construction of a new Tangier-Mediterranean superport along with a new railroad station and other new building is reorienting the city. Moroccans seeking better opportunities gather near the port, looking for ways to cross the straits to Spain. The seedy old Café Central, where in days gone by old men would smoke *kif* and where Burroughs and others hung out or wrote, now looks like Europe, with two flat-screen televisions, air-conditioning, and very clean bathrooms. One of the best views of the city is from the McDonald's. Clearly, Tangier, for better or worse, has entered the age of economic and cultural globalization. From this new horizon, a younger generation of Moroccan critics with no memory of the colonial period have begun to reevaluate the literary production in the city, both by Moroccan and foreign writers. In 2005, the inaugural international conference on "Writing Tangier" was held in the city, and a fourth conference featuring a focus on Beat Writers and Tangier was held in May of 2008. (Many of the papers have been published in a volume of conference proceedings; see Hibbard and Tharaud.) Informed by postcolonial theory, attentive to the political ramifications of representation, and aware of ethical issues associated with expatriation and travel, Moroccan critics are deploying an "exogenous" perspective on American literature, the value of which Djelal Kadir has recently heralded. It will be interesting to see how Burroughs fares under this scrutiny.

Works Cited

Burroughs, William S. *Interzone*. Edited by James Grauerholz. New York: Viking, 1989.

———. Introduction. In *The Letters of William S. Burroughs, 1945–1959*, xv–xl. Edited by Oliver Harris. New York: Viking, 1993.

Edwards, Brian T. *Morocco Bound: Disorienting America's Maghreb, from Casablanca to the Marrakech Express*. Durham: Duke UP, 2005.

Finlayson, Iain. *Tangier: City of the Dream*. London: Flamingo/HarperCollins, 1993.

Green, Michelle. *The Dream at the End of the World: Paul Bowles and the Literary Renegades in Tangier*. New York: HarperCollins, 1991.

Hibbard, Allen, and Barry Tharaud, ed. *Bowles/Beats/Tangier*. Tangier: International Centre for Performance Studies, 2008.

Kadir, Djelal, ed. "America: The Idea, the Literature." Special issue. *PMLA* 118, no. 1 (January 2003): 9–24.

Miles, Barry. *William Burroughs: El Hombre Invisible*. New York: Hyperion, 1993.

Morgan, Ted. *Literary Outlaw: The Life and Times of William S. Burroughs*. New York: Holt, 1988.

Pennell, C. R. *Morocco: From Empire to Independence*. Oxford: Oneworld, 2003.

———. *Morocco since 1830: A History*. New York: New York UP, 2000.

"The natives are getting uppity": Tangier and *Naked Lunch*

kurt **HEMMER**

I f *Naked Lunch* were published today, fifty years after its original publication, and William S. Burroughs were still alive, rather than inciting calls for censorship over its lurid depictions of sex, it would probably inspire a *mufti* to declare a *fatwa* for Burroughs' immediate silencing. Although we tend to view Burroughs in the West as a radical voice against hegemonic control systems, it is possible today to see *Naked Lunch* as reifying certain imperialistic narratives. In *Culture and Imperialism* (1994), Edward Said, referring to conventional Western narratives, writes: "Narrative itself is the representation of power, and its teleology is associated with the global role of the West" (273). By resisting conventional Western narrative strategies, texts potentially resist the imperialistic hegemony that is reified by such narratives. Said reads some aesthetically traditional novels as potentially reifying imperialistic domination despite their possible criticism of imperialism, because the conventional narrative "embodies the same paternalistic arrogance of imperialism that it mocks" (xviii). "[R]epresentation itself," observes Said, "has been characterized as keeping the subordinate subordinate, the inferior inferior" (80). According to this thesis, by dismantling traditional narrative, Burroughs' *Naked Lunch* resists the hegemonic functions of the Western conventional novel. Yet, as Greg Mullins asserts, "While Burroughs lived in Morocco in the years immediately preceding and following independence and national integration, and while one might think that his own struggle against 'control' would have caused him to ally himself with the Moroccan struggle against colonialism, Burroughs remained hostile to Moroccan nationalism" (81). Although Burroughs might not have been completely hostile to Moroccan nationalism, *Naked Lunch* does not make a sustained stand against colonialism and often does not resist the arrogance of imperialism.

While *Naked Lunch*'s antinarrative form has the potential to resist the reifying tendencies Said sees as often inherent in traditional Western narratives, certain aspects of the content of *Naked Lunch* neutralize its potential for resisting imperialistic hegemony. As Mullins argues, Burroughs' concern about his personal freedoms, supported by colonial control in Tangier, superseded any sympathy with Moroccan nationalism. This is in keeping with Burroughs' feeling that individual freedoms are more important than national autonomy, especially if such nationalism is itself oppressive to personal rights. While certain aspects of *Naked Lunch* bring into sharp focus the cruelty of imperialism in Tangier, other aspects appear to reify that oppression. Dismantling traditional narrative form does not necessarily create a liminal space of resistance if the content of the text disrupts this formal resistance. Burroughs may not have supported French colonialism, but he appreciated the personal liberties that it afforded him—and these seep into his text. A close examination of certain routines in *Naked Lunch* reveals it as a text of "desistance," rather than a text of "resistance."

If we recognize *resist* and *desist* as cognates of the Latin *sistere* (to cause to stand), then *resist* is "to stand again" while *desist* is "to cease to stand," or, in essence, to stop resisting. Burroughs uses a narrative aesthetic that resists the traditional European narrative but desists from making a sustained critical stand against certain imperialistic attitudes. In letters to friends like Allen Ginsberg, this aesthetic was arrived at by writing "routines," disjointed and often brutal depictions of nightmarish visions and episodes of black comedy. *Naked Lunch* consists of a collage of "resistant" material that did not conform to a traditional linear narrative. This catered to Burroughs' desire to create a text that would be unshackled from the constraints of traditional form. The recalcitrance of this aesthetic lends itself to the antididactic content of the material, which may be one factor in the novel's resistance to making a stance of resistance. As Burroughs wrote *Naked Lunch*, the resistance to imperialism in Tangier forced its way into his novel but was met with the desistance occasioned by his sexual desire. Tangier was a place where Burroughs could indulge his desire for young boys, who were plentiful and cheap, without arousing the animosity of local authorities, who seemed to maintain a relatively laissez-faire attitude toward the sexual proclivities of the expatriate population. At the time of Burroughs' arrival, Tangier was a haven for the licentious "where almost any pleasure could be had for a price" (Green, 11). This was certainly one of the major reasons Burroughs was attracted to Tangier in the first place. Yet, what should be focused on is not Burroughs' personal habits—although examining these aspects of Burroughs' personal life may help shed some light on the complexity and ambiguity of his political stance—but on how they manifest themselves in the published text of *Naked Lunch* itself and in relation to the revolution that also found its way into the novel. While Burroughs worked on what would become *Naked Lunch*, the Moroccan fight for independence unwittingly burst into his book in several interesting ways.

Writing for *Esquire* in 1964, Burroughs recalls an ominous event in Tangier occurring while he was still working on *Naked Lunch*. Referring to himself in the third person, he writes:

> 'Twas the rain-riddled late afternoon of December 13, 1955, at the Villa Mouniria Calle Cook. Author Bill Burroughs was writing a letter in his penthouse quarters. Suddenly a stream of men, some carrying guns, opened Burroughs' door and looked in. The explanation is that the Villa Mouniria is for sale and these were guides for the "Black Bernous," none other than the ex-Sultan of Morocco Mohammed ben Arafa. Burroughs, the most politically neutral man in Africa, said: "Ben Arafa? Quién es?" ("Tangier," 118)

Of course, we should not read Burroughs' description of himself as "the most politically neutral man in Africa" literally. One way to interpret this potentially ironic line is as a veiled way of Burroughs suggesting that, rather than being engaged in the politics surrounding him, he is more interested in using it for his own literary purposes, as we will see later. It is doubtful Burroughs is honest about his ignorance of Sidi Mohammed Ben Moulay Arafa el Alaoui. He knew of Ben Arafa's predecessor, Ben Youssef, whose return to the throne precipitated Ben Arafa's move to Tangier. In a letter to Ginsberg and Jack Kerouac in October 1955, Burroughs mentions "the inevitable picture of Ben Youssef, The Deposed Sultan" in an Arab café (*Letters*, 296). After exiling Morocco's Sultan Sidi Mohammed Ben Youssef for his support of Moroccan nationalism, the French installed Ben Arafa in August 1953 (Green, 111). The last words of Billy the Kid, as Burroughs knew, where "*Quién es?*" before Pat Garrett killed him. Recalling Ben Arafa bursting into his apartment, Burroughs is imagining himself as a literary outlaw about to be gunned down by the Moroccan nationalists.

Support for the deposed Muslim spiritual leader Ben Youssef rapidly became widespread:

Nothing could have harmed the French position as severely as the banishment of ben Youssef. Moroccans who had been indifferent to the cause of nationalism were outraged by the insult to their imam, and the people rallied behind the Sultan as never before. Forbidden to speak his name in public, his subjects regarded him as a national martyr; peasants claimed that they could see his face in the full moon. In the following months, the Istiqlal [the predominant nationalist party] and its rival parties launched a campaign of terrorism that included an attempt to kill the detested ben Arafa, and few of their countrymen took issue with their methods. (Green, 111)

In the midst of a violent Moroccan revolt for independence, Ben Youssef was restored to the throne, and Ben Arafa was sent to Tangier. On November 6, a little more than a month before Burroughs' encounter with Ben Arafa, Morocco's independence was promised by France (Green, 160–61).

Just as Ben Arafa's guides burst into Burroughs' apartment, Morocco's revolution burst into the fiction of Burroughs' *Naked Lunch*. Burroughs arrived in Tangier in January 1954, and his relationship with the indigenous population was complex. To say that he was completely unsympathetic to the plight of the Moroccans would be unfair. He writes to Ginsberg in January 1957: "ARABS ARE NOT VIOLENT. [. . .] Riots are the accumulated, just resentment of a people subjected to outrageous brutalities by the French cops" (*Letters*, 349). Yet, in a letter from February 1956, Burroughs says to Ginsberg, "I believe I wrote you the natives are getting uppity. [. . .] Time for some counter-terrorism, seems to me. The police are quite worthless, the Arab police now quite openly taking sides against Europeans or Americans in any *contretemps*. A number of queers got notes warning them to leave town, and signed 'The Red Hand'" (311–12). As a homosexual, Burroughs' concern for his personal safety interfered with his possible empathy for the plight of the Arabs.

Burroughs' fear of religious fundamentalism spawned from nationalism in Morocco was confirmed when "the campaign against undesirables— con men and dead-beats and tax dodgers, as well as those who slept with the wrong companions" became an urgent topic for foreigners in Tangier (Green, 203). For Burroughs, a man with a penchant for drugs and young boys, Tangier was initially "the Promised Land" (*Letters*, 241). As he began to appreciate more and more his privileged position in Tangier, Burroughs stopped sympathizing with the Muslim population that suffered at the hands of the expatriate community's licentiousness. What was a haven for Burroughs was a nightmare for many Moroccans, and when the privileges spawned from imperialism ended in Tangier, he would miss them.

Just before dawn on 20 August 1955, the second anniversary of Ben Youssef's dethronement, fighting started in which dozens of Frenchmen and hundreds of Moroccans lost their lives. It ended days later, in a scene which could have easily been a Burroughs routine, with General André Franchi telling the masses of surrendering Arabs before him that they "behaved like stinking jackals" and would all be dead if it were not for the benevolence of France (Green, 157). Tangier's susceptibility to the ubiquitous violence in Morocco left the European contingent in Tangier thinking about leaving the country, but Burroughs was eager to see the carnage. In the beginning of August, an Arab whom Burroughs previously had refused to lend money to and who had chastised Burroughs for sleeping with boys ran amok killing four people before being apprehended (Green, 158). "Amoks trot along," writes Burroughs in *Naked Lunch* in a surrealistic rewriting of the event, "cutting off heads, faces sweet and remote with a dreamy half smile. [. . .] Arab rioters yip and howl, castrating, disemboweling, throw burning gasoline . . ." (32–33). In October, Burroughs writes to Ginsberg and Kerouac, "There's a war here I want to dig" (*Letters*, 292). Depictions of riots occur throughout *Naked Lunch,* but the violence associated with Arabs in *Naked Lunch* severs their connection to imperialism's despotism by becoming so shocking as to eclipse any semblance to the immediate politics behind the images: "Arab rioters send smoke signals by throwing great buttery eunuchs—they make the best smoke, hangs black and shit-solid in the air—onto gasoline fires in a rubbish heap" (173). For a man interested in the entropy of systems of control, the riots in Tangier were stimulating not only intellectually but, more important, aesthetically: "The chaos in Morocco is beautiful" (*Letters*, 339). It is the aestheticizing of the riots that comes across most clearly in *Naked Lunch.* Burroughs' routines can often be simultaneously read as symbolic and literal, realistic and surrealistic, fragmentary and connected, funny and revolting. On one level, they can be seen as politically disruptive in their thwarting of our expectations as readers. Yet, an immediate engagement with the Moroccan revolution is lost in the excessiveness of both form and content.

Burroughs' romanticizing of Arab riots reached a fever pitch in 1956 as the violence in Tangier showed little sign of ceasing, and the town began to have what Burroughs described as the "*jihad* jitters" (*Letters*, 336). "Really, rioting must be the greatest," Burroughs writes to Ginsberg, "like snap, *wow.* I mean I dug it watching them Arabs jumping around yelling and laughing, and they laugh in serious riots" (341). Burroughs was surely drawn to such paradoxical scenes because they resembled and could be used as models for his routines. Rather than approaching the violence of the Moroccan revolution with compassion, Burroughs used what he saw to spur his imagination to create grotesque scenes in an attempt to affront his readers' moral apathy. He is showing us the naked truth on the end of the fork—and maybe he wants us to be sick.

Here is one of Burroughs' exemplary routines:

> A group of sour Nationalists sits in front of the Sargasso sneering at the queens and jabbering in Arabic . . . Clem and Jody sweep in dressed like The Capitalist in a Communist mural.
>
> CLEM: "We have come to feed on your backwardness."
>
> JODY: "In the words of the Immortal Bard, to batten on these Moors."
>
> NATIONALIST: "Swine! Filth! Sons of dogs! Don't you realize my people are hungry?"
>
> CLEM: "That's the way I like to see them."
>
> The Nationalist drops dead, poisoned by hate . . . (119)

While Clem and Jody are caricatures of the Ugly American, the Nationalist is also a caricature. The routine ridicules shameful American attitudes, but it also does not align itself with the plight of the Nationalist. Burroughs is aware of the suffering of the Moroccans, but it seems his allegiance is more with the form of the routine than to any particular political cause.

Certain routines appear to depict political scenarios while stripping them of their political essence:

> Riot noises in the distance—a thousand hysterical Pomeranians.
>
> Shop shutters slam like guillotines. Drinks and trays hang in the air as the patrons are whisked inside by the suction of panic. [. . .]
>
> The Market is empty except for an old drunkard of indeterminate nationality passed out with his head in a pissoir. The rioters erupt into the Market yipping and screaming "Death to the French" and tear the drunkard to pieces. [. . .]
>
> Squads of police with thin lips, big noses and cold grey eyes move into the Market from every entrance street. They club and kick the rioters with cold, methodical brutality.
>
> The rioters have been carted away in trucks. The shutters go up and the citizens of Interzone step out into the square littered with teeth and sandals and slippery with blood. (120–21)

By turning the rioters into a pack of Pomeranian dogs, Burroughs is creating a comic scene to be juxtaposed with the brutality that follows. If Burroughs chose Pomeranians because of their ridiculous appearance and annoying bark, this would contradict the empathy he shows for the rioters in his January 1957 letter to Ginsberg. The routine is grotesquely funny, but its worth as a political statement regarding the Moroccan revolution is questionable. The police are morally corrupt, but so are the rioters. What we are left with is a statement about brutality in general, not politics specifically. Although it is certainly arguable that the passage was influenced by Burroughs' actual experience of watching riots, the scene he depicts in his novel becomes entirely his own. The routine could have taken place in another country in another century without influencing its impact.

"Islam Incorporated and the Parties of Interzone" begins:

> A rout of Mullahs and Muftis and Muzzeins and Caids and Glaouis and Sheiks and Sultans and Holy Men and representatives of every conceivable Arab party make up the rank and file and attend the actual meetings from which the higher-ups prudently abstain. Though the delegates are carefully searched at the door, these gatherings invariably culminate in riots. Speakers are often doused with gasoline and burned to death, or some uncouth desert Sheik opens up on his opponents with a machine gun he had concealed in the belly of a pet sheep. Nationalist martyrs with grenades up the ass mingle with the assembled conferents and suddenly explode occasioning heavy casualties . . . (122)

The depictions of Arabs as perverse, violent, and irrational reads as a Western racist trope that falls into the imperialist narrative of control, turning the Arabs into monsters. Burroughs' image of suicide bombers is particularly striking to the reader fifty years after the novel's publication, in an age when every newspaper seems to bring reports of heavy casualties, statistics on our porch steps. The Arab as automaton for violent religious fervor eclipses the Arab dehumanized by imperialist practices.

In seeking to satisfy his own desires in Tangier, Burroughs also takes advantage of the economic hardship of the indigenous population. He writes to Ginsberg and Kerouac, "Did I ever tell you about the time Marv and I paid two Arab kids sixty cents to watch them screw each other—we demanded semen too, no half-assed screwing. So I asked Marv: 'Do you think they will do it?' and he says: 'I think so. They are hungry.' They did it. Made me feel sorta like a dirty old man . . ." (*Letters*, 293). This disturbing scene, whether it literally took place or not, seeps into *Naked Lunch* nearly verbatim:

> Met Marv in front of the Sargasso with two Arab kids and he said:
> "Want to watch these two kids screw each other?"
> "Of course. How much?"
> "I think they will perform for fifty cents. Hungry, you know."
> "That's the way I like to see them."
> Makes me feel sorta like a dirty old man. (50)

The narrative voice eerily echoes Clem's words, "That's the way I like to see them," from the "Nationalist" routine, making the scene even more lurid and repulsive than the original letter and making the narrative voice even more repulsive. Clearly, Burroughs' strategy is to heighten the sense of repulsion he puts in front of his reader. *Naked Lunch* is certainly bereft of a simple moral compass. The nuances of the text lend themselves to outrage, but where should the focus of the reader's ire be leveled? This text of desistance refrains from making the type of definitive moral statement a text of resistance would warrant. If Burroughs has a moral purpose, this unsettling text does not relinquish it easily. The reader will need to stand alone in judgment of imperialism in Tangier.

The horrors of imperialism are still on the front pages of our newspapers. In the West, we have Islam on our minds more than ever before. A few years ago, I heard a paper delivered at a conference by a Muslim woman graduate student examining how *Naked Lunch* did not follow the teachings of the Qu'ran. A mostly liberal, white, scholarly audience listened politely and clapped when the presentation was over. Maybe they were just happy to see a Muslim deal with Burroughs' text at all. But I questioned why this type of reading was now tolerated. Would a paper examining how *Naked Lunch* did not follow the teachings of the Bible by an evangelical graduate student be received with the same response? I asked the graduate student how she felt *Naked Lunch* was received in the Middle Eastern country where she was born. She told me that it would be forbidden to be read because of Burroughs' homosexuality. Maybe that is partially why a *mufti* never declared a *fatwa* for Burroughs' immediate silencing. Perhaps the contemporary reception of *Naked Lunch* will now focus more on Burroughs' use of Tangier in its historical context when the book was written and his complex and ambiguous engagement with Islam than on the infamous pornographic scenes that have aroused readers for the last fifty years.

Works Cited

Burroughs, William S. *The Letters of William S. Burroughs, 1945–1959*. Edited by Oliver Harris. New York: Penguin, 1993.

———. "Tangier." *Esquire*, September 1964, 114–19.

Green, Michelle. *The Dream at the End of the World: Paul Bowles and the Literary Renegades in Tangier*. New York: HarperPerennial, 1992.

Mullins, Greg. *Colonial Affairs: Bowles, Burroughs, and Chester Write Tangier*. Madison: U of Wisconsin P, 2002.

Said, Edward. *Culture and Imperialism*. New York: Vintage, 1994.

"Paris is about the last place . . . ": William Burroughs In and Out of Paris and Tangier, 1958–60

andrew **HUSSEY**

For us, "the right place" was the famous Beat Hotel in Paris, roughly from 1958 to 1963.
—Brion Gysin, *The Third Mind*

William Burroughs arrived in Paris in early 1958. He was in a sour and discontented mood. His first experiences of the city had been to note how expensive it was, especially compared to Tangier where he had been based since 1954, and that its citizens were cold, bad-tempered, and hard to know. "I hear on all sides hair-rising stories of the Paris prices. No rooms etc." Burroughs wrote in September 1957. "I have a lot a work pending that I must be settled to do [. . .] I have run over allowance and must settle down and recoup. For this, Paris is about the last place" (*Letters*, 364).

There is little in Burroughs' chief biographers to contradict this view. In his reasonably comprehensive text on Burroughs, Ted Morgan gives no real justification for Burroughs' frequent long stays in Paris in the late 1950s, other than the presence of his friends Gregory Corso and Allen Ginsberg and the availability of reasonable quality *kif* at his lodgings at 9 Rue Git-le Coeur in the so-called Beat Hotel (274–75). In his entertaining account of daily life in the Beat Hotel in his biography *El Hombre Invisible* and his book on the Beat Hotel itself, Barry Miles is not much more forthcoming: he describes Paris in the 1950s as an "exotic" destination for an American Midwestern male (which it no doubt was) and sets out a garish parade of tourist clichés about the intellectual culture of the Left Bank—cafés, whores, poets, and gangsters—which, even though true, hardly distinguish the city from New York, and certainly not Tangier. In August 1957, Burroughs wrote to Ginsberg: "As for myself, Paris doesn't attract me at all. Like I say don't like the French, nor am I partial to the anachronistic Bohemianism of St. Germain des Prés . . . I mean you can dig it in the San Remo" (*Letters to Ginsberg*, 193). The reference to the Beats' favorite Greenwich Village bar is especially apposite, of course.

Certainly, Burroughs' gloomy mood as he approached and finally settled in the French capital did little to dispel the notion that Paris was no more than a temporary, accidental refuge from America. Indeed, like all of his quixotic travels—through Latin America, North Africa—Paris can be properly understood as part of Burroughs' imaginative landscape, so this logic goes, when set in contradiction against the United States.[1]

All of this is true. But it is also to underestimate both the extent and nature of Burroughs' direct links with the Parisian avant-gardes during this period. Some of these were, of course, entirely personal, such as his friendship with the bilingual painter and poet Jean-Jacques Lebel or the junkie fantasist Jacques Stern (see Morgan, 293–95, and Miles, 79–80). But there were also rather more stringent reasons for Burroughs' presence in Paris: his intellectual links with the likes of Jean Genet and the baleful influence of Louis-Ferdinand Céline—the great chronicler of Parisian low-life during the interwar period and later notorious as a Nazi collaborator—are, indeed, well documented elsewhere.

I want to ask the question whether Burroughs' arrival and subsequent sojourn in Paris were really quite as random as biographers and critics have thus far indicated. In particular, I consider Burroughs' itinerary between Paris and Tangier with the specific aim of tracing a growing political consciousness during this period. *Naked Lunch* has hardly (if ever) been considered as a postcolonial novel. Burroughs' travels between Paris and Tangier, between the center of colonial power and the colony, must, however, reveal a real set of political tensions that, I suggest, both inform and shape the imaginative landscape of *Naked Lunch*. More to the point, Burroughs' encounters and interest in Parisian avant-garde groups of this period cannot be discussed outside the context of political developments in Paris and North Africa and the way in which these developments were, in turn, interpreted by radical groups who were articulating for the first time the language of European anticolonialism.

Secondly, I investigate whether there were cross-currents already at work in the intellectual climate in Paris that Burroughs found both complementary and conducive to his intellectual development and that, indeed, would go on to shape his literary language. One of the most ambitious academic texts in recent years is a study by Timothy S. Murphy that provides a fairly comprehensive overview of French theory before, during, and after Burroughs' period in Paris and aims to situate him alongside such names as Deleuze, Derrida, and Lacan, amongst others. Murphy describes Burroughs' critique of language, subjectivity, and capitalism as part of an argument that aims to place Burroughs outside the dialectic of modernism/postmodernism, which Murphy sees as the central conflict of American writing in the postwar period. He describes Burroughs as "amodern" in his ability to sidestep this dialectic; as far as Murphy's argument runs, it is successful within its own terms.

The same might well be said of earlier studies by Brian McHale, Charles Russell, and Frederick Dolan, who all argue, with varying degrees of persuasiveness, that Burroughs' chief contribution to twentieth-century writing is as a theorist. Perhaps the most convincing example of this academic subgenre is Robin Lydenberg's *Word Cultures,* where she makes the case that "the ideas we now recognize as characteristic of post-structuralism and deconstruction were being developed independently by Burroughs almost thirty years ago" (inside front flap). Lydenberg reads Burroughs with Derrida, Barthes, and Kristeva in support of this argument and reveals in the process much of the inner mechanics of what would become the established Burroughsian framework of an antinarrative.

None of these texts make any reference at all to the *Internationale situationniste* or the *Letteristes,* two avant-garde groups with whom Burroughs came in direct contact (unlike, say, Derrida or Barthes) and who, more to the point, seemed to be in areas directly adjacent to Burroughs in Paris at the same times as he was there. And yet, there are great parallels to be found in both the theories and practices of these groups and Burroughs' own burgeoning experimentation. This much has already been suggested by Will Self, who places Burroughs unequivocally alongside the *Internationale situationniste* and the *Letteristes,* two of the most politically and artistically radical groups at work in Paris in 1959.

It would be too much to say that Burroughs was an assiduous reader of the texts produced by either of these groups, but, as Self points out, the similarities in technique and approach of both groups to Burroughs is simply too important to ignore. At the very least, I suggest, Burroughs was receptive to the big ideas of the Parisian avant-gardes that were then in the air; more interestingly, there are specific parallels to be drawn between Burroughs' writing and Situationist/Letterist activity that both mask and reveal the true nature of this intellectual synchronicity.

Tangier to Paris, via Algiers

In recent years, Burroughs has frequently been described as a "colonialist," an "Orientalist," and, less intellectually but nonetheless damagingly, as a predatory sexual tourist (certainly each of these categories forms the prevailing view of him amongst Moroccan critics). In support of these arguments, critics cite Burroughs' apparent disdain for the politics of anticolonial Arab nationalism, his ignorance of Islamic culture, and his widely advertised contempt for conventional sexual morality (from an Islamic or Christian point of view). And it is true that, at least until his later years in Tangier, Burroughs had demonstrated no more than a superficial and possibly racist understanding of the political tensions of the break-up of the colonial world.[2]

It is, of course, possible to argue, as Greg Mullins does, that by introducing homosexuality, in real and literary terms, into the stable order of the colonial framework (by "queering the colony" [70–71]) Burroughs is already subverting the colonial project. But this is to ignore or severely underestimate the unequal nature of the relationship between the European and the Arab "native": to give just one example, Mohamed Choukri, a writer who spent his adolescence as a male prostitute during the period that Burroughs was in Tangier, has given powerful and convincing accounts of the humiliating nature of this traffic.[3] Indeed Burroughs' casual remarks, in letters and conversation during his early period in Tangier, betray no real understanding of the political situation and reduce all Arabs to sexual and racial caricature ("I meet an Arab in native dress, and we repair to a Turkish bath. Now I am almost (but not quite) sure it is the same Arab [. . .] It's like I been to bed with 3 Arabs [. . .] every time better behaved, cheaper, more respectful" [*Letters*, 196–97]). In a letter from 1956, he reduces the political tension that grips Tangier in the wake of the independence struggle to the "*jihad* jitters," writing in prose worthy of Somerset Maugham or any of the lesser propagandists of the British Empire comically but inaccurately: "[*J*]*ihad* means the wholesale slaughter by every Moslem of every unbeliever" (336).

And yet, it is also possible to trace how, during his years in Tangier, Burroughs slowly shed the prejudices he had brought with him to the city. The first and most important of these is his notion of Tangier as an Oriental utopia of unbridled sexual license. His first fascination with the place, coming from Latin America, is as the "Orient," and all his references at first are to "Oriental" boys. He realizes that this is a fiction that he has created and writes to Ginsberg, "[D]on't ever fall for this inscrutable oriental shit" (*Letters*, 195). With this realization comes the acknowledgment that beyond the economics of sex traffic, there is a symbolic order—the United States, the "System," the "West"—that must be opposed or destroyed. This is how Burroughs arrives at what is not in strict terms a postcolonial vision but rather, more accurately, a postnational vision. He had no interest in Moroccan nationalism but rather a politics of total liberty that transcended all forms of nationalism. This is the key trope that is developed throughout the Tangier years.

This is also the trope that is brought most closely into focus when Burroughs arrives in Paris in 1958. That same year from a Tangier in the throes of change, Paul Bowles, with a cold forensic eye on the stupidity of foreigners, reported to Burroughs in Paris: "Two ladies have moved in upstairs. [. . .] They hope to drive to Mombasa but the thing is obviously impossible from here. 'But it's not a real war in Algeria. It's just a few areas of disaffection. That's what the French told us.' So they wait" (365). The point here is that both Bowles and Burroughs, tacitly understanding, identifying, and despising the innocence of foreigners, are, in a negative sense, acknowledging their own real grasp of the fraught realities of the situation (this atmosphere of apprehension is caught by Bowles in his story "The Time of Friendship").

After an unfortunate interlude with the police in Tangier in early 1959, Burroughs returned to Paris and would not return to Tangier until 1961. In part, this was clearly a practical decision, driven by the need to avoid yet another police conviction. Another reason for staying on in Paris was that, without really knowing much about it beforehand, Burroughs had arrived in 1958 in a city that was on a knife-edge. Although the Second World War had been over for more than a decade, the city still had to come to terms with the traumas and unfinished business of that dark period. Physically, the city was in a shabby state, its poorest citizens were seriously underfed and the streets were regularly packed with violent demonstrations against America, against the government, against the war in Algeria.

As Burroughs arrived in Paris, the city was in the throes of a new tumult. These were the regular convulsions caused by the Algerian war—the "war without a name" that had been festering since an insurrection launched in Algeria by the National Liberation Front (FLN) in 1954 had forced the French government's hand and precipitated military intervention. Having lost the territories of Indo-China, Tunisia, and Morocco, the government of Mendès-France was determined not to go down in France as the government that gave away the last French colonies. The problem was made even more complicated by the presence in Algeria of a French settler population, *les pieds noirs* or "black feet," so-called because their polished black shoes marked them out from native Algerians. This population called upon the

French government to refuse all concession to the Algerian side. When the government looked like it was caving in, the response was terrorism in Paris in the form of shootings and targeted bombings of intellectuals on the Left.

By late 1958, the Algerian war had become an inescapable and shameful fact of French life. Particularly in the capital, where riots in the streets and the use of Algerian informers in the communities of Barbès and Belleville had created a near war mentality, there was a palpable tension in the air. Nearly all groups on the Left, from the centrist parties to the wilder fringes of the avant-garde, perceived very quickly that the French response to the struggle for independence in Algeria posed a threat to the functioning of democracy in France itself. Most notably, in the months before Burroughs' arrival in Paris, the communist Henri Alleg, editor of *Alger Républicain,* had had his book *La Question,* an account of torture at the hands of French paratroopers, clumsily banned by the French government. Far from being the "exotic" terrain of unbridled artistic, political, and sexual freedom described by Miles, Morgan, and others, the Paris where the Beats made their temporary headquarters at the cusp of the 1950s was a heavily policed city, where officially sanctioned murders took place under the rubric of "public security" and where censorship, government lies, torture, and terrorist actions were daily occurrences.

This climate of hate and repression is, of course, very familiar to all those who have read *Naked Lunch,* the "work pending," which was written in Tangier and finally assembled in Paris. More important, it is also clear that at the moment that *Naked Lunch* is published in Paris, Tangier had to some extent served its purpose as the landscape of Burroughs' worst and most powerful nightmares.

But as (again) Greg Mullins points out, it is at this point that Tangier as Burroughs' "composite city" ceased to exist in both real and imaginary terms. Put simply, as foreigners began to leave Tangier in the face of growing colonial conflict (or like Bowles retreated into silence and cunning), the city was no longer historically an "International Zone," or "Interzone," but a mere component in the future construction of Moroccan national identity—a project in which Burroughs had no interest whatsoever. Colonialism, like communism or fascism, is indeed only one of such crimes against the human spirit; what Burroughs pursued in Paris is quite different.

Down to the Bone: Tangier in Paris

It is not so simple as to say that Paris here replaces Tangier as the central focus of Burroughs' imagination. But what Burroughs did find back in Paris was a matrix of avant-garde movements, all of them deeply marked by the tensions of their age and with an absolute belief in revolution as real experience rather than metaphor or theory. This notion is indeed key to any close reading of *Naked Lunch* as a text that is directly aimed against systems of control—the Virus—which are destroying the human species. The more obviously rigorous academic studies of Burroughs' relationship to Paris all emphasize to some extent or other this aspect of Burroughs' work: indeed Burroughs (and Brion Gysin) are frequently placed in a now-familiar lineage of pan-European creative dissidence that begins with Dada and, via Surrealism, traverses *Letterisme* and Situationism.

The fact that all of these movements have, or have had, their headquarters in Paris at some point has been discussed, if at all, as a mere accident of history. If this is the case, then it is an intriguing coincidence that the year 1959 saw the publication and distribution in Paris of a journal called the *Internationale situationniste*, edited by the poet, drinker, and strategist Guy Debord.

This was the house journal of a group of artists, political radicals, and intellectuals who also called themselves the *Internationale situationniste*. They argued against what they called "the society of the spectacle" or the "civilization of the image." They called for a return to experience as the first source of knowledge, hated modern art, and wanted to create a new utopia—New Babylon they called it—where thought and feeling were merged into what they called *situations:* this was the new art of the future, halfway between science fiction and a post-Marxist religion. It's hard to imagine that Burroughs would not be friendly to such currents, particularly as he was acquainted with the painter Ralph Rumney and the Scots poet and fellow junkie Alex Trocchi, both prominent in Paris as the English-speaking wing of the *Internationale situationniste*.

Most intriguingly, like Burroughs, the Situationists, were fascinated by geography as the main fact of creative potential and historical circumstance. They did not travel continents, however, but explored the urban hinterland of Paris in a stoned or drunken quest for the real meaning of the city. They coined the term *psychogeography* to describe the poetic possibilities unleashed by the coming together of their fiercely intoxicated, subjective visions and direct experience of the world; most important, they were inspired by the multiple angles of vision unleashed in that experience. Psychogeography was defined in 1955 by Guy Debord as "the study of the precise laws and specific effects of the geographical environment, consciously organized or not, on the emotions and behaviour of individuals" (qtd. in Hussey, 54). In line with this manifesto, the Situationists produced a broad range of proposals: the abolition of museums and keeping of art in bars, keeping the Metro open all night, streetlights with an on-off switch.

The tangential relationship between the Situationists and Burroughs is discussed by Timothy S. Murphy in his essay "Exposing the Reality Film: William S. Burroughs among the Situationists," as essentially diachronic: in other words, the art of Burroughs and the theories of the Situationists share a common if unconscious terrain. This is clearly demonstrated in the essentially ludic spirit of psychogeography—which aims to reassemble the city according to the laws of subjective reality and chance and that, I would suggest, is even by coincidence extremely close to the fragmented and partially reassembled version of Tangier that forms the geographical and historical core of *Naked Lunch*. From a strictly biographical point of view, it is obvious that Burroughs had set out to write this version of the city long before he could have encountered Situationism or Situationists; by the same token, it was when he was planning to assemble the text that he became friendly with Rumney, who was then making his own "psychogeographic map of Venice" and was then a founder of the Situationist International.[4]

It also worth noting that Situationism, in its embryonic form in 1959, was also directly related to Letterism, a theory of poetry refined and developed by the Romanian poet Isidore Isou. Both the Situationists and the Letterists, who had at one time been part of the same organization, were concerned with the problem of "leaving the Twentieth Century," conceiving of a postrevolutionary world where desire, play, sexuality, and intoxication replaced work, money, order. Isou's route towards this was the product of his theory of the creation of art, which was based on what he called *amplitude* and *ciselant* ("chiselling" or "paring away"), which were diametrically opposed but interchangeable.

However, unlike Dada, which had much in common with Isou's negative method, Isou's key notion was that since Baudelaire's discovery of "auto-destruction" as an artistic process, all poetry was a lie and a sham. True poetry, Isou says, lies not in the "plasticity of sound" but in its opposite: the separation of meaning from sound. Letterist poetry aimed, therefore, at the annihilation of meaning by reducing poetry to its most basic element, the letter. Letterist poets, following Isou's advice, would thus chisel language down to its essential preliterate sounds, which could be depicted as signs on a page.

More to the point, it is obviously a short step from this method to the experiments with cut-ups, vision, and magic that Burroughs would shortly initiate in the Beat Hotel. Burroughs came late to writing, and it may well be argued that his authentic literary voice only began to emerge as he had exhausted, in the most literal sense, the possibilities of his experiences and travels: it is indeed his assault on the negative potentialities of language, the Word, which provide the richest insight into his thinking—and, as I have tried to signal earlier in this essay, this includes his thinking on postcolonial issues (even if he would never have used these terms) as well as mere problems of technique.

Most important, Burroughs had brought with him to Paris the problems and contradictions of Tangier culture. At a personal and poetic level, this included a set of occultist beliefs that formed the center of his creative method. On a political level, he was making a journey from the postcolonial periphery to the center, seeking to subvert the latter with the beliefs and practices he had acquired in the former: Tangier was then both a vision and a reality that he unravelled and only properly understood in Paris.

The Last Place

One of my aims in this essay has been to puncture one of the most persistently recurring myths surrounding Burroughs and in particular the publication of *Naked Lunch* in 1959—which is that during his period in the French capital, Burroughs was either ignorant of or contemptuous towards developments in the French avant-gardes of his era. Although *Naked Lunch* was famously published in Paris, so the argument runs, this was with a marginal expatriate publisher, Maurice Girodias, whose main interest was not literature but money and whose links to the center of Parisian intellectual life were tenuous to say the least.

The parallels between Situationism, Letterism, and what Self identifies as Burroughs' ambition to "rub out the word" are indeed clearly demonstrable. This does not, however, make Burroughs the precursor or prophet of deconstruction or poststructuralism. Indeed both Situationists and Letterists were deeply hostile to all forms of postmodern theory, which they saw as the enemy of revolutionary praxis. Rather, they harked back to the Surrealists in their fundamental and unshakeable belief in the possibility of transferring transformative experiences into the social sphere: this was what was meant by revolution—or as Trocchi put it, the "invisible insurrection of a million minds."

It is, therefore, I would argue, both more realistic and helpful to think of Burroughs as complicit or even participating in this form of avant-garde activity—albeit in an instinctive, unguided manner—than sketching out theories that may or may not apply to his works. In other words, by placing him alongside the Parisian cross-currents of his era, Burroughs emerges not as a theorist but—and I am sure that he saw himself in this way—as a magician, alert to the secret languages and codes of his era, and then as an artist.

One of the most fascinating features of *Naked Lunch*, then and now, is not only the distinctive tone of its author but also his approach to the use of language—an approach that emerges directly from the author's voice and multiple perspective. It is this technique that has made Burroughs a hero to those of his readers who wish avant-garde status upon him. In a parallel sense to the dialectical techniques of the Letterists, the voice that Burroughs adopts to introduce the hipster world of *Junky* becomes in *Naked Lunch* a polyphonic assault on the very possibility of meaning in a world that has long since been evacuated by real human beings. Under these conditions, however, that is to say the conditions of a negative visionary experience, this is not science fiction but a clear and straightforward vision of dystopia; a voice reporting directly from the edge of the abyss.

Burroughs' antipathy to Paris was not sustained for long—overcome in the first instance no doubt by his varied interests in the specific aspects of its underground culture that I have tried to outline. But these are also mere suggestions. What really happens to Burroughs in Paris in 1959 is that, in the most literal terms, Burroughs had brought with him to Paris the psychic map of Tangier in the form of the manuscript of *Naked Lunch*. It was, of course, Ginsberg, Gysin, and Sinclair Beiles (editor for Olympia Press) who did the hard work of assembling the text for the galley proofs to be ready for publication in July 1959.

But by then, Burroughs had learned enough from Paris not to be afraid of rolling the dice and forcing the hand of chance.

Notes

1. This is a key trope developed by many of Burroughs' more academic critics. See, for example, the introduction, Lydenberg, or Mullins, 17–18.

2. For a discussion of these themes, see Mohammed El-Kouche, "Tangier Speaks," Allen Hibbard, "Tangier at the Crossroads: Cross-cultural Encounters and Literary Production," and José Pérez, "Tres Construcciones verbales de Tanger: tres ejemplos de la narrativa espanola," in special issue *Writing Tangier*, ed. Khalid Amine, Andrew Hussey, and Barry Tharaud, *Journal of Middle-Eastern and North African Intellectual and Cultural Studies* 3, no. 1 (Spring 2005).

3. Mohamed Choukri, *Le Pain nu* (Paris: Gallimard, 1998). Choukri described Burroughs as "a predator" (interview with author, Tangier, 11 February 2002).

4. See Ralph Rumney on Burroughs, *The Map Is Not the Territory* (Manchester, UK: Manchester UP, 2001), and interview with author, *Manosque*, August 2001.

Works Cited

Bowles, Paul. *In Touch: The Letters of Paul Bowles.* Edited by Jeffrey Miller. London: HarperCollins, 1994.

Burroughs, William S. *The Letters of William S. Burroughs, 1945–1959.* Edited by Oliver Harris. New York: Viking, 1993.

———. *Letters to Allen Ginsberg, 1953–1957.* Edited by Ron Padgett and Anne Waldman. New York: Full Court, 1982.

Dolan, Frederick M. "The Poetics of Postmodern Subversion: The Politics of Writing in William S. Burroughs's *The Western Lands*." *Contemporary Literature* 32, no. 4 (Winter 1991): 534–51.

Hussey, Andrew. *The Game of War: The Life and Death of Guy Debord*. London: Jonathan Cape, 2001.

Lydenberg, Robin. *Word Cultures: Radical Theory and Practice in William S. Burroughs' Fiction*. Urbana: U of Illinois P, 1987.

McHale, Brian. *Constructing Postmodernism*. London: Routledge, 1992.

Miles, Barry. *The Beat Hotel: Ginsberg, Burroughs, and Corso in Paris, 1957–1963*. New York: Grove, 2000.

Morgan, Ted. *Literary Outlaw: The Life and Times of William S. Burroughs*. New York: Holt, 1988.

Mullins, Greg. *Colonial Affairs: Bowles, Burroughs, and Chester Write Tangier*. Madison: U of Wisconsin P, 2002.

Murphy, Timothy S. "Exposing the Reality Film: William S. Burroughs among the Situationists." In *Retaking the Universe: William S. Burroughs in the Age of Globalization*, edited by Davis Schneiderman and Philip Walsh, 29–57. London: Pluto, 2004.

———. *Wising Up the Marks: The Amodern William Burroughs*. Berkeley: U of California P, 1997.

Russell, Charles. "Individual Voice in the Collective Discourse: Literary Innovation in Postmodern American Fiction." *Sub-stance* 27 (1980): 29–39.

Self, Will. "Living with Dead Time." *New Statesman*, 27 August 2001.

Burroughs: The Beat Hotel Years

jean-jacques **LEBEL**

iven the cosmic scheme of things, it is quite logical that so many scientific or artistic breakthroughs occur by accident. The discovery of the cut-up method by Brion Gysin in room 15 of the Beat Hotel (9 Rue Git-le-Coeur) and its systematic application to textual production by William Burroughs is but one example of the positive impact such accidents can have.[1] Genius—in the arts as well as in science—often consists of letting an accident happen, then exploiting its full, unprogrammed potential. Another such instance is LSD, which Albert Hoffman stumbled upon by "mistake." Jackson Pollock didn't invent dripping, he just let it be and expanded it, whereas tens of thousands of other draftsmen, whose liquid paints or inks also dripped, behaved as taught by wiping it off or by covering it up. So, when Brion showed Bill the surprising scriptural combines he had involuntarily begotten by cutting through several layers of newsprint—under one of his drawings—Bill adopted that technique as the nongrammatical writing process he needed to wage his "no holds barred" uprising against the official discourse of Amerika.

Never mind the comparison between the cut-up method and Tzara's picking out words from a hat and other such procedures. In my view, the dynamic clashes produced, in the minds of readers or listeners, by randomly slicing through linear story lines and breaking apart linguistic structures is more akin to visionary schizo-writing and preverbal sound-speech as practiced by Kurt Schwitters or Antonin Artaud. As a matter of fact, I vouch for an Artaud/Burroughs connection via the use of cut-ups as a tool, or a weapon, they both used to mount attacks on the dictatorship of normalcy, that is, the grammar and syntax of social and sexual normalcy. Way back in the days of the Beat Hotel—I think it was in 1958—I had the honor of introducing Burroughs, Ginsberg, Gysin, Corso, and Somerville to the sound and the fury of Artaud. R. C. Richards' English translation of *Theatre and Its Double* was not yet a must, and all they knew of Artaud was his legend, which Carl Solomon—who had witnessed Artaud's historic public breakdown at the Théâtre du Vieux Colombier, in 1947—had brought back from Paris and shared with Ginsberg at the New York psychiatric hospital where they met. Burroughs as well as Ginsberg was eager to find out more about Artaud, his struggles with opiates, and reinventing of language. I had put my hands on a fresh copy of the original tape of Artaud's *To End the Judgment of God*—which had been "liberated" by an anarchist friend of mine from a locked metal cupboard at the ORTF (the French National Radio Station, which had banned it and never aired it until after May 1968). So I invited them to my home to hear it.

We got stoned, sat on the floor, and huddled around a cumbersome tape recorder. We placed the reel on it and pushed the buttons. The result was a flow of high-pitched beastly blasts, in languages (plural) unknown to us, which we listened to in stupefied awe. When the tape came to an end, we were transfixed and puzzled, knowing that Artaud had indeed been fluent in idioms current only in his own mind. Then Ginsberg, always the practical one, said, "Let's hear it again," and, as we struggled with the tape recorder, we discovered we had put the reel on upside down. Stoned as we were, we had not listened to the radio-play as recorded by Artaud—with Roger Blin, Maria Casares, and Paule Thévenin—but to an accidentally reversed version of it.

Which goes to say that art is not only in the eye of the beholder but also in his ear or, as John Cage put it, NEW MUSIC = NEW LISTENING.

At last, we got the tape on right and were able to catch Artaud's magnetic mix of schizo-sound poetry and sublime antireligious, antimilitaristic, and anticapitalist imprecatory hollering in classical French. Burroughs was visibly impressed. As for Ginsberg, he borrowed the tape from me, made several copies, and mailed them in the United States to Judith Malina and Julian Beck, to LeRoi Jones (later named Amiri Baraka), and to Michael McClure. And that, ladies and gentlemen, is how the Artaud rhizome crossed the Atlantic and spilled over into the American counter-culture. On several other occasions, in Paris, London, or New York, Burroughs and I discussed the hallucinatory substance of Artaud's aural language that he seemed to have put together from fragmented audio snippets heard by him in many "foreign" tongues all mingled together and retransmitted by him through his singular ultrasound mental radio system (in 1962, as a tribute to him, I constructed an electric sculpture entitled *Radio Momo*). Burroughs once told me that, when sitting completely stoned on a Paris street bench near Saint-Michel, he had absorbed unrelated bits and pieces of conversations spoken in French, Italian, English, German, Greek, and other lingoes, by people walking by him, all adding up to a transcultural sound collage of phrases chopped up and put together again by the listener, in a transformational way resembling the cup-up method. To this day, I wonder if Artaud and Burroughs weren't pursuing a similar goal.

There was an ongoing conflict between Gysin and Ginsberg on how to best "translate" the contents of the extraordinary illustrated mixed-media Burroughs scrapbooks—made of texts and images from various sources, pasted into large black accounting books Bill had bought in a Paris stationery store—so as to deliver a printable manuscript to a publisher. Ginsberg won, and he mailed his version of *Naked Lunch* to Ferlinghetti in San Francisco (City Lights Books), who rejected it ("too much sex and violence"). Then the manuscript was handed to Maurice Girodias (Olympia Press, in Paris) by Corso, who was under contract with him for *American Express*. That seemed like a good idea because Girodias' father had published Henry Miller's Paris novels, and he himself had printed books by Samuel Beckett and Jean Genet. But Girodias too rejected *Naked Lunch*, and though he was to falsely claim to have "discovered" Burroughs, he did finally put the book out but only after bowing to the strong pressure put to him by Corso, Ginsberg, and many others. Some years later, Gysin retaliated with *The Third Mind,* a groundbreaking collaborative work he produced together with Bill, that has yet to be recognized for what it is: a cut-up masterpiece.

The years Burroughs, Gysin, Ginsberg, Corso, and their associates spent at the Beat Hotel in Paris were absolutely essential to the consolidation and expansion of their specific creative projects. Although short-sighted, nationalistic American academics and historians have done their best to ignore and hide that fact, one has only to consider the works produced then and there to understand how true that fact is. The Burroughs scrapbooks are probably one of the most important literary/artistic accomplishments of the second half of the twentieth century. Corso's Paris poems are superb. As for Ginsberg, he wrote many major poems while in Paris, including "Europe! Europe!" "To Aunt Rose," "The Lion for Real," "Death to Van Gogh's Ear," "At Apollinaire's Grave" (a fundamental text), and, most of all, he there began writing *Kaddish*, a seminal hymn if there ever was one, indeed as powerful as "Howl." In a weird way, the Beat Hotel residents related to the extraterritorial mythical place called Paris that, before them, had attracted no less English speakers than James Joyce, Samuel Beckett, Henry Miller, Scott Fitzgerald, Ernest Hemingway, Gertrude Stein, Nathalie Barney, Nancy Cunard, Sylvia Beach, Mina Loy, Peggy Guggenheim, Djuna Barnes, Man Ray, and scores and scores of poets, artists, philosophers, musicians, political activists in need of existential umbilical-cord cutting. Were not Joyce's *Ulysses*, Miller's *Tropics*, Beckett's *Molloy*, and Nabokov's *Lolita* first published in Paris? The Beat Hotel was cheap and dirty, a very far cry from the Ritz, where Fitzgerald and Hemingway had hung out, but the great Henri Michaux lived around the corner (Ginsberg wrote admiringly of his pioneering use of psychedelics and his visits to Burroughs and he). Burroughs' first recorded LP—the magnificent *Call Me Burroughs*—was taped in the vaulted medieval basement of the English Bookshop (42 Rue de Seine) and produced by the owner, Gaït Frogé, who asked Emmett Williams (the Fluxus poet) and me to write the liner notes for the album cover. We obliged.

In that tiny cellar took place many a bilingual poetry event including some by Burroughs, Gysin, Corso, and myself. On another such occasion—across the street, at the Galerie 55 in 1962—Corso, American jazz bassist Max Harstein, and I, with other poets, held an international poetry fest. Burroughs sat in the audience next to Octavio Paz, Mandiargues, James Jones, and a host of French poetry freaks mixed together with American expatriates. Corso read "Marriage" and "Bomb," and among the poems I read, I included "Épitaphe pour les morts de la guerre," an exhilaratingly funny antiwar tract by Benjamin Péret, which Burroughs liked a lot. He often mentioned that to me in our subsequent encounters. One of the most hilarious historical events of those Beat Hotel years was the one I had managed to engineer—who knows how—at my father's home, bringing together Burroughs, Gysin, Ginsberg, and Corso with Man Ray, Marcel Duchamp, Péret, and André Breton's wife, Elisa (Breton himself was bedridden with the flu). Burroughs was stoned and mute as always. Corso got drunk and cut off Duchamp's tie with a pair of scissors, emulating what he thought was a typical Dadaist action. Allen, too, was drunk, he went down on his knees in front of Duchamp and kissed the bottom of his trousers. Believe it or not, the grand Dadaists laughed like crazy and actually took a liking to my Beat friends, although my mother never forgave me for inviting such "durty bums" to her literary party. Ginsberg gives a rather cold description of that intense evening in a letter to Peter Orlovsky.[2]

Most parts of Burroughs' life are well documented except the Beat Hotel years. Why is that? We know almost all there is to know about the Columbia years, the New Orleans years, the Tangiers years, the London years, the Chelsea Hotel, and the Bunker years (thanks, mostly, to John Giorno, who has safeguarded Bill's windowless, orgone box-like room as if he had just left it), even the last years spent in Lawrence, Kansas, are known. Why and to what end, one wonders, have the Paris years been overlooked by most Burroughs scholars—except for Barry Miles, who did an excellent job in Beat historiography—and why has that part usually been edited out of textbooks and by whom?

Another crucial component of Burroughs' biography and intellectual output that tends to be minimized or blacked out—in compliance with the Nixon/Reagan/Bush doctrine of global submission to the Pentagon propaganda machine (a.k.a. *"Amerika Uber Alles"*)—concerns the clear-cut political stance he took in the sixties. How many of us remember the telling photograph—published in *Esquire* of all places!—in which Burroughs is pictured marching in a Chicago demonstration alongside Ginsberg, Genet, Mailer, and Terry Southern? This was during the Grant Park mass rally orchestrated by the Yippies and Abbie Hoffman to protest the 1968 electoral convention of the so-called Democratic Party and the ongoing Vietnam quagmire—the My Lai massacre of nearly five hundred unarmed civilians by mad-dog U.S. soldiers under the command of Lieutenant Calley having occurred in March of that year. Genet had smuggled himself into the United States without a visa to visit and support the Black Panthers and had joined up with that bunch of "un-American pinkoes" to explore the possibility of an international alliance of subversives, hoping to radicalize the antiwar and civil rights movement. That worldwide project dreamed up by elements of the American Rainbow left, of the Japanese *Zengakuren*, of the French *Mouvement du 22 mars*, of the German SDS, of the Italian *Movimento*, of the Prague anti-Stalinist resistance movement (amongst others) never materialized, yet the all-out attack on Washington's imperialistic war machine that many read into Burroughs' statements and books was definitely one of the inspirational sources—as was "Howl" or Rimbaud's *Season in Hell*—of that collective dream. I prefer another snapshot of Burroughs—no doubt perceived as less sexy than the *Esquire* one, therefore less appealing to worshippers of literary icons—that was taken in Chicago on 27 August 1968 by Raymond Depardon. Burroughs and Genet are seen in the middle of a sit-in, surrounded by youthful demonstrators, one of whom is holding up behind them a poster of *Ramparts Magazine* (not the same cup of tea as the glossy radical chic *Esquire*) entitled "TEAR GAS IN THE PUMP ROOM," which sounds quite like a line from *The Ticket That Exploded*. Genet is wearing blue jeans, like the kids around him, but Bill looks at once awkward sitting in the street and impeccable in his dark suit, white shirt, tie, and hat. In those days of mass revolt—in deep contrast with today's boring Dark Ages—when asked by underground-press reporters about his participation in such protests, Bill would answer, "You've got to put your ass where your mouth is." A sharp political declaration that, as articulated by him in his unmistakable metallic tone, can, of course, also be heard as an obscene double-entendre.

In the last and mainly solitary period of his life, spent in a hidden-away, isolated country house in Kansas, Burroughs was lured—but to no avail—into producing mainstream (i.e. linear and commercial) literature, practically devoid of the cut-ups, the sex, and the inventive, subversive "madness" that were the trademarks of *Minutes to Go, The Soft Machine, Nova Express, The Ticket That Exploded, The Third Mind*; in other words, he was made to renege on his genius. What a tragically ironic climax.

Nevertheless, I couldn't agree more with Jonas Mekas when he states that for him and his friends, the discovery of the first chapters of *Naked Lunch,* published in *Big Table* magazine, was an "event of monumental proportions," "like a new beginning in American literature." I might add: in world literature.

What better tribute is there to that great innovator than to dedicate to him the cut-ups we keep stumbling upon when doing our stuff? Here's to you, Bill:

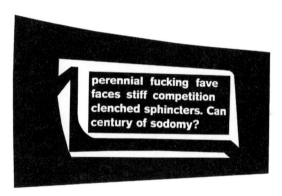

As ever,
Jean-Jacques

Notes

1. As for the method, it's best to go straight to the source which, in this case, is Brion Gysin's essay, "Cut-Ups: A Project for Disastrous Success," included in *Back in No time, the Brion Gysin Reader,* brilliantly edited by Jason Weiss (Middleton, CT: Wesleyan UP, 2002). As an example of the many far-reaching changes in writing techniques brought about by this method—even beyond the realm of so-called avant-garde poetry

or underground cinema—let's mention *Ritournelles* (Paris: Lume, 2007) by the major thinker/activist Félix Guattari, coauthor with Gilles Deleuze of *L'Anti-Œdipe, Rhizome,* and *Mille Plateaux.*

Concerning the schizoid grammar of phonetic collages, I refer the reader to "Schizologie," Gilles Deleuze's preface to American author Louis Wolfson's opus (written and published in French) *Le schizo et les langues* (Paris: Gallimard, 1970), 5–23.

2. See Allen Ginsberg and Peter Orlovsky, *Straight Hearts' Delight: Love Poems and Selected Letters 1947–1980,* ed. Winston Leyland (San Francisco: Gay Sunshine, 1980), 175.

dossier THREE
ian MACFADYEN

Files Comprising: Extreme Cuisine, Vomitorium, A Mess of Eels, *Merde*, Just For Jolly, Laissez-Faire, Atrophied, South American, Boy-Cries, The Candy Butcher, Raise, Jargon City, Zones Of Influence, Always A Body To Trade, Schizoid, Factualist, Visionary, Gone To Persia, Roller-Coaster, Greenback Readers, The Entire Serpent.

Extreme Cuisine

"Tarantulas, deep-fried with salt and pepper, are a speciality of the small town of Skuom, about two-hours drive north of Cambodia's capital, Phnom Penh. Villagers collect the arachnids from their burrows, taking care to avoid the poisonous fangs (which are trimmed with scissors before cooking begins). The spiders are properly cooked when the legs are crispy but the thorax still retains its moist, gooey, interior texture. The experience of eating bears some resemblance to that of a plate of soft-shell crab" (Hopkins, 192).

Vomitorium

In *Naked Lunch*, what is consumed is regurgitated, appetite becomes sensual greed fed by procured sickness, the feast requires an emetic, repletion is bypassed in favor of endless consumption. It's the culture of the Black Meat eaters who eat the nauseating stuff "and vomit and eat again until they fall exhausted" (47). In Petronius' description of Trimalchio's dinner party, Encolpius breaks open a pastry egg and thinks he sees a repulsive embryo inside—but it's a figpecker (a garden warbler) in egg yolk and pepper. Yummy. This is reminiscent of The Sailor's "pink scrotal egg [. . .] Black fur boiled inside translucent flesh of the egg" (171) and the huge, "unspeakably toothsome" (50) worm in a little yellow-brown egg, a gourmet delicacy which hatches in the human body, the kidney an eggshell host for the worm. . . . We are informed that this is "so-called lunch" (50), and like Encolpius' fantastic creation, the "food" here is perverse, repugnant, and possibly delicious. It's true defilement, and really, you haven't lived until you've swallowed *that,* my dear—and swallow it you *must.*

A Mess Of Eels

What is finally eliminated is nothing less, nothing more, than ourselves, used up, the literal *end* product, lunch for worms. It is the idea of devourment which gives the book its title—we are *Naked*/Meat *Lunch*/Eaters, consuming and rejecting ourselves endlessly unto death. Betty Fussell: "I can turn murder into blessing by symbolic salt, but excrement into sacrament is a harder trick to turn. God owes me there. My guts are serpentine as a mess of eels, but the inward darkness of Genesis shakes out as farce. Farce is my exodus. I know that after a lifetime's wandering through a wilderness of snakes and swine, no amount of murdering, no amount of laundering, will change my promised end as meat and gravy for rutabagas, pudding for worms" (225).

Merde

"Flaubert [. . .] conscious of the role of anality in the emergence of narcissism, promoted excrement as a symbol of the 'I'" (Corbin, 219)—and in Burroughs' writing, shit is an expression of unfettered personal license, a refusal of politeness and delicacy of feeling, an insistence upon his own linguistic liberty as well as a way of "privileging the anus" and shamelessness. Burroughs would have known Verlaine and Rimbaud's infamous, collaborative sonnet, *"Sonnet du trou du cul,"* the "Arsehole Sonnet," although as late as 1962, it was absent from the Pleiade *Oeuvres complètes* of Verlaine because it was considered obscene. "'Tis the swooning conch, the fondling flute, / The tube from which the heavenly praline drops, / A female Canaan cocooned in muggy air" (qtd. in Robb, 142). Like Rimbaud, Burroughs attacks the "decent" canons of literature and ridicules conventional notions of beauty through the affirmation of the functioning biological body, even though his sense of physical abnegation and his desire to escape the doomed, mortal flesh is everywhere evident.

Just For Jolly

In 1944, Kerouac wrote the word BLOOD in his own blood on a manuscript, smearing it throughout a section of *Vanity of Duluoz*. Burroughs is not so literal, but he cites a definitively bloody source. The "Atrophied Preface" is subtitled "Wouldn't You?" and the phrase is taken from "a letter to The Press" (Rumbelow, 177), supposedly written by Jack the Ripper and (mis)quoted by Burroughs, the original letter running as follows: "The next job I do I shall clip the lady's ears off and send to the police officers just for jolly wouldn't you" (118). The letter, posted on 28 September 1888, was the first, out of thousands received by the police, to be signed "JACK THE RIPPER," though its authenticity is doubtful. Its significance lies in the way the author of this purported confession flaunts and taunts his readers, relishing the twinned bloody acts of murder and confessional writing—"I saved some of the proper red stuff in a ginger beer bottle over the last job to write with but it went thick like glue and I can't use it. Red ink is fit enough I hope *ha ha*" (Rumbelow, 117–18). This is a model for *Naked Lunch*'s misogyny, its gloating satisfaction at the breaking of every taboo and the relinquishment of all human feeling—it suggests that at one level, Burroughs' book is a self-confessed Ripper routine.

Laissez-Faire

Feel the ecstasy of absolute irresponsibility, the jubilant overthrow of all control. Hear the cry we may always have been secretly waiting for, despite or because of ourselves: *Let it come down!*

Atrophied

Kerouac saw the despair beneath Burroughs' disdain and the profound sense of loss felt by the autodidact and ruthless analyst, the melancholy which runs throughout *Naked Lunch*—the work is a great lamentation for atrophied human potential buried in ideologies and civilized mores, written in mourning for life frozen "under the heavy lid of morality and custom" (Kerouac, 159).

South American Boy-Cries

"'Joselito! . . . Paco! . . . Pepe! . . . Enrique!'" (43). There are some names which must be repeated endlessly, whispered or cried aloud, a litany of the lost to be called back through time, and this is Burroughs' Mexican Mantra as well as his Tangier Threnody, his own ghost-dance chant, and while the "plaintive boy cries drift in on the warm night" (43), it is the one who knew them way back when who recites their names, summoning their own young voices at play in "street ball games, bull rings and bicycle races" (43), even though this paean to innocence and loss is delivered by the one who paid them so very little for his pleasure, even if it was the going rate. It is like Humbert Humbert hearing "the melody of children at play" in the streets, "the vapour of blended voices, majestic and minute, remote and magically near, frank and divinely enigmatic," and realizing the "hopelessly poignant" absence of Lolita's young voice "from that concord" (Nabokov, 308). The Mexican boys cost Burroughs three *pesos* a piece but Brion Gysin would remember how Burroughs *whinnied* these South American boy-cries, suggesting a knowing, self-abasing lament as well as a magical invocation. The line almost certainly derives in part from Lorca's poem, "Fable and Round of the Three Friends," published in *Poet in New York by Federico Garcia Lorca* (English translations were published in 1939–40 and 1955), with its haunting refrain, "Lorenzo, / Emilio, / Enrique" (Belitt, 7). The excoriating elegiac style of Lorca's book profoundly influenced Ginsberg's *Howl* (1956), and Burroughs' own hallucinatory, savage desecration of capitalism, civilization, and the city is indebted to Lorca's great and terrifying *Duende*.

The Candy Butcher

Burroughs sells *Naked Lunch* like a Candy Butcher in a burlesque theater on Forty-second Street—step right up, room for one more inside, sir, c'mon, kid, get it while you can. The Candy Butcher sold dirty postcards and nude magazines from the stage during intermissions to the captive, ogling, titillated audience—along with toothsome candy. This is, of course, a risky, rather than risqué tactic for an author of "literature" to employ but absolutely typical of Burroughs' streetwise aristo persona and renegade but strategic confusionism. Here, the disreputable, shameful object of desire, the ultimate pornazine is *Naked Lunch* itself, the forbidden book *in hand*, coming on to you urgent and ineluctable with a lubricious built-in sales gimmick which cannot be shut off.

Raise

"Ever notice how many expressions carry over from queers to con men? Like 'raise,' letting someone know you are in the same line?" (4). This is also true of pornography and drug parlance, and between these and queer and con parlance, an "every which way" set-up is created, a matrix of interconnecting fabulations and codes. Sexual outlaws, criminal cons, sex traffickers, drug dealers, they move in and out of each other's illegal worlds in which money and the exploited body are always at stake. The richness and ambiguity of *Naked Lunch*'s language lies in the way discreet, specialized discourses overlap and merge, signalling and triggering multiple meanings and suggestive echoes, the relished and *knowing* blurring of codes.

Jargon City

The *pleasure* of shape-shifting linguistic codes is incredibly important to Burroughs—as if to speak and to write certain locutions is to enter, *open sesame*, the forbidden, unstable domains through which meanings float and transmutate. *I speak, and that I am*, except, that *I* is immediately and continually undone by the very instability of the meanings of the words, written or spoken, which have, literally, underground *lives* of their own, parlance signifying something/someone *other*, differences which Burroughs celebrates as an escape from fixity and stasis of "self," the homosexual's ability "to crack a code and enjoy the reassuring exhilerations of knowingness [...] to buy into the specific formula 'We Know What That Means'" (Kosofsky, 204). Argot takes the gay writer where he wants to go, to the forbidden places—it is a linguistic *dérive*—it liberates him, allows him to wander adventitiously through the coded addresses of marginal milieus in which words play hide and seek, and nothing is ever as it seems or *says*.

Zones Of Influence

Only a decade separates the grey room of Orwell's *Nineteen Eighty-Four* and the psychedelic camera obscura of *Naked Lunch*. Orwell wrote about his novel to his publisher in 1948: "What it is really meant to do is to discuss the implications of dividing the world up into 'Zones of Influence'" (Orwell, xii). The four-party Interzone of *Naked Lunch* is not "Tangier," but a model of geopolitical partition, a trial run for planetary dystopia. The racial groups of Interzone are not, however, "absorbed into more collective identities" as Thomas Pynchon observes (Orwell, xvi), but preserved in all their human variety and uniqueness. If Burroughs celebrates "all human potentials" and the "blood and substance of many races" (89), it is because *difference* is an economic necessity, the literal life-blood of the world marketplace, its rich and variegated merchandise.

Always A Body To Trade

It really is the very latest thing and I want . . . *that one*.

Schizoid

And then the schizoid volte-face, the unbearable dialectic which would become a key Burroughs' strategy: outraged polemic turning on a dime into gloating perversity, vicious voyeurism flipping to passionate demands for liberation at all costs . . . An ideal either-which-way set-up for the terminally split operator.

Factualist

If Burroughs is a subscriber to the Factualist party of Interzone, then he has a curious attitude to so-called facts—his anthropological interjections and explanatory parentheses parody and usurp any notion of logic and credibility. The more the autodidact explains and explicates, the less likely we are to believe his recondite hokum, his *curiosa*, his *oeuvres galantes*. Maybe Burroughs was a Sender all along, with a "rabid fear of any fact" (136). "*See the facts and myself*, an old man with the wasted years behind, and what ahead having seen The Facts? A trunk full of notes to dump in a Henry St. lot?" (Burroughs, *Letters*, 226).

Visionary

His son remembered Burroughs on the rooftop in Tangier, "transfixed and absolutely motionless, right hand holding the perpetual cigarette, lips parting to the sun. [. . .] When it was finally, absolutely night, again, the sudden rush to the typewriter" (43). Burroughs was a visionary literalist—if you haven't *seen* it, you can't write it. *Yagé* transport, *kif* dreams, and those images behind the eyes irradiated by the light of dying suns. . . . And then the pencil racing across the notebook page, the typewriter hammered to destruction, words gushing beyond the speed of transcription . . .

Gone To Persia

In 1973, Brion Gysin took a copy of *Naked Lunch* to the remote fastness of Alamout, the ruined fortress of the Assassins in Persia. It would become, effectively, the last book in the great mythic library of Hassan-i-Sabbah, the final text of heterodoxy, rebellion, and esoteric learning.

Roller-Coaster

Like *Naked Lunch*, the manuscript of *Tropic of Cancer* accumulated through osmosis and happenstance over a long period of time, including the use of letters as vital medium and source. The process resulted in abrupt formal jumps and detours, a material, textual homage to

Spengler's theories of nomadism and apocalypse. It would have a crucial influence on *Naked Lunch*. "The rails fall away into the canal, the long caterpillar with sides lacquered in Chinese red dips like a rollercoaster. It is not Paris, it is not Coney Island—it is a crepuscular melange of all the cities of Europe and Central America. Railroad yards spread out below me, the tracks looking black, webby, not ordered by engineers but cataclysmic in design, like those gaunt fissures in the Polar ice which the camera catches in degrees of black" (Miller, 3–4).

Greenback Readers

In the early 1960s, dealers, customers, and cognoscenti of the porn trade referred to sleazy magazines as "books," and so actual books were referred to as "readers," and the paperbacks of the Traveller's Companion Series of the Olympia Press became known as "greenback readers," in recognition of their infamous green covers. Yes, that's where *Naked Lunch* was placed: on a shelf in a Soho backroom or basement, between *The Wisdom of the Lash* and *The Sexual Life of Robinson Crusoe*. Those references to greenbacks unwittingly punned upon the monetary trade in human readers and printed merchandise, both calculated in "greenback" dollars. Some sincere, uninitiated purchasers of *Naked Lunch* must have felt short changed, though others almost certainly got considerably more than they had bargained for. Such is the erotic, economic lottery when a *green* reader invests in a *greenback* reader, and burns a hole in his pocket. *That's not pornography, that's writing!* . . . Hang on, this is *hot* . . .

The Entire Serpent

Baudelaire: "We can cut wherever we want, I my reverie, you the manuscript, the reader his reading; for I do not bind the latter's recalcitrant will to the endless thread of a superfluous plot. Remove one vertebra, and the two pieces of that tortuous fantasy will reunite without difficulty. Chop it up into many fragments, and you will find that each one can exist separately. In the hope that some of those segments will be lively enough to please and divert you, I dedicate to you the entire serpent" ("Paris Spleen," qtd. in Lyu, 137).

The Danger Zone

eric ANDERSEN

You can't fake quality any more that you can fake a good meal. NAKED Lunch—a frozen moment when everyone sees what is on the end of every fork.
—William S. Burroughs, *The Western Lands* and *Naked Lunch*

Come Right in Boys, Grab a Seat

You see him sitting there, the man in a narrow snap-brim hat and colorless suit, dunking a small cake into his coffee at a nameless lunch counter. You sit next to him and casually strike up a conversation. Something about his flat Midwestern drawl and incognito eyes draws you in. You talk about what ails. He speaks in steady, dry, matter-of-fact tones. You are impressed with his vast knowledge of pharmaceutical matters. It makes you wonder if he's some kind of traveling psychopharmacologist . . .

William Seward Burroughs, with his gaunt skeletal face, thin build, gray spectral eyes, and rumpled banker's suit to match, may not be the first person you would bring home to meet mom and little sister. Residing within the conservative style, behind the dead, impassive eyes, and lurking just beneath the flat, hypnotic Missouri drawl is a man with a perilous history of darkest travels, menacing tales, criminal worlds, and years of drug addiction. A face that presented the world with a new version of pain.

Burroughs almost always looked this way, the same at age thirty as age seventy-eight. He was born a young man in an old man's body that never seemed to age. His nickname was *El hombre invisible* (the invisible man) to the Tangier street regulars. His disguise was a nondescript suit. Dress codes aside, Burroughs never disguised his intentions nor pulled any punches about his meanings. Yet, there was a cool watchfulness without his seeming to look. And wasn't William S. Burroughs always careful with words?

Step Right Up, Welcome to the Funhouse

With brutal honesty, cool surgical eye, and scalpel pen, William S. Burroughs instinctively peeled back the skin on issues American novelists rarely dared address. The stuff of his adventures, narcotic addictions, criminal experiences, exotic disease, and substance research (including opiates, sophisticated pharmaceuticals like scopolamine and LSD-25, and South American jungle poisons including curare), plus other myriad flora and fauna investigations, would quickly amass; then afterward, he would return with his discoveries to a room to assemble the material within the lab of his own skull. In *Naked Lunch*, he utilized much of the imagery he gleaned from his exotic wanderings and personal experiments to chilling effect. Fellow Tangier writer and friend Paul Bowles observed that Burroughs "was using his own life as an experiment."

In the preface to his short-story collection *Trouble Is My Business*, one of Burroughs' mentors, Raymond Chandler, wrote, "Their characters lived in a world gone wrong, a world in which, long before the atom bomb, civilization had created the machinery for its own destruction, and was learning how to use it with all the moronic delight of a gangster trying out his first machine gun. The law was something to be manipulated for profit and power" (viii). By his hard-boiled lights, things were not looking good for mankind. Early on, young Burroughs, like Chandler before him, was innately skeptical of the planet's future, predicting that *Homo sapiens* (his "homo saps" in *Ghost of Chance*) was a flawed, reckless species that would eventually self-destruct, "people of such great stupidity and such barbarous manners."

A few miles from his ranch school in Los Alamos, New Mexico, the first atomic bomb had been developed. Looking back, it wasn't the majestic purple-blue mountain vistas that Burroughs would remember but the dust, Gila monsters, and malevolent centipedes creeping under the rocks.

With exceptional powers of observation, a sharp ear for plainspoken American speech, keen sense of telepathy, and scathing wit, he assembled the shards of his multiprism world with awesome skill, elevating himself to the master of shock comedy and hilarious liberator of *noir*. Compared to all the early American *pre*-Beat writers, Burroughs' prose still remains vibrant, unbridled, and remarkably fresh. If Jack Kerouac would go on to make spiritual maps of the road, Burroughs would soon provide blueprints for the future.

In his *New York Times* book review (25 November 1962), critic Herbert Gold described *Naked Lunch* as "booty brought back from nightmare." More precisely, it's a drunken boat, besotted with sinister ghoulish laughs and comic *noir* scenes, a mind voyage without charts. In the party scene in *Naked Lunch*, Burroughs would give the term *gallows humor* a new twist.

Forks Up! The First Course Is about to Be Served!

Naked Lunch was written fifty years ago in a style so revolutionary that Burroughs could have waited and written the same book fifty years in the future. The prose never ceases to startle and amaze. It strikes home while depicting the darkest, bleakest visions that somehow possess the ironic, dark power to *illuminate*! The precision of his language is remarkable, blasting through obfuscation while never failing to roll out one delicious nugget after the other.

Naked Lunch is William S. Burroughs' document of his own consciousness. The book is exceptionally human, sensual, and physical, containing many erotic and homoerotic scenes that spill uninhibitedly and unpredictably in many orgiastic and hilarious ways. Like Lenny Bruce's tireless crusade to liberate and legitimatize the so-called dirty word in America, the shock factor of words always intrigued Burroughs. Bruce had often preached, "There are no such things as dirty words, only dirty minds." Burroughs possessed no word-prison etiquette. His method of word enforcement was "take no prisoners." This was the litmus test. If Burroughs could locate and employ the most-shocking subject matter and language that would be guaranteed to horrify his parents' privileged insular world, the words stayed.

One of his talents was his amusing ability to play two roles at once: the sarcastic protagonist and comic narrator. He was the out-of-orbit visionary and the downhome spinner of commonsense Midwest yarns. His role could range from a carnival pitchman in a Martian midway freak show hawking surrealistic promises to the crowd—step right up, boys—to a corn porn vaudevillian stage hoofer who can make us wince, smile, or laugh as he unleashes his droll, astute observations, and merciless routines that seem to cascade forth effortlessly from the funhouse of his mind. He never shrinks from his task: To think the unthinkable, then write it down.

Naked Lunch continues to be a sexy book overflowing with guilty pleasures both terrible and hilarious. The novel opens like a thriller in New York's Greenwich Village: "I can feel the heat closing in" (3). He involves us immediately in a series of astonishing adventures much as the old seafarer buttonholes the Wedding Guest in *The Rime of the Ancient Mariner*. We suddenly shift roles, becoming aiders and abettors to his mental outrages by becoming leering accomplices slipping down his dark comic trails that can jettison the gentle reader, without warning, from the comical terrors of the present into the wasteland horrors of the future.

Harvard, What, Me Worry?

Burroughs hailed from the Anglo-Saxon Protestant, patrician American ruling class. This was the class of entrepreneurs that believed they were destined to run the American show—the privileged super-rich that produced the Astors, Carnegies, Morgans, Rockefellers, Fords, and the Burroughs family. All of them were bankers, creators of industries, inventors, or self-made capitalists who were destined to become the invisible, all-powerful hands shaking events and moving policies behind American business, industry, and politics, leaving the rest of the populace behind, awed and envious of their power and complexity.

It was not lost on him that Harvard College was blue chip, *the* school for the privileged and elite. Later, after graduation, he would turn his back on all normal values of entitlement, eventually subverting them, while still retaining the ingrained sense of superiority and sang-froid that readily accompanies a privileged background instilled since childhood. The patrician blueprint was a carefully measured blend of ruthlessness mixed with acts of kindness towards anyone possessing the same blue-blood ruling-class background along with a backyard as big as your own. Their motto: *Always keep your eagle eyes as sharp as your talons*, and always keep a stiff upper lip in the face of adversity. As Henry Ford III cynically put it, "Never explain and never complain."

Though a scion of the famous adding-machine family, a corporate American Burroughs would never be. He just wasn't a "company man." Burroughs well understood the machinery of control and how the system worked because his forebears invented it. In *Naked Lunch*, he examines the concept for the need of control as a hooked narcotics user sees his pusher and sees its flawed logic: "*You see control can never be a means to any practical end . . . It can never be a means to anything but more control*" (137).

The store of his own early confidence in his abilities and views, mixed with a strong sense of authority and innate no-nonsense approach to life, would later serve him well as a writer. It gave him verbal superiority and self-assurance to pursue a guiltless, aim-for-the-jugular literary style. Despite his Harvard literature studies, he was comfortable speaking and writing in the unadorned American Midwestern vernacular. His approach was as low key as his drawl. As a personality, he could have just as easily been your sociable local gun-shop owner or friendly neighborhood society columnist, as he could have been your anonymous CIA interrogator and torturer.

He knew money could buy you out of problems; it was a quick fix. But he would soon discover there were some things money can't buy, much less "fix." His life on the run, cavalier lifestyle, and unruly heroin habit revealed something truly frightening: a demon he would call the Ugly Spirit had taken up residence deep within. Money couldn't free him from the demon this time so he vowed to write his way out after committing the most stupid, reckless act of his life, resulting in the tragic death of his wife. In addition to his chronic heroin habit, he would soon add a new one—*writing*.

It's Cut-Up Time. Grab the Knives and Start Carving

Burroughs believed that the purpose of writing was to "make something happen [. . .] in the mind of the viewer or reader [. . .] to create a character who'd be able to walk off the pages" (*Painting and Guns*, 32, 33, 34). When he confronted his existential crossroads, after shooting his wife, he chose to write his "way out" by describing a world even more shocking and perverse than the actual crime he'd so mindlessly and recklessly committed in Mexico City. Allen Ginsberg recalled how Burroughs would spend long sessions sitting at the typewriter thinking in pictures, seeing images moving against the dark, "hands pulling in nets in the dark."

In 1957, Ginsberg wrote Burroughs suggesting it might be wise to impose linear continuity on the novel. Burroughs replied tersely that he considered "any attempt at chronological arrangement extremely ill-advised" (*Letters*, 367). In truth, his novelistic style is one big cut-up—but not of the scissor and paste variety, that of books, magazines, and news clippings—but rather cut-ups from his own singular approach to narrative novel writing. In one of the final sections, Burroughs states, "You can cut into *Naked Lunch* at any intersection point" (187). Looking back, it's true. Entire episodes could have easily been juxtaposed with each other just as easily as some sections of *Western Lands* could be interchanged with *Naked Lunch*.

About writing, he also says, "There is only one thing a writer can write about: what is in front of his senses at the moment of writing . . . I am a recording instrument . . . I do not presume to impose 'story,' 'plot,' 'continuity'" (*Naked Lunch*, 184). Later, he offers insights into his fictional world: "What are writers trying to do? They are trying to create a universe in which they have lived or where they would like to live. That is, are you making your universe more like the real universe, or are you pulling the real universe into yours?"

Close Your Eyes, Boys, Peek into the Crystal Ball

While most writers fictionalize characters, Burroughs fictionalized places. Real places in his mind could never compete with the summoned geographies tucked away within his head. He had already given the expression of having been there a new slant and interpretation when we gaze upon the vivid dreamscape settings, outlandish routines, and bizarre episodes in his writing. He had a memory full of impressions, remembered dreams, and places imagined—not necessarily the physical realities that had often surrounded him—New York, Tangier, Paris, London. He deftly created his own theatrical settings within his own imagination; realms of never-before-seen cities, deserts, rivers, tropical forests, and swamps of his fantasies. He once said, "I'm creating a world in which I would like to live." Add to this his seductively rhythmical language, and you have a recipe for trance literature. "You know," he admitted, "they ask me if I were on a desert island and knew nobody would ever see what I wrote, would I go on writing. My answer is most emphatically yes. I would go on writing *for company*" (Lotringer, 81; emphasis added).

Club Med—Club Dead

It appears that over the years, Burroughs had, in fact, carried his own portable desert island around with him because, for someone who had traveled so widely, he was oddly incurious of his surroundings. His created literary vistas were as far-flung as his real-life landscapes were restricted. He rarely ventured very far from where he lived. Once in the winter of 1953, he met his friend Alan Ansen in Rome and hated it. It was cold and inhospitable, and the ancient churches to him were no more than piles of old stones.

Locales where he took up residence, writing habits, along with his drug and criminal activities (noted in parentheses) were variations on a theme. In the early 1940s, he seldom left Manhattan (morphine syrettes, forged prescriptions, and firearms). Upon leaving New York City, he stayed on a small ranch in Texas (attempts at growing marijuana and arrested for fornication with his wife on the side of an east Texas road). In Algiers, across the bridge from New Orleans, he made forays into the Quarter only to make hasty returns (scoring heroin while his wife was scoring over-the-counter Benzedrine inhalers). In Mexico City, he stayed close to his house with the exception of visits to Chapultepec Park (scoring H. and later getting arrested for manslaughter). In Peru, in search of the psychotropic vine *yagé*, he stayed close to the main road that led to and from the hut where the substance was administered to him by an Amazonian medicine man.

In the late fifties, while living in Tangier writing *Naked Lunch*, his range was limited, toes barely touching the sand, much less making footprints in the Sahara. There are amusing photos of Kerouac and Peter Orlovsky cavorting and posing on a Tangier beach while Burroughs lies motionless on his stomach in the sand wearing a suit and shoes (*kif*, opium, and heroin). In Paris, in the sixties, he stuck pretty close to the Beat Hotel in the Latin Quarter (heroin). The same pattern continued in London when he lived on

Duke Street in the seventies and also at the Bunker on the Bowery in New York in the eighties (heroin, cocaine, hashish, and alcohol). In Lawrence, Kansas, he made weekly excursions to Kansas City for his methadone prescription. Basically, he liked to stay close to home within the comparative comfort and safety of his own private danger zone.

What Rhymes with "Moon and June"? "Spoon." So Start Cooking One Up!

In *The Place of Dead Roads*, the horse-hating hero Kim Carsons was known to carry an edition of Rimbaud's poems in his breast pocket. Besides his smart, imaginative, concise, and often-offensive lyrical poems, Burroughs was impressed by Rimbaud's vast chemical intake of substances like absinthe, laudanum, and hashish, which gave rise to Rimbaud's furious writing edict: *"Rearrange all the senses!"* There was also Rimbaud's fascinating definition of the artist as one who "exhausts all poisons in himself and keeps only their quintessences" (307).

In *Naked Lunch*, Burroughs produced powerful imagery and small poems of vividness and economy. Take, for example, his description of shooting up: "A red orchid bloomed at the bottom of the dropper [. . .] watching the liquid rush into the vein as if sucked by the silent thirst of his blood" (56).

Standing before the judge at the Boston obscenity trial of *Naked Lunch*, Allen Ginsberg quoted lines from the novel, recalling images surrounding his own New Jersey tidal flat childhood: "Motel . . . Motel . . . Motel . . . broken neon arabesque . . . loneliness moans across the continent like fog horns over still oily water of tidal rivers . . ." And another image: "through the tool-house window whitewash whipping in a cold spring wind on the limestone cliff over the river . . . piece of moon smoke hangs in china blue sky . . ." (188).

Hmmm . . . Looks Like Danger Ahead, Let's Investigate

The taste for danger developed early, with morphine syrettes and illicit firearms. Getting involved with guns and narcotics in 1940s New York often ended tragically and sent people up for life. In the Beat view, drugs shouldn't be criminalized in the first place. Drug consumption for them was strictly a personal and never a criminal matter. The Beat writers carried on their lives and work with an almost naïve impunity (or more likely, a false sense of immunity). But in the manner that Burroughs and Kerouac dressed—and their dress code as practicing hombres invisibles—the unspoken creed was always: don't draw unnecessary attention to oneself.

The description *literary outlaw* was not a stretch of the imagination in his case. Unlike the uncaptured outlaw Jesse James, Burroughs survived the "slings and arrows" of the American literary establishment and was presented with a major tribute. In the 1980s, with considerable effort and lobbying, Allen Ginsberg managed to have him initiated into the American Academy and Institute of Arts and Letters. William S. Burroughs was probably the only academy member ever admitted who had written masterpieces while high on heroin, along with other illegal substances, often at the same time.

For a lucky outlaw, he had stood by his motto: Live fast, die old.

Smile, It Won't Hurt to Laugh

Burroughs routinely committed literary outrages while maintaining courteous and courtly manners in his personal affairs. He once divulged: "I have crippling depressions. I wonder how I can feel this bad and live. I've survived by confronting it. I let it wash through me." As any professional comedian will tell you, comedy is really all about pain, either yours or somebody else's.

Burroughs' panoply of hilarious characters, lethal animals, and comic situations spices his works. His great comic alter ego was Dr. Benway, the inept surgeon and master manipulator, an "expert on all phases of interrogation, brainwashing and control" (19) who could carelessly drop cigarette ash in the wound of an open incision while performing surgery. There is also the wincingly funny, misanthropic, misogynistic story in *Naked Lunch* of Araknid, Andrew Keif's worthless chauffeur who runs down the pregnant Arab woman. She miscarriages the bloody, dead baby on the street, and while the chauffeur waits for the cops, Keif sits on the curb and stirs the blood with a stick. While questioning the chauffeur, they arrest the woman for a violation of the sanitary code. Pure Burroughs.

Get Ready, Boys, This Is the End

At the close of his life in Lawrence, Kansas, Burroughs surrendered to the inevitable. He'd always known the mind doesn't age like the body—a sixty-five-year-old can still feel the same glowing desire for love as that of a thirty-year-old. But the dunes drift on, and the sands slip down the body's hourglass until time runs out. William's favorite quote was the final line of Fitzgerald's *Great Gatsby*, "So we beat on, boats against the current, borne back ceaselessly into the past" (182).

"Thinking is not enough," Burroughs concluded. "There is no final enough of wisdom, experience—any fucking thing. No Holy Grail, No Final Satori, no final solution. Just conflict. Only thing can resolve conflict is love [. . .] Pure love" (*Last Words*, 252–53). By the end, surrounded by his beloved cats, Burroughs scribbled: "Love? What is It? Most natural painkiller what there is. LOVE" (253).

Burroughs never minced the meanings of words. He said what he meant, and although he was capable of tenderness, we must remember that, like his great creation Dr. Benway, William S. Burroughs was not averse to making an eight-inch incision where it should have been four. Remember, Dr. Benway studied appendectomy at Harvard in the class of 1910.

Works Cited

Burroughs, William S. *Last Words: The Final Journals of William S. Burroughs.* Edited by James Grauerholz. New York: Grove, 2000.

———. *The Letters of William S. Burroughs, 1945–1959.* Edited by Oliver Harris. New York: Viking, 1993.

———. *Painting and Guns.* New York: Hanuman, 1994.

Chandler, Raymond. Preface. *Trouble Is My Business.* New York: Vintage, 1988.

Fitzgerald, F. Scott. *The Great Gatsby.* New York: Scribner's, 1925.

Lotringer, Sylvère, ed. *Burroughs Live: The Collected Interviews of William S. Burroughs 1960–1997.* Los Angeles: Semiotext(e), 2001.

Rimbaud, Arthur. *Rimbaud: Collected Works, Selected Letters.* Translated by Wallace Fowlie. Chicago: U of Chicago P, 1966.

I Am No Doctor

r. b. **MORRIS**

I am no doctor, no PhD, no master of this or that, no scientist or journalist, no veteran of any particular front, no literary scholar. I am a poet well outside the academic world of letters with only a few books to show, a songwriter, and occasional recording artist. Thanks to the unparalleled referencing of the Internet, I can be located in obscure recesses, but otherwise you haven't heard of me. But, then, the world of recording artists is a wasteland, and a book of poetry perhaps the most ineffectual art form in the culture. So, what would it matter if I was more renowned or notably qualified? If the subject is William Burroughs' *Naked Lunch* and how it fares in fifty years of the world, why would we trust a doctor or scientist, a scholar or artist of any make in today's society to offer any particular insight into him or this fifty-year-old work that is most often referred to as a novel?

I can only lay it out as a layman. Half a century is a long time in the mercurial world we have become. Things get lost. Heroes come and go, eras come and go. Generations die off. Centuries pass. Millennia pass, and new ages begin. All in the span of these few years. William Burroughs is dead. All the Beat writers are dead, except Ferlinghetti, who'll be ninety the year of the fiftieth anniversary of *Naked Lunch*. Burroughs (1914–1997) lived for thirty-eight of those fifty years since *Naked Lunch* first saw publication. He continued to write books that still live on shelves of literature. There were celebrated CDs of recorded readings with musical accompaniment. A loose composite of *Naked Lunch* was made into a feature film bearing the book's title. Burroughs himself had small roles in a number of films. There were conferences and articles and documentaries, a few biographies. Like Henry Miller, he also became a painter of some renown. There were always sightings, a cameo in a Laurie Anderson video, a half-sung track on a Tom Waits record, even a voice-over at the beginning of the first episode in the last season of HBO's smash hit *Sopranos*. Ever a shadowy icon, Burroughs remained reclusively at large and a sometime-inspiration to subsequent generations. But on the whole as with everything and everyone else, he fades more and more from public knowledge. *Naked Lunch*, the dark masterpiece, and William Seward Burroughs, the always astute and well-attired enigmatic figure, slip a little further into the footnotes of history. But, let's not get ahead of ourselves.

Naked Lunch was surely the most controversial, most rumored, and most buzzed-up book to be released in the United States since James Joyce's *Ulysses*. From the first excerpts published in American magazines in 1957 through its various obscenity trials and eventual U.S. publication in 1966, it had a book launch that lasted nearly a decade. Bootleg copies were widely circulated in the States after it was published in Paris in 1959. Its cult popularity and illegal status combined to give it tremendous notoriety. The success of Allen Ginsberg's *Howl* and Jack Kerouac's *On the Road* paved the way for it, all riding shotgun on an exciting countercultural expedition that promised new brilliance and new truth.

Naked Lunch made good on that promise. It was brutal genius. A merciless story regarding a merciless subject told in merciless terms. Like the author, the work had international savvy and human import beyond borders. In fact, *Naked Lunch* made a mockery of all borders, physical, social, and psychic. It created a parallel civilization both real and unreal, current as well as futuristic and prophetic. It revealed a truer nature of human nature, of civilization, of ruling classes and slave classes and the driving *need* that rules them all. *Wouldn't you?*

Burroughs had the Joycean ability to create written language in ways previously unheard. It was language at once shocking and masterful, not only immediate and point blank but hidden and coded. It was a new poetry as much as novel or biography. It was a new literary form really, Burroughs' *routines*. It allowed for all the narrative and dialogue of drama and prose while paced like a series of interconnected short stories with the periodic exactness of essay or scientific paper. But it was still infused with the heightened lingo and obscurity of poetry. All this was colored further with rumors of Burroughs' "cut-up method" for structuring the work, as handed down through Brion Gysin, a link to exotic North Africa and Europe as well as the Surrealists. Artistically, *Naked Lunch* was a tour de force on every possible level. Add to this the scandal and status of being banned in the United States and the subsequent trials.

Not only did *Naked Lunch* present a new language that laid bare the taboos of narcotic addiction and homosexuality but it also lifted the subject from its usual context and gave it far-broader meaning. "The Algebra of Need" revealed the junk addict to be the preeminent example of modern man at the mercy of his modern condition. The pushers, the higher-ups, the controlling classes, along with the addicts and those who are controlled, are exposed as the primal forces at play in civilization. Much was made of this in the Boston court case where Norman Mailer, John Ciardi, and others spoke of the book's thematic portrayal of dominating and competing parties and classes as a grave social malady. But the ruling went against it then. The sex and drugs were just too prominent, too pornographic to be swallowed for a while. Burroughs takes you all the way to the party and makes you join the dangerous dance. He wants the full revelation of porn, a ravaged search for the most erotic language of the erotically depraved mind. But, yes, greater causes are addressed and dramatized as *Naked Lunch* is served.

We should probably go back fifty years before the publication of *Naked Lunch* to get a better reckoning of the context in which it occurred. I recall Burroughs saying something somewhere about "1910," a time he idealized as being prior to major changes and shifts in western civilization. A world war soon left the art world full of cynicism for everything including itself, and Dada was born. The photograph had freed painting, and the "moving picture" kept moving. For a while, fine art's unbridled stepchild, film, would go on to claim popular and economic command over all other art forms long before the end of the century. America embraced Europe's wars and its art. It was only in the decade preceding *Naked Lunch* that America became dominant in the world theater. That ephemeral yet discernible shift in civilizations was the birthing time of *Naked Lunch*. As major art movements often follow major world events, so it was with World War II. America emerged as the new big kid on the block. Its confluence with Europe during the Dada and Surrealist movements evolved into a leading role in art, music, and literature after the Second World War. All three traditions converged around the motif of *improvisation*, a notion and technique both intuitive and big spirited, and America had the strong arm and strong will to lead it. The era of jazz became finely tuned to the spontaneity of bebop. Abstract Expressionism was the natural extension of the psychological realms of Surrealism. The Beat writers, who often took their cues from jazz, leapt from the literary ivory towers to the street, a modern reclamation of Whitman's breath. Their youth and exuberance were infectious but also masked a depth of expression and connection to history. All of these movements were major turns in traditions and media. They each occurred in varying stages over a decade and more but were intrinsically linked and often in personal cahoots. All of them had their birth in American cities, primarily New York.

Naked Lunch was, unfortunately, more of a prophecy than any beginning of a trend in artistic form. True, the boundaries were widened on certain subjects for artistic presentation, and subsequent works—whether science fiction, mainstream or literary, written or film—have delved more often than before into subterranean themes such as addiction and mind control. But from my particular perspective of working songwriter and poet, I see only a lost handful of artists whose work bears noticeable resemblance to the dimensions and intent of *Naked Lunch*.

Bob Dylan broke through, first and foremost, closer on the heels of the Beats. From a troubadour with a poet's soul and street credentials, he evolved into a world-class jester and prophetic bard borrowing much from his predecessors of the printed page besides just a famous name. His ascension may have signaled a fading for the printed word and the Beats, but it also lifted them as well to a greater audience than they would have had without him. There's no doubt that he was greatly influenced by Burroughs' wild juxtaposing of images and scenes, as well as subject matter. This is most visible in *Tarantula* (his first book, written in 1965 and published in 1971) where Dylan's episodic series spinning off of "Black Nite Crash" evokes and emulates Burroughs' "Withdrawal Nightmares," as well as many other examples of spitfire scenes surrealistically exploding left and right in rapid sequence. One could say *Tarantula* is something of a Dylan version of *Naked Lunch*, replacing Burroughs' underworld of madness and addiction with his own version of sixties terrain and structured in a very similar, semifragmentary layout of prose sketches and cut-up scenarios. But this influence is also evident in the more renowned verses of many of Dylan's popular songs, especially from the revelatory period of *Bringing It All Back Home*, *Highway 61 Revisited*, and *Blonde on Blonde*—the period that most established him as poet. "Subterranean Homesick Blues," "Desolation Row," and "Visions of Johanna," for example, are all titles directly linked to Kerouac titles, and the lyrics of the songs are poetically linked to Burroughs, Ginsberg, and Kerouac. Through this time, Ginsberg became a noted friend and influence on Dylan's work no doubt, but because of this more public connection, it shadowed what Dylan took as well from Burroughs, not to mention what Ginsberg and Kerouac took from Burroughs.

Not only Dylan but also the Beatles, the Rolling Stones, Van Morrison, Leonard Cohen, David Bowie, Jim Morrison, Steely Dan, and later Tom Waits and various heavy metal and punk acts, as well as countless others

Erewhile

The County Clerk has his office in a huge red brick building known as the
Old Court House. Civil cases are, in fact, tried there, the proceedings inexorably
dragging out until the contestants die or abandon litigation. This is due to the vast
number of records pertaining to absolutely ev...
that no one but the County Clerk...
spends years in the search...
damage suit that was...
House have fallen...
The County Cl...
have lost th...
trapped in...

the case tr...
lest the ca...
these fact...
rarely get...
Old Court Ho...

zone. The...
are people...
has seen fit...
iron bricks...
signs: "Urb...
nothing but...

Lee's...
fering from pass...
without paying th...
of affidavits and...
Frontier. The Urba...

...amels, donkeys (overloaded, dropping
...cream like castrated pigs) lamas,
...and goats and long horned

...nches, lime-
...ty leather
...drink
...per
...dy

...is
...spun
...el throw-
...r... A
...over whim-
...little
...c, I suspect
...Pea under the

...three grains
...n pervert
...es choose
...nces.
...This
...self

William Burroughs
Lee Burroughs

Self Portrait

he trills. His cock and balls...
and taxes.

Armed with a meat cleaver, the Author...
the Midway and into the Hall of Mirrors, trap h...

just akickin. So I get up on the Nigger...o finish him off and Ted Bane tell me,
'Don't shoot him again. Just let him die.' Good old boy too. Not a finer man
in this valley than Ted Bane."

"Did you evah burn a nigger?"

XXXXXXXXXXXXXXXXXXXXXXXXXXX a nd orde red a d

ond before looking around the room to see i

a s alone at a table tipped back in a chai

e other holding a bottle of beer on ^{his} ~~one~~ k

o acheive a greeting at once freindly a nd

casual) designed to show interest without pushing a short a cquaintance.
             ghastly.
The result was uXXXXXXXXX.As Lee stood aside to bow in his dignified

old world greeting,there emerged instead a leer of nakedlust wrenched in

the pain and hate of his deprived body,and in simultaneous double expos

a sweet child smile of liking and trust shockingly out of time and plac

mutilatted and hopeless.

   Allerton w   He

Feb. 7, 1954
Tangiers.

Dear Allen,

Here is my latest attempt to write something
saleable. All day I had been finding pretexts to

Tanger. Dec 4, 1957

Allen,

        I enclose two samples of pr
cient bits.. One o is iromUSA sect
n..Either one should do ior Carrel
somme or the other.. I literally c
glued to this fucking type wrtie

well ant'i
if the started
that too
had put out a
belligerent Bu

The Word is divided into units which be all in one piece and should
be so taken, but the pieces can be had in any order being tied up back and
forth, in and out fore and aft like an interesting sex arrangement. This book

  SUPER XX

my 1920 crystal set with antennae of jissom. Gentle reader, we see God through
our ass holes in the flash bulb of orgasm. Through these orifices transmute

Campus of Interzone U in the Market... Camels, do[...]
bales, crushing the feet of pedestrians who scream lik[...]

So I am assigned to engage the services of Doctor Be[...]
Benway has been called in as advisor to the Freelan[...]
given over to free love and continual bathing. The citizens [...]
cooperative, honest, tolerant and above all clean. But the ev[...]
indicates all is not well behind that hygienic façade...Benway[...]
and coordinator of symbol systems [...] all phases [...]
brainwashing and control... [...]
from Annexia, where his a[...]
first act was to abolish [...]
limited and special circu[...]

"I deplore brut[...]
prolonged mistreatment, [...]

1

THE WORD

William Seward Burroughs

The Word is divided into units which be all in one piece and should [...]

[...]er being tied up back and
[...]g sex arrangement. This book
[...]e of vistas, medley of tunes

Junky furnished room opens on red brick slum -- young addict, sculpted
to bone and muscle, probes for a blue vein with a brass needle in his mouth [...]

and tilts his body forward. They put on the suits which hang on them in folds and
posture in parody of drunken machos, spitting, patting .45s, flashing police badges
and nude pictures of Chapultepec blondes. Exit boys without a sound. Sun rise.
Vultures settle, peck at dark glasses.

Modern apartment à la swish. Fags and old women gabble and giggle faster
and faster, scream past each other at supersonic speed. Blue walled Arab whore
house. Outside, the yipes of rioters; shop shutters slam, Arab music blasts from
loud speakers mixed with Radio Cairo like a berserk tobacco auction. Fades to
flutes of Ramadan.

Porch of East Texas farm house. Full summer moon. Boy rides up bare-
[...]rinking corn on the porch.
[...]we goin to cut the rest of

[...]I can pick up without FM on
[...]le reader, we see God through
[...]h these orifices transmute
[...]e blacker blasphemy than spit
[...]s those castrates who equate their

[...]side one leg up in the air
[...] off and Ted Bane tell me,
[...] boy too. Not a finer man

[...]less asshole) read Baby Doll
[...] in pathic dismay. "Revolting!"
[...]ve inna thervith of shit death

[...]chase a gentle reader down
[...] impaled on crystal cocks.

THE OLYMPIA PRESS

8, Rue de Nesle - Pari
Téléphone : DANton 1
Télégrammes : Olymp

Dear Mr Burrough

What about letti
us have another loo
"The Naked Lunch"?

I would very mu
like to meet you an
discuss this.

Yours,

M. Giro

June 6, 1959

S. A. R. L. AU CAPITAL DE 100.000 FRS — R. C. SEINE 374.987 B

April 18,1958
9 Rue dit Le Coeur
Paris 6, France

Dear Mr. Ferlingetti,

Regards selections from my Ms which is not easy to
find one's way around in I offer the following suggestions: The whole last
section entitled WORD to be ignored since I have finally cooked same down to
three pages which herewith enclose and suggest this be the beginning and
the title be Have You Seen Pantapon Rose?...Omit Andrew Keif and Ky scandal which
is beginning of Ms.. In Voices, which is section 11, start on page three:
"when I was on the junk I minded my junky business" ect to end of that section
County Clerk omit if you want to follow a straight coherent junk line...
Omit Interzone U, Islam Inc, and AJ's Ball.. And Hassan's Rumpus Room
Include Hospital (except for the Micky Spillane part in the smiddle.)
Include Benway (except for the theoretical part on addiction and schizophrenia.)
Include The Technical Psychiatry Conference and take whatever you want from
The Market...
Now thats one way of doing it holds together in some sort of coherent line..
Of course you may have different ideas.. It could be presented as a series of unrelated
unrelated, short peices.. All I mean is the arrangement I suggest is more or less
all in one peice.. Also have avoided the more obscene sections w which would
involve difficulties of a legal
nature...

WSl, only a suggestion..

Sincerely,
William Burroughs.

WILLIAM BURROUGHS
THE NAKED LUNCH

CORGI

WILLIAM BURROUGHS
THE NAKED LUNCH

BC-115 $1.25
FIRST PAPERBACK EDITION OF THE COMPLETE $6 GROVE PRESS BEST-SELLER
NAKED LUNCH
BY WILLIAM S. BURROUGHS
"THE ONLY AMERICAN NOVELIST LIVING TODAY WHO MAY CONCEIVABLY BE POSSESSED BY GENIUS."—NORMAN MAILER
WITH MASSACHUSETTS SUPREME COURT DECISION AND EXCERPTS FROM THE BOSTON TRIAL

ÇIPLAK SÖLEN

William S. Burroughs

WILLIAM BURROUGHS
THE NAKED LUNCH

WILLIAM BURROUGHS
THE NAKED LUNCH
nᵒ 76
THE TRAVELLER'S COMPANION SERIES

NEW PRICE NF 18
Francs : 1.500
NOT TO BE SOLD IN THE U.S.A. OR U.K.

in the pop-music culture inherited that part of the previous generation that was primed by the Beats. But Dylan, more than any other artist of any other medium, was able to claim it and move it. Putting the Beats' poetics and social landscape into popular songs hip to current events unfolding propelled him and his medium to a new prominence in the modern world of art and entertainment. The significance of Dylan going electric and taking traditional acoustic folk music into the current realm of rock and pop expression was actually secondary to the significance of him taking the "poetic voice" off the page and putting it into music. The poetic voice became a more active and vital force in social and political affairs than at probably any other time in American history.

The rare and disturbed air at such artistic heights within a rapidly expanding pop culture and society soon became untenable, and it was a position Dylan was either unable or unwilling to hold for long. Quite understandable perhaps but the torch of the poetic voice playing a lead role in current social affairs was dropped along the way. This, along with the demise of the Beatles and John Lennon's proclamation of "the dream is over," sucked the air right out of the cultural sails. We don't want to hang our historical hat on the peg of any pop star's legacy, but it's good shorthand for the way it went—the way the wave of mass consciousness in a generational dream raised its head and rolled back over. There were, of course, countless elements at play in this rise and fall, not the least of which was a series of prominent assassinations and the Vietnam War, which left the nation and a generation torn asunder to such an extent that many emerged severely wounded, confused, disillusioned, and primed to be rewired by the more selfish but safer forces of decadence, compromise, and subversion. Ultimately, the Western world of art was put on the auction block, divided up like a subdivision, and parceled out to the public as bankers and corporate gods saw fit. Artistically, a subsequent era began that for all the run of trends and styles and technological advancements and a few generations is still much the same era. An era retro in coined and neutered vision that still produces brilliant artists, master surfers through the American genres but without as big a wave to catch.

All this is worth mentioning because such social and cultural swings may have much to do with the lifespan of certain works of art. The Beats gained a great deal of public notoriety early on, which was a two-edged sword. They soon devolved into a cultural cliché—*the beatniks*—enough so that their shortcomings became politicized into a partisan stance among otherwise-knowledgeable observers of art and literature. Their work is generally lumped together, disparate as it may be, and when the tide that lifts all boats recedes, all boats so linked will fall in turn. There have been resurgences, but none have brought the rush of the initial surge. This may be only natural, predictable, and understandable. But how significant are these social and cultural shifts, and what do they mean for the arts in general?

From my perspective a great diminution has set in among the arts. Yes, art survives in all media but foremost as a corporate accomplice, a flourish or detail in service to the gross income; or else in certain small societies, academic, traditional, or otherwise. It may even thrive in these settings, but these can be controlled and kept from having any substantial effect outside their realm. Art in America is held prisoner. It is more employed and higher paid but vaguely impotent as a coalescing force for social change.

"The Algebra of Need" played out in a much less dramatic yet far more thorough and effective guise than we might have suspected. But here it is all the same, pushers and addicts aligned, international corporate controllers and their political, religious, military, and otherwise partisan henchmen all well placed around the big tables while the masses robotically huddle in strip malls, stadiums, racetracks, and traffic jams when not recharging in front of the ever-varied, always glowing, omnipresent screens. A conspiracy? Yes, of course. As Burroughs famously notes, "Paranoia is just having the right information." But it is never just the pusher but also the addict to blame. Corporate advertising, fashioned to fleece the loose herd and suckers in general, has become in this same fifty years the very air we breathe. In the meantime, we've neither cultivated the beauty of our traditions nor weeded out the fundamentalist baboonery that has plagued the race so clearly through the last millennia.

The Western world where *Naked Lunch* occurred lives a far more virtual reality now. If society in the forties, fifties, and sixties was less advanced in all the more prominent and measurable ways, slower and uncomputerized and far less politically correct in manner and legality, it was also less cynical and more potent for change, more open for possibilities, more imbued with a natural faith for human potential. The air and the airwaves were not so bought up and bought off. The brain police were not so prevalent. The disconnect with nature not so thorough. Our antennae are withering and falling away, being bred out of us. We've been conditioned, coerced, manipulated, and hustled into some kind of modern zombie state. Nothing that crosses the television, movie, and computer screens of today ignites any significant change. It's all entertainment. Reality shows take the place of reality. Nothing satisfies for more than a moment or lifts us beyond our sensory bonds. We are progressively sedated to greater degrees of numbness.

Of course, many people, artists, teachers, social workers, politicians, journalists, scientists, diplomats, doctors, lawyers, and Indian chiefs constantly speak out and try to bring clarity and urgency to the crises of civilization, the injustice of societies, the strangled and destructive politics of the day, the uncharted realm of the mind and heart. But the forces set against those voices have been steadily fortified over the last fifty years to the point of misdirecting, confusing, waylaying, making light of and destroying almost every effort of their effectiveness. There is no counterforce shaking the doors and windows of the status quo enough to bring about a collective epiphany. Turns out, we were much weaker than the almighty dollar.

So, what's the endgame, and where does *Naked Lunch* play in? I don't know. I'm just a lowly poet with no answers, a voice in the wilderness, a fellow down at the bar talking to whoever will hang around and listen. No, I don't know what happens to *Naked Lunch* in another fifty years. I would suggest it has a certain staying power in the wide world of literature. It may be exiled but I think quite difficult to kill off. I believe it has the endurance of the roach bug and will bear up even as a dark age persists. *Naked Lunch* remains a brilliant work of art, a wild novelistic tromp through the netherworld that casts light upwards on a devolving situation. It offers behind-the-scenes glimpses of what really goes on. It holds its place in the chorus of those voices tuned to this sort of endeavor. There's not enough negative energy to silence them. Still, the powers that be recognize it is no longer necessary to remove works that challenge the new order. The success of the current milieu derives in part from its knowing that even though most all things remain available to the public, the public no longer has an interest in them.

That's the unspoken plan. *Naked Lunch* has been relegated to an elegant graveyard we've been allowed to visit but are now advised to stay clear of, and that has a punitive admission if we dare enter again. Still, I find that I am a paradoxical and foolhardy optimist at heart, whistling by these old bones. I have an insane hunch that a reversal of course will come, that some clarity will win out over confusion, and the general virtue of collective beliefs will prevail over the fear and lack of virtue that now rules. Somewhere from the Burroughsian right half of my brain, I hear faint voices clearing their throats. That's my plan.

The Naked Lunch in My Life

barry **MILES**

I n 1960, when I first began to hitchhike up to London on weekends from my provincial art school, I usually stayed on the couch at the communal flat run by John Hopkins, who was then a photographer. Living in one of the rooms was Peter Wollen, who spent each afternoon and evening travelling to distant suburban cinemas to fill in gaps in his study of the cinema. He later wrote *Signs and Meaning in the Cinema* and became head of the UCLA Film School. One afternoon Peter came in, glanced around the living room, and announced, "This is such a cool pad, man. There's always a fresh copy of *Naked Lunch* on the table." And indeed there was. Anyone visiting Paris always smuggled a copy back with them, usually down the back of their shirt as the customs would always find and confiscate it if it was in their baggage or pockets. The book had a legendary status. It *looked* different from all other books: it was a paperback but with a dust wrapper; in England, only hardbacks had dust wrappers. And what a dust wrapper. British book design at the time was pretty dire: Gollancz still put cheap yellow wrappers on their books, intended to be thrown away; Faber used the same typography on every book and refused to even accept the existence of paperbacks, calling theirs "paper covered editions"; John Calder printed everything in obscure Iron Curtain countries on terrible paper with terrible jacket designs; Penguins were a uniform orange for fiction, green for crime, and so on. No one considered that the jacket should reflect, and act as an advertisement for, the content of a book. This jacket did, though it was only later that I learned that the glyphs were by the author himself. *The Naked Lunch* (all three Olympia titles, *The Naked Lunch*, *The Soft Machine*, *The Ticket That Exploded*, took the definite article) had an uncompromisingly modern, yet somehow sinister cover. The orange-yellow lettering on a purple ground made a discord designed to jolt the eye, and all across the jacket were glyphs, like shorthand, or an unknown language beyond the point of intelligibility, demanding to be read. They continued all across the back cover where normally one might find a polite review from a weekly magazine, calligraphic writing like the drawings and paintings of Brion Gysin and Mark Tobey. The book's cool quotient was enhanced by the notice inside the back flap: "NOT TO BE SOLD IN THE U.S.A. OR U.K."; so, not only banned but forbidden, even though Girodias obviously didn't mean it.

Also, the book had been known to make people throw up; this was a significant plus in terms of mythmaking: a book so powerful that it could cause a physical reaction. A woman visitor to Hoppy's flat just made it to the bathroom in time but Jeff Nuttall, in *Bomb Culture* (1968), reported, "*The Naked Lunch* actually caused at least one unprepared square to vomit on the carpet" (108). Naturally, it showed how cool you were if you were able to read the book without flinching. It was like smoking pot without getting "the horrors." Many of Burroughs' early readers were marijuana smokers, and sections of the book would be read aloud, of an evening, to the accompaniment of much hysterical laughter. Sometimes, it would be five minutes before the reader could continue among the splutters and giggles. I heard about half of it read this way before I was finally able to secure a copy of my own, and there is no doubt that this colored my view of it. *The Naked Lunch* was the hippest, coolest book ever written, and for a seventeen-year-old art student, that was quite something to have on the shelf. Most, if not all of the book was written when Burroughs was under the influence of cannabis, and it is filled with pothead humor that becomes especially potent when the reader is also stoned.

The myth surrounding the book came partly from the fact it was published by Maurice Girodias' Olympia Press. The distinctive olive-green wrappers of their Traveller's Companion series, of which *The Naked Lunch* was number 76, were associated with hard-core pornography in the minds of most young travellers, which is why these books were eagerly sought out and smuggled back to Britain or the States. This was the reason that every single Olympia title was banned in Britain, though how Gregory Corso's *American Express*, or Raymond Queneau's *Zazie dans le métro* could be construed as pornographic is hard to imagine; nonetheless, it was a blanket ban designed to stop impressionable British and American readers from getting their hands on such filth as *Tender Was My Flesh*, *The Whip Angels*, or *The Sexual Life of Robinson Crusoe*. Girodias attempted to get around it by putting dust wrappers on his more literary titles to hide their green wrappers and distinguish them as being in a different class to his normal output, but the customs officials were not fooled.

Copies of *The Naked Lunch* could be obtained in London only with great difficulty. In the early sixties, Peter Russell's short-lived Gallery Bookshop on D'Arblay Street in Soho sometimes had copies under the counter, literally, but you had to wait until the shop was empty before asking. Finally, the book benefited from the legends surrounding its author: Burroughs was already known in London circles for his advanced ideas concerning sex and drugs, and rumor had it that he had murdered his wife in a bizarre game of William Tell. The jacket-flap photograph, taken by Allen Ginsberg in New York in 1953, shows Burroughs as an anonymous-looking, middle-aged man and gave no indication of what he might be like in person. When he was invited to visit Oxford, he arrived looking every inch the model of sobriety and respectability but with a rent boy in tow, shocking even the ultra-cool students who had issued the invitation. Homosexuality was just not mentioned in the early sixties; it was an illegal, hidden, secret business, and for Burroughs to so casually reveal his preference for young men was seen as appalling.

He was also a heroin user at a time when this was virtually unknown; something only associated with jazz musicians. Heroin was a subject of great interest to him, and he would talk for hours about different drugs and their effects, about drug dealers and the drug subcultures of the many countries he had lived in. The public can usually distinguish clearly between an author and his book but in Burroughs' case (and with Kerouac and *On the Road*), book and author were entwined in his readers' minds. This is because the book quickly became a symbol: it represented an attitude, a state of mind, the detachment of the cool hipster from the mundane crowd. It was a shorthand way of saying you were cool, which in those days meant you listened to Cecil Taylor, John Coltrane, Eric Dolphy, Ornette Coleman, and Thelonius Monk; you appreciated the work of Jackson Pollock, Franz Kline, Willem de Kooning, Francis Bacon, and Mark Rothko; you smoked marijuana and hash when you could get it; you read Beat Generation writers along with Ezra Pound's *Cantos,* T. S. Eliot's *The Waste Land* (another definite article), Paul Bowles, Flann O'Brien, and Samuel Beckett. As Jeff Nuttall points out, "It depicts the world and existence as a nightmare obscenity and it describes accurately how we felt the world to be at that point, the early sixties" (108).

We first heard of the book through Allen Ginsberg, who included Burroughs in his extended dedication to *Howl and Other Poems* in 1956. Then, bits of the text began to appear in magazines such as *Yugen*, *Black Mountain Review*, and the *Chicago Review*. Blackwells in Oxford sometimes had copies of *Big Table*, the first issue of which published a fifty-eight-page excerpt billed as "Ten Episodes from *Naked Lunch*." Blackwells probably stocked the magazine at the request of Michael Horovitz, who printed "Two Scenes" from *Naked Lunch* in the first issue of his *New Departures* magazine in Oxford in the summer of 1959, just before the book was published, the same time as *Jabberwock*, the magazine of Edinburgh University, printed "And Start West," the opening section of the book. The Olympia Press edition of the book quoted extensively from Burroughs' article, "Letter from a Master Addict to Dangerous Drugs" in its footnotes. This was first published by Dr. John Yerbury Dent in his *British Journal of Addiction* in January 1957, copies of which were in circulation in London. Dr. Dent was the inventor of the apomorphine cure for drug addiction and alcoholism that Burroughs had taken, a treatment that stabilized the body's metabolism, thus providing a real cure. This was another one of Burroughs' favorite topics of conversation, alongside drugs themselves, and a subject of great interest to the small community of junkies living in London, many of whom he knew.

Burroughs' main proselytizer in London was his boyfriend Ian Sommerville, who was completing his studies at Corpus Christi, Cambridge. Sommerville was a mathematician with a somewhat prickly demeanor but who could be very funny. He tirelessly promoted Burroughs' work, mostly through word-of-mouth; he was very fond of marijuana, and it was largely through him that pot smokers in London, Oxford, and Cambridge became aware of the book. He was also the technician who designed Gysin's Dreamachine. His biggest influence on Burroughs in this respect was to explain how to cut up tape recordings and to set up a pair of machines to enable Burroughs to do this. The advent of cut-ups provoked a series of multimedia performances in Paris, London, and Cambridge, one of which was held on Thanksgiving Day 1960 at the Heretics' Club at Corpus Christi organized by David Bonavia. Burroughs read a text, Gysin made an action painting, then destroyed it, and Sommerville played an earsplitting tape-collage soundtrack. It drew attention to the work, but none of the books were available in Britain at that time; Burroughs remained the stuff of legend with *The Naked Lunch* at the center of it.

A suggestion of the desirability associated with the book is glimpsed in Derek Jarman's memoirs, *The Last of England*: "In 1962 I moved to London from home. I was twenty, and out on my own. Things changed quickly. At King's I read my tutor's copy of *Howl*, and learnt of William Burroughs. [. . .] In late August [1964,] I left Ron and took the Greyhound bus to San Francisco to visit the City Lights Bookshop. I'd crossed the world to get to that bookshop, to buy Burroughs' *The Naked Lunch*, banned in England. I bought my copy of it along with Ginsberg's *Howl*, and Kerouac's novels" (22, 36). Of course, what Jarman bought was not the same book that Olympia had published. Grove Press had wanted a longer text and had used a slightly longer, earlier draft of the book for their edition. This means that my generation, who virtually memorized the Olympia edition of the book, have in our heads a somewhat different version than American readers or the later British Calder edition readers; Calder used the American text.

When he moved to London in the early sixties, homosexuality was still illegal, and through friends such as Brion Gysin and Antony Balch, Burroughs found himself a part of the West End gay scene. He got to know the art dealer Robert Fraser, who was both homosexual and, from 1965 onwards, a heroin addict, and through Fraser, he met the Rolling Stones and the aristocratic members of the Chelsea set. Though not very sociable, throughout the sixties, Burroughs was able to move easily and with impunity between the company of the Piccadilly rent boys whom he patronized, the literary salon of Sonia Orwell from whom he once sublet a flat, the Portland Place apartment of Lord Goodman, the guardian of Burroughs' boyfriend Michael Portman and through him, Burroughs' lawyer, and the editors, publishers, and writers of the underground press such as myself, who published him and whose company he appeared to enjoy.

Rock musicians were quick to pick up on Burroughs: in 1963 John Sebastian and Zal Yanovsky, both later of the Lovin' Spoonful, got together with Cass Elliot and Denny Doherty, both later of the Mamas and Papas, to form a group they called the Mugwumps. The book had been published in the States the previous year; it was to provide rock 'n' roll with numerous band names and words: "A Near East Mugwump sits naked on a bar stool covered in pink silk" (63). Similarly, in 1972, when Donald Fagen and Walter Becker were looking for a name for their new band, they flipped through the pages of *The Naked Lunch*: "Mary is strapping on a rubber penis: 'Steely Dan III from Yokohama,' she says, caressing the shaft. Milk spurts across the room" (77). Walter Becker, interviewed in 1974, said, "There always used to be a Beatnik corner in the bookshop—Ginsberg, Corso, Snyder and so on, and that's where I first came across *Naked Lunch*. Naming ourselves from something in the book shouldn't be taken too literally, though [. . .] but we have certainly picked up on some of his world view. I admire Burroughs a lot."

When asked to appear at the Nova Convention, a celebration of Burroughs and his work held in New York during three days beginning 30 November 1978, Frank Zappa, inevitably, chose to read from "The Talking Asshole" routine on stage. Burroughs' appeal to the rock community came because he was essentially working in the same area: libertarian, Dionysian, antiauthoritarian—he was the literary equivalent of rock 'n' roll. Jimmy Page, then with Led Zeppelin, was a follower of Aleister Crowley, and saw many parallels between Burroughs and Crowley: they both believed that humanity was held back by conditioning and controls, and once free of their shackles could become gods. (Incidentally, Burroughs became very interested in this aspect of Crowley towards the very end of his life.) There was also the all-important drug connection, a subject dear to very many rock 'n' roll musicians, and Burroughs was seen as the world expert. In terms of influence, it has been Burroughs' cut-up technique that has been of the most use to musicians rather than *The Naked Lunch*, though the term *heavy metal* has its origin in the book. Burroughs' ideas and techniques have been used by bands as diverse as Soft Machine, Social Deviants, Gong, David Bowie, Blondie, Insect Trust, Throbbing Gristle, Psychic TV, Sonic Youth, R.E.M., Laurie Anderson, Material, and Kurt Cobain.

In terms of literature, Burroughs' influence has been gradual and insidious. There are obvious examples of influence: J. G. Ballard has always acknowledged a huge debt to Burroughs, and books like *Crash* would have been impossible without him. The New Worlds Sci-Fi group that Ballard was initially associated with—Michael Moorcock, Norman Spinrad et al.—obviously took many of their ideas from Burroughs. But it was not until the 1980s that his impact began to show in a big way with writers such as William Gibson, whose enormously successful 1984 *Neuromancer* is seen as the first cyberpunk novel. Other writers in this genre include Rudy Rucker, Pat Cadigan, Charles Platt, Neal Stephenson, and Bruce Sterling. In an interview quoted in *Mondo 2000, a Users' Guide to the New Age*, Gibson said, "I'm deeply influenced by Burroughs. [. . .] I was like fifteen when I read *Naked Lunch*, and it sorta splattered my head all over the walls. I have my megalomaniac fantasy of some little kid in Indiana picking up *Neuromancer* and POW! I had to teach myself not to write too much like Burroughs. He has that kind of influence. I had to weed some of that Burroughsian stuff out of it" (70). Twelve years later, Gibson's work still showed the Burroughs affect. In his 1996 novel *Idoru*, for instance, one of the protagonists, Alison Shires, has "23" (Burroughs' special number) as her door code, and in the same novel, the Death Cube K bar smacks of Hassan's Rumpus Room and Burroughs' later interest in giant centipedes: "a bar of artfully corroded steel [. . .] the high backs of their chairs molded from some brown and chitinous resin. Insectoid mandibles curved above the drinkers' heads like scythes" (3).

In an essay by Richard Kadrey and Larry McCaffery in *Storming the Reality Studio: A Casebook of Cyberpunk and Postmodern Fiction*—the book's title, of course, is taken from *Nova Express*—the authors openly acknowledge the role of *Naked Lunch* in the development of the genre: "The influence of this book is enormous. Without *Naked Lunch* there would probably be no cyberpunk" (18). This view was reinforced by minimalist composer Glenn Branca in a 1991 conversation with fellow New York composer Elliott Sharp: "My hope is that Cyberpunk is going to end up simply becoming Burroughs. I'm just looking for more Burroughs. To go beyond Burroughs, I can't even begin to imagine." Subsequent authors have reworked his themes or made further explorations using his techniques, but none would claim to go beyond him. Kathy Acker, for example, told me that she sometimes felt his influence on her work was too great. Both Will Self and Iain Sinclair have acknowledged his influence. Patti Smith, though not so obviously affected, had a pristine copy of the first edition of *The Naked Lunch* as the centerpiece of an altar she had set up to her heroes in her New York apartment at 1 Fifth Avenue in the late seventies. Burroughs was in the good company of Rimbaud, Bob Dylan, and Keith Richards.

The Mugwumps are not the only Burroughs characters to escape the book to live outside as a part of popular culture: Dr. Benway is given a name-check in a hospital scene in Alex Cox's cult movie *Repo Man* (1984) when a voice comes over the Tannoy, "Paging Dr. Benway." At the time of writing there were over seventy-five thousand hits on Google for "Dr. Benway," only a few of which are about legitimate doctors.

In December 1981, twenty years after Peter Wollen's comment about the added value brought about by a fresh copy of *The Naked Lunch* on the coffee table, Lauren Hutton introduced Burroughs on *Saturday Night Live*, then the leading network television show in the world, saying he was "in my opinion the greatest living American writer." After the obscenity trials and the hostile reviews on at least two continents, Burroughs had won; he was now part of mainstream American culture, a type of name recognition that would in the future enable him to make ads for Nike Shoes. Two years later, he was made a member of the American Academy and Institute of Arts and Letters, inducted by Norman Mailer, and so entered the canon of American literature. He was already a Chevalier des Arts et des Lettres and wore the tiny red rosette on his lapel with pride. Burroughs' career trajectory had always been solidly based upon *The Naked Lunch* more than any other novel, and it was all the more extraordinary to see his final acceptance by the American literary establishment, though it must be said that not everyone was in favor of his joining.

For me, *The Naked Lunch* was always more than a good book. Burroughs said himself that it was not a novel but more a how-to manual, a way of seeing. It really did show the world raw, naked, on the end of the fork, stripped of all pretence, hypocrisy, and spin. I felt a great affinity to what he was saying, and as a teenager I became one of those boring people who is forever quoting their heroes. Fortunately, I did not go as far as to imitate his voice—unlike some people. I got over that, but he remained a major influence in my life. My interest in promoting and propagating Burroughs' world view led to a close association with him. I published him in various anthologies, magazines, and newspapers, I interviewed him for the press, and in 1972, I assembled and described Burroughs' and Gysin's archives—now in the New York Public Library—working with him every day at his flat in Duke Street, St. James's in London for several months. By this time, Burroughs was already established as a major avant-garde writer. Although I knew from my friendship with both his French and German translators that he already had a considerable international reputation, it was not until I began taking notes for my future bibliography that I realized quite how well known he was. By 1973, for instance, *The Naked Lunch* had appeared in translation in German (1962), French (1964), Italian (1964), Japanese (1965), Danish (1967), Norse (1967), Finnish (1971), Spanish (1971, Argentina), and Dutch (1972). I was very conscious of the historical importance of what I was doing and had every confidence that *The Naked Lunch* would in time rank alongside *Ulysses*. This was one of the reasons I compiled his bibliography for the Bibliographical Society of the University of Virginia (together with Joe Maynard, who had been working on a similar project). I wanted to assemble the information while it was still relatively easy to do so, and I also thought that a bibliography would help to promote the work. For the same reason, I wrote a portrait/biography, *William Burroughs, El Hombre Invisible*, in which I attempted to make his more difficult cut-up novels more accessible, though that was commissioned. Both of these projects were done with the collaboration of Burroughs himself. After Burroughs' death, together with James Grauerholz, I edited the text of *The Naked Lunch* itself for the restored-text edition published by Grove Press in 2003. *The Naked Lunch* has been central to my life. I still use it as a template, and for me, it still works.

Works Cited

Branca, Glenn, and Elliott Sharp. "We Are the Reality of This Cyberpunk Fantasy." *Mondo 2000* 5, 1991.

Burroughs, William S. *The Naked Lunch*. Paris: Olympia, 1959.

———. *The Soft Machine*. Paris: Olympia, 1961.

———. *The Ticket That Exploded*. Paris: Olympia, 1962.

Gibson, William. *Idoru*. Harmondsworth: Penguin, 1997.

Jarman, Derek. *The Last of England*. London: Constable, 1987.

Kadrey, Richard, and Larry McCaffery. "Cyberpunk 101: A Schematic Guide to *Storming the Reality Studio*." In *Storming the Reality Studio: A Casebook of Cyberpunk and Postmodern Fiction*. Edited by McCaffery. Durham, NC: Duke UP, 1993.

Maynard, Joe, and Barry Miles. *William S. Burroughs: A Bibliography 1953–1973*. Charlottesville: UP of Virginia, 1978.

Miles, Barry. *The Beat Hotel: Ginsberg, Burroughs and Corso in Paris, 1957–1963*. New York: Grove, 2000.

———. *A Descriptive Catalogue of the William S. Burroughs Archive*. London: Covent Garden, 1973.

———. *William Burroughs, El Hombre Invisible*. 1992. 2nd. ed. London: Virgin, 2002.

Nuttall, Jeff. *Bomb Culture*. London: MacGibbon and Kee, 1968.

Rucker, Rudy, R. U. Sirius, and Queen Mu, eds. *Mondo 2000, a Users' Guide to the New Age*. New York: HarperPerennial, 1992.

A Bombshell in Rhizomatic Slow Motion: The Reception of *Naked Lunch* in Germany

jürgen **PLOOG**

You must remember this:
How random is random?

I remember struggling with my own early writing in the 1950s. Not only did I come out of the cool terror and domesticity of the Adenauer era (equivalent to the "gray flannel" Eisenhower era) but I also experienced the cultural trauma created by Nazism. In Germany, war had been more than the horror of the killing fields, it was the traumatizing experience of spiritual destruction and devastation far beyond the physical and material. This made intellectual and artistic orientation extremely difficult.

Where to go in the aftermath of Armageddon?

The search for cultural and artistic identity in those years was conducted as a kind of name game, catching up on the past. Had you heard of Henry Miller, Jean-Paul Sartre, James Joyce, E. E. Cummings, John Dos Passos, Ezra Pound? Everything from abroad, from Surrealism to Existentialism was up for grabs. A wide-ranging literary field lay open for the reader to explore, untouched by mainstream culture. However random the choice of road taken, the reader could not fail to be rewarded.

The results of this period of orientation obviously varied according to age and experience. Although there was a definite interest in the modernist and avant-garde approach, a traditional tendency prevailed, especially in literature. However, many from the postwar generation leaned towards formalistic and experimental expression based on Dada and Constructivist elements, thus avoiding subjective, personal experience (with the exception of novelist and short-story writer Arno Schmidt, who combined a very personal narrative with formalistic fragmentation).

I am taking these shortcuts through a diverse area of literary enterprises in order to indicate the gap that existed between the more conventional writing of the time and the formalistic "progressive" direction that revealed little inclination for personal expression and *Lebensgefuhl*.[1] With the emergence of Beat literature, an opening for spontaneous, individual, and "free-style" writing appeared.

In the 1960s, the artistic search in Germany changed from a formalistic orientation to questions of an existential nature. Writing became more political and addressed contemporary issues. What had happened in Auschwitz suddenly mattered in the way a poem was written. Conscience and consciousness, with all their traps and angles, now played a role in writing.

The discovery of these key facets of expression coincided with the problems I faced in my own literary work. I felt a more direct approach in handling experience was necessary. Working as a commercial pilot, my life had literally become a cut-up, so that the unrestricted pace and change of scene in Burroughs' prose immediately struck me as structurally liberating. It wasn't style but structure that showed the way forward—a way out of a complex and accelerating reality film.

The German versions of *On the Road* and *Howl* had been published in 1959. In 1962, a landmark of Beat writing appeared: *Beat: Eine Anthologie,* edited by Karl Otto Paetel. Walter Hollerer, a professor and influential promoter of literary trends, organized readings with Beat poets like Gregory Corso. All of this laid the ground for the controversial publication and reception of *Naked Lunch* in 1962, which turned out to be a bombshell in rhizomatic slow motion. The book's iconoclastic barrages confused most readers and critics. This outspokenness was exactly right for those who could already sense the shockwaves provoking the uproar that would follow in the decade ahead.

A scrutinizing view (leading to sight and insight of "what was actually there") emerges as the imperative and basic requirement in a world of blurred semantics and manipulative spin tactics. Taking a hard look could be the credo of the Factualists in *Naked Lunch* who are "Anti-Liquefactionist, Anti-Divisionist, and above all Anti-Sender" (140). Their function seems to be to prevent the worst from happening. They reject the attempt to flood the planet with "desirable replicas" that "constitute an unspeakable menace to life on this planet" (140). In mock political-party talk (which thrives on "for" and "against") the anonymous entity of the Sender is identified as the evil force of the Human Virus.

To look in silence (i.e. without the interference of words) promises to reveal what is actually there: a picture that can only be seen after emotional and associative detachment. Amidst the turmoil of competing opinions and detailed analysis surrounding the parties of Interzone, an illuminating sentence stands out: "Artists will confuse sending with creation" (141). Sending is defined as a one-way message system that never stops even when there is nothing left to send. But artistic creation might also be the disclosure of what is actually there, as opposed to any interpretative "realistic" representation. The actual/factual picture appears as a mere outline or draft. A blueprint. If nothing else, this is the model structure of *Naked Lunch* and stands in blatant contrast to traditional literary concepts, just as Burroughs' book was initially perceived by open-minded readers as a radical antibourgeois statement: "the exact counter piece to the normal bourgeois world," according to Peter Erik Hillenbach.

A division was revealed between a limited, traditional concept of "engaged" literature and a widening "political" approach that emerged in the 1960s and that eventually included sexual politics and behavior in general, highlighted by the slogan, "Everything is political." In particular, the poet and writer Rolf Dieter Brinkmann insisted that literature does not progress but expands into all areas of life (an early indication of Pop Art tendencies). But the conventional premises and repressive expectations of traditional art still obliged the artist to serve an elevated purpose. In this context, *Naked Lunch* presented a radical and seemingly extreme leap out of these inherited parameters. Burroughs was thus labelled a "peripheral eccentric" (by Helmut Winter) writing about "an exotic scrap yard of the marginal" (Bernd Klähn).

What became known as the "open mic phase" of the 1960s had many facets, and it is nearly impossible to sort them out. In Germany, an emerging literary establishment had formed around the *Gruppe 47*, which included writers like Gunter Grass, Heinrich Boll, Hans Magnus Enzensberger, Uwe Johnson, and Martin Walser. In his novel *The Tin Drum*, Grass found a unique way of reproducing the suppressed and uncharted era of World War II by constantly shifting from first to third person in his narrative about Oskar, the drummer boy, thus creating a virtual schizophrenic perspective that was typical in its way of the postwar state of mind. As a conglomerate of writers, critics, and publishers, the group had the power to make or break a writer and decide which works of fiction were publicly noteworthy. Whatever the group's standards, they were destined to become mainstream.

The avant-garde was exemplified by a movement called *Konkrete Poesie*, a vague adaptation and extension of Dadaist intentions. It was primarily concerned with experimentation and the visual potential of texts. In Austria, the *Wiener Gruppe* had formed in the 1950s around Konrad Bayer, H. C. Artmann, Gerhard Ruhm, and Oswald Wiener. Bayer wrote sketches and plays that consisted of sentences patched together in montage, defying sense, logic, and psychological reference. Artmann, on the other hand, produced poems using the Vienna idiom. It was a radical attempt to let language speak "for itself," to find meaning beyond the rules of semantics. Anything that did not fit the two categories of mainstream expectations or textual experimentation was confined to little magazines and marginalized as "underground," below the media and public horizons.

On the other hand, dissident consciousness was occupied by a strong extraparliamentary movement, with Rudi Dutschke as the prominent political figure, who made his point rhetorically and theoretically (realizing that, he kept pushing towards "direct action"). The *Frankfurter Schule* (with academics and intellectuals such as Theodor W. Adorno and Max Horkheimer) was the nucleus of an increasingly militant generation of students. With its *Critical Theory*, it insisted that popular culture (called *Kulturindustrie*) was the product of advertising, movies, radio, television, and rock 'n' roll, which devalued art through replicated, kitsch versions and commercialized surrogates. Protesters flocked around the SDS (a socialist student organization) in and outside the universities, using campuses for teach-ins, sit-ins, and demonstrations. Anti-fascist, anti-imperialistic, anti-bourgeois, and anti-authoritarian, the group pushed for reforms to dismantle the hierarchies and institutions that dominated society and culture. In this atmosphere of upheaval and liberation, literature was declared "bourgeois," some going so far as to proclaim its death.

The *circle of marginalization* had closed. In this context, the *Feuilleton* (the art and literature section of most newspapers) came under attack and was ignored by many who believed in a revolution that would change everything. Independent discourse was forced into underground or "alternative" publications, which actually thrived during this period. This is not an incontestable historical framework but a necessary background that must be considered in order to understand the *Zeitgeist* that prevailed during the time (and beyond) when *Naked Lunch* was published in Germany—this was the context for the book's reception and for the controversy that it evoked.

The fact that a first limited edition was only sold after the buyer signed a prepared form stating his or her age (thus treating the text like pornography) is proof that the time of publication marked a cultural turning point. Considered subversive, controversial, and obscene by traditional standards, the book was, nevertheless, hailed by a progressive minority as a statement against outdated moral and political consent, and by 1972, as Hans Christian Kosler said in *Frankfurter Rundschau*, it had become "legendary." Going through the bulk of reviews about the book, I cannot avoid the sneaking feeling that as a critic, you could not go wrong, no matter what your conclusions were. The choice was either to condemn the book or accept it as a work of radical innovation: in both cases the critical efforts hardly touched upon, let alone grasped the true value of the book and the complexity and diversity of its contents. Burroughs himself insisted that a work of art had to be controversial to serve its purpose, and that is exactly what happened with *Naked Lunch*.

The first German edition of the book (1962), in a less-than-inspired translation and with the most explicit "obscene" sections left in English, reached mainly insider circles and remained within the realms of "Beat literature." It was seen as an exotic American import, typical of a rising youth culture, its visions marginalized as just another example of a remote subculture entangled in what Horst Krüger, writing in *Neue Rundschau* magazine, termed "the spinning merry-go-round of addictions." The book was understood as a world seen through a lens, a world dehumanized by drugs, reducing man to the role of patient with the author as his best diagnostician.

The critical trap had been sprung, practically inviting a dismissive reader response: Why read about the ups and downs, about the salvation and agony of a junkie? The book (one critic notes) follows in its literary structure the pattern of addiction, and its author—medically speaking—is closer to psychosis than to neurosis. Nevertheless, Burroughs is granted brilliance for his handling of "language" (the favorite fetish of most critics) and for the way he achieves, to quote Krüger again, "highly literary effects" through subtle twists and rearrangements of jive, slang, and colloquialisms.

Again, content becomes the unsurpassable obstacle for assessing the structural impact of a radical assault on the Western fabric of reality. What appears as threads of thriller and detective novels, elements of science fiction and even facets of the *Nouveau roman*, does not yet have its place within the panorama of popular mythology that only decades later emerged as the vivid background for postmodern fiction (as with William Gibson or Thomas Pynchon). All in all, these contemporary critical statements linger helplessly around the book, leaving the critics in the position of shocked viewers, much like those confronted with early modern art by Duchamp, Kandinsky, or Kirchner, pointing out details but missing the formal statement and the underlying intention. Overall, the written comments were as diverse and multifarious and irreconcilable as Burroughs' own work, which only contributed to its fascination. "His books," wrote P. Klaus in 1974, "are real experiences that enable us to intensify and understand ourselves and the world around us and to take our fears away because everything that is described here lies within us."

The first German edition was limited to fifteen hundred copies and had an epilogue by Terry Southern in which he stressed the importance of Burroughs' humor, saying that it displays "an absolutely devastating ridicule of all that is false, primitive, and vicious in current American life." Some of the statements read like a premonition of the prevailing criticism of "Americanism" that has intensified as this is written: "Abuses of power, hero worship, aimless violence, materialistic obsession, intolerance and every form of hypocrisy." Southern warns the reader to read the book as a political commentary and states that no translation could capture Burroughs' sensitivity for the English language, and that any attempt would be as imprecise as a translation of Gottfried Benn's lyrical diction into French or English. There was indeed no equivalent at the time for a sentence like: "Itinerant short con and hype men have burned down the croakers of Texas" (13). Southern's remarks serve as hints for the European reader on how to cope with a difficult and shocking literary confrontation.

As may be expected, the sections left in English are the hanging scenes in "Hassan's Rumpus Room" and the part where Mark, Johnny, and Mary engage in a fuck-and-hanging orgy. This precaution was hardly enough to hamper the overall statement of the book, because the average reader could master enough English to understand the impact of these passages. The resentment stirred by the book's subjects and views was confined to the shock wave of Burroughs' uninhibited language and approach to sex: his depiction of basic carnal and traumatic events based on immediate, visceral experience. In the cultural understanding of the early 1960s (especially in Germany), literature was expected to move cautiously and with moral responsibility. Traditionally, cultural expression was seen separately from any political involvement in a broader sense. It had to serve a "higher" ethical purpose. The elements of provocation, subversion, and dissent evolved only years later. In consequence, Burroughs' deep aversion to the prevailing American way of life was neglected and overlooked in most reviews. Criticism of American policy was left to political agitation and focused mainly on the war in Vietnam. Burroughs' much deeper approach was seen only years later and contributed to the growing legacy of his stature as an outspoken and controversial figure.

Categorical prejudice kept the critics from seeing both the formal and the sociopolitical impact concealed by the layering of subject matters and the atmosphere of an alien, outlaw milieu. The gap between the translation by Katharina and Peter Behrens and, sixteen years later, that of Carl Weissner was mostly due to the development of the German idiom itself during those crucial years. Despite the defiance of American policy (especially against the war in Vietnam), in the 1970s, there was an undercurrent of attempts in the literary scene to expand the scope of aesthetic expression.[2] This was the result of exposure to Beat and affiliated literature by writers like Charles Bukowski and Frank O'Hara. The idiomatic range of German had widened, not only verbally but also through music. The words had not changed but after listening to Jim Morrison or the Stones, their sound had. Weissner had hung out in jazz joints in Heidelberg frequented by GIs, and he'd spent considerable time in the States. He was the man to get the rude and loose intonation across. Where the Behrens had to say "opiates," Weissner was able to go straight to "junk." A comparison of the two translations shows the tricky depth of Burroughs' winding and twisting "abstract slang," which is hardly slang at all but a reverberation of slang.

In 1978, the second edition (in the congenial, new translation) was published and triggered a wave of reviews. *Naked Lunch* was now labeled as "classical" and "legendary" by Helmut Winter in 1978, its reception jumping from frowning dismissal to the acknowledgment that it was an undeniable landmark in American and modern literature. The middle part—mediation—was strangely missing. In the same year, Helmut Heißenbüttel (a leading figure in the avant-garde *Konkrete Poesie* movement) made it a point to compare his first reading of the book to the second and found "mostly boredom instead of excitement." What had happened? At the initial encounter with the book, he had apparently been impressed by the disregard of taboos, now with this effect gone he saw it mainly as *a sickness report*: "The pathological motive surpasses the literary."

Noteworthy also is the fascination with the author's biography, which almost takes on a fictionalized form in itself. There is the exaggeration of Burroughs' family background with its hints of inherited wealth. And there is the accidental death of Joan (in one commentary on the William Tell scene, it is even a champagne glass that is tragically missed). By highlighting the sensational elements of Burroughs' personal background, his life becomes an image that reflects his novel and so projects a provocative simulacrum of antibourgeois and antimainstream attitudes. Here is a man who went through hell never to return to the rationalization of a sober life. We are looking at an outcast, not an outlaw, "the so called drug writer and old beatnik," as Hans-Peter Kunisch put it. A revolting portrayal for anyone who knew him.

The chronotopical structure of *Naked Lunch* exemplifies a temporal approach. Time as an element of deconstructing language . . . and ultimately fragmenting the reality film—a process that appears to be technical if not mechanical, as hinted at by the frequent appearance of an anonymous technician. "The Technician, naked, his body burned black, staggers about like a figure in *Götterdämmerung,* screaming: 'Thubber thonic!! Oth Thu thair!!!' A final blast reduces the Technician to a cinder" (54). At another point, "an anal technician mixes a bicarbonate of soda and pulls the switch that reduces the earth to cosmic dust" (141). Semantic nuclear disintegration serves as the pivotal force behind Burroughs' writing, which gives it a sense of urgency. "The grand actuality of fact" is never approached on its own terms. Reality is fragmented into bits and pieces until it appears as a disparate arsenal of props, make-believes, grotesque coincidences, and malicious absurdities that are tackled with hilarious, iconoclastic verve. Even the term *black humor,* often used to describe and interpret the spectacle of Burroughs' "routines," falls short when faced with this total assault on the components of the "rumpus room" and the effects of shock and disorientation on the reader. The surface of a world gone wrong has long been torn to shreds, and after T. S. Eliot's survey of the remaining wasteland, Burroughs seems to be scraping the bottom of the American Dream and indeed the Western world.

It must be seen as a miracle of the publishing business that Limes, the original publisher of the book in Germany, caught on so quickly in buying the rights. The self-censoring restriction of leaving several passages in English is an indication that the German publisher realized he was dealing with controversial stuff, but there was nothing that equaled the political and legal strategy that John Calder in England and Barney Rosset of Grove Press in the United States pursued. When Rosset was asked why he was spending thousands of dollars on lawsuits, he replied, "I'll tell you why—if you don't, you go to jail." The German Constitution does not allow censorship but there are other ways of suppressing books under the pretense of keeping them from minors, thus preventing public display. With the outcome of the legal trial in the United States, Limes got around these obstacles, which, of course, immediately increased the interest in the book. The book may have appealed to some because of its status as an "obscene" work, but, in my opinion, this was never a prevalent or dominating factor in the book's circulation in Germany. If there was such an interest, it came from a mixture of libertarian interests, including homosexuals and users of drugs. As with *Ulysses* and *Lolita* or other pioneering books, voyeuristic motives did play a crucial part in the creation of controversial reputations, while their real achievements have been slowly recognized in more public circles, though certainly not in the mainstream press.

For a young writer, *Naked Lunch* was an immediate revelation to me, demonstrating that experimentation must not be free of experience. And what is experience if it cannot become Word? Here was the exemplification of leaving behind all prearranged expectations, here was a challenge to dig down into the unseen and undisclosed matter of what is right there, in front of the inner eye. It was an encouragement to leave no word unturned.

Naked Lunch served as a delineation of how to deal with a deterritorialized, out-of-control reality that defies ideological categories: "Squares on both sides" (15). Modern society can no longer be viewed as a monolithic bloc (run by an anonymous establishment) and its nature deciphered by mere description but rather as an organic, syntactic formation directed and controlled by subtle, subliminal, institutional, and moblike infiltrations and defections. Instead of society and the individual, it is the human body and the central nervous system that move into focus, the gray room as a theater of operations with sex as a form of warfare. Here the cards of perception are mixed and remixed in a bio-alchemistic manner. Word as an element of metabolic expression . . .

In 1960, I had become a commercial pilot, and it was not the myth of flying that confronted me with basic questions about writing in a set of movable experiences and circumstances. My way out of the linear narrative came with the help of cut-ups. If you cut up the disruptive material, you could reach a composite state where time and space interacted. You were not tied to association lines of consecutive succession leading nowhere, the next step taking you into an abyss of redundancy and meaninglessness that, to use Burroughs' term, is the *word virus*. Cut-up did not set me free but my writing was liberated, a writing that does not follow the predestined routes but takes off in all directions (as unquestionably happens in film and music). The scrambling effect of interfering with the rigid structure of language by questioning the very nature of the word opened up a totally unexplored dimension of writing and ultimately extended its potentialities.

For a writer who claimed his aim was to "rub out the Word," Burroughs left behind a lot of words. My reply to this apparent contradiction is: rub out the Word *as we know it*. I am sure, though, that Burroughs meant it quite literally, and perhaps we are dealing with a fading medium in respect to the aura that has surrounded the use of words. The electronic revolution has only just started, and other means of information and communication are appearing on the technological horizon. Burroughs made his mark as a writer, now let's see what others will do with what he has shown in the laboratory of self-determination.

Notes

1. A romantic German term for the state of mind in which conditions of existence are perceived.

2. Rolf Dieter Brinkmann had coedited a groundbreaking anthology of American contemporary writing in 1969 called *ACID* (März Verlag); Jörg Fauser, another German writer, had worked with cut-ups and later followed a narrative tone indebted to Charles Bukowski; Bernward Vesper tried to work with Burroughs' fragmented factual style in *Die Reise* (März Verlag 1977); finally, Elfriede Jelinek published a manifesto-like essay with statements not unlike Brion Gysin's (*TV of the Inner Space*) in *Protokolle* 1 (1970).

Works Cited

Burroughs, William S. *The Naked Lunch*. Translated by Katharina and Peter Behrens. Wiesbaden, Germany: Limes Verlag, 1962.

———. *The Naked Lunch*. Translated by Carl Weissner. Frankfurt, Germany: Zweitausendeins, 1978.

Heißenbüttel, Helmut. *Die Zeit*. 1978.

Hillenbach, Peter Erik. *Frankfurter Allgemeine Zeitung*, 26 October 1981.

Klähn, Bernd. *Frankfurter Rundschau*, 24 April 1992.

Klaus, P. *Sounds*. 1974.

Kosler, Hans Christian. *Frankfurter Rundschau*, 2 March 1972.

Kunisch, Hans-Peter. *Süddeutsche Zeitung*, 3 December 2001.

Winter, Helmut. *Frankfurter Allgemeine Zeitung*, 17 October 1978, 26 October 1981.

The Flaming Voice: *Naked Lunch* in Apartheid South Africa

shaun **DE WAAL**

What was it like to read *Naked Lunch* in the South Africa of the mid-1980s? What did it mean to a nascent queer stuck in a society that was politically oppressive and socially repressive?

The way I have formulated those questions preempts the answers. By the mid-1980s, the apartheid state was ostensibly liberalizing itself while at the same time cracking down ever more heavy-handedly on dissent in any form. It was, we now know, the last gasp of that regime. Yet, state control of image and information had worked, at least upon most white people: until I got to university in 1983, the broader political landscape was only dimly lit for me. What I felt more strongly, and had felt since my early teens, was the social claustrophobia of a white populace that defined itself in terms of Calvinist Christian norms: homosexuality was bad, drugs were bad, rock 'n' roll was a communist plot to weaken the morals of the youth. Conscription into the army loomed for all young white men, either as soon as they finished school or after university; if they could gain entrance to university, they could postpone conscription. (I left the country, dodging the draft, in 1987.) The model of masculinity offered by white South Africa in the mid-1980s was paternalist, militarized, heterosexual, pious. And murderous. The parallels to the postwar world satirized in *Naked Lunch* a quarter of a century earlier, especially the oppressive roles of race and religion in politics, are striking.

That, at least, was clear, even if my first rebellions were against these kinds of social restrictions and norms rather than the apartheid state per se. In that context, *Naked Lunch* and other works by William Burroughs offered a delirious vision of a kind of chaos, disintegration, a craziness that looked like total liberation. Everything was up for grabs. The text itself was wide open, disorganized, impossible to understand in conventional ways, even incomplete, frozen in a state of partial formation; the sexuality it presented was indeterminate, polymorphous, definitely perverse. It was an ungovernable text. The aura of drugginess that suffused the whole book was immensely appealing to one who had taken to heart the Rimbaudian necessity of disordering the senses. The link back to an alternative culture (an elsewhere) was obvious—the Beats and their hippie descendants may have been long gone as any kind of "movement," and they were certainly far away, but their example resonated for anyone trying, at least mentally, to escape Calvinist South Africa. This was an intimation of what *counterculture* could mean.

Naked Lunch, Burroughs' other works, and the image of Burroughs himself as a kind of icon of iconoclasm became a touchstone of resistance and escape for me. In her meditation on this transitional moment in South African history, this "interregnum," Nadine Gordimer wrote in 1983: "The morality of life and the morality of art have broken out of their categories in social flux. If you cannot reconcile them, they cannot be kept from one another's throats, within you" (14). Gordimer's artistic preferences are more Lukacsian and Gramscian than Burroughsian, and she might well have pegged an obsession with Burroughs as one of the "morbid symptoms" of the interregnum,[1] but she captures the sense of a society in violent flux—and some of the flux within. The indeterminacy of *Naked Lunch*, its resistance to category and norm, resonated not just with my inner resistance to Calvinist, white, heterosexual South Africa but even in relation to the antiapartheid political movement at university. That movement's intentions were clearly correct and to be espoused, but its Stalinist approach meant that it felt as mentally restrictive as what it opposed, as reliant on dogmas and shibboleths: think of Burroughs' "Parties of Interzone" and his whole take on party politics in *Naked Lunch*. Several of us working on the student paper were "purged" from the varsity left for having unknowingly taken an unacceptable position (we found ourselves to have stumbled blindly into Trotskyism) and then having refused to submit to a form of discipline that felt like an assault on the freedom of expression we were trying, in however minor a form, to achieve—the "Divisionists are hysterically paranoid" (139). I found a place outside the organized left, in the underground rock 'n' roll scene, which collaborated with some leftist initiatives such as the Anti-Conscription Campaign and the support of political prisoners, but mostly I took the view that if you freed your ass, your mind would follow. The first step was to emancipate yourself from all that Calvinist repression and po-faced moralizing; we wanted a revolution we could dance to.

Likewise, the shape-shifting perversity of *Naked Lunch* appealed: it was bound to, arising as it did as an extreme response to broadly similar social and sexual conditions. I noted Burroughs' viciously satiric take on the lynch-mob racism of the South—"'Roy, that ol' nigger is looking at me so nasty'" (147)—as well as his bitter picture of the policing of sexuality—the examination of Carl Peterson (155–65). *Naked Lunch*'s take on identity politics therefore struck a chord. Coming to terms with my own sexuality at the time, it felt like going from the category "straight" to the category "gay," as then constructed, didn't answer to the sense of inner lability. I had no interest in a gay world that revolved around the glitter-ball discos; it lacked, for me, the rough, dirty, rebellious edge of the rock underground, and in any case its denizens seemed to be clichés. I had no sense of what "queer" might mean as it was later articulated in the queer theory of the early 1990s (which in any case barely registered in South Africa until fifteen years later), but I see now that that was my visceral affiliation: the anti-identitarian identity, resistant to normativity in any way. It's not hard to see the appeal of such a position in a society based, first, on rigid racial identities, imposed and policed by the state, and, second, on social identities (masculine, feminine, familial) that locked one into insupportable roles.

Reading *Naked Lunch* was like taking drugs—specifically acid. It freed the mind, it threw it into a state of disorientation and disorder that felt very refreshing. Burroughs linked to other cultural icons of the "alternative," young (white), South Africa, such as David Bowie, who was not only self-defined as "bisexual" (at that time) but had invoked Burroughs and his cut-up method of destroying the secret regimes of control through language. A boyfriend and I experimented keenly with our own cut-up writing, and I can't see it as entirely accidental that such early linguistic and textual explorations coincided with my first forays into gay sex.

Gay sex was, of course, illegal at that time in South Africa. Sodomy was a common-law offence, and the law had extended itself to encompass all exhibitions of gay sexuality, including the notoriously absurd clause of the Sexual Offences Act, which "provide[d] that acts committed by men at a party, defined as any occasion where there are more than two persons present, and which are calculated to stimulate sexual passion or to give sexual gratification[,] constitute[d] an offence."[2] Now read this from the start of the "Benway" section: "No one ever looked at anyone else because of the strict law against importuning, with or without verbal approach, anyone for any purpose, sexual or otherwise. [. . .] No one was permitted to bolt his door, and the police had pass keys to every room in the city. Accompanied by a mentalist they rush into someone's quarters and start 'looking for it'" (20–21). But if Burroughs' Annexia sounds like my South Africa, compare and contrast with "A. J.'s Annual Party." It is revealing that this section above all has scared off the critics, faced with Burroughs' delirious and disturbing play of Eros and Thanatos, his unrestrained fantasy of submission and domination, bestial ecstasy and aggression, beauty and terror. It is as uncomfortable reading for men as for women, gay as for straight people—for the "Cunts, pricks, fence straddlers" A. J. calls his guests (74)—and certainly, too, for anyone who would like to elide the power relations embedded in sexual interactions. The overwhelming sense of sex, here as elsewhere in Burroughs, is of an extreme and liminal experience. The scenes of spurting fluids, snapping necks, and screams of ambiguous pleasure-pain hosted by A. J. would certainly have offended against the Sexual Offences Act (and representations of illegal acts were deemed almost as dangerous as the acts themselves) and jars against the official conception of sexuality.

> The South African community considers someone's sex life to be a very private matter which is based on respect for the body of the individual and on the relationship with the spouse. Extra-marital intercourse is disapproved of by the South African community [sic] with its pursuit of maintaining a Christian way of life. (qtd. in de Lange, 20)

Censorship in South Africa is a self-justifying book by the chief censor from 1979 to 1989, Kobus van Rooyen. *Naked Lunch* and other Burroughs works would have been banned under the Publications and Entertainment Act of 1963 and its update, the Publications Act of 1974. Section 47(2)(a) of the act deals with obscenity: "A publication is undesirable if it is indecent or obscene or offensive or harmful to public morals" (de Lange, 20). "Public morals" were as important to the self-righteous apartheid rulers (with their rhetoric of upholding "civilization" in the face of primitive licentiousness) as maintaining an affiliation to one's designated racial group.

Of course, the myriad assumptions in van Rooyen's words are easy to unpick. The South African state had already breached the boundaries of this sacredly private realm of sexuality in its legislation against both nonheterosexual and interracial sex—as was also the case in the postwar America that Burroughs escaped in order to write *Naked Lunch*. And a term such as *the South African community*, used in the midst of a situation in which the state denied basic human rights to the bulk of the (disenfranchised) populace, is simply laughable. *Community* here means the ruling white populace. The application of censorship law required the invocation of "the standards of the community as represented by the average decent-minded, law-abiding, modern and enlightened citizen with Christian principles" (van Rooyen, qtd. in de Lange, 20)—precisely the kind of person Burroughs repeatedly pillories. Margreet de Lange, in her commentary on such laws, notes, "It is obvious that in South Africa at the time this could only apply to white people. The notion of a law-abiding black citizen in the South African context represented almost a contradiction in terms" (19).

Undoubtedly, part of the appeal of a text such as *Naked Lunch* for me, in the mid-1980s, had to do with a very determined disidentification from the apparent norm of "the average decent-minded, law-abiding, modern and enlightened citizen with Christian principles"; in *Naked Lunch, decent* is a recurrent term and always used with savage irony. Perhaps one wanted, in some way, to be "modern and enlightened," but it was clear that my definitions of "modern and enlightened" differed radically from van Rooyen's. And there was no way I wanted in fact to be a member of the said "community"—for me, it represented group-think, Calvinist repression, social claustrophobia, self-righteousness, and the hypocrisy of a violent patriarchy. I was not going to be average, decent-minded, or law-abiding, if those were the qualities of van Rooyen's evoked citizen. This imaginary figure was automatically opposed by what Burroughs seemed to represent.

I came to *Naked Lunch* backwards, that is to say working towards it through the then-available Burroughs oeuvre from *Cities of the Red Night*, which I found in 1983 in a good bookshop in Hillbrow, then an area of high-rise flatland in central Johannesburg, a "cosmopolitan" space of relative freedom. One might even call Hillbrow a sort of Interzone, where gay bars flourished, and some interracial mixing took place. I later found in the same shop the Picador edition of *Queer* and, standing at the shelves, read the "Ugly Spirit" preface. The Burroughs myth became more focused for me. *Cities of the Red Night* seems to have been the first Burroughs text to enter South Africa legally and openly, as the regime softened its censorship rules as part of an overall attempt at reforming apartheid (short of actually abolishing it). At any rate, the indigenous political pamphlets advocating revolution, or at least ungovernability, would on their own have been keeping the censors very busy by then. Not that there had ever been much follow-through on the censorship laws: when the security police raided one's house, they scanned bookshelves for politically seditious material, keeping an eye out especially for those big fat tomes with "Marx" in huge letters down the broad spine, and ignored works such as Burroughs', or Gore Vidal's *Myra Breckinridge* (also famously banned); they seemed unaware that such books were as banned as Marx's.

Other Burroughs texts I found in second-hand shops or had sent to me by friends overseas: *The Wild Boys, Nova Express, The Ticket That Exploded*, and *Exterminator!* and, finally, in a second-hand shop in Hillbrow, I came across an already bleached and tattered *Naked Lunch*. The fact that one could find the notoriously banned *Naked Lunch* in such a place indicated that some people were smuggling copies into the country (as they did many restricted texts) and that the censorship regime was relaxing somewhat. Not that the police were likely to bother to raid second-hand bookshops. This edition of *Naked Lunch* was the Corgi paperback, with a stylized Burroughs image, cut off just beneath the sphinx-like mouth, on the cover. The head is shaved and the eyeballs red, but the face is recognizably Burroughs'. This bald-pate floating head seemed the image of a demon of some kind but an impassively implacable one—a sort of assassin, an exterminator of the values espoused by van Rooyen's fictional good (white) citizen.

For years thereafter, Burroughs (as voice, as image) continued to haunt me—and "haunt" is the right word for the way his ghostly presence shadowed me. In the later 1980s, having returned to a changing South Africa, I was working on a small countercultural publication and in the course of that encountered the poet Sinclair Beiles, who had left the country in disgust, apparently in the late 1950s, to become one of Burroughs' Moroccan and Parisian associates. I enjoyed hearing Beiles' stories about Burroughs, told in his staccato, emphysemic way, with jerking gestures (the same way he recited his poetry in public): how Burroughs threw the pages of the manuscript of *Naked Lunch* up in the air and declared that where they fell would determine the order of the book. This echoed my sense of Burroughs the ungovernable, the Burroughs who, Martin Amis opined, never even tried to climb the control tower—even if such images were by then becoming almost nostalgic for me. Beiles, I think, claimed to have been present when this page-flinging happened, though it now seems clear that this story is apocryphal; Beiles was, in any case, usually an unreliable narrator. But his presence felt like an echo of that of Burroughs himself, for all the fan-boy pretensions that evokes. Beiles even suggested that I write to Burroughs in Lawrence, Kansas, and suggest that he visit South Africa on his way to Madagascar, where, Beiles said, Burroughs would be visiting the lemurs he so loved. I visited the U.S.A. in 1997 and near San Francisco heard that Allen Ginsberg had died; soon after my return to South Africa, I read that Burroughs himself had died. It felt, in some weird way, as though a ghost of chance were governing these coincidences.

Twenty years after finding that bleached floating-head edition of *Naked Lunch*, it was odd to see the 2003 edition of *Naked Lunch: The Restored Text*. In 1986, doing a literature degree at what was then one of the two most progressive universities in South Africa, I was not allowed to do an honors dissertation on Burroughs because he was "insufficiently literary" and had, it was said, not yet "entered the canon" (the implication being that he never would). Twenty years later, here *Naked Lunch* had been *Ulysses*-ed into some kind of quasi-definitive scholarly edition! Does that make him less of an icon of what I can only call a counterculture? Does it make *Naked Lunch* less ungovernable? (No, it doesn't.)

Returning to the same university in 2003 to do a master's in creative writing and critical theory, I wrote a long introductory essay on Burroughs. I was able to deploy queer theory to make greater sense of him, I thought, than a work such as Jamie Russell's *Queer Burroughs* (2001), which found Burroughs insufficiently gay-liberatory; queer theory offered a way to understand the resistance of his work to such a reading. It also offered an opportunity to explore what queer theory might mean and to introduce it in some way to the South African academy, a mere decade or so after it began to fade somewhat in the American academy. (It was also very useful in writing a monograph on the South African artist Steven Cohen, for whom I minted a phrase that resonates with Burroughs: "the anus as a site of artistic practice."[3])

Yet, as the external examiner of my master's thesis pointed out, to read Burroughs in terms of queer theory is in a way to naturalize him or at least to put him in his natural habitat. It is not to provide a "queer reading" of Burroughs, which would necessarily be against his grain—which would be what? To read *Naked Lunch* as a model of stable, reciprocal relationality? In this sense, it is perhaps not possible to produce a "queer reading" of Burroughs; he's too queer. Still, the investigation of queer theory began to get me to see more clearly what it was in Burroughs that had so long appealed to me. *Queer* may refuse a determined or overdetermined identity, but even its leading articulators seem to want to at least collocate a series of resonant ideas in relation to it—hence Eve Kosofsky Sedgwick's list of terms that "cluster intimately" in the same region: "To name only a few: butch abjection, femmitude, leather, pride, SM, drag, musicality, fisting, attitude, zines, histrionicism, Snap! culture, diva worship, florid religiosity; in a word, *flaming*" (64). This is the voice I heard in my early readings of Burroughs, the one that spoke to me: the flaming voice. It is a form of the "queer performativity" Sedgwick finds or "nominate[s]" in "the [Henry] James of the New York edition prefaces," "the name of a strategy for the production of meaning and being, in relation to the affect shame and to the later and related fact of stigma" (61). The *flaming* Burroughs speaks in his "routines," the wild freewheeling concatenations of bizarre imagery that develop out of his letters to Allen Ginsberg, become the primary material of

Naked Lunch. Significantly, however, the first written routines had emerged in *Queer*, and Burroughs recycled parts of several in *Naked Lunch*, from Dr. Tetrazzini, whose "operations were performances" (52) to the Duc de Ventre, in whose Hispano Suiza a certain Professor Fingerbottom is strangled by his falling piles, "leaving an empty shell sitting there on the giraffe skin upholstery" (139). There is a revelatory mini-routine in a letter Burroughs wrote to Ginsberg at the time he was halfway through writing *Queer* in 1952. In it, he reacts to a request, sent via Ginsberg, for an authorial self-description, presumably to be used on the jacket of the book:

> Please, Sweetheart, write the fucking thing will you? PLUMMM. That's a great big sluppy kiss for my favorite agent. Now look, you tell [Carl] Solomon [the publisher] I don't mind being called queer. T. E. Lawrence and all manner of right Joes (boy can I turn a phrase) was queer. But I'll see him castrated before I'll be called a Fag. [. . .] That's just what I been trying to put down uh I mean *over,* is the distinction between us strong, manly, noble types and the leaping, jumping, window dressing cocksucker. Furthechrissakes a girl's gotta draw the line somewhere or publishers will swarm all over her sticking their nasty old biographical prefaces up her ass. (*Letters*, 119)

It is fascinating to note Burroughs' distinction between *queer* and *fag*, both equally derogatory terms in the early 1950s (and "queer" as yet had no theory). Why does he object to one but not the other? The term *fag* Burroughs glosses as the "leaping, jumping, window dressing cocksucker"—basically, the queen. And yet, it seems to me, it is precisely the voice of the screaming queen, the *flaming* queen, that erupts in Burroughs' routines—a voice of what Oliver Harris calls "manic garrulity and emotional excess" (introduction, Burroughs, *Letters*, xxvi). These routines animate what will become *Naked Lunch*, will produce its most outlandish flights of fantasy, the ungovernable chaos that sparked my attention as a youth in a repressive, closed society in the mid-1980s. The *flaming* voice provides a countervoice to the deadpan narrator of *Junky* and *Queer*—yet in the letter to Ginsberg, Burroughs disavows it, displays some shame in relation to the appellation. Perhaps, as Sedgwick suggests in relation to James, that shame is generative for Burroughs; look at the way the Lee figure's proto-routines develop in *Queer*, even as humiliation is piled upon the rejected Lee by his love object.

Burroughs, at least, wants to escape pigeonholing, category, even autobiography. He has already offered a wild send-up of the "old biographical preface" and called it a "routine": "Do they have in mind the—'I have worked (but not in the order named) as towel boy in a Kalamazoo whore house, lavatory attendant, male whore and part-time stool pigeon [. . .]' routine[?]"

(*Letters*, 119). This imaginary biography—with its refusal of coherence, its parody of a respectable employment history, its delight in the dirty and the indecent—says much about Burroughs' need to escape, as he eventually did, from a conservative and repressive society. It also says much about the voice of excess that emerged from such repression, a voice that refuses to conform to new shibboleths any more than it will speak the old ones. Fifty years on, it is still a voice that has the queer ring of truth.

Notes

1. Gordimer quotes Antonio Gramsci's *Prison Notebooks* in the epigraph to her novel *July's People* (Harmondsworth, UK: Penguin, 1981): "The old is dying and the new cannot be born; in this interregnum there arises a great diversity of morbid symptoms."

2. Section 28 of the Sexual Offences Act (23 of 1957, amended 1969). This Act, of course, also criminalized interracial sex. After the ratification of the new South African Constitution in 1996, all such laws were repealed.

3. Shaun de Waal and Robyn Sassen, *Steven Cohen*, Taxi series (Johannesburg: Krut, 2003).

Works Cited

Burroughs, William S. Introduction. In *The Letters of William S. Burroughs, 1945–1959*, xv–xl. Edited by Oliver Harris. London: Picador, 1993.

Sedgwick, Eve Kosofsky. *Touching Feeling: Affect, Pedagogy, Performativity*. Durham, N.C.: Duke UP, 2003.

de Lange, Margreet. *The Muzzled Muse: Literature and Censorship in South Africa*. Amsterdam: Benjamins, 1997.

Gordimer, Nadine. "Living in the Interregnum." *New York Review of Books*, 20 January 1983, 14.

South Africa. Section 28 of the Sexual Offences Act (23 of 1957, amended 1969).

"The ideal product . . . No sales talk necessary": The Olympia Press *Naked Lunch* as Collectible and Book Object

jed **BIRMINGHAM**

It has been over fifteen years, and I have yet to awaken from The Sickness. I am in reasonably good health with a full bookshelf and an empty wallet. The addiction is book collecting, specifically obtaining all William Burroughs material from 1953 to 1965. Little did I know in 1993 when I purchased a signed copy of *The Dead Star* (1969), a small broadside stapled in wrappers, that my life would revolve around obtaining books, magazines, posters, and LPs containing Burroughs material.

With his illustrious family tree, Burroughs would appreciate that collecting is in my blood, handed down like a genetic defect or a cursed family heirloom from the men in my family. Both my grandfathers were collectors bordering on hoarders. Some of my earliest memories of my father surround the Adamstown, Pennsylvania, antique malls where we hunted for his latest obsession be it furniture, bottles, or tin boxes. These obsessions were passed on. I gathered Wheatie pennies as well as sports cards of all kinds. I looked into comic books. These pursuits were mere dabbling. I yearned to put my collecting instincts to use. The summer after my freshman year, I read *Naked Lunch*. Like many, I was immediately fascinated. The book cast its spell and triggered my inborn desire to collect. Reading *Naked Lunch* initiated me not into a drug lifestyle but another addiction. Book collecting is not a kick; it is a way of life.

When I began collecting Burroughs, I felt the Olympia Press *Naked Lunch* (1959) would be the final fix. Nothing could top the experience of finally owning the first edition of Burroughs' masterpiece. That experience came and went. Other rarities became the ultimate trip: the *British Journal of Addiction* offprint (1957) or the Digit *Junkie* (1957). Now, the quest revolves around a complete run of Wallace Berman's *Semina* (1957–64), which includes Burroughs material in issue four. This is one of the first appearances of *Naked Lunch* in print.

Yet, looking over my book collection, the Olympia Press *Naked Lunch* still possesses an aura. I take it out of its clamshell box nearly every day. It continues to fill me with as much joy as the day I bought it. The Digit *Junkie* makes my collection special due to its legendary rarity and cover art, but the Olympia Press title is the cornerstone of any Burroughs collection.

I have never read my copy. I never will. If real estate is about "Location, Location, Location," the mantra in book collecting is "Condition, Condition, Condition." My decision not to read my copy is based on the desire not to damage it. But this goes beyond financial considerations. Collectors often speak in an excited manner about their holy grails: those items that a particular collector desires above all. I mentioned a few of mine above. These books and magazines, which have shaped not just my view of literature but my life, have an almost religious significance for me. I hesitate to handle these first editions, these holy relics that get close to the source of my obsession: Burroughs himself. Yet, I always try to remember that the Holy Grail was once a mere cup. It was only through use that it obtained significance. So I research and make available my collection in an effort to keep its treasures fresh in my mind and introduce them to others.

I am not going to discuss *Naked Lunch* textually. Carol Loranger in her essay "This Book Spill Off the Page in All Directions," Oliver Harris in *William Burroughs and the Secret of Fascination*, James Grauerholz in the introduction to *Interzone*, and Barry Miles and Grauerholz in the editors' note to *Naked Lunch: The Restored Text* have explored this territory. Instead, I am going to examine the book's dust jacket, the wrappers, the title page, and the controversial price stamp. In this way, I hope to express the surge of feelings and associations that rush through my mind as I hold my prized copy as well as to provide a fresh look at this much-studied and discussed classic.

In the mid-1990s, a William Reese catalog featured a large Olympia Press library. To this day, I have yet to purchase Patrick Kearney's invaluable bibliography of the Paris Olympia Press (it is something of a collectible in its own right), but for years, the Reese catalog served as my guide to Maurice Girodias's infamous press. The titles in the catalog ranged from the sublime, like *Lolita*, *The Ginger Man*, *Candy*, and *Watt*, to the ridiculous, like *The Whipping Club*, *The Sexual Life of Robinson Crusoe*, and *Until She Screams*. In between lurked literary pornography by the likes of Pauline Reage, Georges Bataille, and Guillaume Apollinaire and the just plain strange, like Norman Rubington's collage novel *Fuzz Against Junk*. As I remember, William Reese offered the entire collection for $7,500, which looking back on it was a tremendous deal. *Lolita* in two volumes can sell for $7,000 alone, not to mention the high prices fetched by first editions of *The Ginger Man*, *Watt*, *The Soft Machine* and *The Ticket That Exploded*.

The packaging of a standard Olympia Press title was a rather plain affair. Often wrapped or shipped in plain brown paper, the Traveller's Companion series was issued in a now-iconic olive-green wrapper with the title and usually pseudonymous author's name in a simple typeface. I am reminded of another famous yet simple paperback series: the black-and-white wrappers of the City Lights' Pocket Book Series. The Traveller's Companion did not draw the attention of the uninitiated, yet at the same time was easy to spot and unmistakable to those in the know. The green wrappers were a golden ticket to a land of sexual fantasy. There were no lurid images on a dust jacket to draw the attention of an unsuspecting passerby or custom official. Yet, in time, word got around, and Girodias frantically changed titles and even the trademark covers to outwit the authorities.

On the back of the book was the key phrase: "NOT TO BE SOLD IN THE U.S.A. OR U.K." Those words were like a highly addictive drug to readers around the world, particularly English and American readers on the lookout for cheap thrills. The Traveller's Companion series drew tourists, overseas military personnel, and mail-order customers like moths to an erotic flame. In Paris, the English Bookshop and Brentano's were a few of the bookstores where porno junkies could get their fix. Smuggling the book into the United States or Great Britain was a crime, and hundreds of tourists carried the book past customs next to their Baedeker travel guides. The series was small and portable: easy to slip in one's luggage or trench-coat pocket.

As *Naked Lunch* was published in the late summer of 1959, Burroughs found himself charged with drug possession. In addition, the French police suspected he was involved in an international drug-smuggling ring. Burroughs faced expulsion from France. Strangely, the fact that he was published by Olympia Press and an author of some notoriety helped keep him out of jail and in the country. Readers of *Naked Lunch* were, like Burroughs himself, suspected smugglers and outlaws. According to an April 1960 *New York Times* article, only two of twelve review copies of *Naked Lunch* made it to the desks of selected critics (Popkin, 4).

"NOT TO BE SOLD IN THE U.S.A OR U.K." echoed the controversy *Naked Lunch* had generated before it was even published in book form. The phrase exploited the storm of media attention gathering around Burroughs and the rest of the Beat Generation writers. The Olympia Press dust-jacket blurb calls *Naked Lunch* "the great 'secret' novel of the self-styled beat generation." Rumblings of a new American literary scene had been growing for years. On 7 October 1955, Allen Ginsberg read from "Howl" at the Six Gallery, and mimeo copies circulated in literary salons in San Francisco. A section of *On the Road* appeared in *New World Writing* in 1955 alongside an early version of *Catch-22* (then titled "Catch-18"). In 1956, City Lights published *Howl* as "Pocket Book Number 4." In 1957, the San Francisco Scene issue of *Evergreen Review* introduced the Beats to isolated hipsters in Middle America. Jack Kerouac's combination of *Huckleberry Finn*, Thomas Wolfe, and *The Wild One* became an overnight sensation when published by Viking in September of the same year.

Soon the literary community heard stories of a cry in the wilderness, an unpublishable masterpiece written in a drug-induced haze. In the first edition of *Howl*, Ginsberg dedicated the poem to Neal Cassady, Lucien Carr, Jack Kerouac, and William Burroughs. Ginsberg wrote: "William Seward Burroughs, author of *Naked Lunch,* an endless novel which will drive everybody mad." *On the Road* hit the best-seller list with tales of Old Bull Lee, a character modeled on Burroughs. Burroughs was ready for publication. A small but growing literary public was ready to read his work. But were the publishing industry and its censors ready for the dark vision of *Naked Lunch*? According to Ginsberg's dedication to *Howl*, *Naked Lunch* was "published in Heaven." Would it remain so forever?

For a time from 1956 to July 1959, it appeared that *Naked Lunch* might never be published in book form. Excerpts published in the *Chicago Review* and *Big Table* generated a firestorm of controversy. In the spring of 1959, *Big Table* faced an obscenity trial that, ironically, caused Girodias to reconsider publishing *Naked Lunch* at Olympia Press. Previously, Girodias had rejected *Naked Lunch* as not titillating enough for his readers, but seeing *Big Table* sell out ten thousand copies proved to him that the book could still be a big seller. Girodias quickly requested a manuscript from Burroughs and hurried the book into print. Girodias ordered a large print run of five thousand copies, highlighting his faith that the book would be a minor best seller for his press. In addition, Burroughs received the princely sum of $800, roughly double what authors normally received to write Olympia Press's standard dbs (dirty books).

The dust-jacket blurb (pulled from John Ciardi's article "The Book Burners and Sweet Sixteen," published in *Saturday Review*) referred to the Chicago controversy, highlighting the obscenity issues surrounding the book as well as its forbidden nature. The blurb states: "[*Naked Lunch*] has not been published as a whole until now: some extracts which were to appear in *The Chicago Review* have caused the University of Chicago to suppress this quarterly. These same extracts, reprinted in the first issue of *Big Table*, have resulted in the U.S. Post Office Department banning the new Chicago quarterly." So, even when Burroughs was a largely unknown author, there was a buzz around *Naked Lunch*. The Olympia Press edition was desirable immediately to a whole group of readers who did not normally purchase the Press' more fleshy wares.

The dust-jacket blurb straddles between high art and pornography. On one level, the flaps make clear that *Naked Lunch* is different from standard Olympia Press fare. The text states: "As in Kerouac's blurb, the writing does, to be sure, contain a number of four-letter words, but the simple fact is that such obscenities—if obscenities they are—are inseparable from the total fabric and effect of the moral message. No less a writer than Dante made it a principle of harmonious style deliberately to coarsen the writing when dealing with debased characters as his subject matter." The book is described as "a masterpiece of its own genre" and continues, "Burroughs is not only serious in his intent, but he is a writer of great power and artistic integrity engaged in a profoundly meaningful search for true values." Dante? Artistic integrity? Moral message? True values? Clearly, such descriptions would not appeal to the core audience of Olympia Press. Girodias banked on the hype surrounding the *Big Table* trial to sell the book to a cross-over audience of readers interested in daring, frank, and explicit literature, like *Lolita* and *The Tropic of Cancer*.

Yet, this high road is quickly undercut. Girodias did not want to alienate his hard-core audience as well as other less-literary thrill seekers. The dust jacket quotes a particularly sensationalistic section of *Naked Lunch*: "She seized a safety pin caked with blood and rust, gouged a great hole in her leg which seemed to hang open like an obscene, festering mouth waiting for unspeakable congress with the dropper which she now plunged out of sight into the gaping wound." The jacket also mentions "the lust for drugs," "sixteen year old girls," and "green ooze." These lines conjure up appropriate images of sex and drugs. The young girl in trouble was a theme familiar to Olympia Press readers, and drug addiction has always fascinated the square public with its scenes of lawlessness and squalor.

Whether appealing to readers of high art or exploitation, *Naked Lunch* was a popular title for Olympia Press as evidenced by the book's reprint history. Quickly, after the July 1959 printing, Girodias ordered an additional five thousand, this time without a dust jacket. In June 1965, Olympia Press ran yet another five thousand copies. In a 1960 catalog for Olympia Press, Burroughs appeared on the cover, and *Naked Lunch* received two pages of hype in the center of the catalog. Burroughs was a star performer for Giro-dias. The media clamored for the story of this international man of mystery, and a cult readership struggled to get their hands on the elusive novel.

Proof positive that *Naked Lunch* was an event for Olympia Press is the fact that the book had a dust jacket at all. Even the literary efforts of Olympia Press, like *Lolita* and *The Ginger Man*, did not have dust jackets for the most part. All of William Burroughs' titles published by Olympia Press, *Naked Lunch*, *The Soft Machine*, and *The Ticket That Exploded*, have dust jackets. Dust jackets hold special appeal for modern book collectors. In some cases, ninety percent of a book's value resides in the dust jacket. To complicate matters, Barry Miles noted that some true first editions of *Naked Lunch* were issued without the sought-after dust jacket. However, for Burroughs collectors, the Holy Grail is the July 1959 printing with the dust jacket.

With *Naked Lunch*, the dust jacket accentuates Olympia Press's more refined approach to selling the novel. The jacket sets the book apart and gives it an added class and dignity. Although published in paperback, there are pretensions to hard-cover publication as befitting a great work of satire and a work linked to Dante and Swift, not a lurid tale of drug lust and hal-lucination. Not until 1964 with the publication of *Nova Express* by Grove Press would a work by William Burroughs go straight to hardcover without the preliminary stage of a paperback edition from the small, alternative-press circuit.

The first thing I notice about the dust jacket is the title: *The Naked Lunch*. I have always viewed the definite article as ironic given Burroughs' distrust of absolutes. Burroughs preferred fluidity and multiplicity. "A Naked Lunch" would have been more accurate. Although it never again appears in the title of most reprints (the British editions, from the Calder 1964 edition onwards, are a notable exception), the definite article speaks volumes and is appropriate in some ways. This Olympia Press publication firmly estab-lished Burroughs' reputation as an author. *Naked Lunch* made Burroughs an international figure of the avant-garde. The book is *the* Burroughs book, *the* drug narrative, and, along with *Howl* and *On the Road*, *the* Beat text. In addition, it frequently makes lists of the best post–World War II novels, if not the twentieth century. In collecting terms, it is a highspot.

In the 1960s, *Naked Lunch* flourished on the collectible market associ-ated with celebrities and rock stars. The book's counterculture and drug cachet appealed to these nouveaux riche. Burroughs' appearance on the Beatles' *Sgt. Pepper* album cover demonstrates this appeal and added to it. But as a collectible, *Naked Lunch* really exploded in desirability and value with the financial rise of the baby-boomer generation. For many of a certain age, *Naked Lunch*, along with *Catch-22*, *One Flew over the Cuckoo's Nest*, or *To Kill a Mockingbird*, was a defining book coinciding with their late adolescence or early adulthood. As these readers aged and grew financially secure, they returned to the objects that fascinated them in their youth.

Yet, it is pretty safe to say that the Olympia *Naked Lunch* will remain a desirable collectible and appreciate nicely for some time to come. But only time will tell. According to book collectors and dealers, the lasting power of a collectible author can only be assessed after fifty years, even longer. We have reached that point. This book appeals to far more than William Burroughs collectors or a single generation. Fans of twentieth-century literature highspots, American literature, the counterculture, drug culture, the Beats, small presses with added points for being from Olympia Press, collectible paperbacks, banned books, and erotica will all find something desirable in this title. In fact, all of Burroughs' work from 1953 to 1965 falls into at least one of these categories, making this period of his career irresistible to me as a collector.

Part of *Naked Lunch*'s appeal is the fantastic cover art. The purple-and-white jacket gives *Naked Lunch* a regal air. Instead of a sensationalistic drug scene on the cover, *Naked Lunch* features abstract art: calligraphic drawings on the front and back covers. Many assume that these drawings are by Brion Gysin. In fact, William Burroughs designed the dust jacket himself and the drawings are Burroughs' own. The trace of Gysin's signature style highlights the importance of Gysin in Burroughs' creative life beginning in the Beat Hotel era. Yet, the initial influence on Burroughs' style came not in the form of the cut-up. Gysin did not rediscover the cut-up until September of 1959. This is at least a full month after the publication of *Naked Lunch*. The cut-up novels of the 1960s received their first impetus instead from Gysin's paintings. In late July 1959, Burroughs writes in a letter to Allen Ginsberg: "I enclose sample beginning of sequel to *Naked Lunch*. I don't know where it is going or what will happen. It is straight exploration like Gysin's paintings, to which it is intimately connected. We are doing precisely the same thing in different mediums. The Soul Crackers who move BETWEEN layers of light and shadow and color I saw first in his pictures (and my own of course)" (*Letters*, 420).

The drug underworld depicted in *Naked Lunch* is full of rites, jargon, and arcane lore. So is the world of book collecting. How do you determine a first edition, first state, first printing, or first impression? Sometimes one must consult a reference book to unlock the mysteries of a collectible's printing history. The presence or absence of a single word, number, illustration, or dust jacket can mean the difference between a $10 book and a $10,000 one. The collector of *Naked Lunch* must be aware of a few arcane points that can mean the difference between a major score and an expensive bust. A *point* refers to a distinguishing characteristic that defines a distinct edition of a publication. For example, the first edition of the Grove Press *Naked Lunch* (1962) must have no roman numerals on the lower spine near back panel of the dust jacket and no zip code on the back panel. In addition, the $6.00 original price must be printed on the inside flap.

According to Miles and Maynard, in the case of the 1965 Olympia Press reprint, "the last signature (the 15th) has only two leaves, and the colophon reads: 'PRINTED IN FRANCE'" (10). This edition also states that it was printed in 1965. In addition, on some copies, a light-green, black-outlined sticker covers the original price reading "9 francs." But what is to stop an unethical bookseller from marrying a *Naked Lunch* dust jacket with one of the five thousand 1959 reprints issued without a dust jacket? Thankfully, the title page of the true first edition is bordered by a ring of green designs looking like the Tristero symbol from Thomas Pynchon's classic *The Crying of Lot 49*. Book collectors, like seekers of the Tristero, must constantly be on the lookout for myriad signs. These are the keys that unlock doors to a secret world, and they can surface on any page. Like Pynchon's characters, the bibliophile understands paranoia intimately.

Many claim to possess a one-of-a-kind copy of *Naked Lunch*. No tears or creases to the bright purple-and-white dust jacket; crisp, bright-green wrappers; no bumps to the corners; the book itself is tight and unread. Few deliver. This brings me to a minor controversy in the collecting of *Naked Lunch* and all the Olympia Press titles. In January 1960, scarcely six months after the publication of *Naked Lunch*, the French government revalued their currency. Normally, the green rear wrapper of *Naked Lunch* possesses a printed price of 1,500 francs. Many copies are stamped in blue with 18 NF over the original price. What this means is that unsold copies of *Naked Lunch* were repriced according to the new currency. There was no change to the content or format of the novel. Some dealers list these copies as a first edition, second state suggesting an alteration to the integrity of the book. Other dealers will assure you that the stamp makes no difference and that the book is a first edition, first state. This seems a personal decision on the part of the bookseller. James Musser, a counterculture specialist and owner of Skyline Books in California, has a definite opinion on the issue of the price stamp on Burroughs' Olympia Press titles. In a 9 August 2006 e-mail on the subject, he clarified the matter:

> When dealers say "second state" that infers later chronologically and in the case of *Naked Lunch* there is no later state since all first edition copies were virtually identical as they came off the press as part of the initial print run. For that reason I think "second state" is misleading.

If some copies had a certain *printed* price and other copies had a different printed price—then the price becomes an issue point because there was a change during the course of the print run—but for me the after-the-fact ink stamp is not a valid issue point since there are no printed changes to the book and the printing plates were not modified. Naturally, I agree that it is an aesthetic point and if I had a copy of each in my hands I would choose the unstamped one too.

To me, the stamp makes a big difference. The stamp compromises the beauty of the book. The wrapper does not look as clean to me. It tarnishes the holy relic. I would be willing to pay more for a copy without the stamp. I think many collectors would agree.

The Olympia Press *Naked Lunch* holds a special place on any book collector's bookshelf. Before *Naked Lunch* ever saw print in July 1959, the book was in high demand by a variety of readers of different tastes. Some readers were willing to break the law to possess a copy. The book rewarded those readers, becoming an experience that could change your consciousness and propel you into a fascinating underworld. Hundreds of copies have survived over the years. Many have reached the rare-book market at this moment. A few even trickle unknown to the shelves of used bookstores. Those are the real scores. Be warned: the book was much thumbed, much debated over coffee and cigarettes, much passed from hand to hand with syringes and joints. So a mint copy of *Naked Lunch* is, like junk, "the ideal product [. . .] the ultimate merchandise. No sales talk necessary. The client will crawl through a sewer and beg to buy" (201). Yet, there is nothing like the high of the initial purchase and the feeling of placing the Olympia Press *Naked Lunch* on your bookshelf. This is the closest I will ever get to the sensation of junk in the mainline. The price is steep, but like any object that arouses great passion and desire, it pays you back for a lifetime.

Works Cited

Burroughs, William. *The Dead Star*. San Francisco: Nova Broadcast, 1969.

——. "Excerpt from Pantapon Rose." *Semina* 4 (1959).

——. *Junkie*. London: Digit, 1957.

——. "Letter from a Master Addict to Dangerous Drugs." *British Journal of Addiction* 53, no. 2 (January 1957): 119–31.

——. *The Letters of William S. Burroughs, 1945–1959*. Edited by Oliver Harris. New York: Penguin, 1993.

——. *The Naked Lunch*. Paris: Olympia, 1959.

Ciardi, John. "The Book Burners and Sweet Sixteen." *Saturday Review*, 27 June 1959, 22, 30.

Ginsberg, Allen. *Howl and Other Poems*. San Francisco: City Lights, 1956.

Grauerholz, James. Introduction. In *Interzone*, by William S. Burroughs, ix–xxiii. Edited by Grauerholz. New York: Viking 1989.

Grauerholz, James, and Barry Miles. Editors' Note. In *Naked Lunch: The Restored Text*, by William S. Burroughs, 233–48. Edited by Grauerholz and Miles. New York: Grove, 2003.

Harris, Oliver. *William Burroughs and the Secret of Fascination*. Carbondale: Southern Illinois UP, 2003.

Maynard, Joe, and Barry Miles. *William S. Burroughs: A Bibliography, 1953–1973*. Charlottesville: UP of Virginia, 1978.

Popkin, Henry. "The Famous and Infamous Wares of Monsieur Girodias." *New York Times*, 17 April 1960, 4, book review section.

Naked Lunch: The Cover Story

polina **MACKAY**

It is only shallow people who do not judge by appearances.
—Oscar Wilde, *The Picture of Dorian Gray*

Proverbially, one is not meant to judge a book by its cover. Yet, publishers, editors, and writers go to great lengths to negotiate its precise parameters. Most people would not admit to buying a book for the cover, but we operate in a world that values first impressions. The *Observer*'s Rachel Cook in her article, "Allow Us to Judge a Book by Its Cover," comments, "It is pretty difficult not to get attached to certain covers, nor to resist their siren call through the fluorescent wastelands of Borders and Waterstones." In the case of *Naked Lunch*, always preceded by its reputation, could the dust jacket have anything to do with buying figures or with its reception? Does the cover of the first British publication (Calder, 1964), which features a monochrome picture of Burroughs' face with red, piercing eyes, attract or repel the consumer? Does the 2004 Spanish publication, which attempts to capture something of *Naked Lunch*'s sexual themes with the image of a fork dangling over a penis, lure in or scare away the Catalan-speaking reader?[1]

Many critics, including myself,[2] have argued that Burroughs' work assaults authorial ownership, mirrored in his claim in the introduction to *Naked Lunch* that he has "no precise memory of writing [it]" (199). The book's last section addresses this lack of authorial mastery in disorganized prose that aims to disrupt an already unstable narrative: "'Possession' they call it. [. . .] As if I was usually there but subject to goof now and again. [. . .] This book spill off the page in all directions" (184, 191). Another significant characteristic of this section is the repetition of "I." Even this does not suggest some superficial authorial control as the narrating I is as unhinged as its story. It mutates from "a recording instrument" to an absent entity ("*I am never here*") to a limited presence ("I am always somewhere *Outside*") and so forth (185). Simply, these literary strategies proffer a shape-shifting text that might collapse into meaninglessness at any moment.

Although the above interpretation of *Naked Lunch* is valid, there is a problem with this approach particularly in terms of the metanarrative of Burroughs' book. As Oliver Harris points out in a recent essay on *The Yage Letters*, this interpretive criticism draws on fables surrounding *Naked Lunch*, such as Burroughs' claim that he does not remember writing it. What is needed instead is a reassessment of the manuscript's history; as Harris argues, "recovering the original circumstances of publication is essential if Burroughs criticism is to undo what amounts to the repression of his oeuvre's richly complex textual history." In the place of interpretive inaccuracies, Harris offers a Social Text–theory analysis: "This theoretical model opens up descriptive potentials by bringing new material objects within the frame of analysis (physical features of the text, multiple states, etc.), as the basis for further critical interpretation" (par. 8). One such feature that deserves similar treatment, I argue, is the book's cover.

If a meaningful discussion of covers is to take place, we must reposition the literary text in culture. If one accepts that covers and other paratextual fences, such as introductions and appendixes, are part of the text's material history, then one must also be prepared to treat the book as an object. As such, it has a place on a shelf, it decorates coffee tables, acts as a shield from the world on the train. In each case, the cover makes a statement about intellectual curiosity and about taste. By extension, covers are complex manifestations of a culture's aesthetic choices. As Ned Drew and Paul Sternberger argue:

> In retrospect, the most intelligently designed covers of American books recall particular moments in our cultural memory. The designs conjure up associations of our personal and collective encounters with the groundbreaking intellectual expressions of our times. They define what we were, what we hoped to be, and sometimes, what we have become. (8–9)

Alan Powers also argues that covers are modern art forms that have impacted greatly on modern fiction including the successful launch of publishing houses such as Penguin.[3] Covers become pioneering tools for new ideas, foregrounding tendencies such as the postmodern attention to parody and metafictional awareness. Many of the *Naked Lunch* designs respond to these trends. As shown here, they also illuminate Burroughs' respect for collaborations and his interest in the representation of the author.

The first *Naked Lunch* cover of note is of course the 1959 Olympia Press publication, which was designed by Burroughs himself. In July 1959, he wrote to Ginsberg about his involvement in the book's production:

> I had exactly ten days to prepare the MS. for the printers. [. . .] Realize that in the last month I have edited the entire MS., corrected the galley-proofs, and the final proofs, and designed a cover, and the book is rolling off the presses right now. (*Letters*, 418)

Reflecting Burroughs' interest in many forms of writing and representation, the Olympia cover features calligraphic markings that would have been familiar to his peers at the time, as a page of similar drawings also appeared in episode 9 of "Ten Episodes from *Naked Lunch*" in *Big Table* in 1959 (132). The Olympia jacket contains six lines of glyphs with each line consisting of four and five symbols alternately. The backdrop is divided into two columns of two different colors with the left column in lilac, containing the author's name on the top left corner and the title on the lower left. These words are partially superimposed on the calligraphy, appearing both behind and in front of the glyphs, suggesting that the two are meant to be seen as intertwined and thus of equal importance.

If we compare the glyphs to East Asian calligraphy, such as *kanji* (Japanese) and *hanja* (Korean), the closest match is the Chinese cursive script.[4] Both seem to have been written without lifting the pen, which advocates a degree of spontaneity in this form. In this context, Burroughs' cover implies, or rather promises, that the writing inside will be equally free-flowing. This links *Naked Lunch* to what one might call Beat philosophy as expressed in the nonfiction writings of Jack Kerouac.[5] Burroughs' cover responds to this Eastern, zen Buddhist discourse by offering a visual manifestation of its main parameters in a series of seemingly spontaneous, sketchy, and loose drawings.

By 1960, however, Burroughs began to turn away from his Beat past and focused on new relationships and collaborations. The most significant of these was his work with Brion Gysin to whom Burroughs owed his interest in calligraphic drawings. In his letter to Irving Rosenthal of 20 July 1960, Burroughs talks of the pending 1962 Grove edition of *Naked Lunch*: "If illustrations are used (And I think excellent idea) they should be presented with drawings from Brion Gysin since my drawings were derived from his.

[. . .] Certainly I could not use my drawings alone without acknowledging their derivation from Gysin" (in *Naked Lunch,* 249–50). In this context, the calligraphy on the Olympia cover, besides the Beat look, also signals Burroughs' turn to the cut-ups and anticipates his next two, collaborative publications, *Minutes to Go* (1960) and *The Exterminator* (1960), both of which featured cover calligraphy by Gysin.

The first American edition of *Naked Lunch* takes us to a different terrain of the book's history. The Grove publication of 1962 was the first to include Burroughs' "Deposition: Testimony Concerning a Sickness" and an appendix containing his 1956 "Letter from a Master Addict to Dangerous Drugs." These additions were designed to ease the censor but have since become essential components of the narrative of *Naked Lunch,* appearing in most subsequent publications. The 1962 cover features the blurred images of a fork, a pair of glasses, a typewriter, and shadows. The cover, therefore, combines literal implements of vision and writing—glasses and typewriter—with the symbolic fork that is invoked by Burroughs in relation to the title *Naked Lunch,* defined as "a frozen moment when everyone sees what is on the end of every fork" (199). Possibly, this subtle rather than sensational treatment was the result of a marketing decision made by Grove Press, which must have decided not to exasperate the censor at a time when the owner, Barney Rosset, was involved in a series of serious lawsuits for the press's publication of Miller's *Tropic of Cancer* in 1961.

The first American publication after the censorship trials concluded was the 1966 Grove edition, which included court transcripts.[6] The designer of this cover is not noted. However, the speed with which it was rushed out and the comparative simplicity of the cover, which is particularly visible if one sees this in light of the Olympia version, makes it unlikely that it was designed by anyone other than Grove's in-house team. It reprints Norman Mailer's endorsement of Burroughs as an American genius, accompanied by the statement that the edition comes "WITH MASSACHUSETTS SUPREME COURT DECISION AND EXCERPTS FROM THE BOSTON TRIAL." The manner in which this information is related to the gazing consumer is intriguing. The borders around the statement make it look like an awarded certificate, which acts both as a mock stamp of official approval and as a sign of the authenticity and quality of the product. This "certificate" has a further function. Note the cover within a cover, a tilted image suggesting that books contain within their borders their own reproduction and advertisement. This other framed book introduces the possibility that the novel within might not fit perfectly with the image on the cover. Crucially, the "certificate" of officialdom overlaps these borders as if it were the glue that held the two potentially contradictory texts together. Its central position in a narrative that is so consciously aware of the significance of the branding of literature illuminates the fact that the way in which a text is repackaged and sold is closely linked to the history of its legitimization and its moment of entry into mainstream culture.

This "authorization" of the novel was followed by a number of covers that appeal to the biographical "authority" of the author, for the image that appears regularly on the front covers is that of Burroughs himself, either in photographic form or in various mutations.[7] Perhaps the most famous example of this approach is the first U.K. publication (Calder 1964), which features an image credited to Ian Sommerville. Although barely recognizable, this is actually part of a photomontage—similar to the one used on the cover of the first edition of *The Ticket That Exploded* (1962)—superimposed over Burroughs' face in monochrome with demonic red eyes. In the first instance, the eyes defamiliarize Burroughs, in that they make him look unearthly and possessed. The face, which lacks a background and other features such as hair, appears as a cut-out, inviting us to imagine a new framework. Because the image is obviously decontextualized, the cut-out's untold history is never really silenced, becoming part of the new narrative that this cover communicates, namely that of a demonized authorial figure whose anxieties haunt this text. A similar version of this visage is repeated in the popular 1974 Corgi publication that features one quarter of a face, hence asking us to imagine the rest. This process of recycling the dispossessed face or mask in the promotion of *Naked Lunch* suggests episodes in the ongoing metanarrative of the book. At the same time, the history of a book's cover design is usually known only to specialists, so that most readers of *Naked Lunch* remain unaware of the place that their particular copy holds in the larger picture.

Many publications of *Naked Lunch* place Burroughs on the front cover. The Russian 2003 translation, for example, has a close-up picture of his wrinkled face with eyes closed and a shadow across the left side. The face resembles a death mask and creates a powerfully elegiac mood. Similarly, one of the latest translations, the Italian publication of 2006, shows Burroughs in late middle age with shadows running across his face. These covers feed into the Burroughs myth as an encompassing presence that is already uncannily absent. This is why many feature images of faces (in many cases resembling Burroughs' own) that are reappropriations of the human face bordering on the grotesque. One such example is the 1986 U.K. Paladin publication, which shows a face whose mouth is distorted in a scream of horror. Echoing Munch's painting, this scream expresses suffering and makes the human *monstrous*. The likeness of such images to Burroughs implies the problematics of identity for the author.

This assessment of the author's presence on the cover is not as distinct from the book's literary history as it might originally seem. The cover's narrative positions *Naked Lunch* as a personal story told in a confessional mode. One might expect the protagonist in the text to be a damaged junky who attempts to beat addiction. His psyche is restored in the end, an act with metanarrative dimensions as many editions are framed by Burroughs' introduction, the "Deposition," and the appendix from the *British Journal of Addiction* that charts his rehabilitation progress. This story, to which the covers contribute, has two interrelated effects. The first one renders *Naked Lunch* as the text that responds to *Junky* which suggests a thematic continuity to Burroughs' work that is not there in such a simplistic way.[8] The second consequence of having Burroughs on the cover is the reintroduction of the prospect of authorial control.

The disappearing author who is never fully gone instigates a carefully orchestrated intimacy with the reader. This aspect of the novel, coupled with its notorious reputation as the Beat book that bares all, is responsible for its global success. *Naked Lunch* is translated into several languages, including Czech, Japanese, and Turkish. Almost all use different covers that, like the British and American publications already discussed, respond to aesthetic and market choices of a given culture. Attention to these covers foregrounds the material existence of *Naked Lunch* in multiple contexts of history, geography, and culture. The covers of foreign editions challenge us to recontextualize the work as we try to imagine the experience of reading in another language, in a different culture.

The cover of the first Turkish translation of the novel, published in 1998, employs a black-and-white photograph of the author taken at his home in Lawrence, Kansas. Burroughs stands beside a rocking chair, his back to the camera, looking at the black, faceless silhouette of a hatted figure on a screen door. This shadow is a reproduction of one of Burroughs' self-portraits as well as a lookalike of the *noir*-ish plywood cut-outs that he used in his shotgun paintings. In contrast to his larger-than-life double, who looks back on his creator in a cool, sinister pose, Burroughs is forced to depend upon a cane, signifying his age and the deterioration of the physical body. It is a haunting confrontation between the creator and the icon that he has fashioned. In his last full-length novel, *The Western Lands* (1987), Burroughs' protagonist and alter-ego, an old writer named William Seward Hall, is a flawed imitation of the legendary writer who once wrote *Naked Lunch*. The Turkish cover captures the poignancy of this nostalgic, elegiac confrontation between iconicity and physical corrosion, between the mortal man and the legendary author.

Is Burroughs' shadow image already inside the room or behind the screen door, awaiting entry? Is this doppelganger a mere simulacrum or a threatening entity? *Naked Lunch* contains a number of instances of misrecognition of the self, such as the moment when the writer looks up to find himself "reading to the mirror as always" and comments, "Anyone who has ever looked into a mirror knows what this crime is and what it means in terms of lost control when the reflection no longer obeys" (175). Doubles are uncanny and threaten our notions of identity, and the Turkish cover illuminates the central position that this idea holds in Burroughs' work. It also forces us into sharing his viewpoint, because our gaze at the double matches that of Burroughs himself, so that the cover aligns us with Burroughs' confrontation with his own dark image and with the cultural memory constructed around *Naked Lunch*. Fame is a doppelganger, independent and yet inseparable from the creator, fashioning his image, even from beyond the grave.

As long as *Naked Lunch* sells, new covers will be produced. One of the latest front covers, the 2005 U.S. Harper (a paperback edition of the 2003 restored text), features above the suited (in)human figure wild, hand-drawn lettering that seems to be only barely contained by the borders of the cover. This evokes the novel's definition of itself as a text that "spill off the page" (191), as the product of a consciousness with no limits. The lettering resembles graffiti and in this sense deliberately invokes its long-standing status as the means of expression of political activists, nonconformists, and youth cultures. Graffiti is nearly always created on public property—on back walls and railway sidings—advocating the view that art is changeable and transitory. The graffiti-like lettering on this cover is similarly suggestive of the temporariness and immediacy of writing, purposely at odds with the typical perception that this book is a timeless classic.

Cover production tells an aesthetic story; it is also a product of commercial, marketing, and advertising mechanisms which concern the book as a branded commodity that needs to be continuously repackaged. Of course, treating texts as products strengthens the status of the novel as an aesthetic object and a symbol of one's consumerist choices. Such an interpretation of *Naked Lunch* does not go against Burroughs' own image-making. The man who appeared in ads, movies, and concerts and was interviewed by all media was always out in the marketplace.

Notes

1. Many Burroughs covers have been collected by Dave Moore and can be found at http://www.books.rack111.com/burroughs-books/index.html (accessed October 2008).

2. See "Authorship in the Writings and Films of William S. Burroughs" in *Authorship in Context: From the Theoretical to the Material,* edited by Kyriaki Hadjiafxendi and Polina Mackay (Basingstoke, UK: Palgrave, 2007), 111–28.

3. For a history of Penguin cover design see Phil Baines, *Penguin by Design: A Cover Story, 1935–2005* (London: Allen Lane, 2005).

4. See John Stevens, *Sacred Calligraphy of the East* (London: Shambhala, 1995), chaps. 1 and 2.

5. A good example of Kerouac's nonfiction writing in which these ideas are developed is "Essentials of Spontaneous Prose" in *Evergreen Review* 11:6 (Summer 1958), 72–73.

6. "The Boston Trial of Naked Lunch" was initially published in *Evergreen Review* (June 1965), 40–49, 87–88.

7. This is by no means universal. Indeed, the Grove restored hardback edition of 2003 features text on the front cover and a silhouette of Burroughs at the back.

8. Harris has rightly challenged this hermeneutic continuity often used as an over-riding principle to read *Junky* and *Naked Lunch*. For a full analysis that reassesses the material history of the two texts, particularly in light of Burroughs' letter writing, see *William Burroughs and the Secret of Fascination* (Carbondale: Southern Illinois UP, 2003), 46–77 and 179–243.

Works Cited

Burroughs, William S. *Junky*. New York: Penguin, 1977.

———. *The Letters of William S. Burroughs, 1945-1959*. Edited by Oliver Harris. New York: Viking, 1993.

———. *The Naked Lunch*. Paris: Olympia, 1959.

———. *Naked Lunch*. New York: Grove, 1962.

———. *Naked Lunch*. London: Calder, 1964.

———. *Naked Lunch*. New York: Grove, 1966.

———. *Naked Lunch*. London: Corgi, 1974.

———. *Naked Lunch*. London: Paladin, 1986.

———. *Naked Lunch*. London: Flamingo, 1993.

———. *Çıplak Şölen*. Translated by Ucel Birlik. Istanbul: Altikirkbes Yayin, 1998.

———. *Голый завтрак*. Translated by Victor Kogan. Moscow: Simpozium, 2003.

———. *El Almuerzo Desnudo*. Translated by Martin Lendinez. Barcelona: Anagrama, 2004.

———. *Naked Lunch*. New York: Harper, 2005.

———. *Pasto Nudo*. Translated by Franca Cavagnoli. Collana, Italy: Gli Adelphi, 2006.

———. "Ten Episodes from *Naked Lunch*." *Big Table* 1 (Spring 1959): 79–137.

———. *The Western Lands*. London: Penguin, 1987.

Burroughs, William S., Brion Gysin, Sinclair Beiles, and Gregory Corso. *Minutes to Go*. Paris: Two Cities, 1960.

Cook, Rachel. "Allow Us to Judge a Book by Its Cover." *Observer*, 16 April 2006.

Drew, Ned, and Paul Sternberger. *By Its Cover: Modern American Book Cover Design*. New York: Princeton Architectural, 2005.

Harris, Oliver. "Not Burroughs' Final Fix: Materializing *The Yage Letters*." *Postmodern Culture* 16, no. 2 (January 2006). http://muse.jhu.edu/login?uri=/journals/postmodern_culture/v016/16.2harris.html (accessed 19 October 2008).

Powers, Alan. *Front Cover: Great Book Jackets and Cover Design*. London: Mitchell Beazley, 2001.

Wilde, Oscar. *The Picture of Dorian Gray*. Oxford: Oxford UP, 1998.

dossier FOUR
ian MACFADYEN

Files Comprising: Money And How It Got That Way, The Big Con, Weaponry, Hang On To A Dream, Solitary, Mugwumps, Untouchable, Agent Provocateur, Insectoid, Bang-utot And The Pure Quill, Showtime, Head West, The County Clerk And Sam Hose, Signs Following, Satire, Progenitor, The Terminal Reprise.

Money And How It Got That Way

A rich man flips a coin to the cold-kicking monstrous addict rolling in filth, like a George Grosz caricature or a Brechtian critique of capitalism—"Mr. Rich-and-Vulgar chews his Havana lewd and nasty" (67). It's always business as usual in *Naked Lunch*, whatever other shit is going down. Welcome to the black market place where you can get death at cost, wholesale slaughter at wholesale. Also available for money is money itself, the perfect Dalinian fashion statement, a suit of bank notes to keep you warm while you wait for the little baby notes to hatch into mature, negotiable currency.

The Big Con

David Maurer in his study of the confidence man describes "the great number of marks which are roped on trains" (99). But when Lee comes on to the advertising-exec-type fruit on the uptown A train, captivating him with his criminal lingo, he is also blowing his cover—as Maurer points out, to speak the argot in public to the uninitiated is crazy, it's just not done. So why does Lee reveal himself in this way? Because Lee is actually addressing the reader (as the parenthetical, editorial asides indicate). Lee's account of catnipping the mark is in fact the initiation of the reader into Burroughs' underworld and constitutes a hipster's linguistic primer. "'Thanks, kid [. . .] I can see you're one of our own'" (4). But the product being pushed in this case, the book *Naked Lunch* itself, is not fugazzy for some patsy, it's the real deal, and a steal at the price.

Weaponry

Naked Lunch's arsenal is filled with every conceivable and unimaginable weapon of torture, maiming, mutilation, and killing—an old rusty six-shooter, voodoo dolls, a stock probe, hanging nooses, teeth, smother mattresses, flamethrowers, a hot shot, electric drills, barbed wire and fire, psychic jiu-jitsu, scalpels, hara-kiri knives, stones, iron claws, clubs, razor, acids, axes, bicycle pumps, a two-man surgical saw, sting rays and sharks and electric eels thrown in a swimming pool, a toilet plunger, a crystal skull, a cutlass, curare, well-lubricated short arms, a pitchfork, shotgun, burning gasoline, switchblade, an old bullfighter's sword, machineguns, grenades, a red velvet curtain cord, meat cleavers, hog castrators . . . And then the atomic bomb, the virus, and the very words which Burroughs has written.

Hang On To A Dream

In 1917, Edith Wharton could still praise the beauty of Tangier's Arab streets while cursing the tourists—she excepted herself, naturally—who were destroying the perfect picture of place. Adventure and mystery lay off the map, in the desert wastes and the roadless passes of the Atlas. Wharton mourned "the romantic and ruinous Morocco of yesterday" and predicted that soon "even the mysterious autochthones of the Atlas will have folded their tents and silently stolen away" (11). Ten years later, she admitted that her memoir of Morocco had been superseded by Ricard's *Blue Guide*, by new roads opening up the land for tourists—while paradoxically closing it down—and by the protectorate's *Ce qu'il faut savoir du Maroc* with its "full statistics on the economic resources of the country" (15). And, yet, paradoxically, she maintained that these European conveniences and intrusions could not spoil the wonder of a country which she compared to an illuminated manuscript, as if she could not give up the dream of exoticism and purity despite her recognition of the signs—the magic carpet replaced by a military transport. Burroughs, Gysin, and Bowles all bought into this dream, and like Wharton felt elegiac for what they had missed. The place was eternal, but the time was already and always terminally gone. Now the Med Harbor container port has opened 30 km east of Tangier, "with a roll-on-roll-off ferry terminal for five million passengers, a million cars and half a million trucks a year. [. . .] That old layabout William Burroughs must be turning in his grave" (Cook, 060). Significantly, the author of that statement notes the attractive reduction in corporation tax and the very low wages paid to workers.

Solitary

During the 1950s, there were fifty thousand expats stranded or hiding out or passing through Tangier, and the role of the explorer which Burroughs had played out for real in South America, even though he parodied the role in his letters, was no longer possible. The sense of the *other* lay elsewhere—in the adventure of writing, the solitary exploration of the psyche as a primeval jungle, threatening yet fascinating and inviting because terra incognita was the dreamed-of destination, the final place. And in a dark alley, lit by a feeble, flickering, fluorescent sign, behind a grilled doorway centuries old, the last distressed reel of von Sternberg's *Morocco* just played out to an empty house forever.

Mugwumps

Mugwump was the term given to Republicans who supported Grover Cleveland, a Democrat, in the 1884 presidential election. Derived from the dialect of the Algonquian Native Americans of Massachusetts, the term signifies an underling who behaves like a panjandrum—a totally untrustworthy and self-important fence sitter, a professional turncoat. Burroughs uses the expression to characterize treacherous, unctuous creatures which slowly undulate and ooze and secrete, caress and sidle and goose, their *mug* on one side, their *wump* on the other. The fluid metabolism and syrup-smooth actions of the mugwumps reveal their concupiscence for all *sweet things* and their absolute unscrupulousness. They have no principles, just as they have no armature, though their purple-blue lips conceal razor-sharp beaks, perfect for the evisceration of their own kind. They are slithery aficionados of the scaffold, and swift and sure with the noose.

Untouchable

Benway's dismissive attitude to the neurally damaged, "I don't hafta look at them is all" (29) is echoed by Sobera de la Flor, the Mexican murderer who says of the woman he has killed, "I don't hafta take that sound" (50), the same phrase later spoken by the immune fake Buddha who metabolizes his own junk. It is Sobera who provides as mitigation of his terrible and "pointless" crimes the adage *Son cosas de la vida* (50). But the police merely "upbraid" him for "blasting this cunt and taking the body to the Bar O Motel and fucking it" (50); just think of all the paperwork. Burroughs wrote in a letter from Lima in 1953 of a bar owner confronted by a lunatic—"The owner sat there picking his teeth. He showed neither contempt nor amusement nor sympathy. He just sat there picking a molar and occasionally taking the toothpick out and looking at the end of it" (*Yage*, 48). This blank, untouchable remoteness is replayed throughout the pandemonium and uproar of *Naked Lunch*. As in the case of the Sender—"Sooner or later he's got no feelings to send"—empathy requires a two-way exchange because "You can't have feelings alone" (137). The Sender is an antireceiver and is, therefore, "defined by negatives"; he's "a sucking emptiness" (140). Atrocities in *Naked Lunch* are perpetrated out of boredom or petulance, a yawning, nail-paring contempt for life: "Do it slow. He's give me a sick headache" (147). "We are not responsible" (186)—so nothing need ever again be suffered or felt.

Agent Provocateur

In James Salter's *A Sport and a Pastime* (1962), there is a brilliant evocation of the writer as secret agent: "I see myself as an agent provocateur or as a double agent, first on one side—that of truth—and then on the other, but between these, in the reversals, the sudden defections, one can easily forget allegiance entirely and feel only the deep, the profound joy of being beyond all codes, of being completely independent, criminal is the word. Like any agent, of course, I cannot divulge my sources. [. . .] I became obsessed with discovery, like the great detectives. I read every scrap of paper. I noted every detail. Some things, as I say, I saw, some discovered, some dreamed, and I can no longer differentiate between them. But my dreams are as important as anything I acquired by stealth. More important, because they are the intuitive in its purest state. Without them, facts are no more than a kind of debris, unstrung, like beads. The dreams are as true and manifest as the iron fences of France flashing black in the rain [. . .] I am the pursuer" (23).

This is Lee. This is Burroughs. This is *Naked Lunch*.

Insectoid

The horror of slithering and scuttling life-forms, the repellent reptilian and the insufferable insectoid, is allied to the creeping needle-nerve horrors of withdrawal, the slither of cold need, the poisonous threat of breath shut off, the injection of a venomous secretion, coke bugs on the neck. It's metamorphosis from Ovid to Kafka to Cronenberg. In *Naked Lunch*, the repetition of entomological horror is a form of self-torment, the exercise of a fearful fascination, like watching a giant centipede sink its razor barbs into your hand, injecting putrid matter into the deep wound—and feeling your own jaw methodically malaxating.

Bang-utot And The Pure Quill

Burroughs refers to Nils Larsen's 1955 article on the subject of Bang-utot, an examination of the mysterious deaths of migrant Filipinos in Hawaii, a phenomenon now known as Sudden Unexplained Death Syndrome. Burroughs also mentions a related article by Erle Stanley Gardner in *True Magazine*. This may be Gardner's "The Case of the Movie Murder," which mentions a man known as Walter or "Whitey" or "Slim" Kirby, whose body was discovered in a swamp west of Calexico in 1922. Had he died of exposure, starvation, a drug overdose, natural causes, or "was he killed by means only known to the underworld of the border?" Gardner's speculations about Kirby would surely have struck Burroughs: "The drugs of underworld commerce are greatly diluted. It becomes only necessary to deliver to an habitual drug user a dose of 'the pure quill' and the man, thinking he has his usual diluted dose, is conveniently removed from the scene of operations" (113). The linking of the symbolic instrument of the writer's art with a "hot shot" would indeed suggest that this death was, literally, *written*, both by Fate and the appropriately named Underworld.

Showtime

Lee's soliloquy in *Queer* delivered to an empty bar is now a group split-personality operation with stand-ins and stand-ups functioning in libidinous fictional congress, playing to an invisible audience of unknown readers to *Grand Guignol* effect. Blue monocle, eye-patch, owl glasses, black glasses, blue glasses, jeweller's glasses. High-society female drag—a diamond tiara, fur pieces, orchids. And then a filthy old naval uniform, a white trench coat, a southwester, a *djellaba*, a glen-plaid suit, mother-of-pearl opera glasses, a cutlass and Jolly Roger, a two-hundred-dollar cashmere jacket—it's all straight out of a costume trunk labelled "NAKED LUNCH BOX," and the final performance is a dress-rehearsal rag, scrimshank, improvised, haphazard, an amateur theatrical production with all the seams showing. It's the Prospero

Show, directed by the guy Vladimir Nabokov dubbed "The Dream Stage Manager."

Head West

From the Vigilante mugger to the Lone Ranger junkies, the carny Sheriff to the Cowboy in the Waldorf, *Naked Lunch* usurps Wild West film and pulp stereotypes—saloon brawls and shoot-outs, hanging parties and escapes to Mexico, reservations and borderlines, desperadoes and citizen rubes, desert suns and vultures, and not much place for women round these parts . . . These tropes have both a structural and philosophical significance, playing an instrumental role in the book's set action pieces, and fuelling its white shirt/black shirt, dime store Manichaeism.

The County Clerk And Sam Hose

Edmund White knew one just like him. "For squirming, sweaty, panicky hours he'd tell us his cursed nigger jokes, spitting tobacco into a cuspidor beside his rocking chair and drawing everything out at a snail's pace . . . " (36–37). Burroughs gets the character of the County Clerk exactly right, but he is a *type*, something less and other than an "individual." But that's how the talk gets around, through the gossip and bigotry which Faulkner described as a wind and a fire, that's how the business and the damage get done. Sam Hose, a young black man, was "burned alive in front of several thousand people, many of them Christians who had left their church services early to enjoy the spectacle. The ringleaders chained Hose to a tree, cut off his ears, poured kerosene on him, and then lit a match. When he finally stopped writhing, the crowd rushed forward and cut pieces from his smouldering body. When that was gone, they chopped up the tree he was chained to, and when that was gone, they attacked the chain itself. Later that day, spectators were spotted walking through town wearing pieces of bone and charred flesh. Hose's knuckles turned up at a local grocery store" (Junger, 66). And then they all sat around at their supper tables and on their porches and in their dooryards, and as the evening shadows lengthened, they . . . *reminisced.*

Signs Following

The infamous sign of the Sundown Town—"Nigger, Don't Let The Sun Set On You Here" (36)—does not exist in Interzone which embraces ethnic diversity because it's great for business. But a glut of injunctions—*"Urbanite Don't Let The Sun Set On You Here"* (142)—plaster the walls of Pigeon Hole, the backwater redneck town outside the Zone, warning off the perverted polyglot riffraff of the unlicensed, unbridled city beyond the swamplands, the prophetic human waste of global refugees who have only their naked lives to offer. This is the Frontier marker which still goes up in National Socialist graffiti form in parts of Texas and South Carolina: *"Get The Fuck Out Of The South"* . . . *"Democrat Don't Let The Sun Set On You Here"* . . .

Satire

Describing *Naked Lunch* as a satire is like crying "Fire!" while being immolated.

Progenitor

It's a book about carnival routines and ignorant cops, magic and mundanity, insects and an Old Chinaman, fake ethnography and the American vernacular, strange foodstuffs and osmotic cities, hermaphrodites and city clerks, La Cucaracha and The Great God Yottle. It's *The Circus of Dr. Lao* by Charles G. Finney, published in 1935.

The Terminal Reprise

Anticipating the severing and recontextualization of the cut-up technique, Burroughs reprises characters and scenes and lines at the end of the show, his actors taking their final bows as if the only possible conclusion is to present an entanglement of cut threads, a conglomeration of motifs, catch phrases and fragments—slivers of a smashed mirror reassembled into vitreous strata. Paradoxically, it may be the very impossibility of concluding which determines this attempt at précis and summation—it is the only *way out*. In my end is my beginning, and this goes on for as long as life itself until life itself suddenly STOPS.

The Book, the Movie, the Legend: *Naked Lunch* at 50

The reception of *Naked Lunch* is embedded in the legend of William S. Burroughs as transgressive artist. When *Naked Lunch* was first published in the United States in 1962 and in England in 1964, its reception was shaped by Burroughs' status as the shadowy guru of Allen Ginsberg and Jack Kerouac, both of whom had acknowledged his influence among their underground circle in the previously published *Howl* (1956) and *On the Road* (1957). The iconoclastic aura of the work was magnified by the initial publication in Paris in 1959 by a press well known for pornography and by U.S. censorship: *Naked Lunch* is the last work of literature in the United States to be censored by the post office, customs, and government (in the Commonwealth of Massachusetts). The successful legal battle and the praise of literary celebrities at the 1962 Edinburgh festival created a controversy that was continued in the polarized critical response following mainstream publication. Noteworthy and acrimonious exchanges went on for weeks in the *Times Literary Supplement* and the *New Republic*. Perhaps more than the works of Ginsberg, Kerouac, and other Beat writers, *Naked Lunch* presaged the cultural revolt of the 1960s and the divided political response to that era. The fact that the author was (in 1964) a fifty-year-old expatriate far removed from the burgeoning youth culture only contributed to his status as mythic outsider and stimulated readers' fantasies about his legendary life.

Upon his return to the United States in 1974, Burroughs' cult image evolved in response to continued experimentation in his work, public readings to youthful audiences, summer teaching at Naropa University, and his interaction with the punk and performance artist scene in New York City. In 1991, David Cronenberg, in his film entitled *Naked Lunch*, created a narrative about the writing of the book with its author romanticized and heterosexualized as the tortured genius, thereby encapsulating the novel within the biographical legend of bohemian artist-hero. By the time of his death, Burroughs' image as "literary outlaw"[1] was consolidated into a popular icon known by those who had never read his work, and the title *Naked Lunch* was merely a reference point, rather than a literary landmark. The obituaries in newspapers around the English-speaking world reiterated and reified a man known for a scandalous life and a scandalous book seen as one, exemplified by the *New York Times* headline: "William S. Burroughs, the Beat Writer Who Distilled His Raw Nightmare Life, Dies at 83."

The purpose of this essay is to direct attention away from the popular icon in order to review the scholarly criticism about *Naked Lunch* since Burroughs' death in 1997. The intention is not to provide a comprehensive, detailed overview but rather to focus on a few major trends and new developments, and this selectivity necessarily reflects the literary and textual biases of the author. Still, I found it impossible to ignore the impact of the film adaptation on contemporary understanding of the text and the history of its reception. Thus, this essay also includes the debate about Cronenberg's *Naked Lunch* and its relationship to the novel.

Contemporary criticism of *Naked Lunch* takes place within the larger context of a general critical consensus on Burroughs' status as a postmodern artist. As Robin Lydenberg and I observed in *William S. Burroughs at the Front: Critical Reception, 1959–1989,* postmodern Burroughs emerged in the scholarship of the 1980s when his work was used to clarify the distinction between modernism and postmodernism, and Burroughs was often seen as the postmodern writer *par excellence* (11). Twenty years later, the postmodernism of Burroughs is taken for granted by almost all Burroughs scholars. Allen Hibbard calls Burroughs the "quintessential postmodern writer" (*Conversations*, x); Richard Dellamora ironically refers to Burroughs as the patron saint of Po-Mo (163); and Marianne DeKoven identifies Burroughs' cut-ups as "quintessential postmodern pastiche" (119). The inclusion of Burroughs in the Norton *Anthology of Postmodern American Fiction* provides the final imprimatur. It should be noted, however, that American literary critics in general—as opposed to Burroughs critics—rarely give Burroughs a central role in postmodernism comparable to more frequently cited novelists such as John Barth, Thomas Pynchon, or Don DeLillo. Academe has been slow to incorporate Burroughs into mainstream criticism, especially during the 1960s and 1970s when postmodernism was being theorized and when writers such as Barth and Pynchon were seen as prominent exemplars, while Burroughs was then categorized as an "outlaw."

For most critics who identify Burroughs as a postmodern writer, it is taken for granted that, ipso facto, *Naked Lunch* is a postmodern work. Postmodernism has always been an unstable concept, and it appears that, as long as critics do not interrogate the theory or its application to *Naked Lunch* too closely, the label is generally accepted as convenient, while more careful scholars provide more-nuanced perspectives. For example, DeKoven distinguishes between *Naked Lunch* and the works that came afterward by calling *Naked Lunch* a work of "emerging" postmodernism, in that Burroughs employs the formal techniques of modernism while writing from within particular, situated subcultures and deploying elements of popular genre fiction that characterize postmodernism (110–11). She sees *Naked Lunch* as a case study of the "simultaneity of the modern and post-modern in 1960's texts" (112). One prominent Burroughs scholar rejects the postmodern label: Timothy S. Murphy categorizes Burroughs' work as an example of "amodernism," which he says contests postmodernism during the same period. Murphy defines amodernism as a "hybrid" position, critical of both modernism and postmodernism and committed to the belief that literature can have a social impact. (See Murphy, "Intersection Points" and *Wising Up the Marks*, 23-25.)

One of the effects of the critical convergence on postmodern Burroughs is a de-emphasis—even a marginalization—of *Naked Lunch* in the scholarly literature. Most of the scholarship on Burroughs since 1997 is focused on the cut-up novels of the 1960s or the trilogy of the 1980s and, to some extent, on his multimedia collaborations and broader influence on the arts. Also, in recent years, more research has been devoted to the fiction that preceded *Naked Lunch*: *Junky*, *Queer*, and *The Yage Letters*. In other words, critics are examining the whole body of Burroughs' work, not one book that loomed large on the critical horizon in the 1960s and 1970s. In this context, *Naked Lunch* is seen as the culmination of Burroughs' Beat period or as a pivotal work based on the author's stylistic breakthrough with the montage structure but not part of the later fiction that captures contemporary critical attention—work that, as Allen Hibbard has so aptly observed, serves "as a ready, viable host to so many strains of the theory virus" ("Shift Coordinate Points," 27). Very few book chapters or articles in recent years are solely devoted to *Naked Lunch* or include an extended discussion; many important articles are devoted to other works.

Current theoretical perspectives have led not so much to new interpretations as to new preoccupations that highlight facets of *Naked Lunch* that were overshadowed in the early focus on addiction, morality, and existential revolt. Analysis of sexuality in *Naked Lunch* is prominent in current criticism, most notably in the books by Jamie Russell and Greg Mullins that draw on queer studies. Russell discusses *Naked Lunch* in *Queer Burroughs* as an attack on the dominant culture's regulation of identity and marginal sexualities. He historicizes the work within the 1950s discourse about sexualities and sees *Naked Lunch* as the final work of Burroughs' Beat period. Greg Mullins' discussion of *Naked Lunch* in *Colonial Affairs: Bowles, Burroughs, and Chester Write Tangier* is situated in a chronological, biographical, psychosexual analysis of several works charting Burroughs' evolving understanding of sexuality and identity. For Mullins, *Naked Lunch* is the work in which Burroughs realizes that sexuality and subjectivity are constrained not only by external controls but by discourse (79).

A second major theme in recent criticism of *Naked Lunch* is the analysis of power and control systems. One of Oliver Harris' major arguments in *William Burroughs and the Secret of Fascination* is that *Naked Lunch* is Burroughs' analysis of power and his relationship to it; that is, his complicity in all he opposes, which is the source of contrary readings of the text. Timothy S. Murphy, in *Wising Up the Marks: The Amodern William Burroughs,* discusses *Naked Lunch* within his larger thesis about Burroughs' work as a critique of the social organization of late capitalism and the logic of representation and textuality that supports it. Andrew Pepper states that *Naked Lunch* foreshadows a Foucauldian analysis of the power of the state. Several critics see in the novel a specific critique of post–World War II technologies of power. Timothy Melley, for example, says that *Naked Lunch* illustrates "agency panic," a kind of postwar paranoia regarding the subordination of the individual to the technology and communication systems of large organizations, which is reflected in discourse about addiction and the war on drugs. Joseph McNicholas points to the public relations techniques of 1950s corporate culture that *Naked Lunch* both mirrors and satirizes. Jonathan Paul Eburne sees *Naked Lunch* as a response to Cold War containment and identity politics. At the same time, the contributors to Davis Schneiderman and Philip Walsh's 2004 collection of essays see Burroughs as a prescient critic of globalization in its contemporary manifestations. Two essays in this collection—by Dennis McDaniel and Katharine Streip—devote significant attention to *Naked Lunch,* and both discuss how Burroughs' aesthetic strategies in *Naked Lunch* model resistance to globalization's control mechanisms.

A new development in criticism devoted to the novel is the textual analysis of the writing, editing, and publication of the work and of the textual variants. Harris has led the way with his edition of Burroughs' letters in 1993 and the textual analysis of *Naked Lunch* in *Fascination*, providing many new insights about Burroughs' complicity with control (as noted above) and his breakthrough as a writer by accepting a fragmentary structure for *Naked Lunch*. Carol Loranger proposes a textual analysis of versions of *Naked Lunch* and its paratexts, pointing toward a postmodern edition that would be "a fully interactive, continually augmented, electronic edition" (14). Her essay reveals that a study of *Naked Lunch*'s history as a text is also a study of legend, aura, narrative voices and multiple identities, intertextuality, and reader response, concluding that "*Naked Lunch*'s enduring appeal arises in large part from its instability, its openness to multiple and alternative readings and its protean ability to seem always to be addressing the addictions and oppressions of today" (12). Harris's essay on the material history of *The Yage Letters* ("Not Burroughs' Final Fix"), which includes some discussion of *Naked Lunch* and a reply to Loranger's essay, is an attempt to theorize this new Burroughs scholarship in terms of Social Text theory.

The other new development in criticism of *Naked Lunch* consists of the responses to the text that William Burroughs didn't write: David Cronenberg's 1991 film. As has been pointed out by many, the film is not an adaptation of the book but rather a movie about the man who wrote *Naked Lunch* told in the form of the standard modernist narrative of artistic genius: the transgressive artist redeems himself through art. Cronenberg retells the legend and incorporates passages from *Naked Lunch* as decontextualized shards recited by the characters in the film. The fragmentary structure of the novel is replaced by a normalizing and familiar narrative, the sexuality is heteronormalized, and fantastic beings (Mugwumps) are transformed into mechanical puppets. In this context, gone is the savage social and political satire, and, for financial and distributive reasons, the unfilmable grotesque scenes of human sex and violence and bodily disintegration are replaced by more palatable (because obviously unreal) nonhuman monsters. At the same time, the movie employs a medley of Burroughsian themes and images that draw from the larger body of his work, at times effectively transposing Burroughs' vision into another medium. Some of Cronenberg's innovations not found in the novel—addiction to bug powder and insect typewriters, for example—fuse his sensibilities with Burroughs'. The jazz soundtrack by Ornette Coleman captures the jazzy structure of the novel, the 1950s cool of the film's setting in 1953, and the artistic parallel between Coleman's free jazz and *Naked Lunch*'s montage of improvisational routines.

Comments by both Cronenberg and Burroughs on the film are instructive. Cronenberg explains his intentions, "It was obvious, for both artistic and practical reasons, I was going to have to do my own version of *Naked Lunch*—a fusion of my own writing with Burroughs's. [. . .] The film has to be something that still deserves to be called *Naked Lunch*, accurately reflecting some of the tone of Burroughs, what his life stands for, and what his work has been—a combination of Burroughsian material but put into a structure that's not very Burroughsian. That was basically my approach" (qtd. in Emery and Silverberg, 57, 65). In his introduction to Ira Silverberg's book on *The Making of Naked Lunch*, Burroughs observed, "David's script is very true to his own Muse as a filmmaker" and praised him for creating a "masterful thriller" from elements of *Naked Lunch* and other works (14). He calls the film "all in all a most admissible interpretation" of the novel and of its protagonist Bill Lee, while expressing his dismay at the portrayal of Bill Lee's shooting of his wife (not in the novel but a fictionalized version of the most notorious event in Burroughs' life) and the odd conversion of Bill Lee into a heterosexual whose sexual experiences with men are treated as an "unwelcome accident" of the plot (14). Finally, Burroughs draws a clear line between the film and the book by quoting Raymond Chandler on the films made of his novels: "Hollywood hasn't done anything to them. They're still right there, on the shelf" (15). These observations by Cronenberg and Burroughs identify the key questions raised by the movie: Does it deserve to be called *Naked Lunch*? Whose psychology is reflected in the narrative? Who or what is served by reiterating the artist-legend?

Some critics have reacted positively to Cronenberg's appropriation of Burroughs' legend and themes. Mark Blagrave sees the film as a "transformative" adaptation—one that creates a parallel work in which Cronenberg's visual motifs effectively replace Burroughs' verbal motifs (e.g., guns, writing, sex) and produces "the essence of Burroughs's novel: its ambivalent relationship with the reader/audience," who is addressed as both distanced from and participant in the bizarre world of Interzone (53–54). Similarly, Jonathan Rosenbaum states that "Cronenberg's approach is an absorption of certain principles and texts from Burroughs into the filmmaker's particular cosmology and style. The resulting portrait [. . .] is [. . .] some mysterious composite, an overlap and/or interface of these two personalities" (218–19).

Other critics take Cronenberg to task for depoliticizing, dehistoricizing, and deradicalizing Burroughs' work. Timothy S. Murphy (in "William Burroughs between Indifference and Revalorization") charges Cronenberg with aestheticizing the radical political impact of *Naked Lunch* by transforming a discontinuous novel into the linear *Bildungsroman* of the Romantic artist cult, which is easily recuperated by capitalist commodification of celebrity; whereas *Naked Lunch,* like all of Burroughs' texts, has the potential of radical critique and the creation of new individual and collective subjectivities. Richard Dellamora criticizes Cronenberg's artist narrative for dehistoricizing Burroughs' biography, normalizing his extreme art, and for stereotyping female characters as Woman in the heterosexual psychological narrative. He does point out, however, that one important parallel between Cronenberg's and Burroughs' work is that both explore the play of male and female difference within masculinity. Nicholas Zurbrugg objects to the "Disneyfication" of *Naked Lunch* through special effects such as the Mugwump puppets; the "puritanical" omission of vitriolic humor, social satire, and burlesque routines; and the conventionality of the biographical narrative. Both Dellamora and William Beard perceptively argue that Cronenberg's transformation of *Naked Lunch* into a movie about the process of artistic creation employing the standard modernist narrative of artistic genius reflects Cronenberg's psychology and aesthetics rather than Burroughs', and both provide extensive psychoanalytic analysis of the movie within the context of Cronenberg's oeuvre. For Beard, it is Cronenberg, not Burroughs, who sees art/writing as a reenactment of a crime or the return of the repressed original sin (829). And Beard, Zurbrugg, and Rosenbaum all point out that Cronenberg's narrative is a tragic or elegiac one ending in loss and despair, in contrast to the tone of Burroughs' work, which I would describe as exuberantly defiant, funny, and empowering.

Overall, the criticism of Cronenberg's *Naked Lunch* is lively, intelligent, and illuminating about both the film and the novel, and this reader found these essays to be more engaging than much of the other Burroughs criticism published since 1997. The film criticism foregrounds two aspects of *Naked Lunch* criticism that have been present from the beginning. Conflicting interpretations and judgments about Cronenberg's *Naked Lunch* eerily repeat the polarized reception and contradictory interpretations of the novel, as if—even in its absence—the unsettling power and undecidability of *Naked Lunch* break through the film's normalizing strategies. The film criticism also foregrounds the continuing fascination of the Burroughs legend, which constantly threatens to usurp the biography and the work with a simulacrum of both.

At this point, the film has entered scholarly discourse, and, at least for the foreseeable future, critics must now contend with two works entitled *Naked Lunch* and their ambiguous relationship. The reframing of *Naked Lunch* by yet another paratext may yield positive results for Burroughs criticism in the long run. The film forces readers to define what kind of fiction the book is in its structure, style, and effects and to explain why Cronenberg's *Naked Lunch* is not *Naked Lunch*. Furthermore, Cronenberg's *Naked Lunch* has instigated the first sustained analysis of the legend, examining the psychology of its appeal and its fictionality. If critique of the legend continues, it will provide a much-needed corrective to years of misdirected criticism and biography and also contribute to the history of bohemianism in its postmodern afterlife. Finally, the discussion of the film among both film and literary critics has generated a genuine dialog, a welcome development in a field where earlier critics were not talking to each other.

Analyzing Burroughs criticism has been a part of my scholarship from the beginning to the present because misunderstanding and resistance have been obstacles to considering his contributions as an artist. Every critic writing during Burroughs' lifetime has had to defend the work against censorship, scandal, legend, moral or political condemnation, or claims of sheer incomprehension. When I published my critical introduction (1985), I had to argue that Burroughs was an important writer/artist/theoretician whose body of work merited serious critical attention and acknowledgment of its place within the history of the avant-garde. I pointed out the problem of legend as a fictional construct and the pigeonholing of Burroughs at that time as a minor novelist known for only one work that had polarized the critics—*Naked Lunch*. I countered that assessment with an analysis of Burroughs' achievement as the creator of a continuous artwork. In my introduction to the twenty-fifth anniversary edition of *Naked Lunch* (1984), I lamented the fact that, in spite of its fame and the attention of several respected academic scholars, the novel had not generated a dialog among critics and a coherent body of criticism: *Naked Lunch* was still considered *sui generis* and outside the canon. By the time of the publication of *Burroughs at the Front* (1991), the situation was changing. Burroughs was now defined as a postmodern writer, his entire oeuvre was under consideration, and criticism went beyond the confines of the literary. Since the 1990s, a consolidation has taken place, as I noted in my foreword to *Retaking the Universe* (2004) and in this essay. Burroughs has entered the canon as a postmodernist, and this classification provides the ground for critical exchange and collaboration. Within this context, *Naked Lunch* is no longer central to the critics and is now being viewed historically as a mid-twentieth-century analysis of sexuality, identity, and power and aesthetically as a breakthrough to Burroughs' mature voice and style. Also in the 1990s, the legend of William Burroughs was consolidated as a popular icon and received powerful expression in Cronenberg's film. However, even as the film reified the legend, it also generated criticism that rejected its normalizing strategies and reaffirmed *Naked Lunch*'s resistance to such closure. A return to the text by critics will benefit from the textual scholarship begun by Harris and Loranger, for, as their work shows, attention to the history of the novel's production, its various texts and paratexts, its several publications and reception, will revise interpretive criticism based on partial knowledge and mythology.

Note

1. The first Burroughs biography, by Ted Morgan, was entitled *Literary Outlaw* (1988). Geoff Ward's essay "William Burroughs: A Literary Outlaw?" takes the outlaw archetype as the key to Burroughs' life and work.

Works Cited

Beard, William. "Insect Poetics: Cronenberg's *Naked Lunch*." *Canadian Review of Comparative Literature/Revue Canadienne de Littérature Comparée* 23, no. 3 (1996): 823–52.

Blagrave, Mark. "The Oblique Addict and His Recharge Connection: Two for *Naked Lunch*." *Wascana Review of Contemporary Poetry and Short Fiction* 36, no. 1 (2006): 42–58.

Burroughs, William S. Introduction. In Silverberg, *Everything Is Permitted*, 13–15.

———. *The Letters of William S. Burroughs, 1945–1959*. Edited by Oliver Harris. New York: Viking, 1993.

DeKoven, Marianne. "The Literary as Activity in Postmodernity." *The Question of Literature: The Place of the Literary in Contemporary Theory*, edited by Elizabeth Beaumont Bissell, 105–25. Manchester, UK: Manchester UP, 2002..

Dellamora, Richard. "Queer Apocalypse: Framing William Burroughs." *Postmodern Apocalypse: Theory and Cultural Practice at the End*, edited by Dellamora, 136–67. Philadelphia: U of Pennsylvania P, 1995.

Eburne, Jonathan Paul. "Trafficking in the Void: Burroughs, Kerouac, and the Consumption of Otherness." *Modern Fiction Studies* 43, no. 1 (1997): 53–92.

Emery, Prudence, and Ira Silverberg. "Production History: Notes and Scenes from the Making of the Film." In Silverberg, *Everything Is Permitted*, 55–75.

Geyh, Paula, Fred G. Lebon, and Andrew Levy. *Postmodern American Fiction: A Norton Anthology*. New York: Norton, 1998.

Harris, Oliver. "Not Burroughs' Final Fix: Materializing *The Yage Letters*." *Postmodern Culture* 16, no. 2 (2006): 58 par. *Project Muse*. 15 Aug. 2006. http://muse.jhu.edu/journals/postmodern_culture/v016/16.2harris.html.

———. *William Burroughs and the Secret of Fascination*. Carbondale: Southern Illinois UP, 2003.

Hibbard, Allen, ed. *Conversations with William S. Burroughs*. Jackson: UP of Mississippi, 1999.

———. "Shift Coordinate Points: William S. Burroughs and Contemporary Theory." In Schneiderman and Walsh, *Retaking the Universe*, 13–28.

Loranger, Carol. "'This Book Spill Off the Page in All Directions': What Is the Text of *Naked Lunch*?" *Postmodern Culture* 10, no. 1 (1999): 24 par. *Project Muse*. 15 August 2006. http://muse.jhu.edu/journals/postmodern_culture/v010/10.1loranger.html.

McDaniel, Dennis. "New World Ordure: Burroughs, Globalization and the Grotesque." In Schneiderman and Walsh, *Retaking the Universe*, 132–45.

McNicholas, Joseph. "William S. Burroughs and Corporate Public Relations." *Arizona Quarterly* 57, no. 4 (2001): 121–49.

Melley, Timothy. "A Terminal Case: William Burroughs and the Logic of Addiction." *High Anxieties: Cultural Studies in Addiction*, edited by Janet Farrell Brodie and Marc Redfield, 38–60. Berkeley: U of California P, 2002.

Morgan, Ted. *Literary Outlaw: The Life and Times of William S. Burroughs.* New York: Holt, 1988.

Mullins, Greg. *Colonial Affairs: Bowles, Burroughs, and Chester Write Tangier.* Madison: U of Wisconsin P, 2002.

Murphy, Timothy S. "Intersection Points: Teaching William Burroughs's *Naked Lunch.*" *Teaching Beat Literature.* Edited by Jennie Skerl. Special issue. *College Literature* 27, no. 1 (2000): 84-102.

———. "William Burroughs between Indifference and Revalorization: Notes toward a Political Reading." *Angelaki* 1, no. 1 (1993): 113–24.

———. *Wising Up the Marks: The Amodern William Burroughs.* Berkeley: U of California P, 1997.

Naked Lunch. Directed by David Cronenberg. Produced by Jeremy Thomas. Twentieth Century Fox, 1991.

Pepper, Andrew. "State Power Matters: Power, the State and Political Struggle in the Post-war American Novel." *Textual Practice* 19, no. 4 (2005): 467–91.

Rosenbaum, Jonathan. "Two Forms of Adaptation: *Housekeeping* and *Naked Lunch.*" In *Film Adaptation*, edited by James Naremore, 206–20. New Brunswick, NJ: Rutgers UP, 2000.

Russell, Jamie. *Queer Burroughs.* New York: Palgrave, 2001.

Schneiderman, Davis, and Philip Walsh, ed. *Retaking the Universe: William S. Burroughs in the Age of Globalization.* London: Pluto, 2004.

Severo, Richard. "William S. Burroughs, the Beat Writer Who Distilled His Raw Nightmare Life, Dies at 83." Obituary. *New York Times*, 4 August 1997, B5.

Silverberg, Ira, ed. *Everything Is Permitted: The Making of* Naked Lunch. New York: Grove, 1992.

Skerl, Jennie. Foreword. In Schneiderman and Walsh, *Retaking the Universe*, xi–xiv.

———. Introduction. *Naked Lunch.* 25th anniversary edition. New York: Grove, 1984.

———. *William S. Burroughs.* Boston: Twayne, 1985.

Skerl, Jennie, and Robin Lydenberg, ed. *William S. Burroughs at the Front: Critical Reception, 1959–1989.* Carbondale: Southern Illinois UP, 1991.

Streip, Katharine. "William S. Burroughs: Laughter and the Avant-Garde." In Schneiderman and Walsh , *Retaking the Universe*, 258–73.

Ward, Geoff. "William Burroughs: A Literary Outlaw?" *Cambridge Quarterly* 22 (1993): 339–54.

Zurbrugg, Nicholas. "Will Hollywood Never Learn? David Cronenberg's *Naked Lunch.*" In *Adaptations: From Text to Screen, Screen to Text*, edited by Deborah Cartmell and Imelda Whelehan, 98-112. London: Routledge, 1999.

Still Dirty after All These Years:
The Continuing Trials of *Naked Lunch*

loren **GLASS**

I n the early 1970s, William Burroughs' career was stalled. Although *Naked Lunch* was acknowledged as a masterpiece and a landmark of literary freedom, his more recent cut-up texts had been skeptically received, and he himself was beginning to feel that the experiments were a dead end. Already in his sixties, bored and lonely in London, he decided to return to the United States. Within days, Allen Ginsberg introduced him to a young Kansan named James Grauerholz, who would become his secretary, business manager, editor, and adviser for the remainder of his life. In order to kick-start Burroughs' career, Grauerholz arranged a series of readings on college campuses and at music clubs across the United States. The dissonant combination of Burroughs' laconic Midwestern nasal twang with the outrageous explicitness of his subject matter was a huge hit; the readings revitalized his career and helped inject his voice and image into the popular imaginary. Although he had done some readings in the 1960s, Burroughs had seen relatively little point in reading from his work and had famously insisted in the pages of *Naked Lunch* that he wasn't an entertainer, but in the 1970s and 1980s, he found both joy and profit in becoming a traveling performer. The familiarity of his voice and image began to supplement, if not replace, the fame of his prose, and he got involved in a number of collaborative projects with musicians, including an album, not long before his death, with musician/activist Michael Franti, then of the Disposable Heroes of Hiphoprisy. *Spare Ass Annie and Other Tales*, a sonic collage of voice and music featuring Burroughs reading, mostly from texts published much earlier, features a parental advisory warning of "Explicit Lyrics." As printed texts, Burroughs' words have long been free of censorship; a half century later, as recorded lyrics, they have again become the subject of official scrutiny.

Over the last fifty years, *Naked Lunch* has traveled the now-familiar trajectory from outlaw to classic; however, unlike its modernist predecessors, its outlaw status has been sustained by new generations of artists and critics. We can understand *Naked Lunch* and Burroughs' career more generally as a point of historical mediation between modernist writing and postmodern performance as the locus for that notoriously overdetermined exception to our First Amendment rights: obscenity. The battles over literary obscenity that generated a series of landmark Supreme Court cases in the late 1950s and early 1960s began with Ginsberg's *Howl* and ended with Burroughs' *Naked Lunch*; between the two were sandwiched the famous cases of the long-suppressed underground classics *Lady Chatterley's Lover* and *Tropic of Cancer*. The Beats, then, helped bring to a close a period of literary censorship coincident with the modernist enterprise, and this overlap has contributed to a critical tendency to understand their work in terms of modernist paradigms that emphasize the aesthetic integrity of the text and the solitary genius of the author. But the Beats diverged from their modernist predecessors in their emphasis on the performative and collaborative nature of literary art. Thus, their work anticipated and partly enabled the larger shift in the focus of censorship to broadcast radio, recorded music, and performance art.

This significantly transitional location is well illustrated by the ambiguity of one of the more famous lines in *Naked Lunch*, where Burroughs speculates upon "the sex that passes the censor" (112); as Oliver Harris has recently shown, it's not at all clear to what these lines refer.[1] Do they refer to "The Talking Asshole" anecdote that precedes them or to the references to popular songs and Grade B movies that follow? Although Harris convincingly proves that, in its original epistolary form, the anecdote was a digression from Burroughs' condemnation of "America's putrefying unconscious," I would like to suggest that, proleptically, these oft-quoted lines anticipate the fate of "The Talking Asshole" and *Naked Lunch* itself as instrumental in altering the very protocols of censorship in the United States and the United Kingdom. When these lines were written, the only possible market for *Naked Lunch* would have been underground, but Grove Press changed all that, not only enabling it to pass the censor but also leveraging its obscenity—in particular "The Talking Asshole" routine—as a marker of its legitimacy as a classic text and, therefore, of a significant realignment of the cultural field itself. *Naked Lunch* didn't so much squeeze "between bureaus" as exploit the authority of an emergent bureaucracy: the literary "experts" whose Supreme Court testimony helped exonerate it. At the same time, the evaluative stratifications indicated by carnivals and B movies have dissolved into the far more heterogeneous proliferation of the postmodern marketplace, where routines like "The Talking Asshole" in essence signify one coterie niche among others.

Not surprisingly, the routine is a perennial favorite with critics (not to mention audiences) and is usually interpreted, despite its resolute ambiguity, as politically subversive. What these critics neglect or more frequently finesse is the fairly obvious fact that Burroughs owes his success to the structural transformations of capitalism in the contemporary era, and that his aesthetic innovations actually helped contribute to these transformations as they have been articulated in the global culture industry, which is increasingly friendly to radical aesthetic experimentation. I would like to offer my own analysis, then, as a cautionary response to the tendency to see Burroughs as providing modes and methods of resistance. I understand the "obscenity" of Burroughs' work as symptomatic of significant structural realignments between capitalism, culture, and the body. However, as part of this process, cultural "resistance" as articulated by specific aesthetic practices becomes increasingly internal to the postmodern corporate order. As a consequence, I hope to prove, critics of Burroughs tend to base their theories of resistance in the very modernist protocols whose supersession they simultaneously celebrate.

This tendency has its origins in the efforts to defend *Naked Lunch* against accusations of obscenity. Barney Rosset, president of Grove Press, and his lawyer Edward de Grazia recruited a veritable army of writers, critics, and professors to provide expert testimony that relied upon frequent references to modernist masterpieces as analogues for Burroughs' achievement. In Norman Mailer's testimony for the Massachusetts trial that would eventually exonerate *Naked Lunch* and inaugurate what lawyer Charles Rembar would later call the "end of obscenity," Mailer states that upon rereading the text, he realized that "there is more to his intent than I had ever recognized before; that the work was more of a deep work, a calculated work, a planned work." He then elaborated that *Naked Lunch* compelled him "to read it further and further, the way *Ulysses* did when I read that in college, as if there are mysteries to be answered when I read it." [2]

Ulysses was a frequent reference in discussions of *Naked Lunch* not only because Joyce's text had by then become the standard by which any modern masterpiece would be measured but also because the landmark case of *The United States v. One Book Called "Ulysses"* had established the legal precedents by which literary texts could be exonerated of charges of obscenity. Most important, the *Ulysses* case legitimated the concept of the "modern classic" as a category of book that could be determined by experts. In acknowledging this category, Judge John M. Woolsey, in his landmark opinion, affirmed that the intent of the author was dispositive, because "in any case where a book is claimed to be obscene it must first be determined whether the intent with which it was written was [. . .] pornographic" (Moscato and Le Blanc, 309–10). Woolsey's ruling, then, not only set a legal precedent against suppressing a book for isolated passages but it also affirmed the modernist theory of the aesthetic integrity of the text as the author's intended and inviolate creation. Once Woolsey's opinion was affirmed on appeal, Bennet Cerf, president of Random House, incorporated it as a preface into the trade edition of *Ulysses*, and so it remained until the much-disputed 1986 "corrected" text. Woolsey's decision, in other words, not only helped legitimate *Ulysses*, it became for many years inextricably connected with the reading of the text.

During the trial, Rosset and de Grazia's impressive panel of experts worked hard to substantiate that Burroughs' book was a "modern classic." But the prosecuting attorney, William Cowin, doubted that *Naked Lunch* had a structure as coherent and intentional as *Ulysses*. Thus, he asked the first expert witness, John Ciardi, "when he put these notes or writings, however you would refer to the book, together, do you feel that he knew what he was doing; that he was conscious that he was actually writing this book called, NAKED LUNCH?"[3] After all, Burroughs himself had claimed (unreliably) in the appended "Deposition: Testimony Concerning a Sickness": "I have no precise memory of writing the notes which have now been published under the title *Naked Lunch*" (199). As one early critic affirmed, the challenge of the defense in this trial was to "prove to the court's satisfaction that *Naked Lunch* is a book" (McConnel, 93).

Indeed, the version of *Naked Lunch* used for the Massachusetts trial had undergone numerous collaborative revisions and would continue to be collaboratively revised and altered after its American publication.[4] Although Ginsberg in his testimony attempted to justify the specific order and structure of the sections, the judge was, not surprisingly, unconvinced, deeming the text obscene and claiming that "the author first collected the foulest and vilest phrases describing unnatural sexual experiences and tossed them indiscriminately" into the book (qtd. in Goodman, 235). His ruling was overturned upon appeal, but only because the United States Supreme Court had, in the intervening months, clarified that a text could only be suppressed if it was "utterly without redeeming social value." What de Grazia calls the "Brennan Doctrine" (after Justice William J. Brennan, who penned the major obscenity decisions of this era) had mandated that the opinions of literary experts trumped the responses of local judges and juries. Thus, the Massachusetts Supreme Judicial Court conceded that "it appears that a substantial and intelligent group in the community believes the book to be of some literary significance," and therefore it could not be deemed obscene (de Grazia, *Censorship Landmarks*, 681).

Rosset, in turn, used these expert opinions as well as the ultimate decision of the Massachusetts Supreme Court to leverage sales of *Naked Lunch*, much as Cerf had with *Ulysses*. In a 1962 letter to booksellers, Rosset compares *Naked Lunch* to "other famous modern classics of American and English literature—including James Joyce's *Ulysses*, D. H. Lawrence's *Lady Chatterley's Lover*, and Henry Miller's *Tropics*" and then quotes a whole series of critics and authors justifying the comparison.[5] These early versions of the text also included the Massachusetts Supreme Court Decision as well as excerpts from the trial. Mailer's testimony was particularly influential, and his resolutely modernist claim that "Burroughs is the only American novelist living today who may conceivably be possessed by genius" appeared on the cover and in much of the advertisements and promotional materials. Thus, the *Ulysses* case not only set legal and literary precedents for dealing with obscenity prosecutions but also established marketing methods for exploiting them.

In fact, Rosset's marketing of *Naked Lunch* went significantly beyond Cerf's tactics with *Ulysses* insofar as Grove actually added significant materials—such as the "Deposition" and the appendix—which were not in the first Olympia edition. The marketing campaign for *Naked Lunch*, then, not only affirmed that obscenity had shifted from a liability to an asset in the literary field but also that the sacrosanct integrity of the text, associated with literary modernism, was beginning to give way to a more fluid relation between text and paratext. If Cerf and Joyce had made sure to delineate clearly the boundaries between text and paratext in the Random House *Ulysses*, Rosset and Burroughs essentially let *Naked Lunch* accrete and absorb its proliferating paratexts.

This development can also be understood in terms of the analogies between literary text and authorial body that were so frequently used to defend against expurgation. The references to high modernism in defense of *Naked Lunch* rely on an essentially metaphoric relation between body and book. Like the human body, this argument goes, the literary text has an integrity and continuity that, by analogy, renders censorship as a form of physical violence. To remove any part, even a single word, is to mutilate this whole. Indeed, it was common to speak of literary expurgation as authorial castration, providing further psychoanalytic ballast to the analogy. *Naked Lunch*, on the other hand, operates as a veritable invitation to mutilate. As Burroughs' "Atrophied Preface" affirms, "You can cut into *Naked Lunch* at any intersection point" (187). As he would later concede, "all my books are one book," and the "Word Hoard" that eventually became *Naked Lunch* and parts of *The Soft Machine*, *The Ticket That Exploded*, and *Nova Express* could have been, and indeed was, frequently organized and reorganized in a variety of different ways without doing any aesthetic violence to any individual instance (qtd. in Miles, 177).[6] Many different versions of all four texts have been published over the years, and all have equal claim to literary legitimacy. Indeed, Grove had to pressure Burroughs to produce definitive editions in order to secure copyright. Which is only to affirm the concrete practice behind what has become axiomatic in Burroughs criticism: the relationship between text and body in his oeuvre is less metaphoric than it is metonymic. The text is not analogous to the body; it is an extension of it.

This tendency accounts both for Burroughs' fascination with recording and transcription technologies, on the one hand, and his enormous popularity as a speaker, on the other. In many ways, for Burroughs, tape recordings of the voice rendered this materiality more effectively than the printed word, which has a more attenuated link to the bodies of either writer or reader. Thus, his tape-recording experiments appear frequently in the cut-up novels. *The Ticket That Exploded* opens with "the sound of his voice and his image flickering over the tape recorder are as familiar to me as the movement of my intestines the sound of my breathing the beating of my heart" (1). Elsewhere, Burroughs reverses the interface, writing "a tape recorder gasps, shits, pisses, strangles and ejaculates at his feet" (49). In these lines, Burroughs attempts to collapse an analogy between externally recorded and internally produced sound into an actual technological interface between body and machine. But he was frustrated with the limitations of print in effectively embodying this relation; as he affirmed in *The Job*, a series of interviews with Daniel Odier that have become a standard reference for scholars of his work: "There are all sorts of things you can do on a tape recorder that cannot possibly be indicated on the printed page" (29).

Thus, it is not surprising that, according to Beat historian Barry Miles, "many people have said that they didn't really understand Burroughs until they heard *that voice*—the voice of a banker saying all those outrageous things" (7). It wasn't only the comic incongruity between his conservative appearance and his obscene speech but also, I would argue, the embodiment of that speech in sound as opposed to print, in a form that feels more palpable and in which, after all, much of it originally existed as routines. Thus, it is

Burroughs' inimitable voice that effectively embodies how, to recall "The Talking Asshole" routine, talking can have "a bubbly, thick stagnant sound, a sound you could *smell*" (111). The printed text in essence enabled the migration of these routines from private improvisations to public performances. And obscenity itself migrated from print to performance in these years as well. Since *Naked Lunch* was legalized, no printed text has been officially censored in the United States. However, censorship didn't end; the focus shifted to broadcast media, recorded music, and public performance. Since the 1960s, the key controversies over the censorship of art have involved Federal Communications Commission (FCC) restrictions on public broadcasting, performance artists such as Karen Finley and Annie Sprinkle, and explicit lyrics in musical recordings. And much of Burroughs' later work has been in collaboration with artists working in these media, including Laurie Anderson, Gus Van Sant, Bill Laswell, John Cale, Sonic Youth, Tom Waits, Michael Franti, and Kurt Cobain.

With this change in media has come a corollary shift in the protocols of censorship that are well worth noting. This shift was most prominently illustrated by the Supreme Court's ruling in *FCC v. Pacifica Foundation* (1978), which legitimated FCC regulation of indecency on the airwaves and ushered in a new regime of censorship that has superseded modernist debates over obscenity. During the modern era, the emphasis tended to be on absolute definitions of obscenity, and a key weapon in the arsenal of artists was the aesthetic integrity of the text. This belief in aesthetic integrity conceptually leveraged the assumption that literature and obscenity were mutually exclusive categories and practically militated against expurgations of literary texts. However, when texts like *Naked Lunch* appeared, as we have seen, these arguments no longer seemed valid. Simultaneously, the legal world was beginning to develop theories of "variable obscenity" that shifted the focus from text to context and therefore justified restricting or even editing work in specific media and for particular audiences (usually children).[7] Thus, Justice John Paul Stevens, who penned the majority decision in the *FCC* case, affirms that unlike obscenity, "indecency is largely a function of context—it cannot be adequately judged in the abstract" and that "each medium of expression presents special First Amendment problems" (*FCC*, 191, 193). Literary texts, then, remain "liberated," but other media that rely much more heavily on the collaborative and contiguous aesthetic that Burroughs innovated are frequently and legally altered and/or channeled for specific retail or broadcast venues. Andrew Ross provocatively suggests that we call these new practices "the fine art of regulation," to distinguish them from older methods of censorship that were dominant in the era of modernism (257).

Burroughs' career in these other media logically emerges out of the reciprocal relations between his emphasis on the materiality of language and the proliferation of a McLuhanesque mediascape in the postwar world. On the one hand, Burroughs' writing, unlike that of the modernists who preceded him, operates by a metonymic logic whereby the text is understood as a mutable extension, not a sacrosanct representation or analogue, of the authorial body. On the other hand, new technologies of sound recording and broadcasting increasingly interpellate the authorial body into other media and venues where this metonymic relation is more readily enacted.

McLuhan himself was a shrewd critic of Burroughs, and one of his insights provides a crucial cautionary check on contemporary critical practice. In his "Notes on Burroughs," published in the *Nation* in 1964, McLuhan claims, "Burroughs is unique only in that he is attempting to reproduce in prose what we accommodate every day as a commonplace aspect of life in the electric age. If the corporate life is to be rendered on paper, the method of discontinuous nonstory must be employed" (69). McLuhan sees Burroughs as a reflection of, as opposed to a rebellion against, late capitalism, and his overdetermined deployment of the term *corporate* illuminates both the centrality and the ambivalence of the body in Burroughs' work. Does it operate as the very substrate of capital's ingestion and expansion, or does it function as a utopian basis of resistance to commodification? As we have seen, critics tend to lean toward the utopian end of the spectrum here, but it is worth noting that Burroughs would himself become a corporation when Grauerholz formed William Burroughs Communications to manage the author's performance schedule and other business matters, and then later Nova Lark Music (administered, of course, by ASCAP) to handle the copyrights to his recordings.

The critical protocol of understanding Burroughs in terms of resistance crucially relies on the apparent clarity of his famous contrast between bureaus and cooperatives:

> Bureaus cannot live without a host, being true parasitic organisms. (A cooperative on the other hand *can* live without the state. That is the road to follow. The building up of independent units to meet needs of the people who participate in the functioning of the unit. A bureau operates on opposite principle of *inventing needs* to justify its existence.) (112)

Thus, Timothy Murphy cites these lines in support of his claim that "Burroughs articulates a critique that is structurally and thematically similar to the critique articulated by Horkheimer and Adorno" in *Dialectic of Enlightenment* (77). But Burroughs' own exposition of the "Algebra of Need" and his entire career attest to the difficulty in maintaining a coherent critique based in this contrast, a difficulty that almost inevitably bleeds into paranoia. Indeed, in the original epistolary version of "The Talking Asshole" episode as reprinted in *Letters to Allen Ginsberg, 1953–1957,* Burroughs offers it as "my saleable product" and, in the place of "cooperatives" as the utopian counterpart to "bureaus," the letter has the word *corporations.*[8] The significant slippage between *cooperatives* and *corporations,* the uncanny homology between *bureaus* and *Burroughs,* and the ultimately prophetic identification of the routine as a "saleable product" reveal the dialectical difficulties of distinguishing modes of collectivity and corporeality under global capitalism (*Letters,* 20). After all, in Burroughs' world, which is also our world, it has become increasingly difficult to distinguish between the discreet human body and its media environment or between collaborative and corporate modes of cultural production. As Harris affirms, "Complicity in all he opposes is the very *condition* of Burroughs' work, its *material ground* as well as its material effect" (31).

The academic need to disentangle these modes, to outflank this inevitable complicity, it seems to me, is in truth a displaced symptom of our own material ground. On the one hand, we continue to produce criticism in a residual, solitary modernist mode that favors the construction of literary canons organized around individual geniuses; on the other hand, our work is completely absorbed into the new postmodern, corporate multiversity, whose emergent bureaucratic authority produced the experts who defended *Naked Lunch.* This might help explain why Burroughs' critics always seem to feel the need to represent him as academically marginal even as they simultaneously participate in making him an academic industry. Burroughs can only represent "resistance" if he stays on the margins, but we can only build our careers around him because he stands at the center.

Rather than mire ourselves in increasingly acrobatic attempts at extricating visions of resistance from Burroughs' actual practice of complicity, it seems more fruitful to understand his career as symptomatic of a realignment of these very terms. Late capitalism thrives on the creative energies of cultural resistance, which is why Burroughs' metonymic collage aesthetic has so successfully fueled his own mass-media celebrity and why academic critics can get tenure by celebrating that very aesthetic as subversive. The very naturalness of this move, it seems to me, should make us suspicious of it. Indeed, Burroughs' symptomatic slide from corporations to cooperatives should signal for us the dangerous reversibility of these terms under contemporary global capitalism.

On the other hand, the new nexus of relations between censorship and intellectual property does seem to afford possibilities for concrete academic intervention. The shift from obscenity to indecency has empowered government agencies such as the FCC and megacorporations such as WalMart and Blockbuster to restrict and edit, as opposed to suppress completely, a wide variety of media. And this new focus on the regulation of content coincides with an alarming consolidation and extension of the corporate ownership of intellectual property. This combination of industry regulation and corporate ownership concretely impedes the availability of content to both artists and audiences. The question, in other words, is not a matter of whether specific texts or authors are subversive but who has access to these texts and for what purposes.

Notes

1. See Harris, *William Burroughs*, 219–24.

2. Trial transcript, *Attorney General vs. a Book Named "Naked Lunch,"* p. 109, Grove Press Archives, Syracuse University Special Collections, Syracuse, New York.

3. Ibid.

4. For a history of *Naked Lunch*'s collaborative composition, see the editors' note to the restored text edition and Harris, 179–245.

5. Barney Rosset to Booksellers, 30 October 1962, Grove Press Archives, Syracuse University Special Collections.

6. For a list of the many versions of these texts, see Maynard and Miles.

7. For a discussion of these developments, see Lockhart and McClure.

8. According to Oliver Harris, editor of Burroughs' letters, this substitution is a transcription error, which he corrected. *The Letters of William S. Burroughs, 1945–1959* (New York: Viking, 1993), 261. However, he also notes that the original, handwritten copy of this portion of the letter is missing. E-mail to the author, July 2005. In other words, the slip between *corporations* and *cooperatives* can be understood as a consequence of the collaborative practices and contingencies that shaped Burroughs' career.

Works Cited

Burroughs, William. *The Job: Interviews*. 1969. New York: Penguin, 1974.

———. *Letters to Allen Ginsberg, 1953–1957*. Edited by Ron Padgett and Anne Waldman. New York: Full Court, 1982.

———. *The Ticket That Exploded*. Paris: Olympia, 1962. New York: Grove, 1967.

de Grazia, Edward. *Censorship Landmarks*. New York: Bowker, 1969.

———. *Girls Lean Back Everywhere: The Law of Obscenity and the Assault on Genius*. New York: Random, 1992.

FCC v. Pacifica Foundation. In Robert Hilliard and Michael Keith, *Dirty Discourse: Sex and Indecency in American Radio*. Ames: Iowa State UP, 2003. 163–99.

Goodman, Michael B. *Contemporary Literary Censorship: The Case of Burroughs' Naked Lunch*. Metuchen, NJ: Scarecrow, 1981.

Grove Press Archives. Syracuse University Special Collections, Syracuse, New York.

Harris, Oliver. *William Burroughs and the Secret of Fascination*. Carbondale: Southern Illinois UP, 2003.

Joyce, James. *Ulysses*. New York: Random, 1934.

Lockhart, William, and Robert McClure. "Censorship of Obscenity: The Developing Constitutional Standards." *Minnesota Law Review* 45 (1960): 5–121.

Maynard, Joe, and Barry Miles. *William S. Burroughs: A Bibliography, 1953–73*. Charlottesville: UP of Virginia, 1978.

McConnel, Frank D. "William Burroughs and the Literature of Addiction." *Massachusetts Review* 8 (1967): 665–80. Rpt. in Skerl and Lydenberg, *William Burroughs at the Front*, 91–101.

McLuhan, Marshall. "Notes on Burroughs." *Nation*, 28 December 1964, 517–19. Rpt. in Skerl and Lydenberg, *William Burroughs at the Front*, 69–73.

Miles, Barry. *William Burroughs: El Hombre Invisible*. New York: Hyperion, 1992.

Moscato, Michael, and Leslie Le Blanc, eds. *The United States of America v. One Book Entitled "Ulysses" by James Joyce: Documents and Commentary*. Frederick, MD: University Publications of America, 1984.

Murphy, Timothy S. *Wising Up the Marks: The Amodern William Burroughs*. Berkeley: U of California P, 1997.

Rembar, Charles. *The End of Obscenity*. New York: Bantam, 1968.

Ross, Andrew. "The Fine Art of Regulation." In *The Phantom Public Sphere*, edited by Bruce Robbins, 257–68. Minneapolis: U of Minnesota P, 1993.

Skerl, Jennie, and Robin Lydenberg, eds. *William S. Burroughs at the Front: Critical Reception, 1959–1989*. Carbondale: Southern Illinois UP, 1991.

"Gentlemen I will slop a pearl":
The (Non)Meaning of *Naked Lunch*

davis **SCHNEIDERMAN**

Unmaking the Meal

Perhaps the strangest aspect of *Naked Lunch*'s slow tromp from the avant-garde margins remains the way that still, after fifty years, the book resists full co-option into the American literary mainstream. There are scant similar examples in the permeable realms of modern and postmodern literature that have become as popular as *Naked Lunch* and yet still remain as thoroughly unmanageable. The book, a self-aware contortionist, performs a series of "innaresting" positions that for many readers familiar with the jump-cut aesthetic of movies, video games, music, and television—but not for god's sake *literature*—make as much "sense" as the mosaic juxtapositions marking the text.

Naked Lunch is a deeply ambivalent book: it remains inconsistent in message, discordant in style, variable in method, and, as recently demonstrated by Oliver Harris, exaggerated in mythos. The situation is complicated by various attempts to make critical "sense" of the novel, which often, to contradictory effect, limit the possibilities for reading *Naked Lunch* and simultaneously assure its continued popularity. To the extent that almost every method of reading *Naked Lunch* promises to unlock its secrets—and so provide textual mastery—the novel gestures in return, at times suggesting a misleading synergy with the critical perspective, at times remaining more obviously hostile.

The critical terrain mapped out by Jennie Skerl in her introduction to the twenty-fifth anniversary edition remains almost unchanged twenty-five years later (with at least one major exception), and after she discusses her own insights, she cites the ways in which readers have attempted to understand *Naked Lunch* during its first quarter century. Significantly, there are academic/critical and popular perspectives: with the avant-garde modernist tradition (xvi); with French writers of "revolt," including de Sade, Céline, Genet, and Camus; with Henry Miller as the link between the French and the American; and with the antiliterature of Beckett (xvii). There is the ubiquitous "Beat novel" pigeonhole (xvii) and an elision of Burroughs' comedic voice in terms of his (a)moral positions (xiv).

Skerl writes that critics of the 1970s and 1980s began to pay attention to *Naked Lunch*'s form, and she notes that two early studies, John Tytell's *Naked Angels: The Lives and Literature of the Beat Generation* (1976) and Eric Mottram's *William Burroughs: The Algebra of Need* (1971), indeed follow the formal path, while still assuming "the same social and moral message that had been discussed in the 1960s" (xviii). Finally, suggesting a notion of *Naked Lunch* as a "radical text rather than a message," Skerl makes her most striking point: "*Naked Lunch* has been placed in many theoretical contexts [. . .] psychoanalytic, archetypal, reader-response, phenomenological, and various definitions of postmodernist, structuralist and deconstructionist. But because critics have for the most part not responded to each other, no unified body of criticism has emerged" (xix).

The exception: As part of the critical renaissance in motion since about the time of Burroughs' death in 1997, Carol Loranger and Oliver Harris have provided a new direction in textual/genetic studies. Harris' important *William Burroughs and the Secret of Fascination* (2003) locates the epistolary origins of the texts that would eventually become *Naked Lunch*, remarking, "Burroughs' pieces do not fit together into a whole novel precisely because they are not fit pieces for a novel" (212). In critiquing Timothy S. Murphy's failure to push through "Beat Legend" for genetic histories, Harris notes that "a false material base must in turn have material consequences for textual interpretation" (187). He ably details the elimination of almost all epistolary traces in *Naked Lunch*, and in doing so, we might slop a pearl: if the texts in *Naked Lunch* are not the texts of a "novel" in any sense of a form arrived at prior to its construction (and, rather, elements of letters), the treatment of the text-as-such results in a series of *impossible* readings, each attempting mastery foiled by the material methodological limits.

Here, Skerl's closing comment assumes even greater import: "[*Naked Lunch*] is a masterful performance that refuses classification: a paradoxical masterpiece by a writer who eschews masterpieces" (xix). In light of Harris' work, we might go further: *Naked Lunch* is an epistolary performance that refuses its own signature: a paradoxical transubstantiation by a writer for whom authority remains a black magic trick of the pen.

Naked Lunch rejects traditional narrative analysis and, accordingly, traditional structures of novelistic meaning. *Sui generis, Naked Lunch* withholds meaning for which there can be no adequate explanatory vocabulary. As we shall soon discover, *Naked Lunch* is coded with its own interpretative counterarguments, and to subscribe to a particular narrative interpretation is to fall into its metanarrative traps. These pitfalls are determined as much by the political economies of Burroughs' literary efforts, as detailed by Harris, as by the intent of a writer frustrated by his own desires (for Allen Ginsberg, for a bestseller, etc.).

Still, the "excess" production of *Naked Lunch*, whether the absent epistolary "sources," or, as we will see, the material that defies linearity, might be taken in at least two ways. Firstly, as-yet-unassimilated material primed for eventual recuperation into a readerly cosmology: think of twentieth-century psychoanalysis or the more hopeful elements of Surrealism that seek to unleash the irrational in order to bring about the eventual *reformation* of the rational world. In the first case, the unruly psyche is daringly explored but only for its eventual Oedipalization; in the second case, the excess world of the automatic mind, the superrational, reveals the absurdity of rationality. This reading suggests the ultimate possibility of meaning-making as an elusive reward for intrepid exploration. And secondly, the converse: as "excess" in the sense that Georges Bataille might suggest—as a means of transgression. In this mode, the agent, through the process of acting outside existing norms, crosses the limiting boundaries of the institutionalized (i.e., nontransgressive) subject's reality. This transgression exposes the limits of action previously unknown to the agent. This mode is revelation: A. J.'s annual party exposes other soirées as tightly controlled exercises in social restraint. Yet, this revelation does not necessarily reveal the means of escape but outlines the shackles one already wears.

Although *Naked Lunch* functions, ultimately, in the second mode, it is the readerly hope that the text can be slotted into the first that powers the continual (mis)readings. This possibility is often predicated on a key analytical flaw: reading what makes "sense" in *Naked Lunch* while dismissing the "excess" text as hallucinations produced through William Lee's drug cure.

This indicates not what to make of *Naked Lunch* but the necessity of *unmaking* its meal. Rewind the condiments. Turn bread back to yeast. And for Ah Pook's sweet sake, rethink the ubiquitous drug-novel line, put down as just another "pin and dropper routine" (10).

The Talking Cure: *Naked Lunch* as Drug Narrative

The most pervasive textual reading, despite the deconstruction of the last four decades, is realistic: William Lee, the novel's "main" character, quits drugs and so engages in a series of withdrawal hallucinations. This is Skerl's perspective, although she complicates the reading with Lee's position as an Agent, a particular "angle of vision" (viii) that "universalizes the addict experience" (ix). The pervasiveness of this perspective goes back at least to *Naked Lunch*'s first publisher, Maurice Girodias, and continues to the present day in both critical aids (Murphy's "Intersection Points" article) and popular "reviews."

Girodias, who published the 1959 first edition (Olympia Press), notes two points of particular interest in his essay accompanying a reprint of "The County Clerk" section in *The Olympia Reader: Selections from the Traveller's Companion Series* (1965). The first underscores the novel's textual ambivalence: "*The impression left by this is perplexing*," followed closely by, "*This would seem to be Burroughs' position, but it is not consistent with his picture of sex*" (460). Both statements accompany an excursus of the contradictions in the novel's warnings against control, and Girodias is astute in recognizing the paradoxes.

A second and earlier point from Girodias' essay plays into the reader's attempt, even so, to make "sense" of the book from the internal, readerly perspective—to see it as essentially more than the random arrangement of randomly composed/juxtaposed materials. Here, Girodias proffers the standard narrative line: "*The action of* Naked Lunch *takes places in the consciousness of One Man: William Lee, who is taking a drug cure*" (456). Comically, and perhaps to undermine this oversimplification, Girodias then lists the novel's "characters," including among the principals "*various boys with whining voices*" (456).

Four decades later, the Resident Scholar of a Web site titled *AllReaders. Com*, Judy Berman, offers a review with more-earnest linearity:

> This novel is a loose collection of its author's drug-induced delusions. It takes place mostly in Tangiers, Morocco, where the writer sometimes lived. He depicts the city as a depraved, sexually deviant, drug-addled, bizarre underworld, known as Interzone. Characters come and go, strange situations and themes play themselves out. A recurring character in Burroughs' work, Dr. Benway, a sadistic quack bent on mind control, also surfaces every once in a while. The only element that draws all parts of the novel's nightmare-esque narrative together is the

idea that all of the visions come from a heroin addict who desperately needs a fix.

The first and last sentences suggest a secondary "reality" to the novel strangely in line with Gilles Deleuze and Félix Guattari's well-known critique of Burroughs' later work as *fascicular* (opposed to *rhizomatic*). In this argument, the "order" of the world reaffirms itself despite the apparent madness of the text. For Berman, also, these "strange situations and themes" ultimately fade into the light of the real.

Graham Rae, in a review of the 2005 Harper Perennial edition of *Naked Lunch*, has recourse in his penultimate statement to the *drug myth* as heroic counterculture pose: "As long as new generations of readers come along looking for something new and revolutionary and revelationary and super-intelligent and rebellious to read, Burroughs will be smiling back at them from the opaque opiate dark, needle in arm and treason in mind." Again, the contrived link between opiate use and rebellion. Not only does Rae's closing note play into an alarmingly one-dimensional hipster mythomania for Burroughs-as-dopehead-guru but also his prurient description of the "needle in arm" is ably skewered in the very opening pages of *Naked Lunch*: "You know how this pin and dropper routine is put down" (10).

Conversely, Rae earlier remarks, "Much of *Naked Lunch*'s reputation as a work of drugged-out madness doesn't bear weight. Burroughs was not wrecked out of his mind when he wrote it, or at least not *most* of it; that's just writer legend." Rae wants it both ways: celebrating and eviscerating the opiate elements of the Burroughsian myth. This ambivalent response to the drug/control vector by even Burroughs' popular commentators remarks, in part, on the inscrutable quality of the narrative's position. Is Burroughs a proud junkie? Do his texts promote an opiate drug culture the way Timothy Leary would hallucinogens in the following decade?

Regardless of the evidence suggesting a negative answer, the association remains the predominant mode of *Naked Lunch*'s popular explanation, as it is for Skerl (metaphorically), Girodias (ironically), Berman (simply), and Rae (mythopoetically). Yet, these drug-oriented perspectives are often counterindicated by the actual text, which offers consistent revision to this reading while concurrently dismantling the authority of the critical impetus pushing otherwise inassimilable prose neatly into a heroin dropper.

This drug-oriented reading upholds the traditional notion of the author as genius, in the Romantic tradition, where the ebullience of the imagination is at once excited *and* explained through the boundaries of the literary act. If Lee is on drugs, quitting drugs, hallucinating through drugs, then our world remains protected outside this altered state. When Alice awakes at the end of her Wonderland jaunt, after the Dormouse, the deck of cards, and the dolor of its outlandishly mad creatures, the child receives the gift of imagination—contained neatly within leather binding. In short, Alice awakes, Lee hallucinates, and we may breathe easy away from their odd nightmares.

There is every reason to think that *Naked Lunch* is still, in 2009, finding itself read as the hallucinatory confession of an American opium eater—and so neutralized—a victim of a conveniently limited critical palette's attempts to novelize a text that in its construction, Harris demonstrates, cannot be considered a novel.

"That Wasn't a Nice Thing to Do, Teach"

The investment of critical and popular discourse in *Naked Lunch* as drug narrative remains surprising, given that the text directly codes its suspicion and even rejection of critical sensibility within its more linear routines. In fact, one of *Naked Lunch*'s most effective parodies involves a professor's interpretation of Coleridge's *Rime of the Ancient Mariner* in the "Campus of Interzone University" section (inspired by Burroughs' 1930s study at Harvard under Livingston Lowes, author of *The Road to Xanadu: A Study in the Ways of the Imagination* [1927], a genetic study of Coleridge's work), where the Mariner stops only "those who cannot choose but hear owing to already existing relation" (73).

Paradoxically, the reader is offered insight into the text, yet the harbinger of that insight, the "Prof.," is quickly deconstructed as an agent of a disturbing critical apparatus. To take the Prof.'s point about the "already existing relation" seriously, the reader becomes no more an *accidental* personage than the results of the random cut-up/fold-in experiments that would consume Burroughs in the next years. The students in *Naked Lunch* do not simply end up as listeners of the Prof.'s lecture by virtue of life's unpredictable vicissitudes. Like the reader, they have been called by the text's mosaic clarion that produces *inevitable* results: they have been "pre-ordained" to listen to the unpredictable spectacle of the Prof.'s tutelage—"Fucked by the Sultan's Army last night" (71)—but this preordainment operates only retroactively. This "already existing relation" is a reverse power dynamic that forces their listening and serves as an early version of Burroughs' experiments with cut-up–induced randomness, where "randomness"—rather than creating chaos—instead arranges with prophetic accuracy. Put another way, the Prof. provides a message of great import that like a cut-up piece assumes its meaning retroactively and recursively throughout *Naked Lunch*: "nothing can ever be accomplished on the verbal level" (74).

As a condemnation of the critical apparatus pumping the text with meaning on the flawed verbal level, this "already existing relation" bears the mark of the occult interconnections of interpersonal communication (the subject *magnetized* by the control discourse of others), as well as a tradition of American hucksterism (from the Ivy Lee side of the family)—both manifest in the one-way nature of the literary transaction. The reader, by virtue of reading, becomes a prefabricated recipient of this same contradictory message: you can't help but listen but don't believe a word.

Even more tellingly, this section further reveals the socioeconomic institutions that prop up the figure of the Author (here, the educational system), particularly one of Coleridge's stripe. For writers such as Burroughs, influenced by the Romantic tradition but operating in a decidedly post-Romantic era, Wordsworth's conception of poetry as "the spontaneous overflow of powerful feelings [. . .] emotion recollected in tranquility" (preface to *Lyrical Ballads*), represents a barrier between the rarified strata of those supposedly special souls who write and those who, sadly, only read. The latter remain located in the form of the pigs that rush the Prof. as he demonstrates how to "slop a pearl: *You can find out more about someone by talking than by listening*" (74). Readers, in the traditional process of literary interpretation—mediated explicitly by modern bourgeois critics and the professoriate, or, more subtly, through an insidious constellation of social apparatuses—become, eventually, those with "fat stomachs and responsible jobs" (73), unable to escape the Mark inside, who, conveniently, is equally unable to dictate literary meaning beyond bland mimicry of the professoriate.

This internal "Mark," grabbing desperately for conventional meaning, operates on at least two levels within the routine. First, the interiority of the self-fashioned, postwar subject becomes stripped of "freewill," to represent the passive half of the power coupling. The "already existing relation" between Mariner and Wedding Guest is the same as that between Prof. and students/pigs and between author and reader—calling into question, as noted above, the conventional methods of explaining the novel.

Second, this questioning transcends the merely intertextual to indict conventional literary authority as processed through the economic engines of authorship (hence the appropriateness of Harris' genetic enterprise). Accordingly, the Prof. calls the students' "attention to the symbolism of the Ancient mariner *himself*" or, in other words, to the "unappetizing person" (72) of Coleridge, the Romantic Author (with capital "A")—from whom literary meaning once traditionally flowed. The lecture hall becomes overrun with pigs not long after the students attempt to rebel against this strain of the Prof.'s metacritical discourse—"switchblades clicking like teeth, move at him" (72). This point is repeated with similar irony later, through the degraded menu from *Chez Robert*, where epicureans are terrorized into consuming "The Clear Camel Piss Soup with boiled Earth Worms" (125). In other words, with added complication: you can't help but listen, but don't believe a word—if you can find a way to stop yourself.

Sometimes an Entity Jumps in the Body

I've taught *Naked Lunch* three times since 2001, twice to students at Lake Forest College and once to an adult-book class, where the group of sophisticated readers seemed to grow more disturbed the farther they traveled into Interzone. They agreed, somewhat hesitantly, to study the novel, largely on the basis that I have published extensively on Burroughs, and they figured that an "expert" might be able to act as guide through the midcentury medina.

They wanted to know, during each of our sessions, what, precisely, the book was trying to convey. In preparation, I presented them with Murphy's article "Intersection Points: Teaching William Burroughs's *Naked Lunch*," although, as Harris notes, the essay errs in the earnestness it attributes to the explanations of the "Atrophied Preface" (reinscribing the novel according to a mistaken manuscript preparation mythology [Harris, 187]), and as well, I would add, in its reinforcement of the unfulfilling trope: William Lee quits drugs (Murphy, 85). I refused, ultimately, to offer what I thought the text "meant" and kept, to their displeasure, only to elaborations on how the text might be operating at any particular point.

Without disregarding the usefulness of context and even conventional criticism for a holistic reading of the sociopolitics of *Naked Lunch*, let me hypothesize that *Naked Lunch* continues to fascinate because of the meaning it *withholds*, rather than the prescriptions it offers to the careful or "turned-on" reader. What causes the text to be simultaneously embraced *and* dismissed, to remain a book perhaps more owned than read is that beyond the few explanatory paragraphs of the "Atrophied Preface" (what Murphy calls "a straightforward practical pedagogy of [Burroughs'] writing" [84]), snake lines less-easily lassoed: "Crabs frolicked through his forest . . . wrestling with the angel hard-on all night, thrown in the homo fall of valor, take a back road to the rusty limestone cave" (190).

These pieces of the *Naked Lunch* mosaic, somewhat resistant to the critical readings that for the most part ignore the material surrounding and asphyxiating those few "straightforward" statements, remain for many readers fundamentally unknowable, extraneous, dangerous—excessive. Unfortunately, in the aforementioned critical views of *Naked Lunch* and despite the novel's meta-fictive attempts to deal with the problem of interpretation in sections such as "Campus of Interzone University," *Naked Lunch* for these same readers is still put down like the "pin and dropper routine"—as a deliberate literary affectation of an alternate drug reality. This returns us to our two modes of reading "excess." In the first, this affected "pin and dropper" routine becomes emblematic of a readerly impulse to police the boundaries of the real, through the mechanism of the outré.

The problem with such explanatory rationales—that a text such as *Naked Lunch* can be understood through the lens of explanatory critical interpretation or reduced to the oversimplified frame: William Lee quits drugs—is that they neutralize the potential of the reader through the act of reading itself. These methods of conventional analysis, which attempt to define a novel from vignettes that as Harris demonstrates "are not fit pieces for a novel," privilege the sections of *Naked Lunch* such as "Hospital" with its "*Disintoxication Notes*" (47).

Yes, a case might be made for the text-as-drug-cure-tale. Yet, these sections contrast with the supposedly "straightforward" declarations of the oft-cited "Atrophied Preface." Statements such as, "I do not presume to impose 'story' 'plot' 'continuity'" (184), if read as modifying the linearity of the drug-cure storyline, offer proof (as Girodias notes) for the work of more "perplexing" counterindications. Given the contradiction between a narrative moment regarding Lee and drugs and the "straightforward" warnings to beware this same straightforwardness, why do readers put such faith in the "explanations" of the "Atrophied Preface"—that *Naked Lunch* does not offer continuity—only to quickly and in the same breath extend the faintest dangling of those linear narrative threads? Significantly, and most likely until the final stage of the manuscript, Burroughs titled this last section "Explanatory Preface/WOULDN'T YOU?"[1]—suggesting by the change that even the casual reader should remain suspicious of its narrative charms.

What, then, maintains the fascination with *explaining Naked Lunch*? Why the rush to inscribe it within the larger trajectory of drug literature? Let me briefly suggest that the book, produced from the flurry of Burroughs' letters, contains these possibilities in just enough substance to remain, when we let down our guard, sublimely intoxicating.

We want to master *Naked Lunch*, to stop *Naked Lunch* from mastering us. To accomplish this, it would take a complete redefinition of "reading" and perhaps an even further genetic refinement of what exactly constitutes the "definitive" text to reveal an alternative. This may well be the work of the next fifty years, and yet such initiatives would bring us no closer to understanding than the text's own excesses *currently* bring us to a "straightforward" plan of action. *Naked Lunch* keeps to the second mode of "excess"—exceeding the possibilities of narrative interpretation—because it refuses to reflect the standard body politic. The book becomes a talking asshole that opens, not toward the light and the way but toward an intestinal economy where the walls are not only lined with shit but also, ultimately, in the drug narrative's failure built from the inassimilable substance itself.

This impossibility of fully explaining *Naked Lunch*'s excesses invokes a more horrifying possibility: Narrative-based explanations, no matter how comforting, are simply not comprehensive enough to *explain* a text that continually announces the impossibility of explanation. And so, gentle reader, despite the best efforts of standard literary criticism, there might be no waking up from the sickness. And for my unhappy students, dizzy in the Rumpus Room, I can only advise, sadly, on how to slop a pearl.

Note

1. William Burroughs, "Explanatory Preface," 2p. tms. SPEC. CMS. 85, box 2, folder 4, William S. Burroughs Papers, Ohio State University.

Works Cited

Berman, Judy. Review of *Naked Lunch*. allreaders.com. http://www.allreaders.com/ Topics/info_24989.asp (accessed June 28, 2007).

Girodias, Maurice. "William S. Burroughs." *The Olympia Reader: Selections from the Traveller's Companion Series.* Edited by Girodias. New York: Grove, 1965. 449–61.

Harris, Oliver. *William Burroughs and the Secret of Fascination.* Carbondale: Southern Illinois UP, 2003.

Lowes, John Livingston. *The Road to Xanadu: A Study in the Ways of the Imagination.* Boston: Houghton Mifflin, 1927.

Murphy, Timothy S. "Intersection Points: Teaching William Burroughs's *Naked Lunch*." *College Literature* 27, no. 1 (2000): 84–103.

Rae, Graham. Review of *Naked Lunch. Pen Pusher* (Winter 2007). http://www.pen-pushermagazine.co.uk/extracts/texts/0701_FOUR/naked_lunch.pdf.

Skerl, Jennie. "Introduction: The Twenty-Fifth Anniversary Edition of *Naked Lunch*." In *Naked Lunch*, by William S. Burroughs, v–xix. New York: Grove, 1984.

Wordsworth, William. Preface to *Lyrical Ballads. Prefaces and Prologues.* Vol. 39. Harvard Classics. New York: Collier, 1909–14. Available at Bartleby.com, 2008, http:// www.bartleby.com/39/36.html (accessed June 28, 2007).

Burroughs' Visionary Lunch

théophile **ARIES**

In September 2005, *UNCUT* magazine asked a hundred musicians and other artists to send a picture of the work of art from the twentieth century that had most influenced them. Rock musician and Velvet Underground cofounder Lou Reed submitted a photograph of himself holding a copy of *Naked Lunch: The Restored Text*. In fact, on the back of this edition, he is quoted as saying, "When I read Burroughs, it changed my vision of what you could write about, how you could write. He broadened people's conception of what makes humanity." Since the early 1970s, William S. Burroughs has indeed become an inexhaustible source of inspiration for many artists seeking creative innovation, something that has not diminished. Combining his dystopian visions with literary experimentation—his own art of montage, such as the cut-up or fold-in techniques—Burroughs opened the door to an unlimited fecundity and managed to transcribe a sense of immediacy and simultaneity, a way out of temporality, that has had a significant influence on innovations in film, music, and song writing. Take, for example, the San Francisco duo Matmos, who in 2006 released an album entitled *The Rose Has Teeth in the Mouth of a Beast,* a series of "sound portraits" of thirteen iconoclasts they admire. It includes, for instance, tributes to director James Bidgood, writer Patricia Highsmith, King Ludwig II of Bavaria, and William S. Burroughs. It is therefore a declaredly queer context that requires from the listener a certain knowledge of the biography and work of each personality portrayed as well as the band itself. What's so original about Matmos is the way they make music and build rhythms with all kinds of unordinary "objects." The piece on Highsmith was made by snails—which feature in two of her psychological horror stories—crawling inside a glass cylinder and interrupting beams of light and so altering the pitch of a theremin. The list of instruments used for *Rag for William S. Burroughs*, an almost fourteen-minute long track of "Arabic ragtime psychedelia," is no less impressive: a *darbuka*, a typewriter, Burroughs Adding Machines, film projectors, a shortwave radio, a tape recorder, and two nineteenth-century printing presses (a Heidelberg Windmill and a Chandler and Price) whose tempo can be adjusted to print in time to music.

Rag is a "blueprint" of Burroughs' life and the writing of *Naked Lunch* and operates through the listener's preexisting knowledge of the author and the book. For instance, the introduction is a mixture of computerized noises mixed with distorted sounds of cats purring and Burroughs saying, "Yasss . . . my little beast," an obvious reference to the writer's love for cats. Although it might seem "touching," Matmos speeded down the band, a technique used to excess by Burroughs in the 1960s when he experimented with audio cut-ups, giving it a frightening aspect that sounds more like a threat than a gentle act of petting. The rag that follows pays nostalgic reference to the 1920s and Burroughs' childhood and adolescence in St. Louis, the birthplace of rag. The piano used in the track is reminiscent of saloon bars and silent movies during which live piano was usually played. It's an evocation of a vanished time, the Jazz Age of *The Great Gatsby* (a favorite of Burroughs). This old American world is abruptly shattered by the sound of a stormy gunshot. The informed listener directly thinks of Mexico City in 1951 when Burroughs accidentally shot his wife. It is followed by a soundtrack-like sequence: music has stopped, we can hear footsteps on bare boards, keys rattled, a door unlocked, opening and closing. The location has shifted. The gunshot works as an aural space-time trip. As in *Naked Lunch*, one has been transported through space and time: in this case, by a time-accelerating gunshot that aurally translates the feeling that after the death of his wife, Burroughs was urgently pressed into writing. Typewriter keys start a rhythm and are rapidly joined by the Burroughs Adding Machine and printing presses. Where are we, and what is being written? The location and the identity of the book are revealed when a *darbuka* is added to the rhythm: we are in the Maghreb, and Burroughs has just started writing *Naked Lunch* in his Tangerine room. The rhythm created by the machines is frenetic; it does not stop and increases in intensity as if the writer were lost in a vortex in which he had no choice but to transcribe data instantaneously given to him. This whirly feeling of lost control is strengthened by the arrival of Moroccan Joujouka music, with swirling rhythms of pipes and drums that weave in and out of the mechanical typewriter rhythm. It is the music of possession that perfectly illustrates the creation of *Naked Lunch*, when Burroughs felt catapulted into some sort of automatic writing, as if the text of *Naked Lunch* were literally creating itself.[1]

Matmos took *Naked Lunch* and Burroughs' life, which they reworked and recombined in their own way. Using the software Max/MSP, they were able to create their own synthesizers from the sounds they first selected in the same way Burroughs was able to create new texts with the cut-up technique, using material he had previously selected. They also resorted to granular synthesis, a method invented by Greek composer Iannis Xenakis, in which samples, instead of being directly used, are split in small pieces called grains that can be layered on top of each other, all playing at different speeds, phases, and volume. The result is a soundscape where many different sounds can be produced through time stretching, multichannel scattering, random reordering, and the like. It is the aural transposition of the cut-up technique, in which Burroughs would split his own writings or those of others in order to create a new, fragmented literary landscape. More than just a reference to the writer of *Naked Lunch*, *Rag for William S. Burroughs* is a piece that is purely Matmos in its vibrancy and its construction of rhythms using both bizarre and ordinary objects. They chose specific objects for each track—a cow uterus (Valerie Solanas), toilet-paper rolls (James Bidgood), cigarettes (Darby Crash), and glassware (Ludwig II)—and used them not as musical instruments or sound effects but primarily as narrative devices. *Rag* is a story in sound. But in the same way David Cronenberg emphasized the insect aspect of *Naked Lunch* and produced a Cronenberg-themed film, Matmos paid homage to Burroughs by absorbing the writer's universe into their own. In the same way that Cronenberg's idea of visually mixing a typewriter with a bug came from his focusing on pictures, Matmos utilized thematic, structural, iconic elements drawn from *Naked Lunch* so as to provide an aural equivalent, consequently transcending mere referentiality and breaking new ground in their treatment of *Naked Lunch* and its author. At the end of the piece, after Joujouka trance music and typewriter keys have built in rhythm and increased in tempo, coalesced, and intertwined before fragmenting and fading, one last sound is heard: the bell of the typewriter; the rag is over, *Naked Lunch* has been written.

With his greatest novel, Burroughs became a prime mover within the tradition of "prophetic" novelists, following on from George Orwell and Aldous Huxley. However, while Burroughs is often considered a kind of visionary, many continue to see his work as inaccessible. Indeed, not only did Burroughs portray his dystopian vision using an extreme carny humor and rawness à la de Sade, exceeding the bounds of conventional prose, he did so through an experimental aesthetic that was as visionary as his ideas. This is what sets him apart from other so-called visionary writers, and this is why he has proved so inspirational for so many artists in so many media.

Annexia

Dystopian novels such as *Brave New World* (1932), *Nineteen Eighty-Four* (1948), and *Fahrenheit 451* (1953) have gained popular status but William S. Burroughs' most famous book remains resistant to such general acceptance, even though the world it depicts seems closer to our present reality. It does so with a whole range of exuberant characters, including Benway, the mad doctor working for Islam Inc. (whose exact objectives remain obscure), and Clem and Jody, two secret agents working for the Russians, whose goal is "to represent the U.S. in an unpopular light." They claim "they are interested in the destruction of Near East oil fields to boost the value of their Venezuelan holdings" (132), and Clem writes a provocative number that goes:

> *What you gonna do when the oil goes dry?*
> *Gonna sit right there and watch those Arabs die.*
>
> (135)

As so often, Burroughs hits the spot with his uncanny foresight. More broadly, he describes a world where the need for control knows no limits. Annexia, where Benway used to work, is a perfect example of a police state where control has taken over human rights. One purpose hiding behind a control system is the provocation of contradictory emotions in people. For instance, to turn pleasures of yesteryear into a sort of modern guilt or a tool of enslavement while at the same time arousing a need for such pleasures, something close to Philippe Mikriammos' definition of Interzone as "the region located between human will and its negation" (45; my translation). In the section entitled "The Examination," Carl Peterson finds in his mailbox a postcard "requesting him to report for a ten o'clock appointment with Doctor Benway in the Ministry of Mental Hygiene and Prophylaxis" (155). Once there, Benway shows Carl pictures of pinup girls and asks him to "pick out the one you would most like to uh make heh heh heh . . ." (162). After Carl does so, Benway excitedly reveals to him that some of these girls "are really *boys*. In uh *drag* I believe is the word?" (163). Benway later accuses Carl of homosexuality, a "deviant" state of being, which enables Benway to label him a criminal. *Naked Lunch* describes a world where criminality has evolved from "doing" to "being" and where Benway is the embodiment of a control system that, though open in communication, actually tries to conceal its reprimanding attitude.

French philosopher Gilles Deleuze wrote in his essay "Post-scriptum sur les sociétés de contrôle" (1990) that "in the societies of control, one is never finished with anything." Such a belief Benway carefully nurtures, explaining that "prolonged mistreatment, short of physical violence, gives rise, when skilfully applied, to anxiety and a feeling of special guilt" (19). It is a special guilt found everywhere today, in airports, shops, on public transport, at customs or in banks, as Burroughs explains in *The Job*:

> Your passport or visa is not quite in order? You have lost your currency control slip? How many times will you *compulsively* repeat the explanation you have prepared in case the customs official starts asking questions. So control measures conjure up phantom interrogators who invade and destroy your inner freedom. (108)

Those phantom interrogators can only be created through a feeling of anxiety, and therefore guilt, something Benway is well aware of, which is why citizens of Annexia have to rush "from one bureau to another in a frenzied attempt to meet impossible deadlines" (20). Such measures are usually justified, as Benway does, as a means to increase public safety. In the United States, since the attacks of 2001, new tools such as biometric identifiers (which verify travelers' fingerprints when they enter the country) have been implemented in order to "improve safety and national security for all Americans."[2] Obviously, the present "war on terror" is a copy of the previous American war on drugs, or the anticommunist witch hunts during McCarthyism, which allowed new encroachments on civil liberties. Everyone is now under suspicion. Following the enactment of the U.S. Patriot Act, privacy and freedom have fast been eroded along with the slowly encroaching reduction to a police state. Such present tools are those deployed in *Naked Lunch* as part of Benway's plan of Total Demoralization, leading to the inevitable desecration of the human image, something obvious in his humiliating questioning of Carl Peterson.

Who Controls the Control Men?

In May 1987, in a talk delivered at the Femis, Gilles Deleuze asserted that Michel Foucault had established two kinds of societies, the *societies of sovereignty* and the *disciplinary societies* (from the nineteenth century to the middle of the twentieth), the latter being organized into enclosed spaces such as the family, the school, the barracks, and then the factory and in some cases, the prison and the hospital.[3] But World War II is, according to Deleuze, at the origin of a new kind of power, which he and Foucault called the *societies of control*, taken from Burroughs' numerous essays on the subject (see *The Adding Machine*). However, Burroughs used the term

Control System rather than society. In old models of power, surveillance had to be limited in space and number. In control systems, rules have changed, as power has been spread throughout society and is not only restricted to closed areas. As Benway reassures Carl Peterson during his examination: "No isolation is indicated . . ." (158). Warders become useless, and control is exercised in an open space, implemented through information, a development Burroughs was the first to address, as Deleuze noted. The ironic aspect of a control society is that freedom, any kind of freedom (of movement, speech, and so on), is necessary for the good use of control. As Burroughs argued (see his essay "The Limits of Control" in *The Adding Machine*), control has to remain partial to be effective. It is therefore a "free-floating control" spread on a fake representation of freedom. The idea is in itself as ironic as the Republic from *Naked Lunch* called Freeland, where Dr. Benway is called in as adviser and where one of his first acts is "to abolish concentration camps" (19).

Since 2001, the Burroughsian idea of the world as a battlefield never seemed truer, reaching a spectacular level, a cosmic fantasy dimension, as if we're all now living inside a Roland Emmerich movie. A conflict has grown, and the most incredible speculations and conspiracy theories (see the documentary *Loose Change*) have emerged to the point that it is almost impossible to know what's going on and who's on whose side—a chaotic confusion that is a key feature in *Naked Lunch*, where Lee, himself a Factualist agent, observes: "You can never be sure of anyone in the industry" (123). In a 1970 interview, Burroughs described how "a junta of colonels" could use the media to establish a control program on the planet and how, their power being not unlimited, they should have pretexts:

> They must have an excuse to proceed. They couldn't start things like that without a pretext of war or some extreme emergency. [. . .] they could put an old style A-bomb over New York which would eliminate quite a bit of the trouble, and then say that the Chinese did it. [. . .] They'd declare a national emergency and arrest anyone. They don't have to know who did it. They'll just arrest everyone who might have done it. (Lotringer, 155–56)

"Arrest anyone" in the same way Hauser and O'Brien were supposed to arrest Lee and Benway summoned Carl Peterson.

A Modest Proposal

Naked Lunch embodied a great range of ideas that Burroughs would go on to develop and theorize in later essays. He once criticized novels from the Bloomsbury Group, including *Brave New World*, for being not "so much novels as treatises, and then if you stripped them down to consider the thought behind them it wasn't particularly interesting or useful" (Bockris, 135). *Naked Lunch* is indeed not a treatise but rather, in Burroughs' own terms, a "How-To" book.

"How to what?" one might ask. How to extend new levels of subjectivity according to the author or how to initiate new forms of subjectivity as suggested by Michel Foucault, an answer that explicitly opposes a "visionary" world against the repressive "reality" and its need to eradicate the "myth of other-level experience" (187). *Naked Lunch* is, therefore, unlike *Brave New World*, *Nineteen Eighty-Four*, or *Fahrenheit 451* a "visionary" novel on two counts: in the prophetic sense of predicting our dystopian world but also in the sense of teaching how to open up realms of unimagined possibilities. Reading it as a how-to book, *Naked Lunch* enables the reader to experience the world in a new way, without having to go where the writer had to go in order to devise the literary form.

Burroughs called his novel a blueprint, which implies a preparation, the expectation of a forthcoming project, a possible call-to-arms, something close to Deleuze's decision to bypass optimism or pessimism and simply to look for new weapons. The only problem was that, at the time of *Naked Lunch*, Burroughs lacked a truly practical weapon to pass on to others. As Oliver Harris points out in his essay "Cutting up Politics": "Any such ambitions depended on an *available technique*—and until he saw what Gysin's Stanley blade had done, Burroughs did not have one" (186). Brion Gysin inadvertently created what would be known as the cut-up technique, precisely the "tool" that *Naked Lunch* pointed towards, which he showed Burroughs in October 1959, only three months after the publication of *Naked Lunch* in Paris.

The cut-up technique was a literary assault aimed at further altering the reader's consciousness, a path to the road of deconditioning, far away from Freeland and Benway's Reconditioning Center (a Burroughsian re-appropriation of Huxley's Conditioning Centre from *Brave New World*), a gate to territories such as those found in Huxley's *Doors of Perception*. Significantly, Huxley had to take psychedelic drugs to realize a creative "visionary" dimension but even then could not invent a correspondingly visionary aesthetic. *The Doors of Perception* was one of the very first texts Burroughs decided to cut up, making plain his awareness of the need to re-vision language itself.

"I Am the Doctor"

Burroughs' addiction played a major role in his consideration of the world, because through the way he was treated as an addict he saw what most people did not usually witness. In the last years of his life, when journalists asked him to speak about the evil of junk, he would answer, "shallow pretext for police state" (*Last Words*, 39). His many arrests, searches at airports, the many routines enacted by cops (see "Hauser and O'Brien," 175–81), the many bureaucratic procedures he had to undergo—all these experiences he went through were intelligently used in *Naked Lunch* but applied to everyone, not only addicts. He extended police encroachments to all citizens, foreseeing that some day everyone might be considered a criminal under obscure, ever-changing laws. By extending the policies applied to drug addicts to all citizens, Burroughs illustrated how his addiction had been relevant for his writing and his way of thinking and why *Naked Lunch*, written in the 1950s, seems to describe the world in which we presently live.

Naked Lunch puts the reader on his/her guard against human nature and its need for power. He warns the reader against trusting in the self, tells the reader to mistrust what the little voice inside says, to keep checking in the mirror to prevent "The Crime of Separate Action" from occurring (186). *Naked Lunch* warns us of our own nature. Deploying a linguistic flair, carny humor, and a new form of montage (predicting his cut-up technique), Burroughs ridicules control and science as exerted and practiced by Benway. He therefore delivers an avant-garde vision whose potent content is expressed in a unique form, a powerful text which changed not only Lou Reed's but any reader's vision of "what you could write about" and "how you could write."

On 7 May 1997, aged eighty-three, William S. Burroughs wrote in his final journal: "So books do exactly that—show us where present policies are taking us" (*Last Words*, 177).

And that's exactly what *Naked Lunch* did—and still does . . .

Notes

1. The possessive and frenetic immediacy of Joujouka was also the basis for later music such as jungle music in the 1990s; see for instance the use of *Drum'n'Bass* in Underwires' *Dr. Benway* (2007) or David Bowie's *I'm Deranged* (1995), whose lyrics he wrote using a cut-up software.

2. U.S. Department of State, Bureau of Consular Affairs, "Safety and Security of U.S. Borders / Biometrics," http://travel.state.gov/visa/immigrants/info/info_1336.html.

3. Gilles Deleuze, "Qu'est-ce qu'un acte de création?" *Multitudes: revue politique artistique philosophique*, http://multitudes.samizdat.net/article.php3?id_article=1559 (August 2004).

Works Cited

Bockris, Victor. *With William Burroughs: A Report from the Bunker*. 1981. Rev. ed. New York: St. Martin's Griffin, 1996.

Burroughs, William S. *The Adding Machine*. 1985. New York: Arcade, 1993.

———. *Last Words: The Final Journals of William S. Burroughs*. Edited by James Grauerholz. London: Flamingo, 2000.

Burroughs, William S., and Daniel Odier. *The Job: Interviews*. 1974. Rev. ed. New York: Penguin, 1989.

Deleuze, Gilles. "Post-scriptum sur les sociétés de contrôle." *L'autre Journal* 1 (May 1990). http://1libertaire.free.fr/DeleuzePostScriptum.html.

Harris, Oliver. "Cutting up Politics." In *Retaking the Universe: William S. Burroughs in the Age of Globalisation*, edited by Davis Schneiderman and Philip Walsh, 175–200. London: Pluto, 2004.

Lotringer, Sylvère, ed. *Burroughs Live: The Collected Interviews of William S. Burroughs 1960–1997*. Los Angeles: Semiotext(e), 2001.

Matmos. *The Rose Has Teeth in the Mouth of a Beast*. Matador Records, 2006.

Mikriammos, Philippe. *William S. Burroughs*. Paris: Seghers, 1975.

dossier FIVE
ian MACFADYEN

Files Comprising: Holy Ghosts, Lunch Calls, Plain Brown Wrappers, Lee And The Chinese, The Script And The Score, Virtual End-Point, Glittering Mosaics, Kicking, From Erewhon To Annexia, Enter The Powers Of Evil, Rock And Roll Oedipus, Trickster, The Doctor Is Expecting You, Criminal Sex, Anything Written, Biomechanical.

Holy Ghosts

In Abel Ferrara's vampire movie *The Addiction* (1995), Christopher Walken asks the heroine, a student writing a doctoral thesis on the nature of evil, "Have you ever read *Naked Lunch*? . . . You'll be hungry all the time . . . " *Naked Lunch* is a work of vampiric, libidinous orality—slurping on Babe Ruths, devouring a sugar skull, suckling paregoric babies, thirsty veins sucking syringes. . . . The naked woman keeps her stash in a Cobra lamp, she gives Lee a shot, pulls out the needle, and "licks a drop of blood off her finger" (191). Like vampires, junkies form "a world network" (7) and though Burroughs assures us that this is not a sacred cult, it is "profane and quantitative" (201), he contradicts this: "Junk is surrounded by magic and taboos, curses and amulets" (6). As Sinclair Beiles wrote in *Sacred Fix*, "I am devoted to a holy cult. / a needle vestal if you wish, / diner from the lotus dish" (23). Junkies are blood brothers of the needle, necromancers fearful of the dawn, ritualists warding off jinxes and hexes in their "blighted, secret place" (23), every score seemingly procured by an act of magic.

Lunch Calls

In Aleister Crowley's 1922 novel *Diary of a Drug Fiend*, the two junkies on the train are stirred from their "whirling trance" by the steward's "first call for lunch" (106). It's a wake-up call, but Crowley's dope fiends are derailed on smack time, for them this is the last and final call for lunch, the steward's voice fading down the corridors of the *train de luxe* . . . *Naked Lunch*: "Train compartment: two sick young junkies . . ." (68). Burroughs' junkies are ostensibly en route to Lexington to take the cure, but as the train "tears on through the smoky, neon-lighted June night" (69) they are already planning to make a stopover in the dry County of Marshall and hit on an old croaker for an Rx . . . Junk doesn't run to schedule and lunch for these lotus eaters is most definitely *over*.

Plain Brown Wrappers

Kerouac didn't prophesy the title, he recognized it. Robert Creeley told me about the times he shared with Kerouac in San Francisco, sitting in a back alley and passing back and forth a bottle of wine hidden in a brown paper lunch-bag. *Naked Lunch* tears and throws the bag away to reveal the addictive pleasure beneath—the illicit but necessary hit which had been secreted in the working man's lunch bag from the very beginning. Like erotic fiction circulated in plain brown paper wrappers, the secret should be made plain for all to see. In Adler Place. In Piccadilly.

Lee And The Chinese

Lee was Burroughs' mother's maiden name and the nom de plume he used for *Junkie*. It is a relatively common Southern name, but in *Naked Lunch*, it takes on an exotic component, redolent of early 1900s New York, when games of fan tan were played and opium smoked in the basements of Chinatown, and old Tom Lee was head of the On Leongs. We don't discover that *Lee* is a surname until the "Hauser and O'Brien" episode late in the book, and both in English usage and in certain transliterations of this common Chinese name, *Lee* may be taken for a first name or a surname, and this ambiguity compounds the play upon identity and "inscrutability" which links Lee to opium—it is his fate to end up trapped in time in the rural Chinese community of Deadwood near Sioux Falls, South Dakota. Lee has two ghost cops along for this terminal ride into the past, and they are traveling together right through the Black Hills of the 1890s and the Gold Rush gaming halls of 1876 into the heart of America, the land before the

Chinese and the Lakota, before Robert E. Lee and every other Lee, and "The evil is there waiting" (24).

The Script And The Score

Did *Naked Lunch*, patently *in parts* an antiheroin book, ever stop anyone in their tracks? And how many decided, even after reading Burroughs' book, especially *after* reading it, to take that ride? As Elizabeth Young asked, "How many lesser, faltering comets have burnt out helplessly in his wake?" (26). When Marianne Faithfull told Burroughs that she felt reading *Naked Lunch* had been instrumental in her own addiction, Burroughs replied, "That is the road and only the person on the road knows how far it goes. It might lead you to Timbuktu, it might lead you to Avenue B . . . or the Interzone . . . But, my dear, I was just stating the facts. I'm not in the business of giving advice." Marianne Faithfull replied, "Well . . . maybe I read between the lines a bit" (99).

Virtual End-Point

Burroughs provides a blueprint for reading *Naked Lunch* only at the book's virtual end-point, the "Atrophied Preface," which promises innumerable new beginnings—the book "spill off the page in all directions," it can be read "back and forth [...] fore and aft," "the pieces can be had in any order" (191), recombined as in a kaleidoscope, continually regenerating and transforming meaning—"You can cut into *Naked Lunch* at any intersection point . . ." (187). This is why all Burroughs' self-confessed attempts to write a "proper" preface "atrophy and amputate spontaneous" (187), because the true beginning of *Naked Lunch* is an intersection point *anywhere within the text* and the only possible introduction to such a reading must come after the termination and abandonment of the paginated, sequential, version.

Glittering Mosaics

Naked Lunch's structure is impossible to grasp because it is essentially *a work in progress*, a moving mosaic reconstituted in variant form by every reader through an endless "piecing together," a continual reassembling of a text without limit through associative recombination, the creation of new, alternative versions from the original bricolage. Burroughs came close to describing this kaleidoscopic process in his blurb for Irving Rosenthal's 1967 book *Sheeper*—"Each word is transmuted by the alchemy of arrangement. Brightly colored beetles move and shift in a glittering mosaic of Mandarin complexity" (Rosenthal, n.p.).

Kicking

Heroin is a disease characterized by its chronic lapses, and in its circular recurrences and emotional spasms, in its manic burlesque cut-ups and dreadful night longeurs, *Naked Lunch* structurally embodies the excruciating tension and explosive release of absolute need, the kicking addict's endless rise for a fall.

From Erewhon To Annexia

"Later the receiving agent will be hanged, convict of the guilty possession of a nervous system" (173). This mockery of judicial authority recalls the trial scene in Samuel Butler's 1872 *Erewhon*. With "majestic severity," Butler's judge addresses a man charged with pulmonary consumption: "You were convicted of aggravated bronchitis last year" (123), he reminds the poor wretch, before sentencing him to life imprisonment. In the land of Erewhon, all doctors have been criminalized and outlawed, while Burroughs' doctors really are criminal, yet esteemed in their lunatic disregard for their patients and their contempt for every medical ethic and rule of hygiene. The maverick artist, the crank ideas merchant, the authority on drugs, the practitioner of control and wreaker of bloody chaos, Benway & Burroughs Burlesque is an unforgettable Siamese double act, a punishment act, a hard act to follow, and to swallow. As Brion Gysin said to Terry Wilson, "It was a great service to humanity that William never practiced medicine."

Enter The Powers Of Evil

Shrieking harridans and lust-crazed matriarchs set out on a mob castration spree—in *Naked Lunch*, the female of the species is always deadlier than the male: "this old hag appear as she thinks resplendent in her diamond tiara. [. . .] All these old witches examining their rocks. [. . .] Old bitch marry so many times [. . .] a *poule de luxe*" (108). The misogyny is worthy of Uncle Charlie, the Merry Widow Killer, in Hitchcock's *Shadow of a Doubt*. It's so blatant and excessive as to suggest a satire on misogyny, but it just won't wash. Burroughs' bourgeois matrons and housewives are transformed through loathing and guilt into fiendish, hideous Furies, like those filmed by Slavko Vorkapich in the virtuoso opening sequence of the 1934 proto-*noir Crime Without Passion*—a woman's staring eye becomes the barrel of a gun, the gun fires, the eye screws up in pain, and blood splatters on the floor, releasing the daemonic painted hags who swoop screaming and laughing through the canyons of the city, shattering windows and skylights, seeking revenge for the female victim, and celebrating with awful ululations the death of love.

Rock And Roll Oedipus

The Rock and Roll hoodlum is more than a mixed-up kid, he's a switch-blade psycho, though he knows his Shakespeare, his Freud, and the Bible. Putting down the old Hamlet routine, he reveals his own take on the Oedipus Complex—"better 'twere to cut your throat and screw my mother playing it straight than fuck my father or vice versa mutatis mutandis as the case may be, and cut my mother's throat" (35). But how straight can our Punk Hamlet play it when, as he says, "Male and female castrated he them" (35)? This rephrasing of Genesis 1:27 ("male and female He created them") explains the kid's professed anxiety about whether to submit to getting fucked by "great big daddy" (or "motherfucker") or to "commit a torso job on the old lady." In Peter Biskind's phrase, he's "the Dead End Kid of the therapeutic fifties [. . .] the perfect patient" (261). "Who can't distinguish between the sexes?" he asks, but that's the point, it's an entirely disingenuous dilemma because he'd really like to slash *both* his parents' throats. Jumping plays, it's a line from *Macbeth,* 2.3, which our Black Leather Oedipus parodies next—"Confusion hath fuck his masterpiece" (35). He means it literal—instead of killing his father, he's "cut the janitor's throat quite by mistake of identity, he being such a horrible fuck like the old man." Castration ends procreation and sexual differentiation, creating confusion which ruins the symmetry of the Oedipus myth for our queer Psycho Killer (truth be told, it was ruined already), and now every couple is a mummy and a daddy just waiting for this Son of Sam to catch them *in flagrante delicto* and terminate conception, *including his own.* This street-corner performance of Sophocles, played for pure brutalist laughs, deliberately mixes and mangles Shakespeare and 1950s American psychodelinquency, starring doomed John Barrymore Jr., the pomaded drug pusher from the 1958 flick *High School Confidential!* as our petulant, callous killer, a perfectly degenerate literary descendant of Pinky in Greene's *Brighton Rock* and a prophetic, narcissistic sketch of *In Cold Blood* murderer Perry Smith, who wants to cut his mother's throat because "it's the best way I know to stem her word hoard" (35) . . . before Burroughs, naturally, declares the unleashing of his own.

Trickster

Naked Lunch is a work of deranged anthropology and spurious, fantastic ethnology, consistently deviant and unreliable. The infamous "Talking Asshole" routine usurps a trickster myth of the Winnebago Indians and totally reverses its meaning. In the mythological story,

Trickster orders his anus to guard some roasted ducks while he sleeps, but despite expelling gas, the anus is unable to ward off a raid of foxes who steal and consume the meat. When he wakes, Trickster is furious: "I will burn your mouth so that you will not be able to use it!" (Douglas, 81). And he burns "the mouth of his anus" (81) with a stick from the fire—only to cry out in pain. The story charts the passage from undifferentiation to socialization, Trickster obliged to learn the nature and limits of his being in the world. But in *Naked Lunch*, the asshole takes over entirely, sealing the "real" mouth with gasoline jelly, the suffering brain going out behind dead eyes—"It's you who will shut up in the end. Not me. Because we don't need you around here anymore. I can talk and eat *and* shit" (111). But the asshole's jubilant use of the first-person pronoun is doomed, the takeover operation is self-inflicted asphyxiation. Playing upon the famous ventriloquist possession scenario in the 1945 film *Dead of Night*, Benway's fantastic "case history" reverses the process of socialization and privileges the death instinct—the asshole's routine is a deranged, suicidal soliloquy, an aberrant will-to-power, a delirious projection of Benway's own loquacious antihomosexual fascism.

The Doctor Is Expecting You

Dr. Benway, so popular and well loved, is a direct medical descendant of celebrity brain surgeon Dr. Walter Freeman, who toured the States from the 1940s well into the 1960s, giving dramatic, live public demonstrations of transorbital lobotomies which he performed with an ice pick, releasing the "black butterflies" of psychosis through a hole in the cranium. Traveling in his specially designed camper van which he dubbed the "Lobotomobile," Freeman believed this exorcism by psychosurgery was ideal for all schizos, queers, and commies. Here's how you do it: anesthetize with electric shock, pull back the eyelid, insert the tip of the ice pick, easy does it, then whack with a hammer right through the orbital plate into the brain, pull back by thirty degrees or so, try not to crack the skull open like an egg, stupid, then yank the thing back and forth in a twenty-degree arc, severing the nerves of the frontal lobe. . . . And there you have it, or rather, there you *don't* have it.

Criminal Sex

Dr. Benway's view of homosexuality is in accord with Edmund Bergler's 1956 description of "the great proportion of homosexuals" as incorrigible "swindlers, pathological liars (pseudologues), forgers, lawbreakers of all sorts, drug purveyors, gamblers, spies, pimps, brothel-owners, etc." (200). Note the inclusion of "spies" in that lineup, mixing up sexual and narcotic criminality with actual treason—by their mark shall you know them, and *they're all the same,* by any other name: Junkie. Queer. Commie. Writer.

Anything Written

Hauser takes a breakfast call from the Lieutenant: "Don't take time to shake the place down. Except bring in all books, letters, manuscripts. *Anything* printed, typed or written. Ketch?" (175). He does not supply a reason. This is ostensibly a bust by the City Narcotic Squad, but there's an unspoken assumption—that Lee's writing is politically subversive and criminally complicit. "Now I, William Seward, will unlock my word hoard" (192) mocks the "confessions" of the House Un-American Activities Committee and, despite of—or because of—its derangement and invective, it is a truly lacerating testament. Prospero: "This thing of darkness I Acknowledge mine."

Biomechanical

In Nathanael West's 1933 novel *Miss Lonelyhearts*, a "'goat and adding machine' ritual" (217) is devised to accompany the execution of a con-victed killer: "the goat would be used as part of a 'sack cloth and ashes' service [. . .] Prayers for the condemned man's soul will be offered on an adding machine" (217). *Naked Lunch* is just such a ceremony, blasphemously blessing the mechanization of monetary profit and the numerical loss of life—"the only universal language" (217)—with an outpouring of sacrificial blood, dumping the slashed, eviscerated carcass onto the magical invention bearing the proud Burroughs fam-ily name, creating a biomechanical pagan altarpiece, dripping with lust and shame.

Sole Survivor a Raving Maniac

gail-nina **ANDERSON**

Before cut-ups, there were cuts—fades, zooms, flashbacks. Scenes were repeated, moments emphasized and reemphasized, inserted, juxtaposed, isolated. That's the magic of the movies. In a world of darkened rooms, these vignettes of absurdly heightened reality could play out, brought together yet connected by nothing more than narrative conventions, and sometimes not even by those. Did the feature and the advertisements and the newsreels and the cartoons and the shorts all run together to create a world where apparently discrete universes jostled for attention? A swift trip to the lobby could take you out of the Wild West and return you to a place where animated orange drinks sang for your attention. The movies were never for the faint-hearted—you checked in your reality at the door and exchanged it for a carnival parade that used your optic nerve as a cable into your brain, and you did it in the dark, in a room full of candy-popping strangers.

And William Burroughs did it and must have been doing it through some of the golden ages of American moviegoing. Must have soaked up matinees and double features with all the trimmings, must have been there as generic conventions blossomed and codified and waned. Must have hunkered down in the sticky availability of the plush seat while wandering the vast scenario that flattened out a universe in front of him.

Scenario—Rick's bar, or something like it. Somewhere between *The Maltese Falcon* (1941) and *The Third Man* (1949), an International Zone where no one is at home, and everyone is dealing in some commodity that shifts and alters its meaning as soon as it is named. Negotiation is endless, closure impossible, violence implicit. Oh, and corruption is so intrinsic as not to be worth naming. This sleazy world is characterized not so much by its lack of heroes as by its seething expenditure of energy on things that slip and slide. Reputation, treasure, vengeance, lust—someone deals in everything, prices change in a breath, and commodities vanish like fairy gold the moment their value is defined.

Even mainstream movies, even within the comparatively strait-laced, closely prescribed morality of post–Hays Code cinema could offer up an amoral world where appetite loomed much larger than social responsibility, where individuals *were* appetites. Sidney Greenstreet or Peter Lorre in *The Maltese Falcon* are grand grotesques who could have come straight out of *Naked Lunch*, Orson Welles as Harry Lime in *The Third Man* could (and probably did) sell any quack cures that Dr. Benway cares to patent. Burroughs has been to the movies, and the silver screen reflects its tropes right back onto the pages of the book.

The desire to view *Naked Lunch* through the lens of classic *film noir* is made more understandable by the way that David Cronenberg, in his 1991 film-of-the-book, does just that. Of course, Cronenberg's *Naked Lunch* isn't so much the film of the book as a mutating riff on the themes of *Naked Lunch*, Burroughs' life, and the director's own magnificent obsessions. Cronenberg's back catalogue reveals a body of work dedicated to the New Flesh—those obtrusions and excrescences whereby the unnavigable interior forces its way outwards, lacking all respect for the previously perceived form of things, redefining the body as a battleground rather than a temple. But the cinematic language of his mature style has come also to reveal a terse elegance, where (as so memorably in *Dead Ringers*) just the glimpse of a tray of gynecological implements can manifest the entire agonizing process of a private world created, then twisted out of kilter.

And so *Naked Lunch*—The Movie eschews massive set-pieces of boys and baboons. That its director can articulate insectoid typewriters and forge a visual relationship with Mugwumps can be taken as a given. The surprise comes with the sense of those locations, places we've all been because we sat in the dark and watched the moving shadows, places Burroughs, too, must have been before he wrote the book, before he went near Tangier. Preestablished cinematic modes locate Lee and co. better than any atlas. Interzone is that postcolonial, postmorality no-man's land where to know the rules is to break them, where everyone has an angle, where it is the shadow rather than the light that defines. Its *noir*-ish atmosphere, laden with the ghosts of private dicks, hopeless dames, and effete exiles, provides a reminder that

Burroughs' text, despite its baroque excesses, also floats on a layering of suggestion and connection, on memories built up in those dark, smoke-filled picture houses where worlds must always collide.

Flickering through *Naked Lunch* are single frames, flashes of light that don't need to be much more than subliminal. We already know where that threshold is, have bought our tickets, and paid into a world crackling with sweaty anticipation, where the sensational can be activated by no more than a hideous implication. Like the director who could translate his text into the required narrative coherence of a mainstream movie, Mr. Burroughs has most certainly been not just to see the gangsters in the shadows but to the horror film.

Returning to the book after putting on the X-ray specs of the film buff and alerting ourselves to possible roots and sources (not to mention subsequent developments in the movies themselves) transforms the experience of reading *Naked Lunch* into the formulation of a compendium of types and motifs central to the repertoire of horror/science-fiction cinema. From the Southern Gothic of Old Ma Lottie and her dead daughter (vultures circling over the swamps) to the dead insect-eye of Salvador with his inappropriately smooth face like someone already embalmed, this is the imagery of those X-rated films that offer up as their key to the mysteries of the human condition the perverse rather than the normal. Tack on as many happy endings as you like, the attraction of such films isn't that it all comes out right in the end. They offer a glimpse into the lurking horrors that defy normalizing, giving a shape to what we know is really there but cannot describe.

Horror films assign a form to the monstrous not so that we can defeat it but to allow us to embrace it, and Burroughs threads just these familiar monsters through the shifting scenario of his work. Almost throw-away references remind us that just beneath the skin (quite literally at one point, a uniform of human skin) lies the fleshless mummy, the invisible man, and our interior vocabulary of cannibals, screaming skulls, and serial killers. (Long before *10 Rillington Place*, Burroughs references Christie—if his Robert is the same as John—alongside that favorite enigma of the horror/detective genre, Jack the Ripper.)

One specific film, though, stands out at once via what are surely intended to be unmistakable references. When Burroughs writes "Room for one more inside" (193), it calls up the lugubrious smile of British character actor Miles Malleson as the conductor whose crowded bus is about to topple over a bridge, killing all passengers. The horror, though, lies not in the disaster itself but (real perversity here) in one man's avoidance of it. A racing driver has seen and heard the conductor in a premonitory dream, inviting him to enter a hearse, so he doesn't board the bus and survives to tell the story. Originating in a short story by E. F. Benson, "The Bus Conductor" was adapted to become part of *Dead of Night*, a British film of 1945 in which four different directors each "told" a strange story or two all wrapped up in a locating narrative that would eventually break down, shatter illogically, and reabsorb elements of the four tales into a wildly fragmented nightmare from which the central character (played by Mervyn Johns) would emerge only to start the whole cycle of events again (and presumably again and again). Structurally, the attractions of this sort of portmanteau film (later a mainstay of British horror movies of the 1970s) to Burroughs are obvious. The stories could be viewed in any order, and though the containing narrative offers an apparently sequential pattern of development, its ending overrides our desire to keep things neatly compartmentalized. While the stories themselves are not sensational by modern expectations, they generate a distinct air of unease while the very restraint of the film acts to create the keynote to which Burroughs must have responded—a terrifying sort of impropriety. The setting is an English country house just after World War II, but the war seems scarcely to have happened. Social mores and expectations—even a few jolly touches of hallowed British eccentricity—remain intact in an atmosphere where friendly informality is really the external form of a well-established code of manners and behavior. An architect (Johns) has been invited for the weekend to discuss building an extension, and nothing looks set to disturb a world of comfortable armchairs, tea, and companionable cigarettes. A chance remark starts a story ("The Bus Conductor") that punctures the bubble of security, leading the house guests to tell tales that lead them further and further away from the notions of security and containment that the house had seemed to offer, and to open up worlds beyond their control. A teenage girl has met the ghost of a boy murdered by his sister, a young married woman has seen her husband transformed into a wife-killer by the influence of an antique mirror, and even an attempt at humor hinges on a tall tale involving suicide, haunting, sexual frustration, and the distinct possibility that a new bride will spend her wedding night with the ghost of her husband's former rival. While the film never overtly challenges the limitations of good taste that its date and setting inevitably imposed, yet there is an unadmitted sexual tension underlying the stories, four of which contextualize their supernatural aspects within tales of courtship and/or marriage and all of which implicitly threaten the cozy, unchanging world view of the participants.

The fifth story, director Alberto Cavalcanti's "The Ventriloquist's Dummy," is justly the best remembered and is less of a traditional ghost story than the others. Michael Redgrave is the ventriloquist, popular enough to be playing in the sort of sophisticated nightclub that is one of the favorite settings of filmmakers of the forties (the decade when Burroughs seems to have been most consistently absorbing the tropes of popular film). Amongst a cosmopolitan atmosphere of evening clothes and cocktails, Redgrave's character is humiliated by his dummy, Hugo, who seems to reject his operator to woo another ventriloquist. On one level, this is a tale of madness, of a disassociation from reality and the assignment of independent awareness to an inanimate object. This is the way it is interpreted by its teller, Dr. Van Straaten (Frederick Valk). This character is the catalyst for the film's central debate, a mysteriously (given the date) German house guest (the host makes the point that he keeps schnapps particularly for the doctor) who could be seen as a nod back to such prototypes as Dr. Caligari. Thickly accented and spectacled, he is clearly a "brain doctor" whose psychological explanations clamp down on the free-floating possibilities presented by everyone else's story. He exerts the control from under which their irrationality is always trying to slip and eventually explains away the possibility that Hugo could really have gained an unnatural life of his own. It was all in the ventriloquist's mind, as evidenced by a final sequence in which he has taken on the character and voice of his dummy. The film could have become fixed at this point, an essay in modernism scaring away the ghosts, but the dream-sequence ending and the promise of repetition bravely deny the heavy-handed brightness of Dr. Van Straaten's reasonable explanations. Almost allowed to be the prophet of clean, rational psychological theory, he becomes part of the nightmare and so joins that line of control-obsessed scientists that stretches from Frankenstein to Dr. Benway, Burroughs' shyster heir to this enduring horror-film trope.

The ventriloquist's dummy (surely the very same one who acts as a simile in "Ordinary Men and Women," where the Latah sucks all the persona out of someone "like a sinister ventriloquist's dummy" [118]?) is also, though, a tale of the part breaking away from the whole, the terrifying and (like so many horrific motifs) visually ludicrous notion that physical coherence is under constant challenge. Dr. Van Straaten could never, in 1945, have suggested with hackneyed Freudian neatness that Hugo is actually the ventriloquist's penis, but viewers may find their own resonances in the little wooden man who wants his own way and who eventually stands up for himself. The hand that crawls in *The Beast with Five Fingers* (1946) or the grafted hands and even the head that apparently gets reattached in *Mad Love* (1935) attest to the power of the animated part that threatens the whole. Both films starred Peter Lorre, whose heavily accented voice and always slightly offbeat physical presence could suggest a decadence that placed him firmly in Hollywood's horror/*film noir* repertoire company. Even at the start of his career, in Germany, he had been most notably cast by director Fritz Lang as the moon-faced child murderer in *M* (1931), and in *The Maltese Falcon*, he played one of the most overtly effeminate characters Hollywood allowed, not a spit off one of Burroughs' camp queens.

In 1946, to show a single autoperambulatory hand required immense ingenuity. Changes in taste, modern special effects, and the revolution offered by computer-generated imagery (CGI) combine to make the morphing and splitting off of the human body almost commonplace in contemporary cinema. Cronenberg's external wombs (*The Brood* [1979]) or the way America's social elite operates by a jokingly hideous merging of its members' bodies in *Society* (Brian Yuzna, 1989) offer riffs on themes that Burroughs had already explored. Professor Fingerbottom's wayward piles gut him with an obscene *schlup* and a curious nod to Isadora Duncan (strangled when, like the piles, her long scarf drifted backwards to get caught in the wheels of a car). Doc Scranton's questing arsehole is the owner's lust on an extension lead. The talking anus described by Dr. Benway (surely referenced in *Zero Patience* [1993], where two gay arses duet on the theme that the rectum is not a grave?) is *Dead of Night*'s Hugo, the part that develops first a voice and then a will of its own, leaving its previous operator an empty shell of his former self.

Naked Lunch's threat to physical coherence and dignity, though, is more free-flowing than even the most extreme horror films of Burroughs' youth could have been. The full impact of Technicolor red blood was notoriously first exploited sensationally by Hammer films in the late fifties, but the cinema still shies away from that irrepressible fluidity of jissom, shit, ectoplasm, afterbirth, piss, and menstrual discharges that defines (if that is the right word) the human condition in *Naked Lunch*. In the movies, coherent visual/physical identity was (especially under the studio star system) paramount, and any threat to its clearly defined boundaries was a shock. One of the most genuinely, ludicrously shocking moments in 1940s cinema comes in Sam Wood's sensationalist exposé of American hypocrisy *Kings Row* (1942) when Ronald Reagan wakes up minus his legs to cry, "Where's the rest of me?" (incidentally, the title of the actor's 1965 autobiography). But if there was a limit to the extent films could desecrate the human body, even during the Hays Code period of imposed good taste, horror films still found ways to explore the idea.

Between the 1930s and 1950s, Universal Studios had, in a sequence of films sufficiently popular to see many sequels, re-releases, and imitations, established a repertoire of those "movie monsters" that still continue to populate our culture. The worlds they inhabit and their repeating plot motifs form a sequence of "routines" that call up many echoes in *Naked Lunch*. These are the riffs that horror films (like comedies) are permitted to play on decency and coherence, the license accorded to the jester and mad doctor alike. For challenges to the flesh, the entire *Frankenstein* oeuvre stakes an undisputed claim. That the sensibilities of gay English director James Whale might not match those of the accredited mainstream is perhaps a given. In the lead of both *Frankenstein* (1931) and *Bride of Frankenstein* (1935), he cast Colin Clive, an actor whose clipped, camp hysteria forged an unforgettable hybrid when linked with his character's (apparent) expertise in medical experimentation. Despite the regulation beautiful and long-suffering wives, these films crested a wave of weirdness in their subversive imagery of procreation. A camp scientist creates a huge man from looted body parts, with the aid of a male assistant who in the first film is a sadistic hunchback (Dwight Frye) who can substitute a (labeled) criminal brain for that of the required genius, and in the sequel is the finicky, effeminate Dr. Pretorius (Ernest Thesiger) whose alchemical expertise has led him to "grow" tiny stereotypical humans (bishop, ballet dancer, mermaid) in bell-jars. The creation of their scientific meddling (Boris Karloff's "monster") subverts by his very being any concept of a "natural order" of things, being put together from their dabblings in dead flesh and unnatural animation.

But Frankenstein wasn't the only mad scientist to flicker somewhere in the shadows behind Dr. Benway. *Dr Jekyll*, in film versions from 1920, 1931, 1941, and beyond, toys dangerously with ideas of control, experimenting on himself to separate the good from the evil selves and in the process creating Mr. Hyde. Hyde isn't just the embodiment of our antisocial impulses: he represents (especially in Stevenson's original novella) that favorite late-Victorian trope of de-evolution. Hyde is humanity without human restraint, not so much evil as innocently but entirely self-centered, an unrestrained id acting out every impulse.

In Rouben Mamoulian's 1931 version, there is something decidedly ape-like in Frederick March's performance, the descent of man from the gentle to the bestial, the baboon that lurks beneath the dress suit. Both this and the 1941 Spencer Tracy version also feature fragmented dream-like sequences that operate to acclimatize the viewer to this state of deterioration and untrammeled sexual alertness. Alongside Dr. Jekyll, one might place H. G. Wells' Dr. Moreau (Charles Laughton in the 1932 film adaptation, *Island of Lost Souls*), who attempts to reverse the process by surgically transmuting wild animals into subjugated humans who still retain something of their natural origins. Order is harshly imposed and violently denied, as flesh refuses to be coerced into an irrelevant conformity. Burroughs more than once uses the phrase *black lagoon*, gesturing towards a later riff on the same theme of evolutionary uncertainty. In *Creature from the Black Lagoon* (1954), a humanoid gill-man represents what we might have been, a living fossil from a dead branch of evolution who (inevitably) attempts to abduct the beautiful scientist-heroine to a life of unimaginably nonhuman affection.

The exoticism of *Island of Lost Souls* and *Creature from the Black Lagoon* strikes its own chord—these things take place somewhere strange and "primitive" where the rules never quite apply. *Naked Lunch* flirts with the concept of the superstitious mind, untutored in Western logic, with repeated references to the Bang-utot death that afflicts Asian men, to cannibals, devil-dolls, and leopard men. This last seems to relate to the real-life (but much contested) instances of murderous attacks by steel-clawed tribal cult-members ritually dressed in leopard skins and particularly newsworthy during the mid-1940s' outbreaks in Nigeria. There might also be a hint of the 1943 Val Lewton/Jacques Tourneur low-budget movie *The Leopard Man*, which could almost be a Burroughs scenario. In a faux-sophisticated New Mexico nightclub where girls with names like Clo-Clo and Kiki are part of the entertainment, a leashed leopard is introduced as a publicity stunt. It breaks free, creating mayhem amongst the diners, and goes on to disrupt the peace of the town by savagely killing three young women before the real culprit is revealed to be a mild-mannered serial killer who runs the local museum. During the 1940s, Lewton emerged as the producer of a distinctive line of subtly nasty B-movies that explored themes of repression, dependence, and control. Burroughs would surely have responded to *I Walked with a Zombie* (1943) or *Cat People* (1942), which features a predatory psychiatrist who attempts to seduce a virginal young wife in the name of curing her obsessive notion that sexual arousal will transform her into a big cat and result in the death of her partner; his fate scarcely requires exposition.

For the ultimate motif of social disruption that comes in a seductive guise, of flesh that embarrasses by breaking taboos and crossing even the boundary between life and death and of sexuality as virus, infecting, destroying, and creating a complex pattern of dependency, all packaged up into a form that can disguise its meaning under the permitted license of the horror film, one should look to *Dracula*. The 1931 version directed by Tod Browning and starring Bela Lugosi in a languorously reptilian reading of the vampire as lounge lizard, includes a character prominent in Bram Stoker's original novel but often omitted from film versions—Dr. John Seward, keeper of a lunatic asylum. It's coincidental but potent that Burroughs' middle (family) name was Seward—Young Seward duels with a hog castrator in "Ordinary Men and Women" (106), and *Naked Lunch* includes many vampire references. Of course, the 1931 movie is far from the novel, and Seward here is a staid and even kindly doctor, father of the heroine, Mina. Still, the narrative context gives a resonance even to this pallid characterization. Seward consults with Dr. Van Helsing, a forerunner of Dr. Van Straaten from *Dead of Night* in all but his attitude to the supernatural. The performance by Edward Van Sloan gives us a decisive, bespectacled traditionalist sporting a tweed jacket and cropped white hair—twenty years on and he could have been the prototype for any Nazi rocket scientist who had moved his allegiances to America. His arcane knowledge involves liberal garlanding with wolfsbane (was garlic too vulgar for film audiences in 1931?) and confrontations with the ostentatiously evening-dressed vampire Count, like whom he represents the eruption of the irrational into—into what? The latter part of the film takes place in Dr. Seward's discreetly well-appointed home-cum-sanatorium, where gracious drapes and flowers on the console tables gloss over the fact that this is a hospital for loonies (to quote one of their keepers, the cheery cockney Martin). Dracula and his sinister, foreign, vampire ways has found his way into a normality already challenged from within—he could as well be an inmate as an intruder. And the main character of this dialogue-bound version (the script was too obviously adapted from a stage dramatization) isn't even the Count—it's Dwight Frye's Renfield, the dapper, prissy little man who travels into the unknown territory of Dracula's Transylvanian castle to deliver legal documents concerning his move to England and becomes hypnotized, addicted, dependant on "the Master." Renfield's descent from precise, polite agent to floor-crawling, giggling madman illuminates that oldest of horror-film themes—all surfaces can crack, all floors slip from under you, all certainties betray you. Renfield is the bug-eater (progressing up the food chain to spiders, birds, and, with luck, a kitten). He's addicted to the life force, to Dracula's eyes, to the fact of being addicted. He's the perfect Burroughs hero.

And let's finish with that happy Seward connection. Francis Ford Coppola's *Bram Stoker's Dracula* (1992), a film that inevitably contained much that had nothing to do with Stoker's novel, did attempt to restore to their original state some of the novel's minor characters. Among them was Dr. Jack Seward, played by Richard E. Grant (already immortally memorable from 1987's *Withnail and I*) as a high-principled, noble-browed young doctor somewhat bowed by the responsibility of the asylum and depressed when the beautiful Lucy rejects his offer of marriage. Coppola reminds us what such a medical man might do in 1897 (the publication year of the novel) but couldn't have been shown doing in 1931. Seward shoots up (the novel specifies chloral hydrate as his drug of choice) in an effort to forget the pain, and what goes around comes around. In the horror film, control is always fought for and always ceded, in a territory as slippery as Interzone and no less fraught with a constant shifting commerce, with deals that dissolve the boundaries and deals that replace them, with flesh that promises coherence and lies in its teeth, with a veneer of order skimming a pit of corruption. That's the magic of the (horror) movies, and like a big fat vein it can be felt pulsing throughout *Naked Lunch*.

Random Insect Doom: The Pulp Science Fiction of *Naked Lunch*

timothy s. **MURPHY**

Funny what you find in old pulp magazines. [. . .] Quite haunting actually . . . the middle-aged Tiresias moving from place to place with his unpopular thesis, spending his days in public libraries, eking out a living writing fiction for pulp magazines . . . good stories too . . .

—Burroughs, "Wind die. You die. We die."

From the very first pages of *Naked Lunch*, William S. Burroughs immerses his readers in the world of "old pulp magazines": narrator William Lee is a junky on the run from "the heat closing in," assisted in his escape by a "[y]oung, good looking, crew cut, Ivy League, advertising exec type fruit" whom Lee quickly recognizes as a "square [who] wants to come on hip" (3). The fruit, conventionally bourgeois down to his Brooks Brothers shirt, gets involved because he is a prurient "character collector" whose expectations of the junky are derived from "B production" movies and their literary correlative, pulp fiction (5). Lee plays into the fruit's genre expectations and hipster aspirations by treating him as "one of our own" in order to set him up for a later con (4). The fruit is clearly a surrogate for the reader of *Naked Lunch*, whose familiarity with the means and ends of pulp fiction is the hook that draws him into the novel's vast confidence game. Although the opening pages deploy the tropes of the hardboiled detective pulps, thereafter the genre markers begin to mutate as surreal, quasi-human characters like Willy the Disk and Bradley the Buyer appear. By the time we are introduced to the mad scientist Dr. Benway (19), the detective tropes have been infected and absorbed by science-fiction images and themes to form the hybrid generic framework that will govern the rest of Burroughs' novel.

The sources of this mutant framework should come as no surprise, since Burroughs was born in St. Louis in 1914 and graduated from Harvard in 1936; thus his childhood, adolescence, and early adulthood coincided with the rise and spread of the much-maligned genres of pulp fiction, especially pulp science fiction, the origin of which is conventionally dated to either 1911 or 1926.[1] Although other pulp genres, including the western and the "spicy" (erotic) adventure story as well as the hardboiled detective story, also influenced Burroughs' style and technique of narrative construction, pulp science fiction suggested several of the most important elements that made Burroughs' work so shocking to readers in the 1950s and 1960s. The *Nova* trilogy is perhaps Burroughs' most systematic application of the tropes that he extracted from the science-fiction pulps, but he had deployed them discreetly and effectively in his earlier fiction, especially his masterpiece *Naked Lunch*. At the time *Naked Lunch* was published and for many years afterwards, the question of pulp influence on the book would have been irrelevant to most readers and critics—who would have cared how a crude and artistically negligible genre like pulp science fiction had influenced a chaotic and obscene curiosity like *Naked Lunch*? But on the fiftieth anniversary of its publication, *Naked Lunch* has secured a place in the canon of American experimental fiction, and at the same time the pulps have been reassessed and recognized as the staging ground for a reinvigoration of vernacular literature that was accomplished by Raymond Chandler, Dashiell Hammett, H. P. Lovecraft, and other popular writers of the 1920s and 1930s. My modest intention here is to celebrate these welcome critical reversals by tracing some of Burroughs' science-fiction tropes to likely sources in the pulps and then to complete the circle by noting Burroughs' own influence on subsequent science fiction.

Burroughs frankly admitted his interest in science fiction on numerous occasions. His early letters from 1953–54 contain references to science fiction and science-fiction writers, including H. G. Wells, whose works were often reprinted in the American pulps (*Letters*, 178, 181), and regular pulp contributor Ray Bradbury (202), and in his most substantial early interview, with Conrad Knickerbocker for the *Paris Review* in 1965, he includes "quite a bit of science fiction" among the sources for material in the working note-books he called "coordinate books" (Lotringer, 69). That same year, he was interviewed for the pioneering critical journal *S. F. Horizons,* which was coedited by noted New Wave science-fiction novelist and historian Brian

Aldiss; in that interview, Burroughs described himself as "a long time reader of science fiction. I remember *Amazing Stories* [the first science-fiction pulp, which debuted in 1926]—what is it: 30 years ago? [. . .] it has always been a genre that interested me exceedingly" (Lotringer, 82). He also explained the reason for his interest: "I have always felt that science fiction is a form that gives you so much leeway that you really can say perhaps more in this form than you can in any other" (Lotringer, 85).

Burroughs first made overt use of that "leeway" in *Naked Lunch*, though it is likely that the hallucination scenes in *Junky* (see, for example, 23, 111) owe their phantasmagoric imagery at least in part to the monsters, aliens, and insects of pulp horror and science fiction (and the fact that *Junky*—or rather *Junkie*—was originally published by Ace Books as an original pulp paperback should not be forgotten either). *Naked Lunch*, however, deploys many more images and themes that had become commonplace in pulp science fiction by the 1950s, including mad scientists (not only Dr. Benway but also Dr. "Fingers" Schafer, both of whom owe something to Wells' Dr. Moreau), thinking machines and their psychopathology ("Benway," 21–22, 32), and functional mutations of the human body ("Meeting of International Conference of Technological Psychiatry," 87–89, and, of course, "The Talking Asshole" routine, 110–13, as well as numerous shorter passages). Some entire routines clearly allude to conventional pulp-narrative situations, such as the Sailor's encounter with his "time connection" in "The Black Meat" (43–47), "Coke Bugs" (167–69), "The Exterminator Does a Good Job" (169–72), and their coda "The Algebra of Need" (172–74), routines that manage to combine the seedy underworld of the hardboiled detective pulps with the alien artifacts, imaginary addictions, and bodily mutations of the science-fiction pulps. Likewise, the three totalitarian "Parties of Interzone" (136–40) are organized around classic science-fiction techniques of domination: chemical dissolution and absorption, for the Liquefactionists; telepathic mind control, for the Senders; and genetic duplication or cloning, for the Divisionists. Thus, it is not inappropriate for *Naked Lunch* to be described, in its "Atrophied Preface," as "a blueprint, a How-To Book. . . . Black insect lusts open into vast other-planet landscapes" even as our own "Planet drifts to random insect doom" under the anti-imaginative rule of the control addicts (187). Among other things, *Naked Lunch* demonstrates how to put the well-worn concepts and tropes of pulp science fiction to use for innovative satiric and parodic ends.

Obvious evidence for Burroughs' interest in science fiction is both easy to find in his fiction, letters, and interviews and difficult to measure in its consequences for his work. On the basis of the list of scenes above, one might think that the impact of pulp science fiction on *Naked Lunch* was random and local. The leeway that pulp science fiction granted Burroughs may not have been limited to borrowed themes and imagery, however. Readers familiar with the pulp tradition will recognize its influence even in places where Burroughs himself does not openly acknowledge it. For any examination of *Naked Lunch*, perhaps the most important of these places is the 23 October 1955 letter to Allen Ginsberg and Jack Kerouac in which Burroughs describes his progress

> towards complete lack of caution and restraint. Nothing must be allowed to dilute my routines. [. . .] The centers of inhibition are atrophied, occluded like an eel's ass on The Way to Sargasso—good book title. You know about eels? When they reach full maturity, they leave the streams and ponds of Europe travelling downstream to the sea, then cross the Atlantic Ocean to the Sargasso Sea—near Bermuda— where they mate and die. During this perilous journey they stop eating and their ass holes seal over. The young eels start back for the fresh water ponds and streams of Europe. Say that's better than *Ignorant Armies* ("Dover Beach" by Arnold) as a title for my Interzone novel:
>   *Meet Me in Sargasso, I'll See You in Sargasso, The Sargasso Trail.*
>   Death opens the door of his old green pickup and says to The Hitchhiker: "You look occluded, friend. Going straight through to Sargasso?"
>   *Ticket for Sargasso, Meet in Sargasso, On the Road to Sargasso.* What I want to convey, though, is the inner pull towards Sargasso: Sargasso Yen, Sargasso Time, Sargasso Kicks, The Sargasso Blues. I can't get it. This is all trivial, doesn't convey those eels wiggling across fields at night in the wet grass to find the next pond or stream, thousands dying on the way . . . If I ever buy a boat, I will call it The Sargasso . . . Sargasso Junction, Change for Sargasso, Sargasso Transfer, Sargasso Detour. (*Letters*, 294–95)

This letter is worth quoting at such length not only because of its focus on Burroughs' newfound thematic leeway but also because of the sheer number of variations that he rings on the image of the Sargasso Sea in his search for a title for the "Interzone novel" that would become *Naked Lunch*. This flood of spontaneous verbal invention unleashed by his musings on the Sargasso Sea suggests that the conceptually unconstrained and speculative universe of pulp science fiction also encouraged him to explore the absurd, the grotesque, and the excessive through radical formal innovation: the disjunctive "routines" that give shape to *Naked Lunch* through their remorseless nonlinear proliferation constitute a structural correlative to the pulp-derived themes and imagery of mind/body mutation.

But what is the "*inner* pull towards Sargasso" that Burroughs wanted to convey, and what does an appreciation of it mean for our understanding of the book? The Sargasso Sea is an area of the mid-Atlantic Ocean, marked by large banks of sargassum seaweed, that, as Burroughs notes, is an important stop on the migration route of several common eel species. However, the Sargasso Sea is also an important locus in the folklore of seafarers and in the fiction that sprang from their experiences. For centuries, the Sargasso had been known to sailors as the "graveyard of ships" because the absence of tides and the thickness of the sargassum weed there threatened to immobilize sailing vessels. By the end of the nineteenth century, these travelers' tales had begun to inspire popular fiction. As Brian Stableford notes, the English science-fiction/fantasy writer William Hope Hodgson, who had been a sailor for many years prior to the start of his literary career, "did more than any other writer to popularise the myth of the Sargasso Sea. [. . .] he was the man who developed the legend into its most fantastic form" (92). In a series of stories originally published in 1906 and 1907 in American and British protopulp magazines and in his first published novel, *The Boats of the "Glen Carrig"* (1907), Hodgson established a pattern for stories of the Sargasso Sea that other authors would later imitate: a first-person account of a sailing ship getting trapped in the Sargasso and its crew and passengers confronting the bizarre and dangerous creatures that live there. As a regular reader of science-fiction magazines during the 1920s, 1930s, and 1940s, Burroughs would have had the opportunity to read Sargasso stories by largely forgotten authors like Robert Welles Ritchie or Edsel Newton, or he could have read some of Hodgson's own stories when they were reprinted in the early 1940s, during the very period in which his introduction to Ginsberg and Kerouac inaugurated the Beat Generation.[2]

In Hodgson's short stories, the creatures encountered in the Sargasso Sea are generally gigantic animals—octopi, crabs, rats—but in *Glen Carrig*, he invents a species of "Weed Men" that he describes as "human slugs" whose arms are "divided into hateful and wriggling masses of small tentacles" and whose faces are dominated by an octopoid "bill like to an inverted parrot's" (90). An army of these creatures threatens Hodgson's narrator and his comrades throughout the novel. Burroughs' character Willy the Disk, the mutant addict with a "round, disk mouth lined with sensitive, erectile black hairs" that "eats a hole right through the door" (7–8), seems to echo Hodgson's Weed Men, as do the Mugwumps with their "[t]hin, purple-blue lips [that] cover a razor-sharp beak of black bone with which they frequently tear each other to shreds in fights over clients" (46), but a more significant connection lies in the claustrophobic sense of entrapment within an environment that is both frustratingly static and actively malevolent that both authors create in their fiction. In Hodgson's work, the ships are often trapped in the endless stretches of weed for decades or even centuries, and the people in them must survive years of monotonous immobility interrupted irregularly by spasms of violence. In *Naked Lunch*, Burroughs similarly describes the American landscape as "a vast subdivision, antennae of television to the meaningless sky" (11). The claustrophobia of the suburbs is a manifestation of "the U.S. Drag [that] closes around us like no other drag in the world" (12). The monotonous repetition of the mundane—"every block of houses has its own bar and drugstore and market and liquor store" (11)—threatens to becalm and entrap Burroughs' junky narrator in the "Undifferentiated Tissue" of the "basic American rottenness" (111–12) as effectively as the expanses of sargassum weed entrap Hodgson's sailors. This "U.S. Drag" may be Burroughs' way of evoking what his 1955 letter described as the "inner pull" of the Sargasso, the seductive or addictive quality that draws prey to its featureless doom. The narrator's concluding recognition that he has "been occluded from space-time like an eel's ass occludes when he stops eating on the way to Sargasso," then, marks his escape from psychosocial entrapment as surely as his killing of the narcotics cops Hauser and O'Brien does. Simultaneously it also brings *Naked Lunch*'s narrative full circle by restaging the opening routine's mutation from the "Heat" of the hardboiled detective pulps to the "not-yet of Telepathic Bureaucracies, Time Monopolies, Control Drugs, Heavy Fluid Addicts" drawn from pulp science fiction (181).

This almost postmodern mood of suffocating paranoia and entrapment may have been Hodgson's most significant contribution to the pulp aesthetic (and later literature), but his representations of desire and sexuality were traditionally Victorian—his narrators somehow manage to marry so as to avoid any hint of immorality aboard the trapped vessels. But such asceticism was atypical of pulp fiction generally, though pulp science fiction was generally more restrained than the other pulp genres. Much pulp cover art and interior illustration was designed to appeal to its readers' prurience, often by focusing on attractive, scantily clad women whose chastity or safety was threatened. In the case of the detective, western, and "spicy" adventure pulps, the women were usually threatened by predatory men, and although this was sometimes the case for horror and science-fiction pulps, the latter often made use of nonhuman antagonists like monsters or extraterrestrials, which complicated the implied threat to conventional sexual morality.

Explicit depictions of nonhuman and interspecies sexual activity would not appear in science fiction until the 1950s and 1960s—just before Burroughs' own explicit depictions of such activity began to appear—in the work of Theodore Sturgeon (a favorite of Burroughs; see Lotringer, 82) and Philip José Farmer, but at least one early pulp writer decided to take the prurient visual and narrative imagery of the pulps literally and see where it might lead. In "The Dunwich Horror" (1928), one of his best-known tales that was originally published in the most famous of all pulps, *Weird Tales*, H. P. Lovecraft posited the apparently consensual impregnation of a human woman by the malevolent, multidimensional alien being Yog-Sothoth, resulting in the birth of two destructive hybrid offspring. Unlike most pulp aliens, Lovecraft's is not even remotely anthropomorphic, and its offspring do not long remain so: Wilbur Whateley's half-human body quickly dissolves into slime after he is killed by guard dogs while trying to steal a copy of the *Necronomicon* (Lovecraft, 174–76), while his even more alien brother is banished back to its father's home dimension after laying waste to the Massachusetts town of Dunwich (194–96). This grotesque catastrophe, Lovecraft suggests, is a more plausible outcome than the conventional erotic titillation implied by the standard pulp subtext of sexually imperiled femininity. "The Dunwich Horror" is thus a work of generic reflexivity that explicates and critiques the implicit fantasy of nonhuman/interspecies sexuality that accounts for a significant portion of pulp science fiction's appeal.

In *Naked Lunch*, Burroughs makes considerable use of the imagery of nonhuman/interspecies sexual activity, generally in the form of predatory sexual exchange or exploitation. Bradley the Buyer's increasing need to "rub up against [junkies to] get fixed" dehumanizes him both psychologically and physically, leading him to "make himself all soft like a blob of jelly and surround [the junky] so nasty. Then he gets wet all over like with green slime. So I guess he come to some kinda awful climax . . . (15). Ultimately, the Buyer is incinerated while consuming the Narcotics Commissioner, "the court of inquiry ruling that such means were justified in that the Buyer had lost his human citizenship and was, in consequence, a creature without species" (17). The most important scene of human-alien sexual activity is probably "Hassan's Rumpus Room," Burroughs' vicious satire on capital punishment, in which Mugwumps sodomize young boys who are being hanged for the entertainment of Hassan's affluent and apparently mainstream clientele. Burroughs' implicit charge that popular support for capital punishment in the United States is based on the scopophilic pleasure that the audience derives from observing executions shows just how radically he was able to displace the conventional social and sexual morality that underpinned the pulp imagery he used. In this, his achievement is not unlike Lovecraft's in "The Dunwich Horror": both authors find ways to use conventional pulp images and techniques to satirize the conventional social and sexual values that most pulp fiction vigorously defends.

This brief examination of the possible influence of Hodgson and Lovecraft only scratches the surface of Burroughs' borrowings from and evocations of pulp science fiction, but nevertheless it establishes the relevance of this line of inquiry for any thorough understanding of *Naked Lunch* and the later fiction.[3] An equally valuable indication of the significance of Burroughs' engagement with pulp science fiction is the extent of his influence on later science fiction. Perhaps the earliest acknowledgment of that influence came when fantasy and science-fiction writer Michael Moorcock, who had defended Burroughs during the "UGH" controversy over *Naked Lunch* and other works in the *Times Literary Supplement* (see Skerl and Lydenberg, 41–51), was named editor of the most important English science-fiction magazine, *New Worlds*, in 1964. In his first issue as editor, he published what has become a widely cited appreciation of Burroughs by J. G. Ballard, "Myth-Maker of the Twentieth Century." "For science fiction the lesson of Burroughs' work is plain," Ballard writes, and he "illustrates that the whole of science fiction's imaginary universe has long since been absorbed into the general consciousness, and that most of its ideas are now valid only in a kind of marginal spoofing" (129–30). Both Ballard and Moorcock, whose novels and stories take that general absorption of the science-fiction imaginary as their point of departure, went on to become defining figures of the so-called New Wave in science fiction, a very loosely organized international movement that took its thematic and stylistic cues from William S. Burroughs instead of Edgar Rice Burroughs[4] and in the process broke open the literary ghetto within which science fiction had enclosed itself since the days of the pulps. Although Moorcock insists, "It was not that we were actually influenced by Burroughs," he has described himself as

> an admirer of Burroughs' use of modern imagery and idiom, for his *metaphorical* use of sf ideas, for his ear for the language and ironies of the drug underworld and of the streets. He seemed the first writer to celebrate the present as well as to lampoon it. (Moorcock, 17; see also Ashley, *Transformations*, 239)

Burroughs returned the compliment in his *S. F. Horizons* interview, where he identified Ballard and Moorcock among the "moderns" who interested him and *New Worlds* as a magazine he read regularly and in which he "found some extremely good stories" (Lotringer, 82–83). Ballard's and Moorcock's demand for wider recognition of Burroughs' significance for science fiction was finally fulfilled in 1982 with the founding of the science-fiction magazine *Interzone*, named for the setting of his most famous novel and dedicated to perpetuating the revolution in science fiction that he had inspired. Thus, the pattern of influence constitutes a feedback loop: Burroughs drew upon his reading of pulp science fiction to create works like *Naked Lunch* that far exceeded the stylistic limits and value system of the pulps, works which themselves contributed to a radical expansion of science fiction's formal and thematic limits, and hence not only to the rise of a New Wave but also to the dawn of a new era in science fiction that could no longer be derided as *pulp*.

Notes

Thanks to the editors of this volume for their very useful suggestions.

1. The earlier date is the one given by Hugo Gernsback, who is widely lauded as the "father" of genre science fiction. The year 1911 is the time that Gernsback's serial novel *Ralph 124C 41+* was published in his technology magazine, *Modern Electrics*. However, science-fiction historian Mike Ashley notes that fiction very similar to that which we now label "pulp science fiction" had been published before 1911; see Ashley, *The Time Machines*, 1, and *passim*. The year 1926 is the date of first publication of the first exclusively science-fiction pulp, *Amazing Stories*.

2. For information on pulp publication and reprinting, see Day, 231. On *Famous Fantastic Mysteries*, which reprinted the Hodgson tales and which was perhaps the first magazine to show an awareness of the historical importance of pulp fiction, see Tymn and Ashley, 211–16.

3. In addition to the intersections between Lovecraft and Burroughs discussed above, there are several others worthy of serious study but beyond the scope of this essay. They shared a disdain for human arrogance and its institutionalization in both religion and science—Burroughs' preference for a polytheistic universe of squabbling and opportunistic divine "hustlers" has obvious affinities with Lovecraft's loosely structured pantheon of inscrutable and indifferent alien "gods." Burroughs also acknowledged the influence of Henry Kuttner, who was a protegé of Lovecraft, and, in collaboration with his wife, C. L. Moore, one of the most widely published and influential contributors to the science-fiction pulps and the magazines that succeeded them during the 1940s and 1950s. Their influence on the *Nova* trilogy has yet to be measured. (On Kuttner and Moore's work, see Gunn.) Finally, there is the role played by the editor and publisher August Derleth in impeding both men's careers: Derleth founded Arkham House to publish Lovecraft in book form, but he also promulgated an interpretation of Lovecraft as a Christian allegorist that seriously distorted the reception of Lovecraft's work for decades after his death; Derleth was also the only writer or critic to assist the Post Office's attempt to suppress *Big Table* 1, which contained the first published excerpts from *Naked Lunch*, on grounds of obscenity. On Derleth's misreading of Lovecraft, see Mosig; on Derleth's involvement in the censorship of *Naked Lunch,* see Goodman, chaps. 3 and 4.

4. This witticism is not mine: in its two-hundredth issue (1970), Moorcock's *New Worlds* published a short story by Philip José Farmer, "The Jungle Rot Kid on the Nod," which presents a Tarzan adventure narrated in the style of William S. rather than Edgar Rice Burroughs (see Moorcock, 491–92, and Ashley, *Transformations*, 252).

Works Cited

Ashley, Mike. *The Time Machines: The Story of the Science-Fiction Pulp Magazines from the Beginning to 1950.* Liverpool, UK: Liverpool UP, 2000.

———. *Transformations: The Story of the Science-Fiction Magazines from 1950 to 1970*. Liverpool, UK: Liverpool UP, 2005.

Ballard, J. G. *A User's Guide to the Millennium: Essays and Reviews*. New York: Picador, 1996.

Burroughs, William S. *Junky: The Definitive Text of "Junk."* Edited by Oliver Harris. New York: Penguin, 2003.

———. *The Letters of William S. Burroughs, 1945–1959*. Edited by Oliver Harris. New York: Viking, 1993.

———. "Wind die. You die. We die" (1968). In *The Starry Wisdom: A Tribute to H. P. Lovecraft*, edited by D. M. Mitchell, 65–68. London: Creation, 1994.

Day, Donald B. *Index to the Science Fiction Magazines 1926–1950*. Boston: Hall, 1982.

Goodman, Michael. *Contemporary Literary Censorship: The Case History of Burroughs' Naked Lunch*. Metuchen, NJ: Scarecrow, 1981.

Gunn, James. "Henry Kuttner, C. L. Moore, Lewis Padgett, et al." In *Voices for the Future: Essays on Major Science Fiction Writers*, edited by Thomas D. Clareson, vol. 1, 185–215. Bowling Green, OH: Bowling Green University Popular Press, 1976.

Hodgson, William Hope. *The Collected Fiction of William Hope Hodgson Vol. 1: The Boats of the "Glen Carrig" and Other Nautical Adventures*. Edited by Jeremy Lassen. San Francisco: Night Shade, 2003.

Lotringer, Sylvère, ed. *Burroughs Live: The Collected Interviews of William S. Burroughs 1960–1997*. New York: Semiotext(e), 2001.

Lovecraft, H. P. *The Dunwich Horror and Others*. Edited by S. T. Joshi. Sauk City, WI: Arkham, 1984.

Moorcock, Michael, ed. *New Worlds: An Anthology*. London: Flamingo, 1983.

Mosig, Dirk W. "H. P. Lovecraft: Myth-Maker" (1976). *H. P. Lovecraft: Four Decades of Criticism*, edited by S. T. Joshi, 104–12. Athens: Ohio UP, 1981.

Skerl, Jennie, and Robin Lydenberg, eds. *William S. Burroughs at the Front: Critical Reception, 1959–1989*. Carbondale: Southern Illinois UP, 1991.

Stableford, Brian. *Scientific Romance in Britain 1890–1950*. New York: St. Martin's, 1985.

Tymn, Marshall B., and Mike Ashley, eds. *Science Fiction, Fantasy and Weird Fiction Magazines*. Westport, CT: Greenwood, 1985.

All Consuming Images:
DJ Burroughs and Me

dj **SPOOKY**

O
ne of my favorite writers, William Gibson, has a great phrase—it's a sample that I trot out every once in a while when I think of how strange the world has become and how strange it's going to get over the next couple of centuries as technology advances, and we begin to question the very foundations of what it means to be human. In the *Economist* (23 June 2000), Gibson observed simply, "The future is already here. It's just unevenly distributed." In a simple phrase, Gibson, whose always elegant and precise prose was the first image many people had of the idea of "cyberspace," created a context where humanity lived in multiple time zones depending on its relationship to text and technology. It goes without saying that this phrase became the staple for a lot of "samples"—it's been quoted ad infinitum, but then again, so has James Brown's drummer Clyde Stubblefield on the track "Funky Drummer"; it doesn't make the sample any less interesting. What I'm pointing out here is a link between text, ideas, and how they evolve in the course of the info-ecology they are created from. It's a great place to think about William S. Burroughs and his impact on twenty-first-century literature.

If there's one of his novels that really stakes the claim of setting the tone for many of the issues that the early twenty-first century sees as core conflicts, it's *Naked Lunch*. The subtle control mechanisms that are on full display throughout the novel—whether it's the "Blue Movies" that reflect and distort human desire or the bizarre "Mugwumps" that prey on the minds of the unaware—are all extremely current. Burroughs' *Naked Lunch* forged a path that many people in the music, literary, and art worlds have followed. For me, the nonlinear aspects of Burroughs' work, especially *Naked Lunch*, really resonate with the eerie displaced quality of America in the early twenty-first century and the Middle East in the twentieth century. It shows the paradox of existing in multiple time zones that seems to pop up over and over these days. Are we in a neofeudal middle ages again? Have the loops and cut-up narratives come back to haunt us as Fox News? Is George W. Bush the "Talking Asshole"? All of these questions linger whenever I think about *Naked Lunch* and its index of loops. One has to wonder—how did one person's imagination engage all of the manifestly convoluted material Burroughs managed to generate? Think of his novels as a Wikipedia "disambiguation"—*Naked Lunch* is made of hyperlinks and fractured texts, just as much if not more so than anything that James Joyce could come up with. Instead of *Finnegans Wake* beginning with "rivverrun," Burroughs would just pull out a pair of scissors to the local newspaper to see what would pop up. It's that complex, and it's that simple. Involution, stories within stories, uncanny links to contemporary affairs: *Naked Lunch* set the tone for most of his novels to come after, and it's the Rosetta Stone of his work if you want to decipher the almost-acoustic connection to text that he set up with his cut-up technique.

A couple of years ago, back in the ancient mid-1990s, I took a name from an old William S. Burroughs novel entitled *Nova Express*—my nickname for many years was basically a nom de guerre: the Subliminal Kid in Burroughs' novel was a sampler. The character was a construct, a synthesis of several concepts rolled into one. On one hand, the character was someone who pilfered meaning from the fragments and detritus of the media landscape of a corrupt and environmentally devastated planet ruled by inept and ultimately destructive alien "controllers"—the Nova Mob—and on the other, he was a projection surface for a kind of information freedom. The blurb that I took from Burroughs was a manifesto for many things that would happen to me over the next decade as electronic music, digital media, and the on-rush of Web culture drove the pace of culture at the speed of light through the fiber-optic cables, wireless networks, and high-speed routers holding the "developed" world together. Burroughs was the shaman of this new era of digital connectivity, and as anyone who owns an Ipod, Xbox, or PS2, has ring tones on their cell phone, or has a computer loaded with mp3s knows—it's all connected. Burroughs was the seer who warned of a new world at the height of the analog era of TV, radio, and the slow, mesmerizing forces of the Cold War, the future of a connected and intimately involuted info world. It's hard to divorce the material that he wrote about from his techniques and the way they're reflected in the world of hyper jump cuts and time/place shifting attention-deficit-disordered perspectives that we all call home now.

Where in the 1950s, the Beat Generation played with language as a way of breaking through the control mechanisms of propaganda and behavioral conditioning the industrial economy placed on the citizens of the "free" world, Burroughs called the lie of the "Enlightenment" West what it was: totalitarian. I wanted to make mixes that I felt would allow people to see how the media landscape was one of technological control through selective editing processes, information overload, and a sense of a loss of identity by way of advertising, mass-produced goods, and the collapse of the civil culture of education for all. The mixes I made when I started out as a DJ, and the "sample" of the nickname "That Subliminal Kid," came from that semiological landscape. Burroughs' cut-up technique for freeing "meaning" from the control mechanisms of limited forms of literacy reminded me of the way Newspeak functioned in George Orwell's *Nineteen Eighty-Four*. All of that has come home to roost—in fact, Burroughs would now probably be regarded as a purveyor of "hyper-realism."

After the era of films like *Blade Runner* and *The Matrix*, it's hard to see what Burroughs *hasn't* affected. But I like to look back even further to a Russian writer by the name of Yevgeny Zamyatin, whose 1927 book *We* influenced George Orwell and Aldous Huxley when he was writing *Brave New World*. I have a feeling we'll all look back at the twentieth century and the rise of mass media as a blip on the historical timeline when people were all watching the same thing at the same time. In the era of youtube, last. fm, myspace, and above all, the chaotic podcasts and blogs that have taken the place of a "central" or "dominant" narrative in the developed world, the old ways of media seem quaint indeed. The near future seems to be a world like Times Square—a pristine, photorealistic, "am I here" experience like 70 mm IMAX, particularly 3D IMAX, and you are the main character of any story you can possibly choose, as long as it's within the framework of the infosphere we live in. It's almost like the remix ecology of the "mindscreen" Burroughs anticipated is even more nuanced at reaching to the very core of what it means to be human, and that's the world that Zamyatin anticipated. Everyone in his dystopian story is a number in a cosmic-sized equation brought on by The One State. An excerpt from the beginning of the story tells the whole deal—its manifest destiny of the nation state, the media, and the mind control of a mathematics of the subconscious all tied into one bite-sized package: unlike Neo in *The Matrix*, it doesn't matter if you take the red pill or the blue pill, they're both equal illusions, it just depends on what branch of the simulation you feel like exploring. The "killer app" of this info ecology is the human mind—and that's what Burroughs explored with a relentless, almost analytic passion. *Naked Lunch* was the touchstone for this kind of Beat-era wireless imagination.

In the year 1915, two seminal works of the twentieth century appeared. One was D. W. Griffith's *Birth of a Nation*. The other was Luigi Russolo's *Art of Noises*. I like to think that each of them set a shadow over art for most of the rest of the century. One, Griffith's film, used editing techniques to condition the viewer's response by creating a mythic landscape of totally false information presented as real historic fact. The other, Russolo's *intonorumori*, created noise as a way of breaking down all aspects of history's controls on how humans would perceive music. I think that my DJ'ing style comes as a result of a different kind of literacy—not the literacy of texts but the literacy of being able to read bar codes, algorithms, and high-speed routers as they accelerate human culture further and further into the realm of the digital. Being able to get a grip on the "metanarrative" was a tool that Burroughs bequeathed to us all. He definitely has his detractors and, yes, let's face it, he was no saint, but the basic premise of his work—of the nonlinear method of creating text, scenes slid together with little care for narrative, the world as a book that could be cut into at any point—it all leads us to a bleak world of viruses, mental epidemics, love lost in a flurry of media constructs: his works aren't in any sense science fiction, but they seem to forecast—with eerie prescience—such later phenomena as AIDS, liposuction, and the crack pandemic. In the era of the World Wide Web, it seems more prescient than ever that one could look at the depredations of the corporate world and the culture industry as mirror responses to his infamous phrase "Nothing is true. Everything is permitted." From the war-torn streets of Baghdad to the prodemocracy protests in the abandoned boulevards of Rangoon, it's a phrase that's still revolutionary in its implication of the artificial structures humans have placed on their systems of governance from the dawn of time.

His *Naked Lunch*'s "Interzone" could easily be seen as a metaphorical vision of what the Internet has become and a signpost on the road to what it will be in the future, but the term probably was derived from the "International Zone" in Tangier, where (as in Interzone), everything could be had for a price. His style of text assembly and his seemingly endless investigations with devices like Brion Gysin's Dreamachine all point to a world where time—past, present, and future—switch places with blinding speed and where the European ideal of the "Enlightenment" has become a dark, gutted house, a place people avoid because of rumors of ghostly infestation.

Like America in the era of Hurricane Katrina and 9/11, his work looks like a mirage—strong and solid from one angle, feeble as a light beam projected through fog from another. His work has a lenticular logic where almost anything can be you, depending on how you look at it. That's the acoustic world he points to: pick a card, any card, the dealer has all the files, but you, too, can play that semiological game and make your own remix. I like to think that his work offers us hope, and like the Dreamachines that he used with Gysin on the North Coast of Africa, they can be made to mix almost anything. In Burroughs' world, like the realm of the DJ, the acoustic imagination is a place we can all think of as a liberated zone—a place where the mix can absorb any pattern, any sequence, and any text. His work, ultimately, is about the noise of liberation.

Naked Life: William S. Burroughs, Bioscientist

richard DOYLE

This is Revelation and Prophecy of what I can pick up without FM on my 1920 crystal set with antennae of jissom [. . .] The way OUT is the way IN . . .
—William Burroughs, *Naked Lunch*

To write is also to become something other than a writer.
—Gilles Deleuze

Illustration 1: This Is Not an Author?

It is perhaps true that one cannot, as Burroughs taught us, *fake* quality writing anymore than you can fake a good meal. As such, most readers who come with an open mind and, yes, "read," rather than merely consume, *Naked Lunch*—Burroughs' early (1959) effervescent novel of experimental verve and poetic genius—recognize, however begrudgingly, the work of a master chef. The cuisine may not be to everyone's taste, this *Naked Lunch*, but it is a work of such stunning novelty and comic timing that the patient and open-minded reader must, finally, laugh.

> Americans have a special horror of giving up control, of letting things happen in their own way without interference. They would like to jump down into their stomachs and digest the food and shovel the shit out. (179)

It is perhaps an only slightly lesser challenge to fake quality science, where inquiry demands the discipline of open mind and the clear, immersive observation that can result. Indeed, robust scientific inquiry would seem to demand what Burroughs dubbed, following Korzybski, the "extermination" of rational thought. The unacknowledged role of rhetorical or "semantic" maps in our consciousness was Korzbyski's quarry, but the goal was identical to that offered by Timothy Leary et al in their remix of the *Tibetan Book of the Dead* (115):

> In the ego-free state, wherein all things are like the void and
>   cloudless sky,
> And the naked spotless intellect is like a transparent vacuum;
> At this moment, know yourself and abide in that state.

Asymptotically, investigators must approach zero attachment to any belief or concept, however cherished it may be, and the first practice of such detachment is to recognize, wherever possible, the slippage between our linguistic models of reality and reality itself. The most replicable form of this thought from Korzybski's enormous opus was simply "The Map is not the territory," and with Burroughs we might add: "The map is not the territory. And neither is the territory!" Burroughs' downright shamanic treatment of language—witness the 1967 text "Word Authority More Habit Forming Than Heroin"—works to erode and even "wash away" the usual semantic webs and habit structures in which we all dwell. In *The Ticket That Exploded* (1962), Burroughs has recourse to the "sensory deprivation" tank invented by John C. Lilly for recounting this work of erasure so fundamental to his own practice, this "blast of silence":

> —Body outlines extend and break here—The stretching membrane of
> skin dissolves—Sudden taste of blood in his throat as gristle vaporizes
> and the words wash away and the halves of his body separated like a
> mold—[. . .] Screaming without a throat without speech centers as
> the brain split down the middle and the feed-back sound shut off in
> a blast of silence. (83)

Korzybski points out that few undertake this form of investigation willingly.

> But exactly the distinctive work of science is the modification, the
> reconstruction, the abandonment of old ideas; the construction of
> new ones on the basis of observation. This however is a distressing
> operation, and many refuse to undergo it, even many whose work is
> the practice of scientific investigation. The old ideas persist along with
> the new observations, they form the basis—often unconsciously—for
> many of the conclusions that are drawn. (5)

Korzybski's work and teaching was devoted in part to overcoming the "either/or" logic of Aristotelian logic, and with him, Burroughs sought to navigate a "Third Mind" available for exploration by those willing to let go of their attachment to "word authority." "Cure is always: *Let go! Jump!*" (185).

By approaching this "blast of silence" or zero degree of attachment to any thought that would understand a living system as "either" an organism "or" a machine, Burroughs was able to observe and represent aspects of living systems that were not on the radar of mainstream life sciences, enthralled as they were with the molecular machinery of life, nucleic acids, and proteins. By offering recipes for making life "naked," Burroughs teaches readers to engage the complex world of our perceptions with what some Buddhist traditions call "diamond mind," and in so doing, his recombinant texts could be seen to be recipes for the alteration of consciousness—the induction of clear mind through the interruption of "ordinary" internal thought. And *Naked Lunch* is, if we are to believe an "Atrophied Preface" two hundred pages into a work of fiction, a set of recipes: "*Naked Lunch* is a blueprint, a How-To Book" (187). As such, *Naked Lunch* is a fundamentally algorithmic text, a set of recipes where "Black insect lusts open into vast other-planet landscapes. . . . Abstract concepts, bare as algebra, narrow down to a black turd or a pair of aging *cojones*" (187). Refusing the opposition between abstraction and mundane, finite, rotting, and shitting materiality, these recipes work to disrupt habitual thought formations and behavior, an alteration of consciousness whose readerly contribution is an active silence:

> How-To extend levels of experience by opening the door at the end
> of a long hall . . . Doors that only open in *Silence* . . . *Naked Lunch*
> demands Silence from The Reader. Otherwise he is taking his own
> pulse . . . (187)

Burroughs offers us training in a silence before which the lunch is indeed naked. Rather than being offered a work to "consume," Burroughs offers his work as a manual for achieving the blast of silence. In short, *Naked Lunch* is a manual for overcoming current conditions through mutation, and in some sense, we must only shut up long enough to mutate. When asked about his message to politicians, Burroughs responded that these science-fiction creatures should "Tell the truth once and for all and shut up forever."

And in silence, we behold a very different and no-less-scientific model of life in Burroughs' writings than that offered by 1950s nascent molecular biology, understandably transfixed as it was by the work of the DNA Word. In the blast of silence solicited and induced by Burroughs in *Naked Lunch*, a recognizable "subjective correlative" to the emerging informatic vision of living systems can be perceived. Here readers must practice introspection and explore *life from the inside*. "The way OUT is the way IN . . ." (191). This way "IN" is itself as manipulable as the external world, where the practices of molecular biology augured complete control over living systems. Burroughs' way "IN," though, was no less rigorous and emerged out of an apprenticeship with both junk, whose addictive potentials pull the user toward the machine state of repetition, entropy, and death, and *yagé*, a plant adjunct Burroughs came to describe as a time-travel technology. In both cases, it is the very difference between living systems and machines that is both blurred and advanced.

Burroughs was, of course, not alone in his advance beyond either mechanism or vitalism. Most recently, Stephen Wolfram has focused on the concept of "irreducibility" in his studies of cellular automata, where remarkable and thoroughly unpredictable complexity emerges out of the (viral?) iteration of simple rules. Wolfram adopts the language of "irreducibility" in order to amplify the epistemological limits reached by his research; only by growing and exploring artificial life forms can they be known. By analogy, Burroughs had to drink *yagé*—and drink it again—in his own quest for what he called the "Final Fix."

This "subjective" aspect of living systems—they must be lived in order to be understood—induced Physicist Niels Bohr to call for a complementary model of living systems akin to the complementary wave/particle model in physics. Bohr sought a theory that included both the unmistakably and irreducible "teleological" pull of life and our capacities to effectively describe and manipulate organisms as mechanistic systems. More-recent work in thermodynamics by researchers Stanley Salthe, Rod Swenson, James Jay Kay, Eric Schneider, and Dorian Sagan suggest that living systems are indeed pulled toward the dissipation of ever-increasing amounts of energy and information.

Bohr's "teleomechanical" model of living systems has not had much influence, and for the most part, the return of teleological thinking to biology has not yet begun to alter our maps of living systems, which are, as biologist J. B. Haldane remarked long ago, stranger than we can imagine.

Hence, the evolution of our imagined maps of evolution becomes crucial to any advance in our ongoing exploration of nature, and by composing both the machinic and irreducible aspects of living systems in one, necessarily disjunctive, text, Burroughs offers us a new map for new territories opened up by emerging biotechnological and biochemical visions of (trans)human beings. The "junkie" approaches the pure form of habit structure, the human outted as biochemical machine. Yet, these exempla of the "Algebra of Need" are also urging, surging "wetware" with what Jean-Baptiste LaMarck called "the inner feeling of being alive."

They gibber and squeal at the sight of it. The spit hangs off their chin, and their stomach rumbles and all their guts grind in peristalsis while they cook up, dissolving the body's decent skin, you expect any moment a great blob of protoplasm will flop right out and surround the junk. Really disgust you to see it. [. . .] Isn't Life peculiar? (6)

And even reading about such "Life" makes me gibber and giggle at the sight of it. It is life viewed from the perspective of naked life, the living need of an addict even as she approaches the pure state of a machine: more more more more, the algebra of need, the ever-increasing demands of addiction, and, indeed, thermodynamics, for more. "Thermodynamics has won at a crawl" (187). It was Philip K. Dick's androids translated by Ridley Scott who spoke the immortal cyborg mantra, "More life, fucker!" but it was Burroughs who was able to most abstract it from his own persona and ego. While Dick suffered the ordeal of VALIS as he experienced what it was to be part of an enormously abstract machine identical to the cosmos, Burroughs' practiced emptiness allowed him a perhaps slightly wider aperture with which he could open his mind to the future in all of its strangeness and otherness:

Wrong! I am never here . . . Never that is *fully* in possession, but somehow in a position to forestall ill-advised moves . . . (185)

Burroughs recalls to our consciousness, again and again, the sheer metabolic fact of our embodiment, as the flows of which we are composed become outsourced with terrified hilarity:

"Yes I know it all. The finance company is repossessing your wife's artificial kidney . . . They are evicting your grandmother from her iron lung." (154)

And while high-quality hoaxes are a veritable tradition in physics, these exceptions prove the rule that "normal" science resists challenges to the status of truth itself, a challenge often posed by the mere existence of compelling fiction. Perhaps, Burroughs was the greatest fake writer ever, a confidence man crossed with an Intelligence Agent. I call Burroughs a "fake" writer not because his writing lacks authenticity or rhetorical effect, both of which it exudes with intensity and quantity. Instead, Burroughs simulated the Writer Archetype and hacked the obsessive figure of the writer himself, a shamanic dismemberment or "cut up" and not Death of the Author. This map of the territory "William S. Burroughs" or "Bill Lee" as a "fake writer" suggests that Burroughs' activities as a writer provided the armature for a thoroughgoing investigation into yet another map and, yet, not one among others—"life." By amplifying the relentlessly teleological aspect of living systems, Burroughs demonstrated that for the sake of scientific inquiry, it is sometimes necessary to pretend to be something other than a Scientist, if only because that archetype, even into the present, demands a separation of the observer from the observed, a separation Burroughs consistently dismembered in his fictional and nonfictional writings. Beginning with Burroughs' experimental ingestion of *yagé* in the 1950s and continuing to his investigation of dreaming in *My Education*, Burroughs' investigations into the biological aspects of consciousness were "involutionary" and "metabolic"; they began with experimentation on and with the self through manipulation of the processes of ingestion (a junky eats through her arm, Bill Lee drinks *yagé* for the "final fix") and digestion (a black turd). Science from the inside, Burroughs' work fits the criteria embryologist and theoretical biologist Stanley Salthe offers to define an "internalist" science:

> Internalism is the attempt to understand ("model" may be too "objective" a concept) a system from within, with the inquirer being a part, inside the system, and therefore unable to see itself as if from outside. In contrast, the mirror would symbolize the stance taken up in standard (externalist) scientific modeling, delivering a spatiotemporally global picture of a whole system, describable in the universal present tense (as in: "organisms reproduce" or "a star's energy dissipates").

In a discussion of animal cruelty, Burroughs points specifically to this internalist perspective, a point of view characterized by a fertile negation whose effect is unmitigated and inspired compassion. His inability to separate himself from other organisms separates him from those who take a more mechanistic understanding of living systems:

> I am using myself as a reference point of view to assess current and future trends. This is not megalomania. It is simply the only measuring artifact available. Observer William: 023. Trends can be compacted into one word . . . GAP. Widening GAPs. GAP between 023 and those who can club seal cubs to death, set cats on fire, shoot out the eyes of lemurs with slingshots. (*Word Virus*, 510)

This separation that emerges from an otherwise thoroughly connective affect (compassion) could be seen to be the very basis of Burroughs' life science, one that queries irreducible aspects of living systems. By contrast, the scientific model of the DNA Word encouraged a perspective Burroughs summarized under the word *control*:

> Like all control systems it depends on maintaining a monopoly position. If anybody can be tape recorder 3 then tape recorder 3 loses power. God must be THE GOD. (*Electronic Revolution*, 18)

With the rise of the well-named "Central Dogma" in molecular biology, which insisted on a static genome beyond alteration by an organism, so too must DNA be THE God of living systems. And, so the Dogma decreed, there was to be no feedback between an environment and DNA during the life of an organism, including the feedback between human consciousness and DNA. To explore those other aspects of living systems that elude this monopoly and closure of control, in *Naked Lunch* Burroughs casts himself as a scientific instrument whose read out is both "Direct" and partial, focusing on "certain areas of psychic process."

> I am a recording instrument . . . I do not presume to impose "story" "plot" "continuity" . . . Insofar as I succeed in *Direct* recording of certain areas of psychic process I may have limited function . . . I am not an entertainer . . . (184)

From his practices with orgones to his vision of the control society and artificial life forms, Burroughs' investigation of "life" offers a conceptual framework resonant with and complementary to recent calls for "First-Person Science," a mode of scientific description that integrates an observer into a participatory universe where living systems and their investigators cannot be neatly separated. In what follows, I splice Burroughs' contributions to the life sciences into an account of my recent work as a participant observer with international organizations in the field of biometrics, emerging technologies of control. Here in the "blast of silence," Burroughs and his creations become practical and useful guides to anticipating the likely effects of any given (bio)technology. A recording instrument, Burroughs *is* a biotechnology reporting on his own, biometric, nature.

Wetware Protocols: A Blast of Silence

The farmer's eye is the best fertilizer.
—Pliny

πάντων χρημάτων μέτρον ἐστίν ἄνθρωπος, τόν μέν ὄντων ὡς ἐστιν, τών δέ ουκ ὄντων ὡς ουκ ἐστιν
—Protagoras

We each live in our own world—together.
—mobius

The forward step must be made in silence . . .
—Burroughs

What Burroughs—or, rather Lee, or the other labels we have assembled together in that feast *Naked Lunch*—labeled *factualism* entails an empiricism of the self, an ongoing and evolving response-ability to the festival of life forms hosting and hosted by the self. Burroughs was comfortable writing texts not "governed" by him; no All Powerful Organizer Author was in charge of the emerging text, and if he were, he would be cut up. When Burroughs writes, then, it is less a representation of life but is, instead, a continuous response to it, a "recording instrument" whose condition of operation is to cut up the Author Himself. "Inside. Outside. Let's call the whole thing off. Suddenly, map and territory meet as One: Tell me: What do you say we play a little William Tell?" What does, in fact, William tell?

> I saw it [. . .] past invading the present, rancid magic of slot machines and roadhouses [. . .] "Selling is more of a habit than using." [. . .] He claimed tea put him in touch with supra blue gravitational fields. [. . .] Causal thinking never yields accurate description of metabolic process—limitations of existing language. (9, 11, 14, 18, 23)

No matter how hard mobius works to differentiate these two worlds—the interior world of his involutionary investigations into Mind and the exterior world that often denies the very existence of Mind—he finds them to be One. Of a piece. All together now . . . mobius is on his bike. Rather, mobius rides the bike, an old French frame single-speed fixed gear that does not allow him to coast. Ever. Pedal pull breath chant must become a reflex. mobius has become bike, mobius is the label for the place where inside and outside call it off. mobius pedals towards the Western Lands, making tight dervish circles singing.

The bike is an interface. The dappled sunlight through the maples and the oaks and the hemlocks cast baroque, curling shadows across a granite sand path. Birdsong seems to synchronize with the rhythms of umbra and penumbra. These fire roads make good stalking grounds for the morel, one of mobius' prey.

Something is on the ground. mobius skids to a halt, the knobbed rear tire tearing at itself.

It is nothing. A piece of birch bark. Native Americans used it as parchment.

Pedal pull breath chant must become a reflex.

That night, a dream had mobius. The dream was like Burroughs' packing dream, the boat is whistling in the harbor, trying to pack, gotta get out of Gibraltar . . .

> A writer's will is the winds of dead calm of the Western Lands. Point way out he can start stirring of the sail. Writer, where are you going? To write. Here we are in texts already written on the sky. [. . .] The texts sing. Everything is grass and bushes, a desert or a maze of texts. Here

you are . . . never use the same door twice. Sky in all directions . . . on the word for word. The word for word is word. (*Word Virus*, 515)

Something *is* there. A scroll of parchment. Birch. The parchment unrolls mobius, who beholds it, blinking, with eyes like a Mugwump. It's typed in twelve-point pico, a typewriter, a Remington by the looks of it. "Twelve Gauge," I think to myself . . . It tells a story:

I can feel the heat closing in, feel them out there making their moves, setting up their devil doll venture capitalist stool pigeons, crooning over a fat roach I feel burning toward my fingerprints, whistling on the exhale and vaulting the railing near the tourist kiosks and drink stands serving the Swiss cave near which I crouch . . . It's a science party, and our quarry's the numbers and levels for the human body. Biometrics, a sound check for Control. "Check one. Check two. Check." To wit: How loud, how bright, how hard, how hot? Idea is, we start designing the machines for our bodies rather than the other way around. Some of the machines will even tell us who we are. Or aren't.

We project to a large screen in a well-designed conference room in a Franciscan Retreat shadowed and sheltered by the Swiss Alps, one hour from Geneva. Our collective is TC 395/WG 0, Quantitative Logos, and their letter symbols. Glyphs and tables flicker on the screen, a cursor blinks and moves back a few spaces from a superscript, as if in terrified awe of its tiny font. Text scrolls. We are bootstrapping telebiometrics, a system for biologically based human authentication at a distance, by working out its vocabulary and units of measure, its protocols.

AJ is in his element, working the screen and the phone and his crew toward an impossible consensus about the fundamental measurements of the human sensory system. I say "impossible" because one of the things I have learned during my investigations of telebiometrics is that "we all live in our own world—together." What with the combinations and recombinations between and among the senses and the attention we give to them, any given scene can be tuned in such a multitude of ways that the world very likely feels different to each and every one of us even as we experience momentary flashes of telepathy, a feeling of what it is to be a body for each and every individuated organism. I say "very likely" because given this sensory diaspora, it is good to remember along with the Count that "the map is not the territory." Burroughs writes:

> Emphatically we do not oppose telepathic research. In fact, telepathy properly used and understood could be the ultimate defense against any form of organized coercion or tyranny on the part of pressure groups or individual control addicts. We oppose, as we oppose atomic

war, the use of such knowledge to control, coerce, debase, exploit or annihilate the individuality of another living creature. Telepathy is not, by its nature, a one-way process. To attempt to set up a one-way telepathic broadcast must be regarded as an unqualified evil . . . (140)

So, each of us, living in our own world, together, shares their world with machines. And this sharing—it's increasingly intimate. "Tele-pathic research" now must be parsed as research connecting bodies at a distance.

AJ's gig is telemedicine—acupuncture at a distance, networks of distributed healing. He comes on real coyote, a trickster, tantric, pantheist, last of the great taxonomists. He cuts the world up into chunks so that we can all connect them. He is the broker, a breakbeat artist of love, ideas, and money whose mix renders the future. His is the path of freedom from fear and attachment to any given outcome, a grinning, laughing mustachioed bow-tie-wearing shaman of emerging technologies, brokering and making deals between those two dimensions, past and future.

And biometrics, the very measurement of living systems now in ecosystemic distress, poses the question of the future: *Shall we have one?* Burroughs' insistence on being a "recording instrument" reminds us of his paradoxical operation as writer—to continually erase the habitual meanings linking "maps" to "territories." As a first-person recording device, Burroughs is a psychonaut seeking the expansion of consciousness through the interruption of Word Broadcasts:

> I feel that the principal instrument of monopoly and control that prevents expansion of consciousness is the word lines controlling thought, feeling and apparent sensory impressions of the human host. (Lotringer, 43)

What is at hand now fifty years after *Naked Lunch* is an ecosystemic distress whose very roots, Burroughs suggests, can be found in our unacknowledged allegiance to a mechanistic model of life, a model tending toward the elimination of affect whose word lines *must* be disrupted if the ongoing elimination of living systems, this extinction event, is to be cut up:

> All political organizations tend to function like a machine [. . .] if the machine absorbed or eliminated all those outside the machine, the machine would slow down and stop forever. Any unchecked impulse does, within the human body and psyche, lead to the destruction of the organism. (Lotringer, 44)

Burroughs' friend and fellow life scientist Timothy Leary wrote of Burroughs as an "Intelligence Agent," an agent acting as a local area problem solver for evolution. mobius imagines Burroughs' Intelligence Agent archetype whenever he gets a little bit freaked out by the flickering projector and the idea of a biometric sensor capturing every bodily sign and signal.

What Are You Doing Here? Who Are You? (184)

The word *wetware* is highlighted on the screen: "*That aspect of any living system that can be treated as an information system.*" From the perspective of the participants of TC 395/WG 0, this is mobius' word. And some of them don't like it a bit. Makes mobius feel all figure/ground uncertain.

An engineer's stomach reacts and speaks: "Disgusts you to hear it come out of my meathole. Slang. *Not human.* Computer Freak Speak."

A delegate rises to general murmuring. mobius slurps coffee. "It reeks of filthy carbuncle. Makes me sweat an avalanche of ear dross. It'll lead to new standards in rectal leakage. An attack on the Lipid Structure Of the Health State!"

So instead of yelling "*Where Am I?*" cool it and look around and you will find out approximately . . . You were not there for *The Beginning.* You will not be there for *The End* . . . Your knowledge of what is going on can only be superficial and relative . . . (184)

AJ's tie bloats with the silence. mobius moves his mouth only a little to begin the flow: "It's a mnemonic device. Installs a tripartite remembrance module for eternal embodiment remembrance loops, a piece o' string about the designer's finger to remind them of their nature. Hardware, software, wetware. Gotta have all three."

A naked lunch is natural to us
We eat reality sandwiches
But allegories are so much lettuce
Don't hide the madness

(Ginsberg, 114)

Works Cited

Burroughs, William S. *Electronic Revolution.* Bresche, Germany: Expanded Media, 1976.
———. *The Ticket That Exploded.* London: Calder, 1985.
———. *Word Virus: the William S. Burroughs Reader.* Edited by James Grauerholz and Ira Silverberg. New York: Grove, 1998.
Ginsberg, Allen. *Collected Poems, 1947–1980.* New York: Viking, 1985.
Korzybski, Alfred. *Science and Sanity: An Introduction to Non-Aristotelian Systems and General Semantics.* 1933. Lancaster, PA: International Non-Aristotelian Library, 1958.
Leary, Timothy, Ralph Metzner, and Richard Alpert. *The Psychedelic Experience: A Manual Based on the Tibetan Book of the Dead.* New York: Citadel, 1995.

Lotringer, Sylvère, ed. *Burroughs Live: The Collected Interviews of William S. Burroughs 1960–1997.* Los Angeles: Semiotext(e), 2001.

Salthe, Stanley. "Internalism Summarized." Stanley Salthe, homepage, Neils Bohr Institute, Denmark. http://www.nbi.dk/~natphil/salthe/internalism_summarized.pdf (accessed September 2007).

dossier SIX
A Little Night Music

ian **MACFADYEN**

Files Comprising: Addict-Ridden, Corpsing, A Little Night Music, Nothing Sacred, Djinns, God's Radio Station, Bounce, Targets, Burial Ground, Out Of The Ether, East St. Louis Toodle-O / Nightmare, Cold, Down On The Farm, It's About Time, Soundtracks, The Sounds Of Silence, The Beggar's Opera, Stardust, The Outlaw Breed, So Long At The Fair, Human Radio, Mockery, Silence Over And Out, Envoi: Avedon's Burroughs Portrait By Jeremy Reed.

Addict-Ridden

The pusher hums the melodies of 1930s and 1940s film songs like *Smiles*, *I'm in the Mood for Love*, and *They Say We're Too Young to Go Steady*. He's the Pied Piper, a musical soul stealer, hypnotizing young kids with his sweet melodies, while the delicious irony of the lyrics invoked, cynically exploiting romantic yearning as a cover for junk need, must really turn him on. "Melancholy Baby dies from an overdose of time or cold turkey withdrawal of breath" (7). Burroughs' choice of the 1912 song *Melancholy Baby* references, among others, Judy Garland and her iconic performance in the 1954 movie version of *A Star Is Born*. Garland sings the song in a Manhattan supper club, in a dream projection of chanteuse stardom, but as Tim Armstrong has noted, "Both in the context of its production, and in its contents," this is "a profoundly 'addict-ridden' film" in which popular culture is continually reproduced and played back, the addict star "'plugged in' to the studio apparatus," and the entertainment spectacle which would eventually destroy her (140). *Smiles* was also a Garland film number, from the YMCA montage sequence in *For Me and My Gal* (1942)—"But the smiles that fill my life with sunshine / Are the smiles that you give to me." The original 1917 song is segued with *It's a Long Way to Tipperary* and *Pack Up Your Troubles*—beneath the honey and the razzamatazz, all three songs are littered with bloody corpses.

Corpsing

"Can you show me the way to Tipperary, Lady?" is answered, "Over the hills and far away . . . Across the bone meal of lawn [. . .] The screaming skull" (109–10). *Over the Hills and Far Away* is a British army song, dating from the time of Marlborough, sung by tens of thousands of corpses-in-waiting. It's as if Burroughs is compelled to sabotage these songs and turn them into a different kind of *show-stopper*, to see the blood beneath the choreographic and militaristic display, the terrible denouement masked by a popular culture of lachrymose, patriotic sentiment, the obscenity of Great War songs given the Hollywood Treatment. "Confidentially, girls, I use Steely Dan's Yokohama, wouldn't you? Danny Boy never lets you down" (117). *Danny Boy* is a song beloved of the Irish diaspora, a long-established Irish American funeral song, an elegy for a very young man killed in battle. Judy Garland would record several heartbreaking versions, and Burroughs' spin on the theme is, of course, spectacularly insensitive and provocative. The congruence of references in *Naked Lunch* points decisively to Garland's anguished routines and her recordings of *Meet Me in St. Louis* and *The Man That Got Away* would have had a special, bitter significance for Burroughs. *Naked Lunch*'s vaudevillian interludes resemble those Garland-Rooney musicals in which our guy and gal burst forth into extempore song and improvise a whole show out of handy props and an invisible full orchestra. *"I know! Let's put on a show!"* And Burroughs does just that.

A Little Night Music

The 1920s Broadway nightclub torch singer Tommy Lyman featured *Melancholy Baby* in his midnight cabarets and it is his signature song which is subversively parodied by Burroughs, so that it becomes a junk lullaby—"Tell me of the cares that make you feel so blue . . . My love is true and just for you . . . I'd do almost anything . . . Could not fail to lull you into peaceful dreams . . ." Junkies are carrying a torch for the only one they really love, and this inhuman, terminally unrequited love is mockingly couched in the parlance of popular romance and crooner shmaltz. Likewise, "Every day die a little," says Sailor (170), pushing to a boy, turning him on, and turning him into a profitable user, transforming Cole Porter's 1944 standard *Everytime We Say Goodbye* (definitively recorded by Ella Fitzgerald in 1956) into a sardonic paean to the coupling of pusher and addict. Here, the erasure of the personal pronoun is devastating, deadly—we are obliged to read: "Every day *you* die a little."

Nothing Sacred

The Star Spangled Banner is sung by a "decayed, corseted tenor—bursting out of a Daniel Boone costume" (53), the platform draped with the American flag. The National Anthem was not sacrosanct for Burroughs, and he had nothing but contempt for this homage to "the Land of the Free" with its "bombs bursting in air"—which Hendrix would brilliantly hijack in 1968 as a sonic protest against the Vietnam War. Of the American flag Burroughs would say, "Soak it in heroin and I'll suck it," and for him, there was nothing sacred about *that* song about *that* besmirched flag of convenience. As for *The Battle Hymn of the Republic*, Burroughs did not believe in "deliverance" after the Wrath of God has passed over the battlefield, and his treatment of the hallowed words of Julia Ward Howe is suitably heartless and monstrous and paradoxically heartfelt and moral, an outrage perpetrated by the truly mortified. Maybe Burroughs was remembering those 1943 advertisements which transformed "The Grapes of Wrath" into "The Blades of Wrath": "There will be blood on the moon tonight in Germany . . . Nash-Kelvinator Corporation."

Djinns

Burroughs himself was clearly *infiltrated* by these songs. Gail-Nina Anderson has pointed out that the "resident djinn" in Burroughs' line, "'He's got this resident *djinn*'" (103) comes from Gilbert and Sullivan's 1877 comic opera about magic and curses, *The Sorcerer*, and the songs in *Naked Lunch* are themselves treated as mischievous, malevolent musical sprites, liable to swarm forth when the stylus hits the groove or that dial is touched. Burroughs clearly wanted rid of these songs, he wanted them out of here, and he did so by twisting and turning them, deforming them, and by exploiting subtexts or imposing meanings of his own. These lines from *The Sorcerer* certainly had a hidden meaning for him—"If you want a proud foe to 'make tracks' / If you'd melt a rich uncle in wax / You've but to look in on our resident Djinn / Number seventy, Simmery Axe." Yes, those old records definitely left their track marks, but all bad things must come to their end: "And then, suddenly, the music dies; the flying djinn has been rebottled. With a stupid, insect-like insistence, a steel point rasps and rasps into silence" (Huxley, 41).

God's Radio Station

In "Megalopolitan Maniac," the final section of *Black Spring*, Henry Miller writes: "This is the city, and this the music. Out of the little black boxes an unending river of romance in which the crocodiles weep [. . .] All in step. From the power house above God floods the street with music. It is God who turns the music on every evening just as we quit work [. . .] It is this *Song of Love* which now pours out of millions of little black boxes [. . .] It is this Song which gives us the courage to kill millions of men at once by pressing a button. This Song which gives us the energy to plunder the earth and lay everything low" (247–48). Miller's 1936 attack on God's radio station as it plugs murderous patriotism and the panacea of sentiment, was clearly a major influence, conceptually and stylistically, on *Naked Lunch*'s musical divertissement, and on "The Prophet's Hour" and the "Atrophied Preface." The sound bombardment and entertainment overload is unstoppable, exponential, ectoplasmic—"from every shop on Broadway the radio answers with megaphone and pick-up, with amplifiers and hook-ups" (244), it is "a séance with megaphones and ticker tape, men with no arms dictating to wax cylinders" (246), the melody of mass entertainment "drowned by its own suppurating stench" (246).

Bounce

Danny Deever sung by a tenor in drag is one of Kipling's *Barrack-Room Ballads* about the military execution by hanging of a young soldier. The musical setting of the poem by Walter Damrosch was Teddy Roosevelt's favorite song—a perfectly hypocritical preference for a president who supported capital punishment. "So it started in Addis Ababa like the Jersey Bounce" (36) not only refers to the 1942 song *Jersey Bounce* recorded by Benny Goodman and many swing bands and Doo Wop groups—"And whether you're hep or not / The Jersey Bounce will make you swing"—but also to wartime B-17 Flying Fortress bombers, their fuselages baptized and painted with the name

"Jersey Bounce" after the song—a prophetic, unholy marriage of pop culture and war machine.

Targets

There's "always a space *between,* in popular songs and Grade B movies, giving away the basic American rottenness, spurting out like breaking boils" (112). It is in this *space between* that Burroughs operates, in which a festering culture suppurates, and he works with the reject matter, the discharge, the *waste products*—he flings it back. In 1945, Paul Bowles wrote, "The same pattern prevails all over the world: the uprooting of natural culture for the implantation of an ersatz culture which can be controlled from headquarters" (248). Burroughs' apparently cheap shots expose the ludicrous, tawdry potency of popular music and ridicule the duplicity beneath which it operates—music as junk, shellac for the war machine, the heartbreak routine and the political rally, the Japanese Sandman selling "new dreams for old."

Burial Ground

Geoff Ward has written of "Fragments of different songs and rhymes . . . cohabiting over time, like skeletons separated by generations finally embracing in the same burial ground" (156). This could be used to describe the effect of Burroughs' musical collage in *Naked Lunch,* and it is not far-fetched to see Burroughs' strategy as comparable with Harry Smith's *Anthology of American Folk Music* as described by Ward—"At once a salvaging of cultural detritus, of lost names on crackling 78s, and a template for the artistry of sampling and collage in an electronic age" (137).

Out Of The Ether

Song lines, snatches of conversation overheard in a bar, a radio program caught for a moment while passing an open window, Burroughs plucked fragments "out of the ether" and redeployed them in ways akin to his St. Louis predecessor T. S. Eliot. What did such phrases mean? Eliot said of *The Wasteland,* "I wasn't even bothering whether I understood what I was saying" (Rainey, 126). Burroughs operated as an extension of the communication apparatus—writer as electrophonic receiver and hooked-up stenographer, creator as possessed transmitter and structural randomizer, and only then as the conscious decoder and interpreter of sound made script, witness to that mosaic of fate which he had apparently constructed with a bloody left hand from shards of brilliant trash.

East St. Louis Toodle-O / Nightmare

Duke Ellington's 1926 *East St. Louis Toodle-O* is the music which name-checks Burroughs' birthplace, reminiscent of home and times lost forever. It was the theme tune of the Ellington Band and is the signature tune of the novel—a melody blown down memory lane, a few magical glints in time, then gone. Its musical nemesis is nowhere mentioned in *Naked Lunch*, but it is a recording Burroughs knew well—*Nightmare* by Artie Shaw, an ineluctable, escalating sleepwalk towards doom, a breathtaking performance that conjures the maniacal Hugo from the film *Dead of Night*, the possessed dummy advancing with his white strangler's mitts. . . . Recorded in New York on September 17 1937, on the same day as a jolly version of *It's a Long, Long Way to Tipperary*, it is a refrain which Shaw would use to even more sinister effect in a bizarre arrangement of *My Heart Belongs to Daddy*—the song's gay connotations would not have been lost on Burroughs—evoking a murderous *noir* scenario in which either the femme fatale or her sugar daddy will not be around for too much longer. Music gives, and it takes away, like the Hakamas, the Arab women paid to sing atrocity songs and rouse the Janjaweed to slaughter: "Once we started singing, the killing would not stop. It was exciting" (Bloomfield, 37).

Cold

Baby, It's Cold Outside was written by Frank Loesser in 1944. As the snow falls and the temperature drops, the male protagonist, "The Wolf," tries to persuade the female voice, "The Mouse," to stay the night at his place. This classic duet of seduction and resistance is used by Burroughs in both his introduction and the "Atrophied Preface," and unlike most of his other song allusions, this is more than *détournement*, it's conceptually employed—"nice and warm in here nice and warm nice and IN HERE and nice and OUTSIDE IT'S COLD . . . IT'S COLD OUTSIDE" (209). This refers to opium smokers who like to hibernate in a warm place unlike "all the dross eaters and needle boys out there in the cold" (209) who won't last long in the freezing, silent, cold world, leaving only their footprints in the snow like the famous scene in *The Invisible Man*. Burroughs writes that junkies *want* it cold, but cold *inside the body*, "metabolism approaching Absolute ZERO" (208). He notes the death of the libido through junk—"I am forgetting sex and all sharp pleasures of the body" (56)—and though some like it hot, the junkie is not one of them, and in any case he has no one to persuade to stay in the warm unless it's that special, fabulous person who just happens to be *holding*.

Down On The Farm

In *Junky*, Burroughs describes the regime at the Narcotic Farm in Lexington, Kentucky, in 1948, but he doesn't mention the jazz soundtrack and the jazz clientele of the place. Many addicted musicians passed through Narco—Chet Baker, Sonny Rollins, Jackie McClean, Elvin Jones among them—and in the late 1940s and 1950s, inmates were provided with instruments and practice rooms and performed concerts in the institution's thirteen hundred-seater theater. There's a radio on the Lexington ward described by Burroughs, but it's switched off, or he pays it no mind, his interest entirely fixed on the jive talk of the hipster bebop junkies, and it is their revolving, hep, coded raps, so intimately bound up with the rhythms and cadences of jazz, which run in riffs throughout *Naked Lunch,* the junk talk combo playing variations on their favorite theme—*loaded, shoot it, on the nod.*

It's About Time

Burroughs has none of Kerouac's passion for bebop. Mary does put on a record of "metallic cocaine bebop" (78) just before she inserts Steely Dan III, cueing speedy, labyrinthine, driving jazz for the frenzied sex action on screen, but whereas for Kerouac, Parker's *Now's the Time* said it all, the music in *Naked Lunch* is distinctly, and in both senses, *out of time.*

Soundtracks

Howard Shore and Ornette Coleman's soundtrack for Cronenberg's *Naked Lunch*, approximates, in part, Burroughs' description of the music of the City of Interzone—"High mountain flutes, jazz and bebop, one-stringed Mongol instruments, gypsy xylophones, African drums, Arab bagpipes . . ." (90). Shore's "harmolodic" *noirish* orchestrations and Coleman's evocative dervish takes, as well as the rock collaborations and tributes of Burroughs' later years, have culturally and historically remade/remodeled the way we *hear* the book, just as many readers today will know the sound of Burroughs' voice—a friend, hearing it for the first time, described it as "like something crawling along the floor"—and are helpless not to *hear* that extraordinary instrument as they turn the pages, which was very definitely not the case for those who read the book in the early 1960s.

The Sounds Of Silence

Burroughs advised that we should learn to read in silence, but we don't read in a soundproofed anechoic chamber, and even there, we would hear the singing and ringing of our own nervous system and the drumming pulse of our circulating blood. As John Cage commented, "No silence exists that is not pregnant with sound" (qtd. in Revill, 163). Burroughs instructs us, "*Naked Lunch* demands Silence from The Reader. Otherwise he is taking his own pulse" (187). But in silence, the reader would be doing exactly that, while *Naked Lunch* is itself a clamorous bombardment, an unholy din of slammed shutters, sirens, explosions, foghorns, air hammers, steam shovels, and endless screaming, relieved only by "heroin silent as dawn" (191), following the brief tap-tapping of the syringe.

The Beggar's Opera

"Over the hills and far away with the dawn wind and a train whistle" (100)—the opening phrase is taken from *The Beggar's Opera* (1728) by John Gay, from a duet between Polly Peachum and Macheath. "And I would love you all the day / Ev'ry night would kiss and play / If with me you'd fondly stray / Over the hills and far away." *The Beggar's Opera* is political satire, a squalid lowlife rogue's gallery, a dark vision of society and a rude comedy, a debunking of the triviality of high art, and a musical parody. Gay's drama inspired Brecht and Weill's 1928 *The Threepenny Opera*, and the fifteen-year-old whore killer in the *Naked Lunch* episode is closer to the cutthroat Mackie Messer, a.k.a. Mack the Knife, than Gay's gentleman thief, but Gay's work is structurally and thematically present in *Naked Lunch*—with its short dramatic scenes, musical interludes, prisons and taverns and low life, its underworld agents and informers, inebriated rogues and whores, the criminal world intertwined with respectable society, it is a paradigm of Burroughs' subjects, sets, and scenes.

Stardust

Burroughs loved Hoagy Carmichael's *Stardust* (1927), and it was the music of the Jazz Age and the Depression which touched him, and to which he was nostalgically attached. This was Burroughs' true musical era—the era of sheet music, piano rolls, and the phonograph, vaudeville theaters and nightclubs, radio broadcasts, player pianos, and song lyrics projected on cinema screens to piano, organ, and orchestral accompaniment. The music of *Naked Lunch* is a 1926 Columbia disc of Fletcher Henderson's *The Stampede*, or the 1937 version, or his 1931 recording of *Sugar* played on an old Victrola. . . . That's the needle scratch and jumping beat and roller-coaster swing and bitter sweet hook of the book. It is this period of popular music and song which runs throughout *Naked Lunch*—a soundtrack which may be lost on some present and many future readers of the book. When Burroughs refers to Louis Alter and Harold Adamson's 1928 *Manhattan Serenade* (129), he is also remembering a radio soundtrack for the *Easy Aces Radio Show* in the 1930s. But all this is disappearing into the past, despite the Web—it is no longer known and felt, except by a cognoscenti, it can be re-called, but not *recalled*.

The Outlaw Breed

Burroughs was in his late teens and early twenties when the Midwestern crime wave hit Chicago, St. Louis, and Kansas City. The Dillinger Gang, the Barrow Gang, and the Barker-Karpis Gang were in the headlines and on the covers of drugstore dime books—sharp suits and Tommy guns and fast cars, a new-style version of the robbers of the old days. Burroughs' fondness for the songs of the 1930s is bound up with his admiration for John Dillinger's scofflaw, devil-may-care exploits, his unbridled individualism in action. Swing and croon, novelty rag and big-band stomp, the music of the period provided the indelible soundtrack to the mythos of the new outlaw breed. Burroughs always thought of Dillinger as an artist, a libertarian, an icon of resistance, and in *Naked Lunch* the music of the Depression is a celebration of and an elegy for this final expression of the true "frontier" spirit.

So Long At The Fair

"Watching you and humming over and over, 'Johnny's So Long At The Fair'" (194). This old nursery rhyme and folk song, treated by Burroughs as an elegy for lost love, contains a secret significance. In the 1950 film *So Long At The Fair*, Vicky, beautifully played by Jean Simmons, discovers that her brother Johnny has disappeared from his Paris hotel room. The authorities conclude that she has lost her mind and that Johnny, despite her protestations, never existed. This is the chimerical heart of the "Hauser and O'Brien" episode in which the living cops become "Dream Cops": "'Nobody of that name [. . .] no Hauser no O'Brien'" (181). The one who watches over the sleeping beloved and hums *So Long At The Fair* is remembering a lover who vanished forever in time, but did that person ever really exist at all? And if he did, then even at the time, "Johnny" was beyond reach, indifferent to the murmur of fascination, lost to the world, unknowing, and unknowable. At the end of *Queer*, the sinister Skip Tracer appears in a dream scenario, and it isn't money he's after but the settlement in regular installments of a sexual contract to be paid in-kind, payments due on a body if not a soul—he's a dybbuk, a demon lover in slimy grave clothes, and he hums *Johnny's So Long At The Fair* as a threatening paean of repossession to his inamorata. . . . This is Lee's revenge projection, he has finally tracked down his young *john*, and that melody of loss and yearning is carried throughout Radio City, "languid and intermittent, like music down a windy street" (133) and blown into the pages of *Naked Lunch*.

Human Radio

Burroughs feared and repudiated human love with its dangers of possession and possessiveness—he preferred the concept of "recognition"—and he found popular songs, so redolent of rejection and loss, excruciating. As Lenny Kaye puts it, in the sensual but ersatz "language of chimera" of the love song, the singer is a "human radio tube. Pure vacuum" (5), while the listener is an electronic earpiece, the terminally hooked-up receiver. It's the perfect cybernetic system for the transmission and reception of addiction, compulsion, and obsession: "Me, you. You, me. Which is to be who. We could even trade places . . ." (4).

Mockery

John McCormack's 1933 version of the parlor favorite *Believe Me If All These Endearing Young Charms*, a song about undying love and mortality, is transmogrified by Burroughs into a fairy faggot tribute by the Flesh Corset brigade, pathos replaced by spurting guts, while Samuel Woodworth's *Old Oaken Bucket*, a sentimental school song about the old childhood country home, learned by rote by millions of American children, is sung by A. J., and the very idea of "the notorious Merchant of Sex" and representative of "a trust of giant insects from another galaxy" (121, 123) perpetrating this terrible hokum must have had Burroughs doubled over in ecstatic glee, a guaranteed laughing jag. Big Bill Broonzy's *Crawdad Song* becomes a racist blues, while *In the Sweet Bye and Bye,* a gospel and Salvation Army hymn, is homaged by a "choir of sincere, homosexual football coaches" (42)—Burroughs' parodic take is light years away from the 1910 social protest version of the song by Joe Hill of the Wobblies, because in these funny and horrible skits, Burroughs scorns every scruple and forfeits all conscience, necessarily so.

Silence Over And Out

All sound is noise and a painful infliction on the junkie's senses, only relieved by a shot which blots out the aural intrusion. Sound in *Naked*

Lunch is the excruciating experience of the world outside the silent cocoon of junk, the uproar which scrapes nerves raw and continually jangles the nervous system, a clamor signified by the profusion of exclamation marks in the text. Heroin is "relief from the whole life process" (30), and scoring is itself a soundless process, the junkie picking up on the "silent frequency of junk" (8). Burroughs, above all, wants inner silence, freedom from the jabbering voice inside, but junk as an exorcism of cultural noise is doomed, it shuts out the source by terminally closing down reception, speeding up the advent of that great night towards which we are all heading at some forty-five hundred heartbeats an hour, that unattended moment when the jukebox glow will flicker out forever, the radio pick up nothing but static, and the world fade out to a vibrating soundless hum . . .

Envoi

There would be many other books and often brilliant writing. The final file of these dossiers contains a telling but tender portrait of the author William Burroughs by poet Jeremy Reed, taking us at speed through Burroughs' second, iconic life. Those were different days. *Naked Lunch* would remain.

Avedon's Burroughs Portrait
By Jeremy Reed

The face is anatomically exact,
a stripped, forensic, near exhaustion shot,
seer and seen acutely locked
into a frame;
the St James' tie like a silk river run
from a deep collar, pocketed, ice-blue,
fitted, TM Lewin, Jermyn Street shirt.
The suit's gun grey: the left hand casually
stops at the navel, like it's a lotus
he's apprehended opening out inside.
Bill looks smoked-out of a fortressed bunker,
a reptile surfaced to sun on a log
beside a muddy Amazonian pool.
He's like his books extraterrestrial,
stoned by a deep river melancholy,
the left eye raised above the right,
fractionally 2cm up,
the eyes occupying separate identities,
the right seeing in gold, the left in green?
He's a chemical lab, dependencies

written into the genial, down-mooded
resignation of a look cooked
by opiates, circa Cities of the Red Night.
He's like an endgame that won't terminate,
a prose-czar bottled in Jamesons,
a mug shot captive in a whiteout space,
dejected, the lines on his face
so grainy they're testicular.
He works at it, the concentrated style
that's cool, but loaded like a luger.
He stares at his reversed image
in Avedon's lens. He's used up
old world stock, hanging in on time,
a man downloading his genes into text,
his novels and celebrity
insignificant to the post-shoot drink,
the full-on Jack Daniels that's coming next.

**works cited and
consulted for dossiers**

illustration credits

contributors

index

works cited and consulted for dossiers

Andersen, Eric. "Goin' Gone." *Memory of the Future*. Appleseed Recordings, 1998.

Armstrong, Tim. "Addiction, Electricity and Desire." In *Beyond the Pleasure Dome: Writing and Addiction from the Romantics*, edited by Sue Vice, Matthew Campbell, and Tim Armstrong, 134–42. Sheffield, UK: Sheffield, 1994.

Beiles, Sinclair. *Sacred Fix*. Rotterdam, The Netherlands: Cold Turkey, 1975.

Belitt, Ben, trans. *Poet in New York by Federico Garcia Lorca*. New York: Grove, 1955.

Bergler, Edmund. *Homosexuality: Disease or Way of Life?* New York: Collier, 1956.

Biskind, Peter. *Seeing Is Believing: How Hollywood Taught Us to Stop Worrying and Love the Fifties*. London: Bloomsbury, 2000.

Bloomfield, Steve. "Can Songs of Peace Bring Harmony to Strife-torn Darfur?" *Independent on Sunday* (London), 15 June 2008, 37.

Bowles, Paul. *Paul Bowles on Music*. Edited by Timothy Mangan and Irene Herrmann. Berkeley: U of California P, 2003.

Burroughs, William S. *The Letters of William S. Burroughs, 1945–1959*. Edited by Oliver Harris. London: Picador, 1993.

Burroughs, William S., and Allen Ginsberg. *The Yage Letters Redux*. Edited by Oliver Harris. San Francisco: City Lights, 2006.

Burroughs, William S., Jr. *Kentucky Ham*. New York: Overlook, 1984.

Butler, Samuel. *Erewhon*. 1872. London: Penguin, 1985.

Clej, Alina. *A Genealogy of the Modern Self: Thomas De Quincey and the Intoxication of Writing*. Stanford, CA: Stanford UP, 1995.

Cook, William. "Into Africa—Tangier." *Monocle* 1, no. 3 (May 2007): 57–63.

Corbin, Alain. *The Foul and the Fragrant: Odor and the French Social Imagination*. New York: Berg, 1986.

Croft-Cooke, Rupert. *Smiling Damned Villain*. London: Secker and Warburg, 1959.

Crowley, Aleister. *Diary of a Drug Fiend*. York Beach, ME: Weiser, 1998.

Dick, Leslie. "Seventeen Paragraphs on Kathy Acker." *Lust for Life: On the Writings of Kathy Acker*. Edited by Amy Sholder, Carla Harryman, and Avital Ronell, 110–16. London: Verso, 2006.

Douglas, Mary. *Purity and Danger: An Analysis of Concepts of Pollution and Taboo*. London: Ark, 1988.

Faithfull, Marianne. *Memories, Dreams, and Reflections*. London: Fourth Estate, 2007.

Ferrara, Abel, dir. *The Addiction*. 1995. Scanbox Entertainment Ltd.

Fussell, Betty. "On Murdering Eels and Laundering Swine." *A Literary Feast*, edited by Lilly Golden, 221–25. New York: Atlantic Monthly, 1993.

Gardner, Erle Stanley. "The Case of the Movie Murder." *Murder Plus: True Crime Stories from the Masters of Detective Fiction*. Edited by Marc Gerald. London: Pan, 1993.

Gheerbrant, Alain, *The Impossible Adventure: Journey to the Far Amazon*. London: Gollancz, 1953.

Hillman, James. *The Soul's Code: In Search of Character and Calling*. New York, Random, 1996.

Hopkins, Jerry. *Extreme Cuisine*. London: Bloomsbury, 2005.

Huxley, Aldous. *Music at Night and Other Essays*. Hamburg, Germany: Albatross Verlag, 1935.

Jones, Louisa E. *Sad Clowns and Pale Pierrots: Literature and the Popular Comic Arts in Nineteenth-century France*. Lexington, KY: French Forum, 1984.

Junger, Sebastian. *A Death in Belmont*. London: Fourth Estate, 2006.

Kaye, Lenny. *You Call It Madness: The Sensuous Song of the Croon*. New York: Villard, 2004.

Kerouac, Jack. *Orpheus Emerged*. New York: ibooks, 2000.

Lotringer, Sylvère. *Over Exposed: Perverting Perversions*. New York: Semiotext(e), 1994.

Lowry, Malcolm. *Under the Volcano*. London: Penguin, 2000.

Lyu, Claire Chi-ah. *A Sun within a Sun: The Power and Elegance of Poetry*. Pittsburgh, PA: U of Pittsburgh P, 2004.

Marlowe, Derek. *The Rich Boy from Chicago*. London: Weidenfeld, 1980.

Maurer, David W. *The Big Con: The Classic Story of the Confidence Man and the Confidence Trick*. London: Arrow, 2000.

Miller, Henry. *Black Spring*. New York: Grove, 1963.

———. *Tropic of Cancer*. New York: Grove, 1961.

Nabokov, Vladimir. *Lolita*. London: Penguin Classics, 2000.

Orwell, George. *Nineteen Eighty-Four*. Introduction by Thomas Pynchon. London: Penguin, 2003.

Rainey, Lawrence. *Revisiting the Waste Land*. New Haven, Conn.: Yale UP, 2005.

Revill, David. *The Roaring Silence—John Cage: A Life*. London: Bloomsbury, 1992.

Ritchin, Fred. "Time Travels." In *Mexico through Foreign Eyes: México visto por ojos extranjeros, 1850–1990*, edited by Carole Naggar and Ritchin. New York: Norton, 1993.

Robb, Graham. *Rimbaud: A Biography*. New York: Norton, 2000.

Rosenthal, Irving. *Sheeper*. New York: Grove Press, 1968.

Rumbelow, Martin. *The Complete Jack the Ripper*. London: Allen, 1987.

Salter, James. *A Sport and a Pastime*. San Francisco: North Point, 1967.

Sedgwick, Eve Kosofsky. *Epistemology of the Closet*. Berkeley: U of California P, 1990.

Ward, Geoff. *The Writing of America: Literature and Cultural Identity from the Puritans to the Present*. Cambridge, UK: Polity, 2002.

West, Nathanael. *Miss Lonelyhearts*. London, Penguin, 1975.

Wharton, Edith. *In Morocco*. New York: Tauris, 2004.

White, Edmund. *My Lives*. London: Bloomsbury, 2006.

Wilson, Sarah. Introduction. *Paris: Capital of the Arts 1900–1968*. London: Royal Academy of Arts, 2002.

Wilson, Terry. *Here to Go: Planet R-101—Brion Gysin Interviewed by Terry Wilson*. London: Quartet, 1985.

Young, Elizabeth. *Pandora's Handbag: Adventures in the Book World*. London: Serpent's Tail, 2001.

Zweig, Paul. *The Adventurer: The Fate of Adventure in the Western World*. London: Dent, 1974.

 **illustration credits**

P.1. Burroughs, "Self-Portrait [1959?]" 8.5" x 11" ink sketch, and "Interzone [1958]" manuscript. Ginsberg Collection, Columbia University, with permission of the William Burroughs Estate and the Wylie Agency, Inc.

P.2. Photographs by Allen Ginsberg (1953). Allen Ginsberg Papers, Stanford University, with permission of the Allen Ginsberg Trust and the Wylie Agency, Inc. Burroughs, "Queer" manuscript (1952). The William S. Burroughs Archive, the Henry W. and Albert A. Berg Collection of English and American Literature, the New York Public Library, Astor, Lenox and Tilden Foundations, with permission of the William Burroughs Estate and the Wylie Agency, Inc.

P.3. Photographs by Allen Ginsberg (1953). Allen Ginsberg Papers, Stanford University, with permission of the Allen Ginsberg Trust and the Wylie Agency, Inc.

P.4. Burroughs, letter to Allen Ginsberg (7 February 1955 [misdated 1954]). Claude Givaudan Collection, with permission of the William Burroughs Estate and the Wylie Agency, Inc. Burroughs, letter to Allen Ginsberg (4 December 1957). Ginsberg Collection, Columbia University, with permission of the William Burroughs Estate and the Wylie Agency, Inc. Photographs by Allen Ginsberg (1953, 1957). Allen Ginsberg Papers, Stanford University, with permission of the Allen Ginsberg Trust and the Wylie Agency, Inc.

P.5. Photographs by Allen Ginsberg (1953, 1957, 1961). Allen Ginsberg Papers, Stanford University, with permission of the Allen Ginsberg Trust and the Wylie Agency, Inc. Burroughs, "Interzone [1958]" manuscript. Ginsberg Collection, Columbia University, with permission of the William Burroughs Estate and the Wylie Agency, Inc.

P.6. Photograph by Allen Ginsberg (1957). Reproduced from *With William Burroughs: A Report from the Bunker* (New York: Seaver, 1981) by Victor Bockris, with permission of the Allen Ginsberg Trust and the Wylie Agency, Inc. Photographs by Allen Ginsberg (1953, 1957). Allen Ginsberg Papers, Stanford University, with permission of the Allen Ginsberg Trust and the Wylie Agency, Inc. Burroughs, "Interzone [1958]" manuscript. Ginsberg Collection, Columbia University, with permission of the William Burroughs Estate and the Wylie Agency, Inc.

P.7. Photograph by Antony Balch (1960/61), with permission of the William Burroughs Estate and the Wylie Agency, Inc. Maurice Girodias, letter to Burroughs (6 June 1958). The Ginsberg Circle, Burroughs-Hardiment Collection, Special Collections, Spencer Research Library, University of Kansas, with permission of J. P. Donleavy. Burroughs, letter to Lawrence Ferlinghetti (18 April 1958). Ginsberg Collection, Columbia University, with permission of the William Burroughs Estate and the Wylie Agency, Inc. Photograph by Allen Ginsberg (1953). Allen Ginsberg Papers, Stanford University, with permission of the Allen Ginsberg Trust and the Wylie Agency, Inc.

P.8. *Naked Lunch* book jackets, with permission of the William Burroughs Estate and the Wylie Agency, Inc.

 **contributors**

keith ALBARN formed "26 Kingley Street" (1964), whose output includes exhibitions "World of Islam" (London, 1974), "Islamathematica" (Rotterdam, 1975) and "Illusion in Art and Science" (London, 1976, and New York, 1977). He has authored *Language of Pattern* (1974), *Diagram: The Instrument of Thought* (1977), and the forthcoming *The Nature of Pattern*. As an artist, he continues to exhibit.

eric ANDERSEN has recorded twenty-two albums of original material, including the critically acclaimed *Blue River* (1972), *Ghosts upon the Road* (1989), *Memory of the Future* (1998) and the double album *Beat Avenue* (2003). His text "My Beat Journal" appeared in the *Rolling Stone Book of the Beats* (1999), and he has written about Burroughs for the Norwegian National Theatre (2000). He has contributed to the National Geographic Traveler and is currently writing his first novel.

gail-nina ANDERSON is a cultural historian and journalist specializing in Victorian Romanticism, Gothic fiction, and the film and literature of the weird. She has written introductory essays for editions of *Dracula* and *Frankenstein* and is currently working on a book about changing attitudes to the vampire myth to be published by the Centre for Fortean Zoology.

théophile ARIES is a French writer, musician, and translator, living in Berlin. In addition to being the translator of *The Yage Letters Redux* (2008), he is the cofounder of Underwires, an electropop musical project, and maintains the leading Burroughs Web site in France (http://theo.underwires.net/).

jed BIRMINGHAM writes occasional articles on Burroughs, book collecting, and the Beat Generation for *Beat Scene* magazine. He is the contributing editor of RealityStudio.org, the premier Web site dedicated to William Burroughs, as well as coeditor (with Kyle Schlesinger) of *Mimeo Mimeo*, a magazine about the Mimeograph Revolution, Artists' Books, and the Literary Fine Press.

shaun DE WAAL is a South African editor and writer of fiction and criticism. Recent publications include *To Have and to Hold: The Making of Same-Sex Marriage in South Africa* (2008) and *Exposure: Queer Fiction* (2008).

richard DOYLE is a rhetorician and professor of English and science, technology, and society at Pennsylvania State University. He is the author of *On Beyond Living: Rhetorical Transformations of the Life Sciences* (1997), *Wetwares: Experiments in Postvital Living* (2003), and *Ecodelic: Plants, Rhetoric and the Evolution of the NoÖsphere* (forthcoming).

loren GLASS is an associate professor of English at the University of Iowa. His most recent book is *Authors Inc.: Literary Celebrity in the Modern United States, 1880–1980* (2004). He is currently working on a history of Grove Press.

oliver HARRIS is professor of American literature at Keele University and the editor of *The Letters of William S. Burroughs, 1945–1959* (1993), *Junky: the Definitive Text of "Junk"* (2003), *The Yage Letters Redux* (2006), and *Everything Lost: The Latin American Notebook of William S. Burroughs* (2008). He has published articles on *film noir*, the epistolary, and Beat Generation writing and the book *William Burroughs and the Secret of Fascination* (2003). He is currently editing the twenty-fifth anniversary edition of *Queer* (forthcoming in 2010).

kurt HEMMER is associate professor of English at Harper College. In addition to writing the award-winning documentaries *As We Cover the Streets: Janine Pommy Vega* (2003) and *Rebel Roar: The Sound of Michael McClure* (2005), he is the editor of the *Encyclopedia of Beat Literature* (2007).

allen HIBBARD is professor of English and director of the Middle East Center at Middle Tennessee State University. He has written two books on Paul Bowles, *Paul Bowles: A Study of the Short Fiction* (1993) and *Paul Bowles, Magic and Morocco* (2003), edited *Conversations with William S. Burroughs* (2000), and published a collection of his own stories in Arabic.

robert HOLTON is professor of English at Carleton University, Ottawa, Canada. He is the author of *Jarring Witnesses: Modern Fiction and the Representation of History* (1995) and *On the Road: Kerouac's Ragged American Journey* (1999) and coeditor of *What's Your Road, Man? Critical Essays on Jack Kerouac's* On the Road (2008).

andrew HUSSEY is dean of the University of London Institute in Paris. As well as publishing books on Situationism and the work of Georges Bataille, he is the author of *The Game of War: The Life and Death of Guy Debord* (2001) and *Paris: The Secret History* (2006). Professor Hussey is currently working on *The Longest War*, a cultural history of France and the Islamic world.

rob JOHNSON is professor of English at the University of Texas–Pan American. He is the author of *The Lost Years of William S. Burroughs: The South Texas Beats* (2006) and a major contributor to the *Encyclopedia of the Beat Generation* (2007).

jean-jacques LEBEL has exhibited in various leading museums and galleries around the world. He is frequently identified as one of the major figures of the Neo-Dada movement. In 1960, he oversaw and participated in the first European Happening (*L'enterrement de la Chose*, Venice). Lebel published the first critical essay in French on the Happening movements throughout the world and produced over seventy Happenings, performances, and actions on numerous continents, along with his pictorial, poetic, and political work. In the 1960s, Lebel translated and published work by William Burroughs, Allen Ginsberg, Michael McClure, Lawrence Ferlinghetti, and Gregory Corso. In 1979, he founded Polyphonix, a recurring festival of performance and sound poetry.

ian MACFADYEN is a writer. His essay "Machine Dreams: Optical Toys and Mechanical Boys" was published in the collection *Flickers of the Dreamachine* (1996). His other work includes *Ira Cohen's Photographs: A Living Theatre* (2000; republished, 2006) and *The Blood of the Poet: Lorca and the Duende* (2005). He interviewed William Burroughs in 1990.

polina MACKAY is an assistant professor of English at the University of Nicosia. She has published work on the Beats, Kathy Acker, the Southern Gothic, and contemporary women's poetry. She is currently writing a book on the Beats' influence on female artists and coediting the first companion to H.D., the modernist poet.

jonas MEKAS is a filmmaker, critic, editor, distributor, archivist, and poet and has contributed heavily to the creation of the modern avant-garde and independent film movements, which he continues to expand. Mekas cofounded *Film Culture* magazine and contributed a "Movie Journal" column for New York's *Village Voice* newspaper. He also cofounded the Film-Makers' Cooperative, the Filmmakers' Cinémathèque, and Anthology Film Archives. Mekas' film work has been shown extensively at film festivals and museums around the world. In 2007, Mekas launched his epic Web-based "365 film project." He continues to work internationally as an artist, filmmaker, and curator.

barry MILES is a biographer and scholar of the Beat Generation. His books include *Ginsberg: A Biography* (1989), *Jack Kerouac: King of the Beats* (1998), and *William Burroughs: El Hombre Invisible* (1993). He coauthored the standard Burroughs bibliography and coedited *Naked Lunch: The Restored Text* (2003).

r. b. MORRIS is a poet, playwright, songwriter, and recording artist from East Tennessee and the author of books including *The Man Upstairs* (1988), *The Littoral Zone* (2004), and *Early Fires* (2007). His musical recordings include *Take That Ride* (1997), *Zeke and the Wheel* (1999), and *Empire* (2007). From 2004 to 2008, he was writer in residence at the University of Tennessee.

timothy s. MURPHY is an associate professor of English at the University of Oklahoma. He is the author of *Wising Up the Marks: The Amodern William Burroughs* (1997) and other essays on Burroughs. He has also written about such figures of the global counterculture as Gilles Deleuze and Antonio Negri.

jürgen PLOOG is a German writer who divides his time between Frankfurt and Florida. He has written several works about Burroughs, including coauthoring *Burroughs: Eine Bild-Biographie* (1994) and *Strassen des Zufalls* (1998). He is featured interviewing Burroughs in the 1991 film by Klaus Maeck, *William S. Burroughs: Commissioner of Sewers.*

davis SCHNEIDERMAN is a multimedia artist, novelist, and associate professor of English at Lake Forest College. He has authored numerous articles and the recent novels *Abecedarium* (2007) and *DIS* (2008) and is the coeditor of *Retaking the Universe: William S. Burroughs in the Age of Globalization* (2004).

jennie SKERL is the former associate dean at West Chester University and a founding board member of the Beat Studies Association. She is the author of *William S. Burroughs* (1985), coeditor of *William S. Burroughs at the Front: Critical Reception, 1959–1989* (1991), and editor of *Reconstructing the Beats* (2004).

dj SPOOKY (Paul D. Miller) is a composer, multimedia artist, and writer. His work as a media artist has appeared in a wide variety of contexts such as the Whitney Biennial and the Andy Warhol Museum in Pittsburgh, Pennsylvania. Miller's first collection of essays, *Rhythm Science* (2004) was followed by *Sound Unbound* (2007), an anthology of writings on electronic music and digital media. Miller's deep interest in reggae and dub has resulted in a series of compilations, remixes, and collections of material from the vaults of the legendary Jamaican label Trojan Records. He also produced material on Yoko Ono's album *Yes, I'm a Witch.*

philip TAAFFE was born in Elizabeth, New Jersey, in 1955 and studied at the Cooper Union in New York. He has traveled widely in the Middle East, India, South America, and Morocco. He lived and worked in Naples from 1988 to 1991 before settling again in New York. In 2008, his work was the subject of a major retrospective organized by the Kunstmuseum Wolfsburg, with an accompanying monograph. His work is in the permanent collection of the Museum of Modern Art in New York.

index

addiction, 207–9, 241, 259; and addict-pusher relation, 251–52; apomorphine as cure for, 117; and Lexington Narcotic Farm, 256. *See also* body, the; drugs; heroin

Adding Machine, The (Burroughs), 202–3

agents, 39–40, 163, 247–48

Algebra of Need (concept), 109, 112, 184, 241–42

alien life form: Bradley the Buyer as, 229; and breaking of taboos, 221; in "The Dunwich Horror" (Lovecraft), 229; in horror films, 216; and human meta-morphosis, 215; and interspecies sex in pulp science fiction, 228–29; and invisi-bility, 36; and Mugwumps, 118, 120, 162, 171, 173, 215, 217, 229, 234, 246; and New Flesh, 215; and "Weed Men" (Hodgson), 227; Willy the Disk as, 227

Alphaville (Godard), 27

amnesia, 36–37, 38–39

And the Hippos Were Boiled in Their Tanks (Burroughs and Kerouac), 18

Andersen, Eric, 41

anomics, 28–29, 31; and abjection (Kriste-va), 33–34; and humans as waste prod-ucts, 27, 29–32, 91–92; and lumpens, 29–30

Ansen, Alan, 23, 39, 57, 103

anthropology, and *Naked Lunch*, 7, 96, 211–12

anti-Semitism, and *Naked Lunch*, 47, 50–51

appendix to *Naked Lunch* ("Letter from a Master Addict to Dangerous Drugs"). *See under Naked Lunch*, part publica-tion of in magazines

argot, 5, 15–16, 27, 94–95, 97, 160–62, 256

Artaud, Antonin, 85–86

ayahuasca. See yagé

Ballard, J. G., 119, 230

Bang-utot, 164, 221

Bataille, Georges, 29, 144, 190

Baudelaire, Charles, 9, 80, 97

Beat Generation writers, 1–2, 29, 39, 51, 63, 74, 78, 86–88, 99, 104, 107, 109–11, 116, 118, 124, 127, 129, 134, 145, 147–48, 154–55, 167, 169–70, 178, 189, 227, 235, 236. *See also* Corso; Ginsberg; Kerouac

Beat Hotel, The, 4, 57, 73–74, 80, 84–87, 103, 148

182, 184; political, 100, 247; war, 88, 254; writer as, 254. *See also* ventriloquism; voice

magic, 80–81, 207

Mailer, Norman, 88, 109, 120, 155, 179, 181

maps: Korzybskian, 239–42, 246–47; psychogeographic, 10–11, 79–80

Marcuse, Herbert, 29

Marx, Karl, 29, 30, 34, 79, 137

Matmos, 198–200

McCarthyism, 28, 58, 213. *See also* Cold War

Mexico: and the Bounty Bar, 19; in Burroughs' composite manuscript, 12–13; Burroughs' travels to, 5–6, 12–13, 43–44; compared to Morocco, 59–60; and cultural difference, 11–12; and drugs, 11–12, 103; and Lee's fate, 11–12; and Lola La Chata, 11; and shooting of Joan Burroughs, 41; and "*Son cosas de la vida,*" 12, 50–51, 163; and South American boys, 93–94; and temporal experience, 11–12

Michaux, Henri, 87

Miller, Henry, 3, 10, 86, 87 108, 123; *Black Spring,* 253; *Tropic of Cancer,* 87, 155, 181, 189

Minutes to Go (Burroughs et al), 89, 155

misogyny, 93, 210

Moorcock, Michael, 119, 230, 230n. 4

Morocco, 56–64, 65–72; colonial conflict in, 76, 78; exotic myth of, 161; modernization of, 63, 161–62; and Moroccan critics of Burroughs, 76; nationalism in, 56, 58–59, 62, 66–72. *See also* Tangier

Mugwumps. *See under* alien life form

music: Burroughs' taste in, 252, 255–59; John Cage and NEW MUSIC, 85; and censorship of, 177–78; and collage, 254; deconstruction of, 251–54, 259; digital, 234–37; of Bob Dylan, 110–11, 120; as elegy for Paris, 10; of film and show songs, 250–53, 255; of Judy Garland, 250–51; and granular synthesis, 200; influence of on language, 129; jazz, 2, 87, 109, 171, 255–57; Joujouka, 200, 205;

nostalgic, 255, 257–58; and patriotism, 252; and possession, 252–54, 259; radio, 253–54, 259; *Rag for William S. Burroughs* (Matmos), 198–200; remixing, 235–37; rock, 110–11, 118–20, 133, 183, 256; in soundtrack to Cronenberg's film of *Naked Lunch* (Shore and Coleman), 171, 256; traditional folk song, 251, 253–54, 257–59; and war, 251–55. *See also* silence; voice

My Education (Burroughs), and dreaming, 243

Nabokov, 165; *Lolita,* 87, 94, 130, 143–44, 146, 147

Naked Lunch (Burroughs), title of, 15, 16–19, 22–23, 24, 26, 30–31, 92, 115, 147, 155, 168, 173, 208, 226

Naked Lunch, editions: Calder (1964), 24, 118, 147, 152, 156; Grove (1962), 22, 24, 26, 118; Limes Verlag (1962), 127–30; Olympia (1959), 16, 19, 22, 24, 108, 114–16, 118, 120, 143–150, 154–55, 167, 181, 191; restored text (2003), xiii, 23, 24, 25n. 5, 49, 121, 138–39, 143, 158, 159n. 7, 186, 198; Zweitausendeins (1978), 128–30. *See also Naked Lunch,* cover designs

Naked Lunch, part publication of in magazines: "And Start West" (*Jabberwock*), 24, 25n. 5, 117; "Excerpt from Pantapon Rose" (*Semina*), 143; "Excerpt: *Naked Lunch*" (*Chicago Review*), 15, 23, 24, 117, 145; "From *Naked* Lunch: Book III: In Search of Yage" (*Black Mountain Review*), 15, 17, 117; "Have You Seen Pantapon Rose?" (*Yugen*), 117; "Letter from a Master Addict to Dangerous Drugs" (*British Journal of Addiction*), 15, 39, 117, 143, 155, 157, 181; "Ten Episodes from *Naked Lunch*" (*Big Table*), 3, 23–24, 89, 117, 145–46, 154, 231n. 3; "Two Scenes" (*New Departures*), 117

Naked Lunch, sections of: "A.J.'s Annual Party," 48–49, 136, 190, 259; "Algebra of Need, The," 225; "And Start West," 16, 24, 100, 117, 160–61, 223; "Atrophied

Carthy, Mary, 47; McDaniel, Dennis, 170; McHale, Brian, 75; McNicholas, Joseph, 170; Melley, Timothy, 170; Mikriammos, Philippe, 201; Miles, Barry, 58, 121, 143; Morgan, Ted, 58; Mottram, Eric, 189; Mullins, Greg, 66, 76, 78, 82n. 1, 170; Murphy, Timothy S., 75, 80, 169, 170, 172, 184, 189, 195; Pepper, Andrew, 170; Rae, Graham, 192; Rosenbaum, Jonathan, 172; Russell, Charles, 75; Russell, Jamie, 139, 170; Schneiderman, Davis, 170; Skerl, Jennie, 168, 174, 189–92; Streip, Katharine, 170; Tytell, John, 189; Walsh, Philip, 170; Ward, Geoff, 175n. 1, 254; Willett, John, 50–51; Zurbrugg, Nicholas, 173

Naked Lunch, literary sources of: Artaud, Antonin, 85–86; Bowles, Paul, 12; Butler, Samuel, 210; Crowley, Aleister, 208; De Quincey, Thomas, 37, 38; Eliot, T. S., 11, 254; Finney, Charles G., 166; Fitzgerald, F. Scott, 105; Gay, John, 257; Genet, Jean, 39–40; Gheerbrant, Alain, 5; Hodgson, William Hope, 227; Lorca, Federico Garcia, 94; Lovecraft, H. P., 224, 229, 231n. 3; Maurer, David, 160–1; Miller, Henry, 96–97, 253; Orwell, George, 95; Rimbaud, Arthur, 88, 92, 104

Naked Lunch, cover designs: Calder (1964), 152, 156; Corgi (1974), 138, 156; Grove (1962), 155; Grove (1966), 155; Harper (2005), 158; Italian (2006), 156; Olympia (1959), 97, 114–116, 144–50, 154–55; Paladin (1986), 156; Russian (2003), 156; Spanish (2004), 152; Turkish (1998), 157–58

Naked Lunch (general): autobiographical basis to, 46; Burroughs' refusal to moralize in, 50–51; as document of Burroughs' own consciousness, 100; genetic history of, 14–15, 17–24, 189–90, 194, 196 (*see also under Naked Lunch*, critical approaches); mythologization of origins, 14–24, 57, 115; as ongoing work, 23–24, 180–82; as open-ended work, 171, 184

Naked Lunch, The (Burroughs), 24, 115, 116, 118, 120, 147. *See also under Naked Lunch*, editions, Olympia (1959)

New Departures. See Naked Lunch, part publication of in magazines

New Orleans, Burroughs in, 22, 43–44, 60, 87, 103

New York, 17, 18, 20, 60, 74, 85, 100, 103, 104, 110, 116, 118, 208

Nova Express (Burroughs), 56, 89, 120, 138, 147, 182, 234

obscenity, 136, 178–86; of *Naked Lunch*, 27, 33, 49, 92, 116, 126–27, 130, 145–46, 178–79, 224. *See also* Boston Trial; censorship

Oedipus complex, 190, 210–11

Olympia Press, 24, 82, 86, 97, 115, 143–50, 154–55. *See also* Girodias, Maurice; *Naked Lunch*, editions, Olympia (1959)

Orlovsky, Peter, 57, 87, 103

Orwell, George, 200; *Nineteen Eighty-Four*, 95, 235, 201

Paris, 4, 9–11; and the Algerian war, 77–78; "anachronistic Bohemianism" of, 74; Beats meet the French avant-garde in, 87; and Burroughs' friendship with Jean-Jacques Lebel in, 74, 84–89; Burroughs' initial antipathy towards, 73–74, 82; Burroughs' nostalgia for, 10; as center of colonial power, 74; conducive to Burroughs' development as writer, 75; copies of *Naked Lunch* smuggled out of, 114, 144; and French theory, 75; Miles' account of, 73–74, 88; modernisation of, 10; as mythical place, 86–87; and politicization of Burroughs in, 74, 77–78; and psychogeography, 10–11, 79; publication of *Naked Lunch* in, 78, 86; and radical art movements, 75, 78–82; Tangier seen by Burroughs from perspective of, 81. *See also* Beat Hotel

"Parties of Interzone" (in *Naked Lunch*), 95, 134, 225

Péret, Benjamin, 87

theatricality, 164–65, 251, 257

Third Mind, The (Burroughs and Gysin), 86, 89

third mind concept, 240

Ticket That Exploded, The (Burroughs), 56, 88, 89, 115, 138, 144, 147, 156, 182, 239

trickster myth, 211–12, 247

Trocchi, Alexander, 79, 81

"UGH . . ." (Willett), 50–51

utopia, 30, 70, 184

vampirism, 207; and blood, 93, 213, 219; and the body as commodity, 95; and Dracula, 221–22

ventriloquism, 37, 217–18, 259; and logorrhea, 37, 253. *See also* silence; voice

Vietnam War, 88, 111, 128–29, 252

virus, 79, 131, 161, 221, 236

visionary, 38, 96, 200–1, 234–36

voice, 182–83, 254, 256; and Burroughs' readings, 177; and Burroughs' recordings, 87, 178; of Candy Butcher, 94; of carnival barker, 27, 33, 100; as extension of the body, 184; and the "flaming voice" of excess, 139–41; in *Junky*, 52; and musical collaborations, 177–78, 183; in *Naked Lunch*, 52; and reading of *Naked Lunch*, 256; and rhetoric as seduction,

22, 33–34; and second person rhetorical repetition, 33; and sound-machine interface, 182; and tape recorders and routines, 182; and writer as recording instrument, 37, 239–47. *See also* music; ventriloquism

Vollmer, Joan. *See* Burroughs, Joan Vollmer

waste. *See* body, the

Wasteland, The (Eliot), 11, 254

We (Zamyatin), 235

Web, 234–35, 258

Wells, H. G., 36, 220, 224, 225

Westerns: stereotypes, 165; and pulp genre, 224

Western Lands, The (Burroughs), 98, 102, 157

Wiessner, Carl, 128–29

Wild Boys, The (Burroughs), 138

Wilson, Terry, 5, 210

"Word Authority More Habit Forming Than Heroin" (Burroughs), 239

yagé, 6, 8, 38, 60–61, 96, 103, 241, 243

Yage Letters, The (Burroughs and Ginsberg), 12–13, 15, 17, 19, 56, 153, 169, 171

Yugen, 117. *See under Naked Lunch*, part publication of in magazines